CREATIVITY CRISIS

CREATIVITY
CRISIS

Toward a Post-constructivist Educational Future

Robert Nelson

MONASH University Publishing

Monash University Publishing
Matheson Library and Information Services Building
40 Exhibition Walk
Monash University
Clayton, Victoria 3800, Australia
www.publishing.monash.edu

Monash University Publishing brings to the world publications which advance the best traditions of humane and enlightened thought.

Monash University Publishing titles pass through a rigorous process of independent peer review.

www.publishing.monash.edu/books/cc-9781925523270.html

ISBN: 9781925523270 (paperback)
ISBN: 9781925523287 (pdf)
ISBN: 9781925523294 (epub)

Series: Education

Design: Les Thomas

Cover image: *Prometheus* by Theodoor Rombouts (early 17th century).

A catalogue record for this book is available from the National Library of Australia

Printed in Australia by Griffin Press an Accredited ISO AS/NZS 14001:2004 Environmental Management System printer.

The paper this book is printed on is certified against the Forest Stewardship Council ® Standards. Griffin Press holds FSC chain of custody certification SGS-COC-005088. FSC promotes environmentally responsible, socially beneficial and economically viable management of the world's forests.

CONTENTS

AT A GLANCE

University education is structurally uncreative and this book suggests how to change it. Contemporary syllabus design has a negative effect on imagination, because the centrepiece of pedagogy—constructive alignment—promotes mechanistic study practices. Even our strategies for student engagement lead to uncreative outcomes. The book unfolds the sympathetic preconditions of imaginative learning: they belong to the subjective dynamics of student-teacher relations and, above all, to the intimacy of the student's autonomous power of projecting images onto material that is initially foreign. Steeped in the history of ideas, the book explores the language that encourages creativity and helps teachers cultivate imaginative enthusiasm; it radically revises the concept of student-centredness and deconstructs student leadership. According to constructivism, students construct knowledge for themselves; but the discourse limits students to an epistemological framework, where they anxiously gather manipulative skills toward assessments. Instead, this book argues for an ontological framework, recognizing that learning takes place optimally when students create imaginative views of themselves that promise creative ownership of new material.

FOREWORD

David Boud

This book is one of a kind. It begins by putting creativity at the centre of learning, not just in fields branded as creative like studio arts. According to Robert Nelson, when we encounter unfamiliar things that we are expected to learn, the imagination has a powerful role in mediating between what we know and what we do not yet know. Certainly, at its furthest reach, creativity results in extraordinary things with boastful inventions; but Robert sees creativity and imagination as crucial to all deeper learning. Imagination determines how we 'come at' material that is initially beyond us.

There is no other book that explores the intimacy of learning in the same way. Simultaneously, the book identifies the trouble that course design gets into when it forces the learning experience into mechanistic models that our institutions, supported by constructivist theory, insist upon. Much to my discomfort at times, the book defies many articles of faith that have characterized educational reform in universities for the past thirty years: the priority of learning outcomes and their alignment with teaching and assessment; active learning and group work; the deployment of marking rubrics; smart techniques of achieving student engagement; cultivating student leadership and responsibility; and encouraging reflection at the end of a period of study.

In each of these themes, Robert identifies a barrier to creativity. He does not delimit imagination and creativity as an independent area of pedagogy but uses them as a lens to examine the culture that we have built around teaching and assessment. His conclusions in each case are radical and far-reaching, claiming that contemporary course design, with its emphasis on specification and constructive alignment, has a negative effect on creativity. His aspiration is to see beyond these limitations. Under the term post-constructivism, he posits learning less as an epistemological technique—that is, absorbing and manipulating knowledge and gaining capabilities—and more of an ontological attitude, that is, a focus on consciousness, an identification of being or belonging with intellectual material that reinforces one's cognitive sympathies as a curious thinking person, creatively capable of extending human potential. Post-constructivism, so defined, has an ontological emphasis because education, when creative, is integral to the learner's sense of self.

Robert's approach is as radical as his conclusions. Using methods from the history of ideas, he takes in the long chronological perspective of language and identifies how artificially fixed many of our pedagogical conceptions are, where historically they have enjoyed a latitude more conducive to the processes of imagination. Often, the metaphors that he unearths in the history of language are telling and at times unsettling. This unusual lateral method makes the discussions illuminating and instructive, even if, ultimately, you do not agree with his conclusions.

Robert's use of the history of ideas is not ideologically overwritten but unprejudiced. An example is his chapter on waste. It would have been tempting for him to use the theme for polemical ends, clinching his argument that discouraging student creativity is immoral, in fact among the worst kinds of waste because it is a waste of human potential. But while momentarily proposing this case, he defers to the evidence of language and philosophy, candidly acknowledging that waste and luxury are also inherent in creative processes, that the concept of waste cannot be invoked mechanically to stigmatize things that you personally do not like.

Methodologically, educational research tends to align with the social sciences and psychology, mostly empirical, in search of tests of or refinements to existing theoretical frameworks. Robert's method has little to do with conventional empirical techniques of research; nor is it linked closely to a single vein of educational theory. Instead, his method is based on a kind of narrative structure, where the story may be hundreds of years old. This intrepid breadth is not cultivated for daring's sake but to afford an independent perspective on the educational culture that we assume and contribute to. In removing himself from so many conventions of the discipline, he strikes an unusual register, with phrases like 'innovation is creativity sanitized' or 'good learning outcomes make good followers' or 'responsibility is a triggering word with a somewhat odious contractual overtone'.

It is fortunate that Robert's writing style is polished and poetic, because the content is provocative and confronting. To denounce the whole structure of current pedagogy in higher education might have been abrasive and polemical; but Robert's interest is positive and goes beyond an imaginary adversary. His purpose, as we also glean from the self-evident relish in the history of ideas, is to arrive at a creative new vision, where education is less constrained, less instrumentalist, more encouraging and open to the imagination.

ACKNOWLEDGEMENTS

This book could not have been written without the generous support of my colleagues in the Monash Education Academy (MEA). Associate Professor Gerry Rayner, Dr Kim Anh Dang, Professor Kris Ryan, Dr Mathew Hillier and Kay Ritchie have been unreserved in accommodating my irregular working hours, as have our Deputy Vice-Chancellor Professor Susan Elliott and Senior Pro Vice-Chancellor Professor Zlatko Skrbiš. I am grateful for stimulating conversations with Dr Joy Whitton in MEA, whose recent dissertation on creativity is so useful, as I am for the rich interchange with our participants in the Monash continuing development program. Equally enlarging were conversations with previous members of our team in its earlier incarnations, Professor Darrell Evans (Newcastle), Associate Professor Phillip Dawson (Deakin), Associate Professor Hariz Halilovich (RMIT), Professor Angela Carbone (Swinburne), Jason Ceddia, Dr Thomas Apperley (UNSW) and Professor Marnie Hughes-Warrington (ANU). I am especially humbled by Professor David Paganin for reading my typescript so thoroughly and with so much encouragement, just as I am overwhelmed and grateful for the penetrating and big-hearted foreword by Professor David Boud (Deakin). Finally, I would like to thank my family for talking every day about some educational or creative experience and also for putting up with me telling them about mine.

SUMMARY OF THE CHAPTERS

1   Creativity and post-constructivism

Universities are creative through their research but not their pedagogy. Thanks to consistent alignment of learning outcomes, activities and assessments, students are effectively trained to game their studies, to read the clues for high marks and study strategically. Imaginative responses are punished for deviating from the optimum conformity to expectations. Constructive alignment, though well-intentioned, favours uncreative study, infusing programs with a regulatory principle of measurability and discouraging learning outcomes that may vary organically. The chapter proposes a post-constructivist approach that is not based on the student's construction of knowledge but the student's identification with beautiful opportunities, an educational ontology rather than an epistemology.

2   The root of all learning

Quantitative methods are unlikely to solve the problem identified in higher education, where institutions boast about creativity and then fail to deliver on it. But a purely subjective method will not serve either; instead, current preoccupations must be triangulated through the history of ideas. Learning outcomes are used as an example, where philology reveals the same limitations and artificiality intuited from experience. A history of learning is proposed, showing the close parallel between teaching and learning as an enchanted narrative, contrary to the emphasis on learning outcomes, which require deconstruction.

3   Engagement

Despite noble origins, constructivist methods have left us with a dismal method for achieving student engagement. It is, broadly, to force students to engage through assessment and to monitor their contact with unprecedented degrees of surveillance. Conducting a history of engagement, this chapter reveals the hidden compulsion in the term, rooted in the European understanding of a pledge. The contemporary wisdom on collaborative participatory learning paradoxically invokes engagement with its archaic and uncreative emphasis on the contractual.

4   Being nice

Among the subjective preconditions of creativity in education is a benign and receptive teacher who creates a safe space for imaginative expression. A great deal in the pressured environment of higher education, however, discourages teachers from realizing this signal benefit to students. Conducting a history of niceness, this chapter reveals that concepts of kindness are twisted and convoluted, explaining much in the neurosis by which teachers feel a need to emphasize uncreative rigour at the expense of the generosity inherent in imaginative thinking.

5   Telling

The contemporary emphasis on group work, team and collaboration obscures a deeper urge on the part of imaginative students, namely to tell someone about their learning. The chapter outlines a history of telling, which reveals rich connexions with counting and accountability. When you tell someone about your learning, you account for ideas to yourself and confirm your view of yourself. Your identity is created through the rehearsal. Learning is thus socialized on an intimate scale according to the autonomous impulse of the student. The deeper internalization of knowledge and desire to imagine the background of knowledge are thus optimally served.

6   Student-centredness

Among many claims to student-centredness—like student choice of syllabus, time and mode of learning—the least persuasive is the contemporary idea that students are empowered and have learning in their own hands thanks to two constructivist precepts: first that learning 'is what the student does' and second the alignment of assessment, delivery, activities and learning outcomes. Historicizing the very concept of a centre, this chapter suggests that a more creative approach to student-centredness recognizes the mutual dynamic between student and teacher.

7   Expectation

The premise of modern pedagogy is that students should know at each stage what to expect in order that they can plan and have their learning in their own hands. There is a problem, however, when this premise encounters the creative, where expectations must organically adjust to opportunities that unfold in the course of doing. This chapter examines the curious link between waiting, attention and expectation. Through a history of waiting, it suggests that attention to an idea without an expectation is integral to imaginative learning and that the creative impulse depends upon a management of patience proper to the individual.

8   Subjectivity

To act creatively, students need confidence in their own subjectivity. With appeal to fairness and an understandable distaste for the arbitrary, however, academies are guarded about the subjective. Subjectivity is poorly understood, because the subject as person is grammatically confused with the subject as topic. Conducting a brief history of subjectivity, this chapter contemplates how much we need to redeem what used to be called the soul—your inalienable singularity, not necessarily depending on metaphysics—to protect the integrity of the student's creative identity.

9   Leadership

Student success depends in most instances on the ability to follow. Increasingly, educational design makes it clear exactly what to follow, what to do and what criteria to satisfy. It makes followers rather than leaders. For all that, the concept of leadership needs to be deconstructed; and, conducting a brief history of leadership and student success, this chapter reveals how closely related they are. To be creative, we cannot remain followers; but our ability to lead in a creative sense is linked to our ability to follow, albeit with an imaginative vengeance.

10   Waste

Waste in education may be necessary, as when we commit time to learning what later seems redundant. But it is less excusable to waste potential; and that is what happens when we systematically discourage student creativity. But there is a twist. Though resented, waste also seems concomitant with creative endeavour. We never know which idea is worth investing in without trying; and so much is tried that ends in failure. Proposing a history of waste, this chapter identifies the necessary peace that we have to make with waste in seeking creative results. The idea of luxury is crucial to the case, because some generosity is needed to afford the licence to be creative.

11   Flux

Lecturers are sometimes despondent with the disparate abilities of their student cohort. They fear boring the advanced students and also losing the struggling students who are all in the one class. This chapter begins with a solution in the form of flux between the sophisticated and the grounded, where the lecturer rises to heights of abstraction but never for long at a time, returning the talk to the concrete at regular intervals. This motif of flux is then used as a metaphor to describe the way that creative processes organize themselves, racing convulsively between tangible examples and lucid extrapolation. It helps for teaching delivery to have the same fluxing character as the creativity that it stimulates.

12   Ownership

We learn best when we feel imaginative ownership of the syllabus. Reflecting on the materialistic basis of ownership, the chapter discovers an unconscious shyness over proprietorial attitudes to knowledge, as if these are selfish, greedy and mean. Noting the closeness of ownership to the self or identity, however, the argument defends high levels of ownership in the name of creativity, which means owning one's impulse and failure. Creative ownership is contrasted with responsibility, which is seen as a negative contractual concept that does not favour imagination. Creativity, meanwhile, entails the individual's ownership of ideas in an expansive self-propagation of purpose and identity.

13   Reflexion

Reflexion is well-recognized in pedagogical literature but has also attracted suspicion. Conducting a history of reflexion, 'a history of second thoughts', this chapter finds a mysterious dimension in the metaphor that makes reflexion peculiarly congruent with creative thinking. Reflexion is a conversation that you have with yourself and which propitiates the intimacy of creative thinking. Reflexion is an inherently poetic condition, imaginatively matching ideas and experience. Through reflexion, one thing equates with another through a jump, an uncertain parallel, which is symbolic: the return of a reality as an image, which creatively invites other realities and images in its train.

14   Conclusion

Summing up the arguments of the book, creativity and imagination are integral to sustained learning and are not confined to paradigm shifts of genius. Given that contemporary syllabus design does not favour creativity or imagination—and given that the current system is unlikely to change in the near future—it is worth contemplating how creativity and imagination can be cultivated within constructivist parameters. Greater use of non-competitive assessment is suggested as well as the teacherly resources of colour that ontologically support creativity and imagination in spite of the constructivist dullness that circumscribes them.

Chapter 1

CREATIVITY AND
POST-CONSTRUCTIVISM

If I am asked to learn something but cannot engage my imagination, I am disempowered. Absorbing the material feels like an imposition and, if I learn anything, I experience the task as burdensome. Instead of an exhilarating promise of new and wider perspectives that improve my intellectual compass and extend my personal autonomy, I feel that I have to endure and digest something unfamiliar, putting up with the learning experience like one in the stocks. But if I can engage my imagination when encountering the same material, the experience of learning is not only full of wonder and potential but becomes intimately a part of me.

Imagination is so much more than an impulse to paint a picture or dream up a song. It is the mind's vouchsafe for thinking afresh and is consequently central to all learning, which is a process of encountering new material and making it your own. It is not your own to start with because, by definition, you do not know it yet. But bringing your imagination to bear on the subject matter is the best guarantee that an idea barely encountered can become your own, that you can entertain the possession of a concept that you are still in the process of understanding. As you contemplate a fact or idea in an effort to learn, something of yourself draws you sympathetically into the unfamiliar: it is your ability to imagine something about it, even if it is a bit naive, a bit wayward and even a bit wrong.

Creativity and imagination are sometimes conceived as a faculty necessary for innovation, for making objects or methods or strategies; and we rightly celebrate inventors and entrepreneurs, brilliant scientists like Albert Einstein or visionaries in business like Steve Jobs or the musical genius of a Franz Schubert. This book does not associate creativity with exceptional gifts but with the regular promise of learning, the daily endeavour to fathom new information or impressions or ideas. Creativity in this conspectus means creating an intimate rapport with the borders of your awareness, a zone which is otherwise alienating, perceived as a mental barrier from which the learner—perhaps timid in no other dimension—forbears and recedes.

Between the learner and the stuff to be learned is a gap of awkward ignorance, rather threatening, where the new material that you are expected soon to understand is still foreign. To mediate in those potentially humiliating moments of exposure to something more advanced, the imagination is a necessary helpmate that reassuringly makes you somewhat conversant, that makes you feel that you can handle the oddness of it. Your imagination is always your own; and so, if you are able to apply your imagination to any concept, you automatically think in sympathy with whatever it is, something new to you, something challenging, maybe even alien, that goes beyond your immediate experience. An idea in mathematics, a new tune, a theory of gender or the laws of physics all require an imaginative undercurrent to enable that deeper cognitive appropriation that we call learning. It is an activity, a creative picture-making faculty in the mind, that takes care of the untried, the unaccustomed departure, an idea that you have not been able to think of before but which is presented to you as if in broad daylight, defying your understanding and almost accusing your ignorance. By reflex, you might resist the strangeness of the new input. With imagination, however, you can also begin to create matches, to support the learning process by generating myriad images, figments and fantasies, those blithe meanderings of intellectual potential that transform noisy guesswork into ownership and future imaginative use. So the imagination assists two moments of potential: first, it recommends the unfamiliar to the ego and, second, it disposes the mind, once having done some learning, to gain a hunger for more learning.

We are used to thinking of learning as an active building process where we construct knowledge for ourselves. For many decades of Vygotskyan educational theory, the emphasis has been on the social relations that seem to be necessary to learning; and we are therefore inclined to think of the construction of knowledge outside the private sphere, among communications between people. But the model mistakes the context for the cause. Learning is an organic process that involves my imagination—much more than other people—as I entertain ideas that I do not yet fathom: it is my imagination, not other people, that allows me to embrace the foreign ideas in my proximity. When expedient, warm and engaged, learning has a secret catalyst in the imagination: we create fertile projections, extensions, fancies, most of which are provisional and dispensable but vital to the agency of the receptive intelligence. Without this lush bed of disposable creative attachments, the learning process has no direct route to ownership. The personal affordance of learning is missing.

All too often education does not invite imaginative activity. If anything, it is suppressed, not because anyone wants to deny students a creative experience but because imaginative activity is messy, hard to recognize and inefficient. If I work imaginatively and creatively, my progress is littered with errors and false starts; there are risks that I pass over necessary information and dwell on tangential details that tickle my fancy, or I misunderstand essential concepts because in my imagination they are co-opted by my convenience. I might creatively make of them whatever I want. Teachers, on the other hand, seek to be responsible to the syllabus. They are alarmed at the prospect of random wilful energies appropriating elements of curriculum that benefit, instead, from being learned in a consistent linear fashion, with careful reasoning supporting the narrative throughout. Finding connexions between syllabus and a personal view of yourself seems like illusion, a process of making things up for your own conceit, upon which education must in no circumstance depend. There is a strong pedagogical impulse to eliminate haphazard approaches to learning and sadly imagination and creativity are a casualty.

Good universities nevertheless make many claims for creativity. As if updating their heraldic motto from the renaissance, universities establish their identity by issuing statements of purpose, listing graduate attributes or capabilities, many of which include creativity.[1] The aspiration that these statements symbolize is noble and also credible. Universities are self-evidently creative, which we can verify by their research output. The scholars who teach are productively creative, publishing new ideas, methods, insights and facts; they write papers and books, compose music, design buildings and chairs, exhibit challenging new art and stage drama. Academics can afford to be confident about their creativity, because the evidence of clever advances from science to business modelling is boastfully apparent.

The question is how, if at all, they teach this vaunted creativity. We could fail to teach it entirely and still feel complacent in our neglect, on the basis that creativity takes care of itself. Our research graduates will go on to become creative regardless of our apathy in cultivating the faculty, because

---

1   A commonplace at variance with delivery: 'despite its ubiquity in higher education discourse, creativity was not found to be explicit as a strategy or approach to practices of learning and teaching'. Erica McWilliam, *Carrick Associate Fellowship Report*, December, 2007 (retrieved December 2016 from www.cci.edu.au/sites/default/files/fellowships_report_erica_mcwilliam_08-2.pdf).

the underlying structure of knowledge-generation, like the jealous substrate of artistic production, competitively encourages innovation. At a certain point, the distinguishing brilliance of students is neither what they know nor how strategically they can rehearse their knowledge and show off their skills, but what they can do with knowledge to produce more knowledge or insight; and research methods, though seldom speaking of creativity, implicitly encompass creative structures. As I write this page, I jealously look around at every scholar in the vicinity, hoping to clinch an idea or expression that has not been thought of before. This zeal for line-honours in novelty operates in all disciplines by default, because we cannot call it research if someone has said it all before. At best, we would call it knowledge transfer; but the big stakes are known to be research, and all the scholars-in-training at a good university are inducted into the method for being in the lead—however modestly—in order to qualify in research education.

So long as the heat is on research, the heat is off with learning and teaching. With ample signs of innovation through the refereed literature, creativity seems best left to itself. After all, if a paper is written on creativity, it is unlikely to give a physicist an unforeseen boost in ideas and, if anything, academics are inclined to view literature on creativity as woolly, as if the field is hemmed by natural platitudes. This scepticism makes no reflexion on the inherent value of creativity, just that it is too ethereal to handle other than empirically. We know that there is a great deal of creativity in science; it is just that we do not believe that creativity can be helpfully spoken for. As with music, we think of these things as sublimely beyond language, unreachable by theory, inaccessible to analysis, other than a suite of commonplaces which disappoint the mystery that we share. Worse still, creativity is a discourse somewhat tainted with self-help books, vacuous exhortations to introspective improvement, to open yourself up to your hidden internal powers, to realize your inner child-genius. Images of finger painting and amorphous sculptures come to mind, impossible to judge and valorized irresponsibly by the mantra of creativity.

Even artistic fields share the suspicion over creativity. The avant garde would rather speak of ideology, critique, discourse, strategy, irony, subversion; the mere mention of the word creativity is enough to discredit an artist's project or proposal. As in science, some kind of creativity is understood to operate throughout production—because art is judged strongly on its originality—but the term is suppressed from the artistic vocabulary. It sounds cheap, populist, vulgar, romantic, immune from intellect, taste, review and discrimination. I too, as an art critic of over twenty years, catch myself blanching at the word, because it seems to signal a naïvety that disqualifies any practitioner from professional ambition. So if even the creative arts shy away from the rubric of creativity, there seems to be no heartland that champions it. So little is to be gained from invoking it in anything other than a high-level mission statement or advertising. In the disciplines themselves, there is little but embarrassment over it.

We could, I suppose, continue in this vein, smug in our prowess of generating new ideas and simultaneously scornful and indifferent to the term creativity, which is tainted with children's art classes and amateurs. The problem, however, is that relatively few of our students go on to become researchers at university or an industrial lab. Those who continue with a research career are indeed served by the unspoken creativity that we teach by induction in the research culture of the university. But most of our students do not cross the line into a research culture where they can finally escape the withering effects of undergraduate pedagogy, where they can enjoy a life of speculation, constantly adjusting their hypotheses in the face of evidence, stretching their minds in the pursuit of yet-unimagined explanations or solutions, forms, sequences, images, melodies.

*

It is hard to estimate how uncreative undergraduate teaching is. It varies according to discipline, departmental culture and each teacher's disposition; but structurally, there is much across universities and colleges that discourages creativity. To illustrate the core problem, let us imagine two students, along the lines of Susan and Robert, two fictitious educational avatars invented by the educational theorist who has so comprehensively renovated tertiary learning and teaching throughout the Anglophone world, John Biggs.[2] Our characters, however, are Anastasia and Nalini, who have both submitted an essay in a generalist first year subject on cultural history. They choose the same topic but go about the essay so differently that they could almost be studying a different subject. Anastasia diligently refers to the subject guide and follows the criteria set out in the marking rubric.

---

2   John Biggs and Catherine Tang, *Teaching for Quality Learning at University* (1999), Open University Press, McGraw-Hill, Maidenhead, Berkshire, 4th edition 2011, pp. 5 ff. (chapters 1 and 2).

She musters the resources listed, either by selectively reading them or noting their content through their synopses. She accurately quotes the sources with the referencing system demanded in the guide. Anastasia does not attempt to propose original ideas but organizes the existing material coherently so that it answers the question. She announces what she will do from the outset and repeats the terms of the question at the conclusion. They are techniques that she has learned at secondary school, with the difference that it is easier to do at university, because the sources do not have to be memorized.

Nalini, on the other hand, is inspired by the essay topic. She reads the resources on the subject website with mixtures of curiosity and impatience, because they contain little experiential pregnancy that she can see in the topic. She notes their existence in her essay but produces an argument which is substantially independent of their contentions. In ambitious colourful prose, she makes her own attempt at cultural history, which is impassioned, if somewhat naive. She concentrates on the primary literature mentioned in lectures rather than the secondary sources in the subject guide, adducing lines by poets which are eloquent but only partly support her argument. She imaginatively connects the verse forms with artworks, albeit of a slightly different epoch, which is ingenious and potentially powerful, though difficult to bring off. She confesses that she is not altogether answering the question but observes that a better question would frame the cultural material in more critical terms.

Nalini gets a begrudging credit for her essay. Her tutor is concerned that there are too many mistakes and that the essay is messy. She feels unsure of some of the wandering structure, with its multiple contentions and wonders where they have come from, especially given that moments in the essay are well written, revealing a phrase-making impulse. She feels uneasy about these colourful flashes, even suspecting that they may be someone else's work, because they have an astonishing confidence about them. Above all, however, the virtues of the essay do not align with the marking rubric, which definitively supports the verdict of a mediocre mark.

Anastasia, on the other hand, receives a high distinction for her essay. She has given the same tutor no room in any of the categories on the rubric to assess the essay as anything but excellent. She has a strong argument, which admittedly comes from the secondary literature. She backs up every claim with evidence, again drawn from the secondary literature. She never trips herself up with poetic links or historical conjecture or dangerous connexions to personal experience. She does not attempt to engage levels of meaning through polemic or even mild disagreement with the terms of the task. She is strategically compliant, acquiring an authoritative air by judiciously assembling the sources in date order and rehearsing their narrative in a coherent structure.

To be fair, Anastasia is not without imagination. It takes skill to organize the words of others into a coherent argument of your own, even if your own argument is only a synthesis of theirs. Anastasia has learned the process well and has the same gift of responsible and compelling case-building that would be needed for defending someone in court. This legalistic imagination, though clearly functional, is not exactly creative. Anastasia has attempted none of Nalini's daring; she never ventures into risk, taking ideas into her own hands and synthesizing an original thought. To be creative involves certain hazard. To advance new ideas in an old field is a risk that Anastasia would instinctively avoid, understanding that she would never have the rhetorical smoothness to sound credible with her own conjectures, which is where Nalini comes unstuck. Being young and unpracticed, Nalini is bound to make mistakes in her attempts at originality; and inevitably some air of immaturity—which she does not conceal with the language of her quotations—will contribute to a lower mark. In a sense she is punished for her creativity.

Undergraduate essays are often constructed around scholarly conventions, in which creative approaches are seen as premature; and in this quest, Anastasia has done well, and has exercised a skill which will be useful in many contexts, including the manipulative task of writing research grant applications. Nalini, however, has exercised a skill of enormous potential, the kind which, in time, distinguishes a brilliant scholar from a good scholar: she already manifests an inclination to make connexions, to upend the question, to query the very terms of an inquiry, to deconstruct the task by matching it with her own experience. Seeing that she only gets mediocre marks in a subject which initially seemed to invite her imagination, Nalini will either suppress her creative responses in future essays or abandon the field in search of one that does not tempt her to use her imagination. Either way, the creativity of this adventurous student is in shock.

Imaginative behaviour is possible within a tightly controlled framework of learning outcomes. Anastasia reveals how it is done, even in the face of an exam. In a well-aligned subject, even this gruelling form of assessment will have been prefigured by learning outcomes, delivery and learning activities, which Anastasia assiduously studies. She knows approximately what question will arise in the exam but not exactly, because the exam questions are kept secret. So she prepares extensive ideal answers for every area likely to come up. However, during the exam, she must exercise her imagination to adapt the exemplary answers to the topic in hand. It is a clever skill. We could call it imagination but we would stop short of calling it creativity. To exercise imagination in the direction of creativity rather than mere manipulation, we would have to observe Nalini's innocence before the challenge, as she takes the exam question on an interrogative journey that explores her experience and takes advantage of her sense of paradox or humour or persuasion. But in exercising episodic imagination rather than strategic imagination, she will not do so well.

The exam or undergraduate essay with marking rubric is by no means the worst academic instrument for suppressing student creativity. As digital learning expands, the role of the quiz expands, offering assessment by robot, without human eye needing to sight the students' work. In the algorithm of the learning management system (LMS) there is no room for creativity and, in most senses, student creativity is not valued for the same reason that it does not fit into the mechanistic structure of a quiz, because it is disruptive and does not match a template. The spontaneous wit of creativity is noisy, messy, unwieldy; it invokes subjectivity and the affections; it is hard to measure and therefore hard to assess reliably. The more a student is creative, the more any two assessors looking at the same piece of work are likely to come to different conclusions about its merit.

Theoretically, it would be possible to set up assessments with a marking rubric that accommodates creativity. Creativity could be one of the criteria, at least signalling to students that creativity is valued and therefore encouraging the risks of unfounded statements, incoherence, excessive colour or metonymy. But there is a problem with this inclusion among the other staunchly measurable criteria, namely that it is a lot harder to calibrate. Engines that help academics write learning outcomes even discourage using the verb 'understand' because understanding is reckoned not to be measurable, not sufficiently demonstrable or capable of proof; it is considered too vague because you do not know what students can achieve when they understand something. Being creative—for which a single verb does not even exist—is even less measurable than understanding, which is the cornerstone of all epistemology and, you might have thought, learning. We cannot say that we have learned something if we do not understand it; further, understanding is not just a precondition of learning to do something but a legitimate end in itself. No one has a problem with understanding in any corner of the universe except in the rarified discourse of learning outcomes, where understanding is reckoned not to be sufficiently solid and attestable relative to describing or demonstrating or naming or calculating. Actually, I am not sure that describing is very measurable either, because one can describe any given phenomenon in so many different ways. But apparently understanding is tainted with even more vagueness. We cannot measure it objectively through an activity; so it should not be used as a verb in a learning outcome. So obsessed are we with measurement that even this stalwart of comprehension is banished from legitimacy as a learning outcome. What chance does creativity have to be recognized as a legitimate learning outcome?

We could insist and overrule the need for measurability in the case of creativity, because it is so important that it features as a university graduate attribute. But even so, the directive to students that they must be creative seems uncomfortable. Is it reasonable to demand that students should have to demonstrate creativity, which in a sense forces them to be creative? Creativity can be accommodated but it is still uncertain how much it can be taught; and every assertion of the teachability of imagination or creativity is a surreptitious challenge to the definition of creativity itself.[3] If students read 'creativity' in the marking rubric, they will feel compelled to demonstrate it. I feel uneasy about this incumbency. Being smart and savvy, Anastasia will have no difficulty developing a strategy to meet the challenge. She will simulate the look of creativity by using clever headings and interspersing the well-referenced text with cartoons and memes. If it is part of the brief, she will introduce the necessary element as a strategic ornament. Meanwhile, Nalini will not necessarily do well because her zeal to enjoin impulse in a piece of academic writing will not necessarily be recognized as creativity—because it is not demonstrably artistic—but rather as wayward and immature daring. Her essay will still be seen as falling short of the tailored appearance of Anastasia's, which is an uncreative essay in creative clothing.

Creativity is not an easy topic to reconcile with university education. Almost as a symbol of our embarrassments, there are many analogous terms in our lexicon of graduate attributes: creativity, imagination, originality and innovation. In most bureaucratic contexts, the term innovation

---

3   See Erica McWilliam, 'Is creativity teachable: Conceptualizing the creativity/ pedagogy relationship in higher education'. Paper presented at the 30th HERDSA Annual Conference: *Enhancing Higher Education, Theory and Scholarship*, Adelaide 2007; and Erica McWilliam & S. Dawson, 'Teaching for creativity: Towards sustainable and replicable pedagogical practice'. *Higher Education*, 56, 633–643 (doi: 10.1007/s10734- 008-9115-7).

is preferred,[4] presumably because it is so strongly associated with prog-ress and positive change; it is understood as profitable for human welfare, equivalent to the visionary and the forward-thinking. Innovation is also highly marketable and features in graduate attributes. There is no downside, almost by definition; because an innovation that is also a failure is some-how expunged from the history of innovation itself: in hindsight it was not innovative but foolhardy or stupid. Stripped of all its false starts, innovation is creativity sanitized, without the wilful mess, the indulgence of caprice or whim that might characterize creativity or even imagination. Innovation is the purely profitable extract of the naturally fruitful waywardness that the mind comes up with.

In all cases, the prior issue is imagination, because no creativity, original-ity or innovation occurs without it. Imagination is also the faculty that was recognized from ancient times, where the word 'creativity' is an artefact of the industrial age. The Greeks had a word to describe creation (δημιουργία) but it normally involved handicrafts, even though it led to the concept of a divine creator or demiurge.[5] The Greeks had numerous conceptions to indi-cate creation,[6] among which the most glamorous is the productive making (ποίησις) which has given us the word poetry.[7]

Even the adjective 'creative' in the English language is an invention of the industrial period. A convenient snapshot of the relevant dates is given in the *Oxford English Dictionary*: the word 'creativity' only appears in 1875.[8] Creativity is an abstract noun derived from the adjective 'creative', which is somewhat older and based, in turn, upon the truly ancient verb to 'create'.

---

4   Beautifully discussed by Joy Whitton in her doctoral thesis *Fostering Imagination in Higher Education Teaching and Learning: Making Connections*, Monash University, 2016.

5   Plato, *Republic* 401a—but could extend to the divine creation of animals, as in Plato's *Timaeus* 41c. There is an adjectival form but this is also understood as 'being of a craftsman', Plato, *Phaedrus* 248e. Occasionally, the word surfaces adverbially, Aristophanes, *Peace* 429. See *LSJ*, sv.

6   *e.g.* ἐργατεία, which could be done by an artisan (χειροτέχνης); *cf.* creator on his or her own (αὐτοκτίστης), a prime generator (γενεσιάρχης), a founder in the sense of beginning things (κατάρχης), the maker of the world (κοσμοποιητής, κοσμουργός), a creator (οἰστρογενέτωρ), creator by hand (χειροτονητής) and life-fashioner (ζωοπλάστης).

7   With adjectival (ποιητικός) and extensions such as creative of life (ζωοποιός).

8   *Oxford English Dictionary*: '1875 A. W. Ward *Eng. Dram. Lit.* I. 506 The spontaneous flow of his [*sc.* Shakespeare's] poetic creativity. 1926 A. N. Whitehead *Relig. in Making* iii. 90 The creativity whereby the actual world has its character of temporal passage to novelty. Ibid. 152 Unlimited possibility and abstract creativity can procure nothing. 1959 *Radio Times* 23 Jan. 3/1 He [*sc.* Burns] was a man of overflowing creativity in so far as the phrase applies to his poetry.' sv.

It is a pattern replicated by 'originality'. First there is a venerable conception of 'origin' (*origo*). Then there is a more recent adjectival form 'original'; and finally, we end up with the abstract substantive 'originality', the quality of being original. Unlike these artificial nouns, however, imagination is an ancient conception, indicating the faculty of generating wilfully an image in the mind. It was recognized by the Greeks in the word that we still use, namely fantasy (φαντασία), though without the modern associations of irreality or delusion, for which the Greeks had other conceptions, like vain belief (κενοδοξία) or wishful thinking. Nevertheless, the deep history of this beautiful cerebral phenomenon is delicate and embodies certain marvellous contradictions which perhaps inhere in the word and lead to some of the embarrassments that we face today. Imagination in ancient Greece denotes an appearing or appearance of something which is implicitly absent and yet also somehow true. The origin of the word relates to a physical manifestation, to appear in reality (φαίνομαι), that is, to have a visual form, whence a verb arose to indicate that this visual form can arise in the mind (φαντάζομαι), whether wilful or involuntary, whether actual or illusory or perceptual or in memory. Already in ancient Greece, fantasy is easily pluralized: it is not one thing, like that unique faculty of gathering ideas from the air, but also inheres in its multifarious ghostly instances. Aristotle says that like feelings (αἰσθήσεις) fantasies are sometimes true and eventuate and sometimes they are false (ψευδεῖς).[9] Plato had already linked feeling and fantasy, but in the sense of perception;[10] but Aristotle is keen to distinguish it as the faculty of imagination, neither perception nor feeling[11] nor belief (δόξα, because faith is absent) nor understanding, mind or discernment,[12] nor even supposition.[13]

Meanwhile, the high destiny of fantasy was prepared by the Greeks in their identification of a certain metaphorical mental agility, in which an ability to see things is used as a cypher for an ability to connect things productively. Thus fantasy already in Greek language could be used for creative imagination[14] and, while these instances admittedly arise in the Hellenistic period, the concept of fantasy happily married a much earlier conception

---

9   *On the soul* 428ᵃ12, or *Metaphysics* 1024ᵇ24; *cf. Rhetoric* 1370ᵃ28.

10   Plato, *Theaetetus* 152c, *Sophist* 264a, 264b.

11   οὐκ ἔστιν αἴσθησις, *On the soul* 428ᵃ5 and 22, 24.

12   ἐπιστήμη, νοῦς, διάνοια *ibid.* 428ᵃ17.

13   ὑπόληψις, *On the soul* 427ᵇ14.

14   'σοφωτέρα μιμήσεως δημιουργός', Philostratus the Athenian, *Life of Apollonius of Tyana*, 6.19.

of poetic inspiration, whence fantasy was used of imagery in literature.[15]
The culture of the muses had given to poetry the divine prestige of contact with ancestral memory, a level of clairvoyance and lucidity. It seems no
accident that one interpreted Homer as the blind bard. His sight is internal.
He is exceptionally in-contact with some inner part of the mind which is
the abode of fantasy, upon which poets with their own imagination always
depend. The Roman conception for imagination (*imaginatio*) which gives
us our word in modern language carries all those poetic connotations but,
like the Greek, consists in a slightly ambiguous relationship with a physical reality, the image. The image is not quite the reality but a reflexion or a
record of the reality. It could be held to be either correct or false.

The ancient world invested much in imagination. It follows a richly promotional trajectory, akin to the generation of the literary masterpieces and
possessing a unique gift for vividness (εὐφαντασίωτος). The Greek conception was conserved throughout the renaissance and beyond, where especially
subtle shades of inventive sensibility were called for. An example from the
sixteenth century is Baldassare Castiglione, explaining how people's dress
should not prejudice your opinion of them; but, he notes, the costume nevertheless is 'no minor element in the fantasy that I carry of the person',[16]
where 'fantasy' is an image that you carry (*portare*). But on other occasions,
the same author in the same text sees fantasy as a phantom, a falsehood.[17]
In the wonderful *novelle* of Matteo Bandello of the same century, fantasy
can be used as a plan, an idea for frightening a husband, for example,[18]
but at the same time it can mean 'liking', as when a man does not even
entertain a woman in his fancies.[19]

As fantasy broadens in its appeal and functions throughout language in
ubiquitous contexts, however, it becomes morally ambiguous. Within the

---

15　Longinus 3.1; 'rhetorical fantasy', 15.2, 15.11 and 'poetic fantasies', Plutarch 2.759c.

16　'non è piccolo argomento della fantasia di chi lo porta, avvenga che talor possa esser
falso; e non solamente questo, ma tutti i modi e costumi, oltre all'opere e parole,
sono giudicio delle qualità di colui in cui si veggono.' *Il libro del cortegiano* 2.28. All
translations are those of the author, unless otherwise noted.

17　'"E' non è possibile che tu non ci vegghi; egli è una fantasia che tu t'hai posta in
capo". "Oimè", replica l'altro, "che questa non è fantasia, né vi veggo io altrimenti
che se non avessi mai avuti occhi in testa'.' Castiglione, *Cortegiano* 2.86.

18　'Era in quel punto montata la fantasia a la donna di far una solenne paura a l'amante,
e per questo invitava il marito a voler tagliar la veste, non perciò avendo animo che
l'effetto seguisse.' Bandello, *Novelle* 1.3.

19　'Essendo adunque Lattanzio a cena assettato, s'abbatté a caso a seder a canto a
Caterina, la quale piú non gli pareva aver veduta, e, se pur veduta l'aveva, non gli era
altrimente entrata in fantasia.' 1.9.

range of opinions about imagination, some enthusiastic and some reserved, we may propose a pattern which becomes telling for the contemporary educational setting. When imagination and fantasy are confined to personal or autonomously creative ends, they are valorized. But when they apply to the social order, they may be held in suspicion. Throughout the renaissance, the word was used of the stubbornness of an *idée fixe*, some preconception or suspicions, imaginary opinions (*sospetti ed imaginarie openioni*) that deceive you but have stuck in the head (*si ficcano una fantasia nel capo*) which are the cause of ruin;[20] they can be a raving in the mind,[21] a tenacious obsession or 'fantasy and crickets in the mind'.[22] The objective in such narratives is to shed the sticky fantasy.[23]

In art and architecture, fantasy is fulsomely honoured, because it sits perfectly in the discourse of personal invention, which is hugely popular in writers like Giorgio Vasari, whose biographical output identified creative impulse so much with the individual genius.[24] We never find the word invention used pejoratively, because it is understood as one of the defining features of beautiful and meaningful art and architecture, work that is in some way extraordinary, ornamented and invested with copious ideas. So closely is fantasy identified with art that the fantasy is counted as the art itself, as when Pollaiuolo does wax reliefs and other fantasies[25] or Giorgione creates his history pictures and other fantasies[26] and, of course, the *fantasia* was to become a staple of music in the baroque. More usually, however, fantasy is something that comes into your head, as it did in Leonardo's.[27]

---

20   'Il Bandello al molto cortese signore il signor Ermes Vesconte', letter at *Novelle* 1.27.

21   'l'era entrata questa fantasia nel capo che non era bastante cosa del mondo a levarle questo farnetico di mente.' 1.27.

22   'né gli metteva fantasia e grilli in capo, essendo il caso tale che quanto piú se ne parlava piú putiva.' 2.24.

23   'l'essortò assai a deporre questa fantasia e pentirsi', 2.22; 'né si poteva levar questa sua fantasia di capo', 2.32; 'E non si potendo cavar di fantasia la sua Beatrice', 2.28; 'questa ladrona di Catella la quale non mi posso cavar fuor de la fantasia.' 2.36; 'Pertanto levati di capo queste fantasie, che sono piú per annoiarti e recarti danno che piacere né utile.' 2.36.

24   There are approximately 150 instances in his *Lives of the painters*.

25   'E molti anni seguitò l'arte, disegnando continovamente e faccendo di rilievo cere et altre fantasie, che in brieve tempo lo fecero tenere (come egli era) il principale di quello esercizio.' 'Vita di Antonio e Piero Pollaiuolo'

26   'Nella quale oltra molti quadri e storie et altre sue fantasie, si vede un quadro lavorato a olio in su la calcina; cosa che ha retto alla acqua, al sole et al vento, e conservatasi fino ad oggi.' Life of Giorgione.

27   'Nondimeno, benché egli a sì varie cose attendesse, non lasciò mai il disegnare et il fare di rilievo, come cose che gli andavano a fantasia più d'alcun'altra.' Life of Leonardo.

But even in these wonderful texts, so much a paean to artistic autonomy, there is some suspicion about fantasy in *the social order*, revealed in discussions about the difficult personality of Piero di Cosimo, whose 'fantastic life took him to a miserable ending', where 'fantastic' has the value of crackpot. If he had been a bit more domestic and lovable toward his friends, says Vasari, his old age would not have been so wicked.[28] His fantasy life made him both insular and unrealistic, fantasizing in solitude and making castles in the air,[29] because even his deformity made him extravagant, bizarre and fantastic.[30]

In today's language, fantasy contains this ambiguity to a heightened degree, where it can be sublime but also ugly, a bit sordid—as in sexual fantasy, which is now distributed to the social order, where it may be suspected of *bad taste*—but above all unreal. These pejorative meanings become persistent in the baroque, as in Boileau's 'fantastic code built from vain laws'[31] or Dryden's 'false fires of a fantastic glory', also applying themselves unhappily in the social order.[32] In the sober eighteenth century, the playwright Carlo Goldoni suggests that when people are so proud that they become ashamed of not knowing something, ignorant judgements are produced by a distorted fantasy, misguided and wicked.[33] As if anticipating Google, the librarian in *Il cavaliere di buon gusto* explains to the Count that one can easily become learned through consulting dictionaries; but his patron deplores the tendency to study without fundamentals. One has recourse to the dictionary and learns superficially; one makes an embryo in one's *fantasy*; nothing is really digested and people themselves become indexes and

---

28   'la stessa vita fantastica gli conduce a fini miserabili; come apertamente poté vedersi in tutte le azzioni di Piero di Cosimo. Il quale a la virtù che egli ebbe, se fusse stato più domestico et amorevole verso gli amici, il fine de la sua vecchiezza non sarebbe stato meschino', Piero di Cosimo.

29   'Era costui tanto amico de la solitudine, che non aveva piacere se non quando pensoso da sé solo poteva andarsene fantasticando e fare i suoi castelli in aria.' Piero di Cosimo.

30   'per la deformità sua è tanto stravagante, bizzarro e fantastico'; also an accusation levelled at Michelangelo: 'Onde ne fu tenuto da chi superbo, et da chi bizzarro et fantastico, non havendo ne l'uno ne l'altro vitio, ma (come à molti eccellenti huomini e avvenuto) l'amore della virtù et la continua essercitatione di lei, lo facevan solitario, et cosi dilettarsi et appagarsi in quella, che le compagnie non solamente non gli davan contento, ma gli porgevan dispiacere, come quelle che lo sviavano dalla meditatione sua', Ascanio Condivi, *Vita di Michelagnolo Buonarroti* (Rom 1553) 44r.

31   'Bâtit de vaines lois un code fantastique', Boileau *Satire* 11.174.

32   John Dryden, *Mariage à la mode* 4.1.

33   'la fantasia stravolta, sconsigliata e maligna.' *Le donne curiose* 3.4.

dictionaries.[34] For the rest, one reads a string of pejoratives, like 'all madness, all tricks of fantasy, tricks of ambition'.[35]

Similar observations may be made of imagination which, as noted, has an analogous structure through its Latin root (*imago*) of something seen as a kind of substitute for reality, which may or may not equate with the truth. As a faculty, imagination is highly esteemed, and for obvious reasons, because poets, architects, scientists and composers can hardly function without it. Even if they function within tight conventions, they need to be able to make as-yet-unimagined connexions to create original verses, buildings, discoveries and melodies. If we think of creative process, the imaginative element is more labile than the construction that results from it. Mechanically, to imagine is easier than expressing something in words; because we imagine things all by ourselves, in the intimacy of our thoughts; whereas expression indicates relationships with others who are either swayed or unconvinced. Already in the fourteenth century, Petrarch described the relation: I could never imagine, much less tell (*nonché narrar*) the effects that the soft eyes make on my heart.[36] Imagining the effect of the eyes is hard enough but speaking about it is harder. The Western genius seldom separates the two phases, because they are organically linked; and in imagining, one also needs a sense of what one might be imagining for, in the same way that when one is building upon something imagined, one needs yet more imagination to find the beautiful techniques and vessels that best accommodate and nourish the imagined potential. Perhaps for that reason, there is sometimes an air of strategy in the term. In Boccaccio, writing at the same time as Petrarch, the word is associated with analysis and planning. Masetto, about to decide on his diabolical plan to infiltrate a nunnery under the cover of dumbness, is described as imagining—after parsing many things in his mind (*molte cose divisate seco, imaginò*)—what his chances will be. Having decided on this plan (*imaginazion*), he set out and achieved his fill till exhaustion.[37] In the sixteenth-century poet Ariosto, imagination

---

34   'In oggi vi sono tanti bei dizionari, che facilmente un uomo si può erudire.' The count Ottavio replies: 'In oggi non si studia più un'arte con fondamento. Si ricorre al dizionario, si apprende la cosa superficialmente, si fa un embrione nella fantasia, non si digerisce bene veruna cosa, e gli uomini stessi diventano indici e dizionari.' Carlo Goldoni, *Il cavaliere di buon gusto* 1.6.

35   'Sior Florindo caro, tutte pazzie, tutti inganni della fantasia, inganni dell'ambizion, che lusinga i omeni, e ghe dà da intender, che la vendetta più facile sia la più vera, e che per vendicarse del reo, sia lecito opprimer anca l'innocente.' *Le femmine puntigliose* 3.5.

36   *Canzoniere* 73.61–63.

37   'in questa imaginazion fermatosi', *Decameron* 3.1.

is equated with design;[38] and even when not set out as a rigid plan, the imagination is tellingly guided by desire, as when one studies a person and imitates her, imagining how she would act and appear; and through this hungry vision, using mirrors and acting, one seeks to replicate the attire, hair and mannerisms.[39]

In the history of ideas, imagination is used in processes of reason and logic but, rather like fantasy, it is not responsible to reason. It is independent and enjoys the same privileges of wilful travel, metaphor and extrapolation conjoined with desire. Unsurprisingly, therefore, it is sometimes coupled with fantasy, as in Bandello in the sixteenth century, where both words in the one sentence indicate a nascent intention.[40] By the same errant instincts, imagination can be wrong but it can also be generative and create the true.[41] And in the renaissance, imagination can be pluralized in the same way that we pluralize fantasies. Bandello speaks of imaginations, meaning things imagined and, as it happens, these imaginations are untrue (*false imaginazioni*) or hysterical phantom worries (*chimerici affanni*).[42] They are monstrous because they constitute an ill-fit in the social order.

Renaissance culture was also passionately attracted to the generative faculties of invention, the idea that you find something or, by the blessing of inspiration, that something comes to you. The motif of an idea coming to you is somehow inseparable from the motif of you going out to look for it. The idea *comes*, a verb which is the origin of the word invention (*venire*), to come. It comes to you personally, not to anyone else in the same way. The art of biographical literature is inflected with a subtext of the peculiar imagination of a person whose destiny is to happen upon certain novelties, either to come to the ideas or for the ideas to come to them. The ambiguity

---

38 'Questa imaginazion sì gli confuse / e sì gli tolse ogni primier disegno', *Orlando furioso* 9.15.

39 'Come ella s'orna e come il crin dispone / studia imitarla, e cerca il più che sai / di parer dessa, e poi sopra il verrone / a mandar giù la scala ne verrai. / Io verrò a te con imaginazione / che quella sii, di cui tu i panni avrai: / e così spero, me stesso ingannando, / venir in breve il mio desir sciemando.' 5.25.

40 'Ora io su questo fatto tutto il dí discorrendo e diverse imaginazioni facendo, non v'ho mai altro compenso saputo ritrovare, se non uno che assai piú di tutti gli altri mi va per la fantasia, che è che io me ne vada a la corte del nostro supremo signore re Mattia.' 1.22.

41 'si vede che talora l'imaginazione fa quello che farebbe il vero, come in questa novella intervenne.' Letter al gentilissimo messer Domenico Campana detto Strascino 3.20.

42 'Andate col malanno e non mi rompete più il capo con queste vostre false imaginazioni. Mò che febre peggio che continova è la vostra? Io non potrò ormai piú con voi vivere. Se avete gelosia de le mosche che per l'aria volano, che ve ne posso fare? Andatevi ad impiccare, e uscirete di questi vostri chimerici affanni.' 1.43.

as to which is the destination and which is the agent is immaterial; it is in all events the peculiar statement of fecundity, where the fertile imagination generates copious ideas that find their way into miraculous works of art and architecture. Vasari speaks often of this gift, like the incessant thinking (*frequente imaginazione*) with which Antonello da Messina constantly (*del continuo*) enriched the art of painting.[43] The substance of imagination is thinking of spectacle beyond your ken, beyond your conception, like the sadness of a compassionate painting showing what 'is so impossible to imagine', the pain of having lost the most precious thing that you have and then to face losing the second.[44]

The more common use of the imagination is coupled with the prolific production of strangeness, the bizarre and capricious, the variety of angels, devils, earthquakes, fire and ruin, nudes and perspectives, as Vasari represents Luca Signorelli 'strangely imagining' his beautiful but terrifying invention of the Antichrist.[45] The bizarre, the ornamented, the sense of plenty and variety are hard to imagine.[46] With Michelangelo, even the ancients would have had difficulty imagining (*imaginandosi appena*) something so strange and difficult that the force of his most godly ingenious wit (*divinissimo ingegno*) achieved with industry, drawing, art, judgement and grace.[47] The quality of a person's

---

43   'e con la frequente imaginazione che del continuo aveva di arricchire l'arte del dipignere.' Antonello da Messina.

44   'Èvvi lo svenimento della Madonna che è pietosissimo, ma molto più compassionevole lo aiuto delle Marie in verso di quella, per vedersi ne' loro aspetti tanto dolore, quanto è appena possibile imaginarsi nel morire la più cara cosa che tu abbia, e stare in perdita della seconda.' Ercole da Ferrara.

45   'la fine del mondo: invenzione bellissima, bizzarra e capricciosa, per la varietà di vedere tanti angeli, demoni, terremoti, fuochi, ruine e gran parte de' miracoli di Anticristo; dove mostrò la invenzione e la pratica grande ch'egli aveva ne gli ignudi, con molti scorti e belle forme di figure, imaginandosi stranamente il terror di que' giorni.' Luca Signorelli.

46   'Dicono che in detta opera erano sei perle come nocciuole avellane, e non si può imaginare, secondo che s'è visto poi [in] un disegno di quella, le più belle bizzarrie di legami nelle gioie e nella varietà di molti putti et altre figure, che servivano a molti varii e graziati ornamenti.' Lorenzo Ghiberti.

47   'Ma quello che fra i morti e vivi porta la palma e trascende e ricuopre tutti è il divino Michel Agnolo Buonarroti il qual non solo tien il principato di una di queste arti, ma di tutte tre insieme. Costui supera e vince non solamente tutti costoro, che hanno quasi che vinto già la natura, ma quelli stessi famosissimi antichi, che sì lodatamente fuor d'ogni dubbio la superarono: et unico giustamente si trionfa di quegli, di questi e di lei, non imaginandosi appena quella cosa alcuna sì strana e tanto difficile, che egli con la virtù del divinissimo ingegno suo, mediante la industria, il disegno, l'arte, il giudizio e la grazia, di gran lunga non la trapassi.' Proemio terza parte.

wit or mind (*ingegno*) is tied to imagination[48] which, in large part, exists outside the social order.

But even in Vasari, imagination is dangerous when it conspicuously intersects with the social order. Leonardo, for example was so intelligent and strove so hard to achieve impossible perfection through his imagination that many of his projects came to nothing. His imagination led him to unrealistic ambitions. Further, his caprices were so many that while he philosophized about science, he formed a concept in his mind so heretical that he distanced himself from any religion, considering himself more a philosopher than a Christian.[49] Even technically, his imagination led him to try painting with oil in plaster, which was disastrous.[50] These somewhat monitory instances of peril, where imagination goes too far, are the grit that proves the mettle of the artistic mind. The great artists do with imagination what you can never do just with the hand,[51] achieving superlative grace or beauty beyond our capacity to understand, as in Raphael.[52] With great artists, you cannot desire or imagine better, because their work is miraculous.[53] The miraculous is so

---

48   'Et è cosa maravigliosa a considerare, che e' penetrasse mai con lo ingegno in sì alta imaginazione.' Tommaso Fiorentino (Giottino).

49   'Trovasi che Lionardo per l'intelligenzia de l'arte cominciò molte cose e nessuna mai ne finì, parendoli che la mano aggiugnere non potesse alla perfezzione de l'arte ne le cose, che egli si imaginava, con ciò sia che si formava nella idea alcune difficultà tanto maravigliose, che con le mani, ancora che elle fussero eccellentissime, non si sarebbeno espresse mai. E tanti furono i suoi capricci, che filosofando de le cose naturali, attese a intendere la proprietà de le erbe, continuando et osservando il moto del cielo, il corso de la luna e gli andamenti del sole. Per il che fece ne l'animo un concetto sì eretico, che e' non si accostava a qualsivoglia religione, stimando per avventura assai più lo esser filosofo che cristiano.' Leonardo da Vinci.

50   'Et imaginandosi di volere a olio colorire in muro, fece una composizione d'una mistura sì grossa, per lo incollato del muro, che continuando a dipignere in detta sala, cominciò a colare, di maniera che in breve tempo abbandonò quella.' Leonardo.

51   'la quale pare impossibile ch'egli potesse non esprimere con la mano, ma imaginare con la fantasia', Antonio da Correggio.

52   'E così la accompagnavano alcuni putti bellissimi quanto si può imaginare bellezza.' Raphael. *cf.* 'La quale invenzione, avendola fatta Rafaello sopra la finestra, viene a esser quella facciata più scura, avvenga che quando si guarda tal pittura ti dà il lume nel viso e contendono tanto bene insieme la luce viva con quella dipinta co' diversi lumi della notte, che ti par vedere il fumo della torcia, lo splendor dell'angelo con le scure tenebre della notte e sì naturali e sì vere, che non diresti mai che ella fussi dipinta, avendo espresso tanto propriamente sì difficile imaginazione.' Raphael; and also 'Il quale fece egli finire con tanta perfezzione, che sino da Fiorenza fece condurre il pavimento da Luca della Robbia. Onde certamente non può per pitture, stucchi, ordine, invenzioni più belle né farsi, né imaginarsi di fare.' Raphael.

53   'Oltra che e' non si può desiderare o imaginar meglio d'un velo postole intorno, lavorato da lui con tanta bellezza e con tanta leggiadria, che il vederlo solo è miracolo.' Andrea Sansovino

marvellously converted into the empirical through art; and imagination is so powerful that its figments can appear to a person or come to the artist in a dream.[54]

The phrase 'I cannot imagine' is not always reserved for something unthinkably great. There is no reason why it would not equally apply to things that are abysmal[55] or even to relief from something negative;[56] though usually it is for marvel and stupendousness, delicateness, abundance of forms that a sophisticated mind of genius can imagine.[57] Capricious inventions are learned, achieved with a poetic pictorial sense of much elegance, and realized in such a considered way that you would consider the figments real rather than imaginary.[58] The word 'imagined' is used to separate work done-from-life and work done-by-memory or construction[59] and sometimes it is therefore synonymous with 'idea'.[60]

---

54 'E dilettossi tanto Spinello di farlo orribile e contraffatto, che e' si dice (tanto può la imaginazione) che la figura da lui dipinta gli apparve in sogno, domandandolo dove egli la avesse vista sì brutta e perché fattole tale scorno co' suoi pennelli.' Spinello Aretino.

55 'Quivi fece nella Pace sopra le cose di Raffaello una opra, della quale non dipinse mai peggio a' suoi giorni, né posso imaginare onde ciò procedesse, se non ch'egli gonfio di vana gloria di se stesso, niente stimava le cose d'altri: per che gli avvenne che, ciò poco apprezzando, la sua fu poi meno stimata.' Rosso Fiorentino.

56 'Et il primo che vi fece, fu in San Petronio in una cappella un San Rocco di molta grandezza, al quale diede bellissima aria et a parte per parte lo fece veramente molto bene, imaginandoselo alquanto sollevato da 'l dolore che gli dava la peste nella coscia, il che mostra con la testa guardando il cielo in attitudine di ringraziare.' Francesco Mazzola.

57 'A San Simeone fecero la facciata de' Gaddi, ch'è cosa di maraviglia e di stupore nel considerarvi dentro i belli e tanti e varii abiti, la infinità delle celate antiche, de' soccinti, de' calzari e delle barche, ornate con tanta leggiadria e copia d'ogni cosa, che imaginare si possa un sofistico ingegno,' Polidoro da Caravaggio; and later in the same text: 'E sopra altre storie lavorate con alcuni vasi d'oro contrafatti con tante bizzarrie dentro, che occhio mortale non potrebbe imaginarsi altro, né più bello né più nuovo, con alcuni elmi etrusci da rimaner confuso per la moltiplicazione e copia di sì belle e capricciose fantasie, ch'uscivano loro de la mente. Le quali opere sono state imitate da infiniti che lavorano in tali bizzarrie. Fecero ancora il cortile di questa casa, e similmente la loggia, colorita di grotteschine picciole, che sono stimate divine. Insomma ciò che eglino toccarono, con grazia e bellezza infinita assoluto renderono.' Polidoro da Caravaggio.

58 'Le quali capricciose invenzioni dottamente con senso poetico e pittoresco ha garbatissimamente finite ... la quale opera fu talmente considerata d'imaginazione e poi sì ben condotta, che non pitture o cose imaginate, ma vive e vere si rappresentano, perché qui si ha paura che non ti cada addosso, et il calor del sole nel friggere e nell'abbruciar l'ale de 'l misero giovane fa conoscere il fumo e 'l fuoco acceso.' Giulio Romano.

59 'parte ritratti di naturale e parte imaginati', Perino del Vaga.

60 'Infelici secoli possono chiamarsi quegli che privi sono stati di così bella virtù, la quale ha forza, quando è da dotta mano, o in muro o in tavola, in superficie di

In many ways, the canonical artistic literature—lauding the irresponsible invention of the bizarre and the copious—did not recommend freedom of imagination to future generations. It accorded with the baroque in Italy but already in the formation of academies in France and England a strong preference arose to regulate, to resist any form of excess, to achieve conformity of taste under the governance of measure and reason. And so begins the contemporary institutional suspicion, already foreshadowed in Vasari's embarrassment over Leonardo's heresy, that imagination might need to be controlled. It leads as much to silly things as to brilliant things. Like a dream, it is impossible to control: individuals may or may not be able to manage their imagination through internal creative process; but any society which enjoys the constancy and pride of orthodoxy may be threatened with impotence over this *runaway thinking*, a conceptualizing without recognized parameters, an errant flow of ideas that leads in unforeseen directions. Imagination needs to be curbed.

The seventeenth-century writer Jean de La Bruyère, himself endowed with fabulous wit and imaginative expression, takes a dim view of imagination as a liberty: lively wits, full of fire and whom a huge imagination transports beyond the rules (*emporte hors des règles*) and beyond niceness (*la justesse*) can never slake their hyperbole. As for the sublime, even among great geniuses, there are only a few at the top who are capable of it.[61] He typifies the taste of women uncharitably, saying that a vain and indiscreet man who is a great talker and a poor friend, who speaks assuringly about himself and scornfully about others, a man who is impetuous, haughty, audacious, with neither manners nor probity, a man of zero judgement but *a very liberal imagination*, lacks nothing to be adored by women if not some nice features and a good figure.[62] As for literature, he declares that we do not need to have too much imagination; it often only produces vain and puerile ideas that do not at all serve to perfect taste and improve us: our

---

disegno, o con colore lavorata, tenere gli animi fermi et attenti a risguardare il magisterio delle opere umane, rappresentando la idea e la imaginazione di quelle parti che sono celesti, alte e divine, dove per pruova si mostra l'altezza dello ingegno e le invenzioni dello intelletto,' Andrea Taffi.

61 'Les esprits vifs, pleins de feu, et qu'une vaste imagination emporte hors des règles et de la justesse, ne peuvent s'assouvir de l'hyperbole. Pour le sublime, il n'y a, même entre les grands génies, que les plus élevés qui en soient capables.' Jean de La Bruyère, *Les caractères* 2.55.

62 'À un homme vain, indiscret, qui est grand parleur et mauvais plaisant, qui parle de soi avec confiance et des autres avec mépris, impétueux, altier, entreprenant, sans mœurs ni probité, de nul jugement et d'une imagination très libre, il ne lui manque plus, pour être adoré de bien des femmes, que de beaux traits et la taille belle.' 4.31.

thoughts have to be taken with good sense and right reason and must be an effect of our judgement.[63]

La Bruyère deplored the artificiality of his contemporaries. In conversation, polite society leaves to the vulgar the art of speaking in an intelligible fashion. Things of little clarity are joined by others yet more obscure; and to their vagueness one attaches total enigmas, always followed by long applause. People end up not being understood by one another. Nothing is needed in holding these conversations like good sense, judgement, memory nor the slightest intellectual capacity: one only needs wit, not of the best type but a false one, where the imagination has too great a role.[64] It is flashy, over-rich, effusive, silly and false, as even La Bruyère's contemporary John Dryden says: 'The gaudy effort of luxuriant art, / In all imagination's glitter drest.'[65] There are cases where La Bruyère uses imagination in a positive way but he also tellingly uses the term to denote phantoms or things that do not exist.[66]

Suspicion over imagination arises in regulatory cultures of any epoch. Uneasy or apprehensive feelings over imagination are not just a historical quirk of baroque culture, because the suspicion is structural. In all periods, imagination has shades of magic, to which authorities once reacted

---

63 'Il ne faut pas qu'il y ait trop d'imagination dans nos conversations ni dans nos écrits; elle ne produit souvent que des idées vaines et puériles, qui ne servent point à perfectionner le goût et à nous rendre meilleurs: nos pensées doivent être prises dans le bon sens et la droite raison, et doivent être un effet de notre jugement.' 6.17.

64 'L'on a vu, il n'y a pas longtemps, un cercle de personnes des deux sexes, liées ensemble par la conversation et par un commerce d'esprit. Ils laissaient au vulgaire l'art de parler d'une manière intelligible; une chose dite entre eux peu clairement en entraînait une autre encore plus obscure, sur laquelle on enchérissait par de vraies énigmes, toujours suivies de longs applaudissements: par tout ce qu'ils appelaient délicatesse, sentiments, tour et finesse d'expression, ils étaient enfin parvenus à n'être plus entendus et à ne s'entendre pas eux-mêmes. Il ne fallait, pour fournir à ces entretiens, ni bon sens, ni jugement, ni mémoire, ni la moindre capacité: il fallait de l'esprit, non pas du meilleur, mais de celui qui est faux, et où l'imagination a trop de part.' 6.65.

65 John Dryden, *Marriage à-la-mode*; cf. 'Seen by a strong imagination's beam, / That tricks and dresses up the gaudy dream'.

66 'les points d'honneur imaginaires', *op. cit.* 11.12; see also 'Ainsi le sage, qui n'est pas, ou qui n'est qu'imaginaire, se trouve naturellement et par lui-même au-dessus de tous les événements et de tous les maux', 12.3; 'Les enfants ont déjà de leur âme l'imagination et la mémoire, c'est-à-dire ce que les vieillards n'ont plus, et ils en tirent un merveilleux usage pour leurs petits jeux et pour tous leurs amusements: c'est par elles qu'ils répètent ce qu'ils ont entendu dire, qu'ils contrefont ce qu'ils ont vu faire, qu'ils sont de tous métiers', 12.53; 'Ceux qui, sans nous connaître assez, pensent mal de nous, ne nous font pas de tort: ce n'est pas nous qu'ils attaquent, c'est le fantôme de leur imagination.' 13.35.

with horror and persecution, chasing witchcraft from contact with a pious society. The enduring distrust of imagination ensues from its irresponsibility to command, its intellectual waywardness, its idiosyncrasy, its eccentric vagueness, its disregard for authority and rules. Though not at all opposed to reason—indeed frequently functioning through reason, in fact intimately a part of advances in reason—imagination represents thought closer to the unconscious, the dream, the joke or rapture, the faulty pattern, the haywire. By that token, though imagination can be a party to advanced reason, it is not intrinsically conducive to measurement, fairness, comprehensiveness or closure. To any bureaucratic process, imagination seems largely aberrant. It self-evidently has a place in art of one kind or another; but its comfort in the creative arts equates to its marginalization in mainstream fields.

Much jockeying has occurred around the concept of creativity in education, which remains the marginal Other, both desired and anomalous, sought and needed but a bit monstrous at the same time. A particularly well-intentioned trend has arisen to redefine creativity in favour of the institutional, to sanitize it so that it is more compatible with the priorities of measuring and sorting students. A good example is summed up by Erica McWilliam, who distinguishes 'first generation creativity concepts' from 'second generation creativity concepts'. In the first category, we have the implicitly outdated romantic concepts of genius, where creativity is aligned with the 'serendipitous and non-economic'; it is characterized by 'singularization, the spontaneous / arising from the inner self'; it is 'outside the box or any other metric', 'arts-based, natural or innate, not amenable to teaching, and not assessable'. Second generation creativity concepts, clearly more advanced, accommodate the '"Hard" and an economic driver, the pluralized / team-based, the dispositional and environmental', something that 'requires rules and boundaries' and is 'transdisciplinary, learnable, teachable, assessable'.[67] By this language, the romantic view of creativity is anachronistic, discredited, backward; and all is redeemed through a new promise of seamless infusion through the agenda of the contemporary academy. Alas, the alignment of creativity with group-work, measurement and teachability contains as much witchcraft as might the romantic view that it would replace; and none of it is any use to Nalini.

---

67   Erica McWilliam, *Carrick Associate Fellowship Report*, December, 2007, retrieved December 2016 from www.cci.edu.au/sites/default/files/fellowships_report_erica_mcwilliam_08-2.pdf.

Contemporary coursework education is a highly regulated business and, all rhetoric over innovation notwithstanding, imagination does not sit comfortably within it. The mismatch may be understood through the need that educators now feel to spell out learning outcomes which, as noted, demand to be measured. Creativity and especially imagination cannot be measured without distortion, because they are about potential, about a process rather than an outcome. Creativity and imagination are like curiosity in the sense that they are about wanting to know more, not wanting strategically to demonstrate what you already know. When education is structured rigidly around those tangible signs of satisfying what is laid out from the outset, the focus on the outcome forecloses on the potential of the process. Imagination and creativity depend on the gestational; they operate on the basis of non-fixity, freedom from linearity, or the finite. In any case, imaginative responses are heterogeneous and culturally inflected. They respect Nalini's vein of reflexion, where she seeks to square an exam question, say, with her personal local experience. Alas, imaginative responses are therefore not so suitable for comparison, for ranking or benchmarking. The education system that follows these regimes of measurement is structurally hostile to creativity, because it intrinsically denies the open-endedness of imagination.

It may be objected that imagination and creativity, if they are worth anything in the cultural sphere, result in monuments, that is, tangible products, and are not merely invested in processes. The same Vasari who applauds the imaginative genius of the masters was the most recognizing of their masterpieces. Could it be that creativity and imagination are just an overactive random generator? If it is a kind of machine that is good for the gestation of anything—silly things as much as clever ones, ratbag ideas alongside clairvoyant ones—then it makes no sense to measure imagination or creativity in any circumstances other than through their results. Certainly, that objection may hold. It makes no sense to measure imagination or creativity. But why would we want to in the first place? Our aim is to cultivate them, not to measure them. If imagination and creativity are suppressed, we will never know what they are capable of in any given individual and in society as a whole.

Today's tertiary education system is governed by a structure that begins with learning outcomes. If syllabus is introduced outside the learning outcomes, it may be deemed not to belong. Imagination and creativity tend inherently to sit outside the learning outcomes, because learning outcomes have to be measurably assessable. Creativity and imagination belong, more properly, to the unknown learning outcome, the outcome that has not been prefigured, the surprise, colour, the unforeseen. When we are imaginative, no one else has been able to see what we are thinking unless by imaginative sympathy. The student who is imaginative is likely in some sense to transcend the learning outcomes. Alas, we can never write this unknown learning outcome. It makes no sense to suggest: 'by successful completion of this unit, you will have thought of something that we cannot predict'. There is no protocol or logic for handling the imaginative process in a learning outcome. Learning outcomes, meanwhile, are good and systematic for uncreative processes. They systematically produce uncreative outcomes.

There are lecturers who feel comfortable writing a learning outcome that includes 'originality', which potentially fills the creative vacuum. If originality is included in the learning outcomes, it might then feature on the marking rubric. There is some scope, then, that Nalini will be redeemed. 'Originality', however, is like 'innovation', an impeccable and sanitized form of creativity which we aim for and seek in our doctoral studies and unfortunately seldom find in great measure. And there is the rub. If originality is hard to achieve or detect, can it be easily measured? And, above all, can it be taught? Are you really teaching it in your unit or subject or module? You might believe that you are personally original and, by dint of some charismatic induction, you are passing on the gift as you teach. That would be ideal; the colour of your own thought and delivery can indeed become infectious. But can you honestly claim that you are teaching your students how to be original? If you are not actively and effectively teaching originality, you cannot include it as a learning outcome. It would be a breach of constructive alignment.

In principle, it is good to call for originality—and heaven forbid that we discourage it!—but in the context of learning outcomes, it remains a difficult fit, because it is also shy of measurement and is liable to overstatement and delusion. Even for professors, originality is a tall order, and few of us can claim it without some shame. As La Bruyère warns us from the beginning of his major work, 'everything has been said and you have arrived too late after seven millennia of people who think'.[68] Nalini is both imaginative and original, but the proof of originality is harder than that of imagination. Unless you define originality as superficially putting a personal inflexion

---

68   'Tout est dit, et l'on vient trop tard depuis plus de sept mille ans qu'il y a des hommes et qui pensent.' *Les caractères* 2.1.

on something already known, the proof of originality would entail a long search for everyone else's thoughts on the topic to distinguish the novel content that Nalini has come up with. If we demand that students themselves conduct the proof of their originality, Anastasia will do a better job, because she will more systematically summarize what everyone else has said and cleverly craft a statement that diplomatically shows a modest but significant detail or combination or inflexion that supposedly exists nowhere else. In order to transform itself into a learning outcome, the labour of originality descends to manipulation.

Invoking balance, the word originality can be used in the learning outcomes alongside other outcomes that reward knowledge and skills of classification, identification, organization or calculation. So fairness would prevail. No academic wants to set up learning outcomes that make life hard for Anastasia or punish her for her diligence. She is not creative and her excellence in acing the assessments up to this point does not compromise her learning. She is a good learner and should be encouraged in her systematic methods. Her view of herself is modest enough to know that she is not original: rather, she considers herself a brilliant plodder, a dogged adept, a persevering strategist. She loves the word 'effective'. She is already thinking, correctly, that she can achieve great success beyond her coursework either in a profession (most likely) where she will valuably clarify complexity and help make decisions, or even become an academic, where she will also make an excellent contribution, judiciously matching offerings with needs and producing research of a highly organized and referenced kind, albeit with unremarkable conclusions. If, as a student, Anastasia sees a unit that demands originality, she may consider it to be too risky and choose another unit instead.

Could we reconcile the two extremes, the system that demands the learning outcomes and the latitude that wants to transcend them through 'irresponsible' flights of comparison, metaphor, extrapolation and imagery (especially, as we know from Nalini, that they are likely to be somewhat embarrassing in their immaturity)? Could there be, as paradoxical as it sounds, an unknown learning outcome that accommodates imagination and creativity? The only unknown learning outcome that could ever embrace imagination and creativity would be 'love for the subject', that is, an investigative affection, a thrill with the speculative content or the delight in the use you might make of it in another context. Alas, we could never contemplate this learning outcome. Love is also not measurable. We cannot adequately assess people's love; and even if we could, it seems unethical to proceed, because we cannot oblige anyone to love anything in the same way that we cannot teach this: compulsory love is a contradiction in terms.[69]

In our allegory of creative approaches to writing an essay or sitting an exam, Nalini is prepared to show more love, which perhaps necessarily has a reckless dimension that can easily lead to embarrassments. Anastasia is too circumspect and strategic to lose control over any emotional investment, other than the zeal to excel with high grades. She is imaginative with her skill of matching available texts to the demands of the task; but this exercise of clear-thinking does not entail much creativity and could easily be fouled up by creative passion.

Creativity does not directly equate with imagination. Although imagination is prior and an essential ingredient, it is not the whole of creativity. As a necessary but not sufficient criterion for creativity, imagination is an important element in human empathy. For example, in a text by Martha Nussbaum, we encounter 'the narrative imagination' which

> means the ability to think what it might be like to be in the shoes of a person different from oneself, to be an intelligent reader of that person's story and to understand the emotions and wish and desires that someone so placed might have. The cultivation of sympathy has been a key part of the best modern ideas of democratic education ... [70]

Nussbaum emphasizes that 'the arts in schools and colleges ... cultivate capacities for play and empathy in a general way, and they address particular cultural blind spots' and describes how important it is to link empathetic imagination to the motif of equal human dignity. She warns that we can have high levels of sympathy for people close to us and none for people of different colour or religion. No humanist panacea, then, imagination can be used toward racist or chauvinist ends[71] and the same, incidentally, can be said of creativity. Creativity may or may not create a bond between people and encourage empathy (one might think of the pugnacious Italian futurists, for example); but the beautiful use that

---

69   It is notable that Martha Nussbaum specifically invokes the concept of love in her analysis of imagination in education when she explains that ethical exhortations 'can only be promoted by a culture that is receptive in both curricular content and pedagogical style, in which, it is not too bold to say, the capacities for love and compassion infuse the entirely of the educational endeavour.' *Not for profit: why democracy needs the humanities*, Princeton University Press, 2010, p. 112.

70   Nussbaum, *Not for profit*, pp. 95–96.

71   Nussbaum, *Not for profit*, pp. 108–109.

Nussbaum finds for imagination—the ability to identify with the experience of others—is a receptive faculty. Creativity, on the other hand, is a productive faculty.

Creativity is a disposition toward the productive use of imagination. Any given person might be very imaginative (anyone who is funny, for example) but the gift is confined to seeing connexions in an inspired instant and without necessarily seeing its operational opportunities, its extrapolations, its borders with the absurd; so the imaginative activity remains a flash, without necessarily entailing a communicative outlet that builds a vision or contributes to culture. Creativity, even in the modest case of learning with which we began, involves a vision of the individual growing toward something within culture. The imaginative response to learning is to see yourself enlarging your identity: you take on material which already exists in a way which embellishes the person that you are or are going to become. The same motif of adding to your identity may extend, in time, to adding to the very culture that has created or enhanced your learning persona. At that point, the zeal to add to common stock, to augment or embroider or extrapolate, means using imagination ambitiously in order to extend not just your own thinking but that of others. The creative part of a person is the disposition to bring imaginative resources to bear on a project. However naïve, it presupposes a rush of passion for a project, for an inflexion that leaves a mark, perhaps a bit big-headed but ambitiously reaching for immanence. It is no accident that in the history of ideas, imagination is sometimes the thing imagined, in the same way that fantasy is both the faculty and the transport, the ability to fantasize and the thing fantasized about; and still for Nietzsche, the two words—concept (*Begriff*) and imagination (*Vorstellung*)—are put together as synonyms.[72] This folding of the quality upon the faculty never arises with creativity. Creativity is always a faculty and cannot be hypostasized. The gift of creativity can never be collapsed into a creation. It is an inalienable dispositional characteristic in anyone who has it.

In education, we may or may not be able to influence dispositional characteristics of students; but there are nevertheless certain preconditions that allow us to realize our dispositional potential. We cannot necessarily teach imagination or creativity; but we can encourage them. Some students have great advantages over others in their readiness to make imaginative leaps, in the same way that some can make jokes or possess an uncanny acting

---

72 'bald auf den Begriff und die Vorstellung', Friedrich Nietzsche, *Die Geburt der Tragödie: Versuch einer Selbstkritik*, 19.

ability. These talents may derive from early upbringing, where a parent or carer rewarded the child for the risks taken for witty purposes. It may be possible to teach; but it is more obvious how creativity and imagination can be drummed out of students. The pedagogical challenge is not necessarily to teach creativity or imagination or invention but just to encourage them. In competitive education, discouragements abound; and many of these inhibitions arise without any conspiratorial plan or intention to diminish the confidence of the student. On the contrary, the machinery of constructive alignment is created in excellent faith to achieve the most effective learning, to empower students with self-regulated learning, which depends on being able to plan according to clearly laid-out learning outcomes and consistency of resources and assessment. There would be no problem if there were never a need or desire for creativity. Perhaps because creativity cannot with confidence be taught, it easily slips from the parameters of the syllabus. But then it is all the more important to find a pathway for the faculty to be encouraged. No one is so naturally creative that creativity will survive an uncreative ambience.

We could be gifted, for example, in conversation or storytelling but find that there are few opportunities comfortably to exercise the talent. Someone is always counting our performance, weighing up our attainments and whether or not we have conspicuously included in our performance a great number of requirements that have been stipulated. Faced with these strictures, students are more likely to become paranoiac about being punished for some non-inclusion than to extrapolate beyond what they have been told. Their comfort with invention is likely to suffer, because creativity requires confidence and withers with anxiety. In order for students to make use of their imaginative faculties for productive ends, the encouragements need to be felt more compellingly than the risks.

Structurally, students are also discouraged from imaginative academic behaviours because they are trained to be dependent on literature. It is understandable and, up to a point, necessary that students develop a curiosity for what has been written in the field, that they base their work on becoming informed, that they begin to read in the spirit of doing research rather than just swatting prescribed authorities. This bibliographic care is also a powerful form of learning and there is clearly nothing wrong with it. But if there are no encouragements to offset the flow of information with the triangulation of experience and imagination, the learner becomes dependent upon the sources, unprepared to reach ideas beyond the texts by comparing them to experience, a sense of justice or humour or paradox, to paradigms set out in other less scholarly sources, such as movies or memes or provocative skits on a video channel. The moment of leaving the bibliographic dependence behind is cause for anxiety and is sometimes not only judged to be too risky by the student but also for lecturers who run research methods units in preparation for masters and PhD. There is pressure to remain bibliographically dependent, because the student feels punished for departing from sanctioned methods. As she bases an essay on 15 scholarly books and articles, Anastasia saves herself the dangers of uncited speculation but also limits her chances of achieving independence.

Potentially, the learning outcome of 'critical thinking'—which is often embedded in university-wide graduate attributes—will encourage Anastasia to exercise sceptical review and rate one author against another; but this excellent faculty of discrimination may still not enable her to generate independent ideas: on the contrary, it may force her to approach her sources with a legalistic vein to the point of pedantry. Her scrupulosity with critical thinking does not necessarily win her independence but reinforces a conceptual imprisonment within the walls of the given. The grid of references is tyrannical; because Anastasia's job in exercising judgement among the sources has no proactive agency; like the juror in court, the apprehension of the case is passive, without opportunities to set independent terms for the discourse.

Achieving independence, as with creativity, requires confidence. It is easy to say that encouragement makes for confidence, but the case is somewhat circular. Encouragement is a beautiful word—etymologically giving students heart—but of course students cannot be encouraged in any undertaking whatever, regardless of its imprudence. It would be irresponsible to encourage students in their conceit or wrong-headedness or a project which is doomed. The teacher's role in education is also monitory, providing corrective advice as well as encouragement. But if the student experiences the balance of influence as benign, there is scope for more emotional investment in the curiosities of a project and consequently greater imaginative growth. This benignity of the teacher, not the alignment of the syllabus, is the condition most consistently reported by students as important and memorable in their studies, alongside the enthusiasm and humour of the teacher.[73]

---

73   In 2016, my colleague Gerry Rayner commissioned students as part of Monash University's 'Winter Research Scholarships' to investigate what students find most conducive to their learning. All the descriptors developed by the students were on the side of the enthusiasm of the lecturers.

*

This book has been conceived as acting out the imaginative independence that is sought in pedagogy. In planning the structure of the argument, I took a radical decision not to base the claims on pedagogical literature in the field, a modest but growing body of scholarship which, however—summarized with an excellent genealogy by Joy Whitton in her comprehensive doctoral investigation of creativity and imagination—brings me no closer to the revaluations that seem due. Instead, I have sought an independent viewpoint subtending chronologies of hundreds of years rather than the last couple of decades. As La Bruyère has reminded us, we have had sophisticated thought for a long time and, with its copious originality still richly accessible in the library, powerful intuitions on education are available to match. Very little of that time-span has involved constructive alignment or marking rubrics or learning outcomes but the most tantalizing incentives for deep thinking, invention, wit, imaginative extension to the ideas of others, sometimes blatant disregard for the ideas of others, cheek, rapture, rudeness, satire, indecency, lyricism and charm. The stock and methods of two millennia before constructive alignment are instructively unsystematic and provide, I feel, all the independence that I need.

For many years, I too have taught the doctrine of constructive alignment. The motives behind constructive alignment are enlightened and there are powerful reasons that the tertiary education sector throughout the Anglophone world has followed it. The impulse accords with all the right concerns related to learning-and-teaching quality but also social inclusion, equity, student-centredness and the democratic impulse behind massification. Constructive alignment is not a product of corporatization or the fiscal engineering of academies. Its tenets are deeply believed as the centrepiece of effective learning. My personal apostasy has nothing to do with a conspiracy theory and I still respect many initiatives created in the name of constructive alignment, clearly well intentioned, dispelling much that is obscure and mystifying and, by creating greater levels of transparency, potentially aiding in the self-regulated learning of students. Rather, my concerns derive solely from observation of syllabus and intellectual growth that are harmed by constructive alignment. These concerns have led me to form a belief that there must be something more, something beyond constructive alignment that is more congruent with creativity; and this desire to reach a more imaginative destiny for education in turn has led me to formulate an idea of post-constructivism, that is, an educational philosophy that is not based upon the student assimilating knowledge but gaining an identification with beautiful opportunities, an educational ontology rather than an epistemology.

Through Piaget, constructivism has given us a powerful model for how we make meaning for ourselves, namely by drawing phenomena to interact with our experiences and ideas. Coupled with the brilliance of Lev Vygotsky, we understand the importance of practical activity in a social context for learning. We no longer see education as a suite of hermetic instructions or lectures or even reading. All cognition, in fact, is mediated by a multitude of signs and symbols of a cultural nature; and consequently cognition itself is somewhat indivisible from the cultural practices, language and traditions that form those semantic conventions. So learning is highly socialized and must be developed in a socialized direction. Further, we acquire new knowledge by grafting it upon previous learning, embodied in the concept that Vygotsky named 'the zone of proximal development', where we make connexions with stock that we already possess. Part of the appeal of these formidable tenets of constructivism is that they make useful models in practice. Aided by the efforts of John Biggs (who coined the term constructive alignment) they have transformed education from a kind of pulpit-paradigm to a more learner-centred activity-rich set of educational practices. These mutations have been valuable and, up to a point, necessary. But they are structurally all based upon learning as knowledge-gaining and skill-gaining. They are fundamentally epistemological. They have little to do with the creative processes of what you do when you have some of this precious knowledge, how you synthesize it, adapt its language, challenge its premises, extrapolate from it, jettison it or worry over its implications. These creative phases are not necessarily about acquiring more knowledge but acquiring a reason to handle conversively the knowledge that one already has. The process within the learner is akin to that of the artist, that is, one discovers within oneself a kind of desire or amusement or vengeance that prompts a fresh treatment of the available knowledge, that pulls it out of indifference and makes it a vehicle for a vital impulse within the learner.

This vein of discovery is ontological because it is integral to the learner's sense of self, to longing and predilection, a host of emotional investments that urge us to make use of what we have already encountered and to seek more of it as we go. We are not talking merely about the individual constructing knowledge in an active way (hence constructivism, the construction of meaning by the learner) nor even an idiosyncratic personal way. Rather, we are talking about prolific constructions—more than you can recognize—circulating in a learner's mind and finding a match with an intuition, a fond idea that reinforces some growing view that the learner may have of herself or himself. Creativity is not a dispassionate process; it evolves amid seething conceits, identifications, frustrations and at times indulgence. Great editorial struggles are involved within the creative learner in an agony of big-headedness and self-containment.

Until we have an ontology of (post-constructivist) learning, we will only handle creativity apologetically, retrofitting unimaginative learning outcomes with an artificial creative spin. Even in arts and humanities, which ought to be a natural haven for the creative impulse, the liberality of students finding their own poetic desire, purpose and interpretation is receding. We have thoroughly bought the idea that constructive alignment is a necessary step toward learner-centredness; and the priority of learner-centredness, in turn, is essential to handling the great diversity of our students. In this mood, it seems aristocratic and utopian to want to return to a pre-constructivist world that had no learning outcomes. We envisage this reactionary backlash as the revenge of the old educational elite, wanting to revert to an exclusive system of self-motivated humanists. To want to abolish all the checks and balances of transparency and accessibility means disadvantaging all but the privileged students who were cast in the glamorous image of their lecturers. I find this dread illogical, because there is an equal and opposite call to democratize creativity; and at the present time, creative cultures are reserved for only a handful of privileged students who compose, make films, write poems and exhibit art and design. To democratize creativity means discovering and nurturing the underlying creativity among people who are not creatives. To extend the blessing to those currently shut out is just as important as the equity push of the last thirty years, that is, enticing into university the great diversity of learners who have until now been excluded.

This book develops a sceptical view of the current episteme that dominates the tertiary systems in our language. If our current emphasis on syllabus design is somewhat unfit to cultivate the autonomous thought of creativity, there is a question of what might be needed to offset it. A generation of academics has been brought up with the belief that greater engagement and student success—and with them greater levels of student-centredness, metacognition and self-regulated learning—can be achieved with better syllabus design. If academics use technology, institute active learning, and align their learning activities, delivery and assessment with the learning outcomes, excellence will prevail, as if educational effectiveness can be achieved with a relatively mechanical fix. I argue instead that we will find a more creative future through less mechanistic means, targeting rather the relationships between student and teacher and the economy of affections throughout the student learning experience. We do not necessarily have to abandon everything recommended by constructivism, as if to bury a mechanistic shibboleth; but for creativity's sake, we must circumvent the more mortifying effects of constructive alignment on the student's imaginative growth.

This book argues for cultivating certain happy aspects of the natural drama between teachers and students. The book rather emphasizes the niceness of the teacher; it seeks to penetrate the very fabric of expectation, student subjectivity, the inner meaning of engagement, the core dynamics of performativity and the live event in the classroom. These topics are conceived to offset the mechanistic emphasis which is the new comfort zone of educational design. I feel that the case is necessary, no matter how disruptive, to reassign these dimensions of learning and teaching to the priorities of educational development; but if we examine them with the long lens of history, the field turns from anxious entrapment in learning outcomes to the promise of a creative future.

Chapter 2

THE ROOT OF ALL LEARNING

Through examining the educational vocabulary, I am proposing a method for revaluating some core assumptions in learning and teaching which are deadlocked by empirical research. I have no polemic against quantitative methods but they tend to function on premises that prove themselves. An example might be the theme of active learning, where we can show that lecturers who have deployed the new wisdom of blended learning—a combination of preclass videos and activities, in-class group work and discussion and postclass reflexion—achieve greater engagement and student success. The advantages of flipped techniques are widely believed and supported by some evidence; but when critical scholars have eyeballed the literature, it turns out to be less convincing. As Lakmal Abeysekera and Phillip Dawson say:

> Despite popular enthusiasm and a somewhat reasonable rationale, flipped classroom approaches could not yet be considered an evidence-based approach; there is little research on the flipped classroom approach and none of it relies on particularly rigorous designs ... The flipped classroom approach is under-evaluated, under-theorized and under-researched in general.[1]

The virtues of blended approaches sound credible and may well be correctly believed; but it could simply be that flipped methods attract the more energetic and enthusiastic lecturers. It could also be that the same old lecturers, who are either self-selected or are dragooned into change, are suddenly caused to think and reflect about education and the student experience rather than direct their affections exclusively to their research. Having settled on a change with increased consciousness that teaching matters, they are determined to make it work; and so they either devote more zeal or greater reflectiveness to the job, experiencing a refreshment

---

1   'Motivation and cognitive load in the flipped classroom: definition, rationale and a call for research', *Higher Education Research & Development*, vol. 34, 2015, Issue 1, p. 1.

through thoughtful reappraisal. If they directed the same reflective enthusiasm to any other paradigm, it would also work well. Much research in learning and teaching is dogged by difficulties of distinguishing cause and effect; and this book is not about to solve such intractable conundrums. Instead, it offers a view of the field that brings together philological and phenomenological perspectives, arguing from the observational and the literary evidence for the philosophical underpinnings of the new vocabulary of learning and teaching.

In synthesizing a critique of globalized educational paradigms—which I see as uncreative—I want to proceed not merely in a subjective way. The observational conjecture may be as insightful or as seductive as it is; but it would be too easy to dismiss it as eccentric and capricious, dependent upon a personal point of view and hence tainted with arbitrariness. Anyone's subjectivity is valuable (and we will later revisit how necessary for education it is for any theme to be apprehended in a feeling subject) but as an element in research method, this observational subjectivity requires other data by which it might be triangulated. In particular, the history of experience revealed by language provides a perspective from which educational terms can be seen in sharper relief.[2]

In order to triangulate my own subjectivity, this book brings together both the phenomenology of education and the language by which we characterize it. Many of the themes are surprisingly difficult to define; so the book proposes a method for identifying educational phenomena which is radical in the sense of seeking roots. In the same way that we may hope to identify a feeling or intuition by observation, so we may hope to find the roots of experience by examining the history of language, distinguishing the roots that strike out in telling parallel with the expansive observational branches above. Accordingly, this book seeks a match between the observational and the philological: it explores learning as a lived circumstance, but it also seeks to relate this phenomenological description to the philological evidence, most of which has never been examined before.

Roots have a double meaning. On the one hand, the root is the etymology, the almost coincidental derivation of a word from old stock, mostly in languages that are no longer spoken. On the other hand, there is a sense of the root as causation, a telling sign that gives the ancestry of an idea, as

---

2   This method is a work in progress and has been explained in similar terms in my article 'The courtyard inside and out: a brief history of an architectural ambiguity', *Enquiry, The ARCC Journal*, vol. 11, issue 1, 2014, pp. 8–17 (www.arcc-journal.org/index.php/arccjournal/article/view/206).

if the idea, having sprouted from a root, is forever bound to its linguistic inheritance, as if it can never transcend to its contemporary acceptation. To add to the ambiguities, there are also cases where an idea or phenomenon did not exist historically. It grows slowly from related concepts to a point where it is common coin. The narrative of these transitions is not intended to be conclusive in itself but simply to bring contemporary ideas into an independent account of meaning, with a sense, perhaps, that ideas have a trajectory, even if our powers of prediction are negligible.

One way or the other, it is difficult to be indifferent to the historical meaning of roots when they are educational. To propose roots for learning and teaching invites a predisposition to be expressed, a grid of preferred images, in which all our aspirations have a former incarnation. This book neither promotes nor ignores such motivations. It has a phenomenological subtext that intermittently contemplates the root of all learning in a psychological sense: the creative magic of a learner's interest, other people's encouragement (like family and teachers) and then some inscrutable part of any learner which is ambition, hunger, geekish personality, a poetic identification with pockets of content, curiosity, the power of command or the mastery of manipulation. The traditional Freudian explanation for curiosity is the child's keenness to know about the sexual practice of the parents which explains his or her origins. Subsequently, the desire to know is sublimated or abstracted from this lush impenetrability, as the learner converts the unprofitable search into a sustainable zeal to know things in general.

If we say that interest is the prior condition of learning, it follows that a large part of the practice of teaching and learning is the stimulation of interest. The techniques are both well known and obscure. In already offering a critique of constructive alignment, this text has contemplated a negative effect on creativity and imaginative autonomy, arguing that the doctrine of alignment promotes relatively narrow learning experiences, which are very good for uncreative modules, subjects or units. In the chapters that follow, we shall consider some of the elements most likely to stimulate interest and create imaginative rapports between subject matter and the learner's sense of identity, items which are never a part of strategic directions at any university in the Anglophone world. They are items such as niceness, student subjectivity, colour, surprise, the opportunity to tell someone about your learning, imaginative ownership. This book is conceived to interrogate the basis of expectations that make for the greatest cognitive engagement; and through the investigation, it also interrogates the tools of engagement and deconstructs the concept of engagement itself.

*

We have established that education today is organized around outcomes. In the previous chapter, however, we have only partly recognized how potent they are and how problematic. Designing any program according to its intended learning outcomes is a responsible way to structure a relationship between student and teacher, because a list of outcomes sets out expectations for the teacher and simultaneously furnishes a plan for the student. Students are not deceived because, from the outset, the learning outcomes have been set and there should be no surprises, no tricks, none of those ambiguities where the student studies one topic and finds that another is assessed or the student is encouraged by learning activities to acquire one kind of cognitive skill only to find that another would have been more expedient for the assessment. We prescribe learning activities, texts and assessments in accord with the learning outcomes in a nice agreement which is usually described—as already noted in the previous chapter—by the term that John Biggs has coined, namely constructive alignment.[3]

There is much to commend in this arrangement of good alignment, where confusion is attenuated and expectations can be cultivated with a degree of conformity with delivery. It now constitutes one of the principal orthodoxies of education throughout the Anglophone world. No one will recommend that an educational program not function according to these premises. It would seem wrongheaded: no one wants to invite a muddle, to neglect the consistency and coherence of the program, to fail to advise baffled students of the expectations or to design learning activities that have nothing to do with the assessment. It is an orthodoxy in the good sense that it is right-thinking. It says: let us provide maximum chance for student confidence in actively owning their own learning, and minimum chance of confounding the learning experience with contradictions and activities in skew relations with one another and with the assessment.

So ingrained are learning outcomes as the point of departure for any learning program that we think of them as prior to anything else. They are the matter that has to be thought about first in the design of the syllabus

---

3   John Biggs, 'Enhancing teaching through constructive alignment', *Higher Education*, vol. 32, 1996, pp. 347–364; J Biggs, *Aligning Teaching and Assessment to Curriculum Objectives*, Imaginative Curriculum Project, LTSN Generic Centre, 2003, and John Biggs, and Catherine Tang, *Teaching for Quality Learning at University*, McGraw-Hill and Open University Press, Maidenhead, 2011.

and then the design of the learning (learning design or educational design). The learning outcomes are scrutinized for accreditation purposes by professional bodies; they are integral to quality control and, above all, they are central to a concept of empowering students with the charge of their own learning because, through the learning outcomes, students know what they should be aiming for and understand what they will be assessed against. They can thus plan and manage their own learning, actively construct their learning, with this leading to a new student-centred paradigm as opposed to a teacher-centred tradition.

While no one will argue against clarity, consistency and transparency, there are grounds to question all the requirements that we impose upon ourselves all the time, as with all orthodoxies. Among the questions that one might pose—beyond the issue of creativity which is our key concern— is how genuine student-centredness can flourish when the preconditions of student-centredness are so compromised, when all the learning activities are so tightly drawn into conformity with prescribed learning outcomes, closely chased by assessment, that student initiative would struggle for a toehold? Although the point of constructive alignment is to provide space for the student to construct his or her learning, one wonders what, in practice, is left for the student to determine, if everything has been stipulated in advance in the expression of learning activities that must align so seamlessly with learning outcomes and the spectre of assessment to seal the pressure? In a later text, Biggs himself used an ingenuous vocabulary to express the new powerlessness of the student:

> The 'alignment' aspect refers to what the teacher does, which is to set up a learning environment that supports the learning activities appropriate to achieving the desired learning outcomes. The key is that the components in the teaching system, especially the teaching methods used and the assessment tasks, are aligned with the learning activities assumed in the intended outcomes. The learner is in a sense 'trapped', and finds it difficult to escape without learning what he or she is intended to learn.[4]

---

4   John Biggs, 'Aligning teaching for constructing learning', *The higher education academy*, 2003 (www.heacademy.ac.uk/sites/default/files/resources/id477_aligning_teaching_for_constructing_learning.pdf). Biggs is also not without his critics on other grounds, *e.g.* Loretta M Jervis and Les Jervis, 'What is the Constructivism in Constructive Alignment?', *BEE-j*, vol. 6, November 2005 (www.bioscience.heacademy/journal/vol6/beej-6-5.pdf).

In this text—and despite the inverted commas—there is no apparent sense of irony or a scruple that there might be something intuitively and ethically wrong with trapping students or casting them into some kind of pedagogical gaol. Where, when she or he is trapped, is the student's latitude in conditioning the learning experience? Given that constructivism seems automatically to confer student-centredness in the construction of learning, there are grounds to fear that in some institutions, student-centredness is at risk of being an empty rhetorical phantom of claims for the cruciality of student choice in general. That definition is weak and disappointing in itself but, for students 'who find it difficult to escape' the rigours of prescription, it borders on bad faith.

One might further wonder what the experiential calibre of the encounter will be, when there are so few surprises. As far as the educator can guarantee, the learning is prescribed and controlled, with all activities held down in proximal relations with assessment. For some students, there is no issue, because the interest will be internally generated as an intrinsic fascination with the subject, as when the physics student is already obsessed with physics. But the grand architecture of constructive alignment is not conceived for the already-inspired student but the vast cohort of mass-education of which the already-inspired are a small percentage. The argument is described through the colourful contrast of academic-Susan and non-academic-Robert. Once upon a time, lecturers could depend on having a classful of Susans, while the Roberts would never have gone to university. Now, under the terms of the Bologna process, we have an obligation to bring Robert up to Susan's standard of performance.[5] The method, which most academies have accepted from Biggs, is that a structure of activities and assessment aligned with learning outcomes will honour the necessary student-centred active learning, which will be optimal for Robert and Susan alike.

The appeal is tremendous. Beautiful alignment makes good pedagogical sense as well as economic sense if it results in more Roberts rising to the competency of Susan. Constructive alignment itself does not achieve the magic but it creates the preconditions for active learning where, on the strength of knowing the learning outcomes, students can plot their learning journey—assisted at all stages by learning activities in alignment—and know that the efforts will optimally prepare them for the assessment or even fulfil the assessment. Yet the principle of student-centredness is not so easy to

---

5   Biggs and Tang, *Teaching for quality learning at university*, , pp. 5 ff. (chapters 1 and 2).

identify, given that there is so little self-determination. It is fine to say that 'learning is what the student does', and that everything should serve that process; but alignment (even if you add the convenient term 'constructive', which makes it sound very cognitive and Vygotskyan) does not itself achieve any self-determination, even if we say that it allows the student to be at the centre.

Further, the learning outcomes with which everything aligns may encourage mechanistic scoping and diminish certain curious aspects of learning, the string of fresh moments that arise in unexpected encounters. Locking up the whole experience on the basis that the student already perceives the inherent magic of the topic seems more and more out of step with our times, when incentives to follow promiscuous interests abound in profligate sensual layers on the internet and in the media.

We live in a culture where surprises and colour are jealously engineered by all forms of art, from the most cerebral to the most naïve in the entertainment industry. On television, series are created to grip our interest with suspense, not just in natural suspense-genres like crime but documentary genres as well. Rightly or wrongly, our culture finds the predictable boring. The idea that our learning can so extensively be prefigured—insulated from diversions, digressions and distractions—suggests a silent uncreative bubble, insulated from the noise of the world by an artificial academic membrane that shuts out the prolific stimulation that surrounds us. We are welcome inside this fragile sphere of denial but on condition that our intellectual autonomy is put on hold. Alas, if my free sense of inquiry is not indulged to some extent, I am unlikely to be happy, regardless of how perfect the bubble. The predictability is somehow stifling, offending the primacy of my interest and investigative self-determination

When the syllabus, delivery, activities and assessment are all aligned with the learning outcomes, our core question has been: what happens to imagination? In that circumstance where learning is so carefully delimited and remote from fancy, imagination becomes a difficult faculty for the student to exercise, much less cultivate, given that so much of the learning is prescribed and the assessment looms in its strict accord with the learning outcomes. There is perhaps an underlying assumption that students are not in a position to use their imagination when they do not yet have the basics of a discipline and need first to apply themselves to acquiring knowledge and skills. If so, I think we could argue that there is no point at which a human can ever be imaginative, given that we all have so much knowledge and skill still to acquire, as was acknowledged in earlier centuries through the phrase, 'I am still learning' (*ancora imparo*).[6] To consign students to the unimaginative because they do not yet demonstrate mastery is to condemn them to an apprenticeship for automatons.

Learning outcomes and constructive alignment have the unintended consequence of privileging assessment in the student's mind, where it spooks the syllabus, haunting all activities, forestalling curiosity and delimiting the more open-ended journey that learning remains. Students know the template: they are judged according to how well they have met the learning outcomes and, as a result, our educational programs predicate the learning experience on assessment. Through constructive alignment we have made the whole educational experience an accessory to assessment. Alas, assessment is a blunt instrument. It can never subtend the huge potential that students can extract from a course of study, with imaginative detours and burgeoning powers of extrapolation. Under constructive alignment, education is led by the dull, not by the sharp: we have chosen the least promising, the least agile, the least visionary and the least inventive dimension of education to dominate the learning experience. The effect on creativity is withering because learning outcomes encourage mechanistic scoping and strategy rather than curiosity.

We could, however, defend constructive alignment on the basis that while the learning outcomes are prescriptive, they only end up determining the most general aspirational level and leave a great deal of scope and colour for both the teachers and the students to fill in. As a percentage of the encounter, the constructively aligned element might only represent a small proportion, allowing for much creative richness in the way that the outcomes are interpreted. But if we argue that so much in the syllabus is discretionary and accommodates plenty of interpretation and tolerance, it sounds as if the learning outcomes are only relevant to a small part of the syllabus and therefore have only marginal value. Essentially, this defence amounts to a confession that learning outcomes are partially irrelevant.

Theoretically, one could install imagination in the learning outcomes, and thus allow the all-encompassing architecture of alignment to subtend impulse and fantasy.[7] Why not just treat imagination like any other learning

---

6   In fact the motto of Monash University, often attributed to the artist Michelangelo, though it neither appears in Giorgio Vasari's nor Ascanio Condivi's *Vita di Michelagnolo Buonarroti*. In all events, the sentiment is ancient, as in Seneca: 'You should keep learning ... even to the end of your life (*tamdiu discendum est ... quamdiu vivas*)', *Letter to Lucilius* 76.3.

7   L. Young. 'Imagine creating rubrics that develop creativity', *English Journal*, vol. 99, issue 2, 2009, pp. 74–79.

outcome: on successful completion of this subject or unit, students should be able to demonstrate imagination? Alas, it sounds somehow stressfully contradictory and, I fear, unimaginative. What, for example, is an unimaginative student to do? It makes no sense to set imagination as a learning outcome because we have no proof that imagination can be learned, even if we agree that it can be encouraged and hence cultivated. Imagination, rightly or wrongly, does not hugely enjoy plans; it is never entirely predictable and may be inclined to mischief. It is that blithe antagonist of accountability which nevertheless accounts for much of the invention in science, art, poetry and music. Imagination facilitates lateral thought, every jump to a special synapsis. But installed as a learning outcome? How? We should of course encourage imagination throughout our educational system at all levels, but the learning taxonomies that we encounter, further sclerosed as learning outcomes, do not easily accommodate it.

It would be educationally foolish to neglect the extraordinary learning processes that occur outside the grid of learning outcomes. When in our lives do we learn most prolifically? The most spectacular learning that we have ever done is as babies, when we learned language. It is hard for us as adults to learn foreign languages, but to learn language from nothing is much more demanding. Acquisition of the other languages that we might fathom in our maturity is all based upon the prior and almost magical learning that we did as babies, from which we are then able to graft foreign syntactical structures, grammar and words. The mastery, in a sense, has already been gained from infantile learning. When we were babies, there were no learning outcomes and no assessment. There were learning activities, as we listened, watched and tried things for ourselves, all on a spontaneous basis. There was certainly no talk of alignment. For babies, the root of all learning is the same as in research for adults: it is largely based on observation, mostly of a chaotic world within which, however, the intellect is free to isolate clever details that form a synapsis. When someone in the traffic says: 'you prick!' that does not mean the 'prick' that happens when you touch a thorn. To appreciate such nuances and build them successively toward an understanding of language is an immensely sophisticated work of cognition, the like of which we never experience at anything like the same rate in our childhood, teen or adult years.

Though Jean Piaget has identified cognitive stages in language development among children, the language acquisition that he theorized is largely framework-free; and learners learn language irrespective of the self-consciousness of the parents or guardians. One wonders why the educational example of babies or toddlers suffers from the same kind of amnesia that suppresses our own memory as infants. It is as if education implicitly dismisses the infantile paradigm as somehow quaint and romantic. Institutionalized learning is of course highly regulated, fraught with accreditation regimes and continuously chastened by quality control mechanisms; and there is no scope for anarchistic defaults to an infantile paradigm, which involves an inscrutable organic cocktail of osmosis, reward, occasional instruction, encouragement or correction and (above all) powerful imagination on the part of the learner. It is indeed a romantic miracle which systematic learning in any institution would be hard pressed to emulate.

In fairness, our learning institutions are charged to be fully accountable and are therefore possessed of the contrary energy, which is to improve the definition of successive stages and processes that yield learning, however mechanistically they emerge; and once defined as certain steps in a sequence, the process can be managed for optimum operation. Alas the scruples are potentially infinite. As with all regulated systems, the more security that one identifies as desirable, the more one identifies contingent risk; and so more safeguards have to be built around the regulatory framework to ensure the delivery of what seems necessary. The bureaucratization of learning is well-intentioned and undoubtedly often prevents scandals that would otherwise flourish, in the same way that crimes would proliferate without laws and punishment. Education is not minded to devolve itself to the innocence of infant-learning, even though there are teacherless counterparts in work experience and work-integrated learning, and the concept of learning-on-the-job or 'informal learning' is well recognized in higher education.

This book is therefore not an anarchistic polemic against contemporary approaches to learning which, it must be acknowledged, are supported by good scholarship. Further, the root of all learning, hyperbole aside, is unknown, because the very act of learning is itself difficult to define or analyse much less scrutinize in its historical beginnings. For all that, we already have an idea, the idea that we optimally learn because we come at new material after having fancied that there is a place for it in our imaginative view of ourselves, that we imaginatively create a place for new things to be learned ahead of learning them or inscrutably alongside learning them or in some way reinforcing the learning after having absorbed it. In our imagination, we narrate a whole relationship between ourselves and the text. Learning is a creative act. The field of learning is thus sufficiently generous to indicate a radical approach, radical in the true sense of the roots (*radices*) for the several conceptions of learning that we assume by language. Let us begin with the root of learning itself.

Even when we know that cultures were enormously keen on learning, we are often no closer to understanding the phenomenon of learning, either for them or for us. For example, the fondness for learning among the ancient Greeks is legendary and can be checked through the iconography of vase-painting which often shows young people learning from somewhat older people. The interest in learning was richly expressed through an impressive vocabulary, with adjectives like fond of learning (φιλειδήμων or φιλίστωρ), verbs like to love learning (φιλολογέω) and nouns like desire for learning (χρηστομάθεια) and love of learning (φιλομάθεια).[8] However, these celebratory institutions of study obscure the great latitude of learning that was understood in practice. The main verbal root of learning (μανθάνω) could mean to learn either by study or by practice,[9] or by experience.[10] One would, for instance learn the Homeric epic by heart.[11] But it could also simply mean 'to acquire a habit of', or 'to be accustomed to', or 'perceive, remark, notice'.[12] It could mean 'understand'.[13] The expression 'what's to learn' (τί μαθών) or 'under what persuasion' meant rather 'why on earth?'[14]

Even greater latitude arises in another verb for learning (δάω) which could definitely mean learn but also cause learning, in other words to teach (διδάσκω), which is normally described in the origins of our word didactic or teacherly. In an old Homeric infinitive form, it could mean search out (δεδάασθαι).[15] It is also tempting to see an Indo-European link between Greek teaching (διδάσκω) and Latin learning (*disco*) which could mean learn in the sense of study but also more generally to acquire knowledge, to know, to receive information or recognize. These patterns are worth accounting for, since in some languages there is no distinction between

---

8   Examples taken from *LSJ*, i.e. Henry George Liddell, Robert Scott, *A Greek-English Lexicon*, revised and augmented throughout by Sir Henry Stuart Jones with the assistance of Roderick McKenzie, Clarendon Press, Oxford, 1940.

9   Aristotle, *Nicomachean ethics* 1103ª32—which famously defines active learning *avant la lettre*: 'For the things we have to learn before we can do them, we learn by doing them (ποιοῦντες μανθάνομεν)'—cf. *Metaphysics*1049ᵇ31, 980ᵇ24.

10   Aeschylus, *Agamemnon* 251.

11   Xenophon, *Symposium* 3.5.

12   Herodotus 7.208; Xenophon, *History of Greece* 2.1.1.

13   Plato, *Euthydemus* 277e, "ὡς μάθω σαφέστερον" Aeschylus, *Libation bearers* 767.

14   Aristophanes, *Acharnians* 826, *cf. Clouds* 402, 1506, *Lysistrata* 599, *Plutus* 908.

15   *Odyssey* 16.316. Again, words *s.v.* in *LSJ*.

learning and teaching, as in Danish (*lære*); and in others, they proceed from the same root, as in German (*lernen* and *lehren*). There are always further words in all languages for instruct, in the same way that there are terms for discover, study and ascertain. Further, the word that we believe translates as learning often turns out more to designate an unacademic practice. An example is the Italian verb to learn (*imparare*) with its origins in Latin for acquire or procure (*parāre*).

In the writing of the sixteenth-century poet Ludovico Ariosto, for example, learning might involve unacademic motifs like gaining consciousness of other people's costs or expenses.[16] Learning might involve understanding the names of the English knights[17] or the art of surgery gleaned in India.[18] Normally learning is not academic, as when Orlando learns to hurl the torch[19] or how one has to give aid.[20] The large corpus of stories of the Milanese writer Matteo Bandello is a good reflexion of urbane spoken Italian in the sixteenth century. The suave priest hardly ever uses learning (*imparare*) of anything academic. He advises ladies to learn not to trick other people if they do not want to be tricked back, with perhaps double vengeance.[21] Or after a dance, a man from Ferrara follows a lady to learn where she lives, a motif that arises in the very next story.[22] Occasionally the uses of learning (*imparare*) are academic, like the young man whose mother sends him to Barcelona to learn letters and the good civil customs of a gentleman.[23] Young women, it seems, gain great profit from learning to speak modestly, whereas young men receive similar benefits from restraining their unbridled desires.[24] With few such constraints, a man

---

16 'Bene è felice quel, donne mie care, / ch'essere accorto all'altrui spese impare', *Orlando furioso* 10.6.7–8; *cf.* 'ch'a spese lor quasi imparar che costi / voler altri salvar con suo periglio', *Orlando furioso* 27.67.3–4.

17 'e dei signor britanni i nomi impara', *Orlando furioso* 10.90.4.

18 'E rivocando alla memoria l'arte / ch'in India imparò già di chirugia', *Orlando furioso* 19.21.1–2.

19 'Potea imparar ch'era a gittare il brando, / e poi voler senz'arme essere audace', *Orlando furioso* 24.11.3–4.

20 'Per imparar come soccorrer déi', *Orlando furioso* 34.56.1.

21 'imparate a non beffar altrui', *Novelle* 1.3.

22 *Novelle* 1.8, 1.9.

23 *Novelle* 1.27; *cf.* 'Avevagli Ambrogio fatto imparar lettere e sonare e cantare e tanto bene accostumare quanto l'etá loro comportava', *Novelle* 2.36.

24 *Novelle* 1.43; *cf.* 'imparino a por il freno a l'appetitose voglie e piú temperatamente amino, imparando a l'altrui spese di quanto danno il non regolato affetto sia cagione', *Novelle* 2.5 (letter to signor Paolo Antonio Soderino); or 'per ammonir i giovini che imparino moderatamente a governarsi e non correr a furia, la scrissi', *Novelle* 2.7 (letter to messer Girolamo Fracastoro).

sighs in a high demonstrative style that he had learned from the Spanish.[25] Meanwhile, people come to Bologna to learn sense.[26] Learning is cultured, even when not scholarly. Whenever Bandello himself frequents the house of signora Argentina d'Oria e Fregosa, he never leaves without having learned something.[27] Much learning is about manual or sporting skills, such as learning to fence[28] but it can be the more culturally challenging learning of practical arts in Rome.[29] A man with a Milanese brogue resists learning a more courtly Italian accent.[30] In most cases, however, when Bandello wants to talk about academic learning, he uses the word study (*studio, studiare*), only rarely combined with learning (*imparare*).[31]

If learning across languages and time is a slightly weak concept, there is a question of when—or with what artificiality—the concept in English became robust, institutionalized and examinable. Oddly, the history of learning in our language is especially stressful. Dictionaries draw a sharp distinction between learning and teaching, exhorting us not to use the verb 'learn' as teach, as in the slang 'that'll learn you'. But lexicographers are quick to acknowledge that earlier writers did not observe this ban but freely used 'learn' in either sense. An example is Shakespeare: 'a thousand more mischances than this one / have learn'd me how to brook this patiently.'[32] In Shakespeare, the pattern can go both ways in the same breath, as with Caliban's haunting lines: 'you taught me language, and my profit on't / is, I know how to curse: the red plague rid you, / for learning me your language!'[33] Or, more positively: 'sweet prince, you learn me noble thankfulness'.[34] Or Juliet: 'Come, civil night, / thou sober-suited matron, all in black, / and learn me how to lose a winning match'.[35]

---

25   *Novelle* 1.54.

26   *Novelle* 2.1 (letter to la signora Ippolita Torella e Castigliona); *cf.* the motif of learning sense: 'Credetelo, che averebbero imparato senno a le spese loro e così di leggero non veniva lor fatto di far dispregnar Calandrino e fargli l'altre beffe', *Novelle* 2.10.

27   *Novelle* 2.26.

28   *Novelle* 2.27.

29   *Novelle* 2.50 (letter to Gian Michele Bandello).

30   'imparerebbe quell'idioma', 2.31.

31   as in a letter to signor Enea Pio da Carpi, *Novelle* 2.56.

32   *Two gentlemen of Verona* 5.3.

33   *Tempest* 1.2; *cf.* 'Unless you could teach me to forget a banished father, you must not learn me how to remember any extraordinary pleasure.'

34   *Much ado* 4.1; *cf.* Or 'my life and education both do learn me / how to respect you', *Othello* 1.3.

35   *Romeo and Juliet* 3.2; or again reflexively 'where I have learn'd me to repent the sin / of disobedient opposition', *Romeo and Juliet* 4.2.

More than in Bandello, from which Shakespeare drew *Romeo and Juliet*, learning equates with study; but there are still legion instances of learning being unacademic, as in to 'learn to jest in good time'.[36] Sometimes to learn means little more than to hear a report or gain news: 'let's go learn the truth of it',[37] or 'I learn you take things ill which are not so,'[38] meaning 'I have figured out something about you'. In dealing with information, the word 'learn' often just means 'observe' or 'ascertain', as in 'I will presently go learn their day of marriage.'[39] It is often hands-on: 'Hast thou not learn'd me how / to make perfumes?' and is seldom moral.[40]

Certain conclusions can be drawn from these converging patterns. First, though learning can mean teaching, teaching in any given language cannot easily translate as learning. Admittedly, you can use the word reflexively and say: I taught myself Spanish; but this claim is a special case of autodidacticism, where you acquire knowledge and skill as a result of studying without a teacher. Meanwhile the flexible activity is learning: it is capable of reflexiveness, because as well as taking on content you might sometimes help someone else take on content. Second, though we think of teaching as mostly institutional and academic, learning is often informal, ranging from the observational to the acquisition of practice, as in love: its compass has no bounds and its centre no authority.

The roots of the respective English words confirm the more rhapsodic character of learning relative to teaching. Teaching derives from Teutonic roots that mean 'to show' (like modern German *zeigen* or like our own 'token') which must be very old, connecting with Greek to show or shine forth (δείκνυμι). Learning, on the other hand, is an enchantment, connecting with *lore* or myth. You make yourself a repository of *lore*, that is learning which is simultaneously poetic content, as you fathom the stock that you then take on yourself. It is intrinsically steeped in imaginative narrative structures.

Of both earlier conceptions, the contrast with contemporary thinking is most striking with learning. It makes a poor fit with its new steward, learning outcomes, and prompts an inquiry into the whole concept of an outcome being predicated with the noun 'learning'. Outcome itself is a new word, a

---

36   *Comedy of errors* 2.2.

37   *Measure for measure* 1.2; *cf.* 'I learn in this letter that Don Pedro of Arragon comes this night to Messina. *Much ado about nothing* 1.1; 'So that by this intelligence we learn / the Welshmen are dispers'd', *Richard II* 3.3.

38   *Antony and Cleopatra* 2.2.

39   *Much ado* 2.2.

40   Respectively *Cymbeline* 1.5; 'One of your great knowing / should learn, being taught, forbearance', *Cymbeline* 2.3.

term without roots. Its mediocre etymology is exactly as it looks: to come out or that which comes out. In the same way that the Latin for 'go out' (*exitus*) could also mean 'result', early uses of 'outcome' meant something quite different: people who migrate to our country are outcomes—that is, foreigners—because they have come out, come out of their place where they implicitly belong and now inhabit the territory where we belong. This somewhat xenophobic conception of outcomes might be compared with arrivals, that is, people who come to your banks or shores (*rives*, *ripas*). The modern sense of the word outcome began in the industrial period but was first used not to describe an expectation but rather a resolution in which there was some doubt. For example, two men might commit their differences to a duel. What is the outcome? One spoke of the outcome of a story, meaning the ending. Outcome in that sense is a situation that has ensued from doubt, the turn that chance takes after uncertainty. It is, in that sense, almost the opposite of what we mean by a learning outcome; because, as things could have gone either way, there seems to be equal validity among contraries.

For the word to have become *de rigueur* in all fields of bureaucracy, it was necessary that it shed the motif of chance and represent only specified results. Every office wants to see outcomes, especially if they yield profit or lead to public good or public confidence, privilege or prestige. In academia, outcomes are hardly confined to learning and teaching but are equally a part of grants in research, belonging to a sometimes inscrutable string of nouns like aims, objectives and outcomes, all to be stipulated alongside methodology. Today, there is an epidemic of outcomes. In learning and teaching alone, if you isolate the terms in a search as "learning outcomes", Google comes up with 8,340,000 examples. We will never look at them all. Even when finely predicated with shades of hope, as "intended learning outcomes", the Google search yields a quarter of a million hits. There are sites that guide us in the use of the correct verbs to use, so that the ILOs, as they are known in educational offices throughout the Anglophone world, will conform to Bloom's taxonomy, again a logical, well-intentioned and reasonable classification of educational goals.[41]

Like the Pyramid of Giza, the edifice of learning outcomes is both admirable and impossible to shift without extreme belligerence. The structure could be suspected of being admirable on account of internal consistency

41   B.S. Bloom, M.D. Engelhart, E.J. Furst, W. H. Hill & D.R. Krathwohl, *Taxonomy of educational objectives: The classification of educational goals. Handbook I: Cognitive domain*, David McKay Company, New York, 1956.

more than any intrinsic necessity; and, like the majestic tombs of Egypt, it can be viewed from a certain iconoclastic angle as both anxious and vain, paranoiac and overwrought, authoritarian, lugubrious and fearful both in the sense of inspiring fear in slaves and as a Pharaonic symbol of dark horrors on the other side of a life-threshold. The reason one might value a verb-calculator to determine intended learning outcomes (ILOs) is that the exercise of declaring in advance what learning is to take place is structurally fraught. If in very few words I have to tell you what learning you are to do, I risk either asking too much or too little, either proposing learning that could be done in a flash—if needed at all—or learning that is likely to remain beyond reach at the end of the program. The chances of describing a suitable challenge that is neither too ambitious nor too undemanding are slim. So, perilously navigating a narrow pass between platitudes on the one hand and intimidation on the other, I readily clutch at any safeguards on offer. A table that matches verbs with qualities, carefully ordered by a taxonomy of cognitive domains, provides welcome reassurance and allays my anxiety.

Until recently, educators described their programs by their objectives; but early this century, the term of 'subject objectives' was abandoned in favour of learning outcomes. An objective was felt to be too much in the teacher's domain, describing what the teacher intended to cover as his or her delivery target rather than what the student might take away to some benefit. Learning outcomes—sometimes predicated as student learning outcomes, or more modestly, as noted, 'intended learning outcomes'—are the competencies that the student can be expected to acquire by doing the program. The appeal is obvious, in that (a) the culture seems more student-centred and (b) the attainment of criterion-referenced standards is implicitly clinched. But one happy element of the old term 'objective' could be seen as its intentionality: we try to do something but may not entirely reach it or own it comprehensively; and even after a sterling effort, it remains an objective, such as gaining an understanding of what a dog thinks (which you will never know). So perhaps acknowledging that lovely open-endedness, the term 'learning outcome'—which has no intentionality of itself—is retrofitted with hope and tolerance by the addition of 'intended', hence intended learning outcomes (ILOs). It is perhaps one sign of liberality within the mechanical, as if it is acknowledged that you might have the intention to come out of a program with certain competencies but instead you either emerge with a lot less or with plenty of different ones and possibly better ones. The intended learning outcome might be to gain a perspective of

Shakespeare's morality; in fact, after the semester's reading and talking, you remain confounded by the bard's ethics and instead emerge from your studies with a deeper understanding of Shakespeare's metaphoric language. It was not quite the intended outcome but a very good outcome anyway, with great poetic integrity. More likely, however, the predication of 'intended' simply softens the otherwise rigid stipulation of an absolute outcome, allowing for degrees of shortfall. You still might not understand the compass of Shakespeare's morality, as intended, but you at least have some grasp of it and fulfil the intention to some degree.

Mind you, Shakespeare himself had no knowledge of outcomes (as he never used the word), much less learning outcomes. Centuries of scholars who mastered ancient and modern languages, humanist discourses, poetic forms of the most exacting rhythmic structure—all maintained while engaged in a clerical, teaching or diplomatic career—managed to achieve more or less what they wanted from their learning but without a blueprint for what they would learn at each stage. The same must be said of their socially inferior learners in the sensory arts: musicians, sculptors, painters, architects. Their learning was also extensive and lifelong, admittedly sometimes confined to an inspired elite, but the learning itself was evidently ambitious, organic and immersive. The goals in learning were not anatomized as learning outcomes but were superintended by a desire to contribute to culture, around which there was a certain awareness of progress, risk of slipping backward, cycles of advances and degeneracy in which one's learning and practice might distinguish one's efforts for posterity.

In our own epoch, when admittedly there is no longer a humanist tradition that unifies the culture of teacher and student, it is still not clear that 'learning outcomes' are more student-centred than subject or unit objectives. In speaking of the objectives of a course of study (which now sounds retardataire), there was blissfully no sense of a straight-jacket imposed on students that would be checked upon assessment. Alas, educators backed away from the aspirational term 'objectives' because they do not seem to be about what the student does. But paradoxically, teaching objectives gave students more freedom. The teacher said: this is the journey that I want to take you on; but you then go on your own journey and tell me where it takes you. Throughout pre-constructivist education, there were implicitly two journeys: the teacher's and the student's. Why do we now insist on collapsing them as one? There is so much more integrity in distinguishing the two, providing relative independence for both. To define the educational program in terms of what the student does or even gains—the outcome—is unnecessarily prescriptive and limits the scope for student autonomy and especially imaginative growth, with a somewhat unpleasant industrial sense of yield, result or product.

Outcome is not an easy word to translate into other languages and the attempt to do so reveals how fragile the idea is. The most usual translation is result, as in German (*Ergebnis*) or French (*résultat*). These are yet more cumbersome locutions, which are today overwritten with those very tangible signs of student success: the result or grade. But the assumption with a result or grade is that you have earned it; the result is the result of your effort or knowledge or skill. Your accomplishments are recognized in the result; and the result, through an unprejudiced process, is only a reflexion of your attainment.

But in its origins, the concept was both less moral and less mechanical, more dramatic and full of suspense. In the renaissance, the spectre of fortune presides, as with the uncertain outcome of a battle, whose satisfaction to either side—as noted—lies in the balance. For that reason, the term in the plural (results, *Ergebnisse*) is still standard vocabulary for scientific experiments, which are conducted on an unprejudiced basis. In science, the results may reveal evidence of a certain chemical reaction, say, or not. You might have an inkling beforehand but the experiment is conducted for proof's sake, which is carefully recorded. The experiment is conducted on the basis that you do not know beforehand. Etymologically, too, the German (*Ergebnis*) is what is given out, what is dispensed as if by fortune, what obtains, implicitly what logic or fate determines. While we identify the word with results in science, in its origins, the concept suggests more the opposite, as still survives in the nineteenth century in Nietzsche when he declares that the influence of science has resulted in a wholesale disavowal of all philosophy (*mit dem Ergebniss einer Gesammt-Verstimmung gegen alle Philosophie*).[42]

The Romance term (as in French *résultat*, with its root in leaping or jumping, *saltare*) is dramatically the toy of fortune: what springs back or leaps out or jumps back at you. This gestural image of response has a capricious bounce: it springs into a condition that is not necessarily what you might have predicted: agreement or backlash, harmony or discord, profit or loss. Result is not a common word in preindustrial cultures and does not appear much in poetic literature. For example, Shakespeare never uses it, even though there was much metaphoric potential, as you can see from the beautiful

---

42   *Jenseits von Gut und Böse* 204.

lexicography of the *Oxford English Dictionary* (*OED*), which observes that early uses of the word retain the metaphor of bouncing or snapping back, as with the reverberation of a string. When authors call upon the term, it is more often as a verb than a noun; and in the active mood, it describes things that lie in the balance and can jump either way, as when the poet Ariosto asks at the end of a stanza in his epic: what merit results or 'comes your way' if everyone insults you like a traitor?[43] and in the same position at the end of a stanza, he says: it could have remained a secret among us but now open infamy has resulted for me.[44]

Often 'result' can be translated as cause, as in causing you harm or enmity, according to Alberti,[45] or the sober Francesco Guicciardini speaking of the harmful consequences of poor government.[46] But positive things can also result. In Castiglione's *Courtier*, one of the interlocutors avers that gravity and authority result when archaic language is deployed in writing.[47] Everything that a courtier does should result in, and be composed of, virtue.[48] Elsewhere, he explains that just as body and soul result in a mighty composite, so male and female result in the robustness of life,[49] like the knowledge, grace, beauty, humanity and wit of his patronness, which result in a virtuous chain that constructs and adorns.[50] One can find an economic reflexion in the renaissance, where Guicciardini says that it is better to spend on warfare

---

43   'oh che merito al fin te ne risulta, / se, come a traditore, ognun t'insulta!', *Orlando furioso* 21.30.7–8.

44   'Saria stato tra noi la cosa occulta; / ma di qui aperta infamia mi risulta', *Orlando furioso* 21.44.7–8.

45   'te ne risulta o danno o nimistà', Alberti, *Della famiglia* 2, 'a te non risulti danno troppo grande', *Della famiglia* 3.

46   'Se el danno che risulta delle cose male governate si scorgessi a cosa per cosa, chi non sa, o si ingegnerebbe di imparare o volontariamente lascerebbe governarsi a chi sapessi più', Guicciardini, *Ricordi* 137.

47   'e da esse risulta una lingua più grave e piena di maestà che dalle moderne', Castiglione, *Il libro del Cortegiano* 1.29.

48   'di sorte che ogni suo atto risulti e sia composto di tutte le virtù, come dicono i Stoici esser officio di chi è savio, benché però in ogni operazion sempre una virtù è la principale', Castiglione, *Il libro del Cortegiano* 2.7.

49   'anzi, se sempre producesse maschio, faria una imperfezione; perché come del corpo e dell'anima risulta un composito più nobile che le sue parti, che è l'omo, così della compagnia di maschio e di femina risulta un composito conservativo della specie umana, senza il quale le parti si destruiriano', *Il libro del Cortegiano* 3.14.

50   'la signora Eleonora Gonzaga, Duchessa nova; ché se mai furono in un corpo solo congiunti sapere, grazia, bellezza, ingegno, manere accorte, umanità ed ogni altro gentil costume, in questa tanto sono uniti, che ne risulta una catena, che ogni suo movimento di tutte queste condizioni insieme compone ed adorna', Castiglione, *Cortegiano* 4.2.

than to spare battle expenses; because poorly supported campaigns in the long run result in (or incur) greater costs beyond comparison.[51]

Results lie in the balance. Bandello describes the social type of the buffoon, a kind of joker or clown who makes his livelihood by amusing the nobility with somewhat malicious humour: though these practical jokes might give offence to some, they nevertheless result in pleasure for many (*la beffa risulta in piacere*).[52] In his sensual epic of the seventeenth century, Giambattista Marino describes how the beauty of consonance results from the harmonious elements of music,[53] which is a little like the conception of the string resulting in sound in early English. And Milton's line 'With Trumpets regal sound the great result',[54] uses the word result in the same way that earlier authors used the word 'report', like the report of a gun or a gong, literally what is 'carried back' to the ears. Like 'result', 'report' is now almost entirely a bureaucratic conception, even though its origins are demonstratively physical.

The relation that academic results bear to the bouncy physical origins is partly coincidental and partly telling. Academic results or marks might be said to lie in the balance; because you can never predict the results till the grades have been finalized and passed through a board of examiners; and even that degree of rigour does not prevent some cases from being capricious. Above all, the results are collectively the thing that springs back at the student from the institution: the student has made a submission and the marks jump back at him or her as the official reaction. This jumping back at the student by the institution assumes total significance for the student. Good marks are the *summum bonum*, the most tangible sign that a student has done well. They are sought on competitive terms, because students like to do better than one another; and few enjoy the prospect of low marks even if they perceive that there might be some justice in receiving them and are

---

51 'chi manca per risparmiare danari allunga le imprese tanto più, che ne risulta sanza comparazione maggiore spesa', Francesco Guicciardini, *Ricordi* 149.

52 'Molte fiate ho io, Silvio mio vertuosissimo, tra me pensato la varietá de la natura, che tutto il dí si vede tra questa sorte d'uomini che noi volgarmente appellamo buffoni e giocolatori, veggendo i modi loro l'uno da l'altro diversissimi, essendo perciò il fine loro per lo piú di guadagnare senza troppa fatica il vivere ed essere ben vestiti, aver adito in camera e a la tavola de li signori da ogni tempo, e scherzar con loro liberamente, e insomma dare gioia e festa a ciascuno. Si vede chiaramente che cercano tutti dilettare, se bene talora offendeno chi si sia, facendoli alcuna beffa, che nondimeno la beffa risulta in piacere a chi la vede o la sente recitare', (letter to Paolo Silvio) *Novelle* 4.26.

53 *Adone* 16.148.

54 *Paradise lost* 2.515.

reconciled to the relatively low academic regard as a fair reflexion of their efforts. High grades are invested with much vanity, because high distinctions are assumed to be created by native talent as well as determination. Students may reject units, subjects or modules on the basis of their results in any attempt; so there is a reciprocal jumping back, this time from the student to the institution. A department which marks meanly will be punished by poor student uptake, unless special prestige and high professional stakes support the severe grading practices. Sometimes, alas, departments are happy with their harsh marking if it discourages the less talented—judging by the marks—from patronizing their field and leaves them with an elite.

Student success is therefore highly overwritten with results. Because most other student priorities pale by comparison, the results spring back at the student experience of learning with a challenging accusation. Students who study for the test are suspected of doing better than those who seek enlightenment, who have a liberal view of education and who accept the invitation to speculate, to grow intellectually and broaden their minds. If you have a mechanistic and strategic view of your study—guided by hunger for good results at the end—you will achieve higher grades. In his famous case of Susan and Robert cited earlier,[55] John Biggs defines his two archetypes by their relation to results: Susan has an academic and inquiring mind whereas non-academic Robert is opportunistically in it for the marks. After an alienated beginning, he catches up with Susan by dint of strategy.

The implicit line along which learning outcomes line-up with delivery, learning activities and assessment does not necessarily mean that assessment is privileged. Theoretically, one can maintain alignment with lite assessment, that is, either deliberately undiscriminating assessment (like pass grade only) or assessment which errs greatly to the generous. But in practice discriminatory assessment rules: it determines most aspects of the student learning experience and forms the point of greatest stress in otherwise cordial relations between students and teachers.

Our learning outcomes are met to differing degrees by the cohort, which explains the spread of results. So the learning outcomes present a little bit like a contract, against which the student's performance matches

---

55   John Biggs, 'What the student does: teaching for enhanced learning', *Higher Education Research & Development*, vol. 18, no. 1, 1999, based on a distinction between deep and shallow learning in F Marton & R Säljö, 'On qualitative differences in learning. 1—Outcome and process', *British Journal of Educational Psychology*, vol. 46, 1976, pp. 4–11.

expectations or not. Even the plural term 'the results' sounds philologically strange. In earlier centuries, 'result' was mostly a verb and tellingly did not have this fixed presence as a substantive. Among the rare occasions when the noun is used, the term indeed equates with outcome. For instance, in the eighteenth century, Lindoro says in a play by Carlo Goldoni: 'the meeting is over; either by love or by force, Zelinda will tell me the result'[56] or what came out of it. But in other cases, the verb has a great sense of narrative about it, as in different opinions that result in our various minds.[57] But now the results, generally pluralized to indicate a number of individuals' achievement or study fields, are both reified and prosaic, a fetishized cypher of congealed performance. They have lost the connexion with their previous structure of narrative.

If we were to write a new protocol for learning outcomes, we would feel it necessary to muster all previous prescriptions for making them more explicit, more measurable and more certain. It would then seem incumbent upon us to add something to the precision, so that they might be yet more explicit, yet more measurable and yet more certain. But in all probability this elaborate transactional machinery would only add to the anxiety of students and staff. The assessment will still separate students by high or low marks; and the more guidance that is offered, the more opportunities students have to worry if they have memorized the guidance rather than profited by the syllabus. The cues with which we helpfully ply the students resemble telling students the answers before the exam. It sounds fondly benign but it favours the mechanistic exam exponents who strategically memorize the language of the desired answers rather than think independently and learn for themselves.

It is not that the current academic apparatus of alignment is an illogical shibboleth: it undoubtedly has its place. We need to deconstruct alignment rather than abolish it. We must see the whole educational vocabulary with fresh eyes and, as the ancient Greeks already began to say, to tell new (καινολογέω). Through the history of language, for example, we were able to note that the term 'result' historically reveals the opposite emphasis: an acceptance of chance, the unpredictable event that emerges from the balance of possibilities, brought into unforeseeable dialectical relationships with one another and fortune. Those ancient resonances are more congruent

---

56   'me ne dirà il risultato', Carlo Goldoni, *La gelosia di Lindoro* 1.4.
57   'Il diverso parer che nelle varie / Nostre menti risulta, / Pensar mi fa che utile più saria / Introdurre fra noi la monarchia', Carlo Goldoni, *Il mondo alla roversa* 2.1.

with the deeper meanings of student success and genuine and inventive student-centredness. If we put these insights together with our idea of the root of all learning, a pattern emerges. We can take our cue from learning itself, the origins of which are a story that lends itself to poetic enchantment (lore), inviting an imaginative reception by symbols and metaphor and thus proffering numerous moments of identification with the audience. For each listener, the story unfolds with a parallel trajectory of self-images, fantasies, places in the rhythmical narrative where we seem to belong. We learn in the sense of find out about; but the attention is not linear but rather full of imaginary analogies where we see the material symbolizing aspects of ourselves. The best kind of teaching narrates creatively what is marvellously to be learned; it does not commence with a measure and anxiously calibrate itself at each stage according to a contract. Instead, the story that ends in a further event, what one used to see as the outcome or result, is more like a ritualized point of arrival than a stressful contractual proof that stipulated promises have been fulfilled. Learning as a set of tales, each with an ending that begins a new story, one that you want to hear and love to live with because it seems to have you in it: that ontological dimension, that you come to love the subject, is the supreme learning outcome which trumps all others. At this stage, however, this post-constructivist ideal would be seen as a utopian song in defiance of a pragmatic industry.

Chapter 3

ENGAGEMENT

Student engagement is highly prized and for obvious reasons. It is a key element in a satisfying student experience and, insofar as it is created by teachers, it reflects on the quality of teaching. One assumes, rightly or wrongly, that it correlates with learning, on the basis that disengaged students do not appear to learn much and are more likely to drop out. There is every reason to encourage student engagement and to cultivate whatever yields the happy outcomes associated with it.

As for what student engagement is or what creates it, we have plenty of ideas; but they are not generalizable beyond platitudes about involvement, attendance and collaboration, and seldom rise above the obvious. We can ask students what they found engaging and can therefore measure the identified qualities using survey instruments. For years, therefore, we have known the obvious, namely that students consider subjects or modules or units engaging if their lecturers or tutors make the class interesting and demonstrate a personal interest in the topic, if they involve the class and encourage participation, if they make you see the relevance of the material, maybe if they have a flair for language and demonstrably love explaining the content, maybe are a bit eccentric but in all events are entertaining and bring the class with them.

Today, we hardly want to hear these dear old verities. They are all true, of course, but they do not support contemporary approaches to education. Following John Biggs, we are interested in learning as 'what the student does', not what the lecturer does. The many surveys that we once might have commissioned to discover what students find engaging have to be called off, lest they prove that teaching is influenced by 'what the teacher does' and still matters in the minds of students. Rather than ask students for their impressions, we count their behaviours, defining engagement as their aggregated activity on the learning management system (LMS). This appropriately named management system has arrived just in time to complete the managerial view of students. We now count student engagement and seek, in the next click, to manage student engagement through the very same system.

Now that we have achieved a perfect virtual panopticon of the student's learning experience, we feel in a position to direct their every move, to micromanage their learning, to ask them to do X before proceeding to Y and not to allow them to see Z until they have fulfilled all the conditions of completing Y. Even their conversation is mandated and monitored. They must post opinions on the LMS forum and also respond to other students in the same forum, whether they feel inclined to or not. They are not allowed to withhold or brood or adopt a sultry indifference in the face of material that they are sceptical about or find odd or creepy or misguided. They are all lined up in digital files of exhaustive completeness and are compelled, watched, recorded: their learning has no privacy and no liberty. It is a humiliating digital prison, in which an unprecedented level of control is now legitimated because it yields superior levels of engagement. Bordering on abuse, this relentless culture of orders and inspection is inimical to imagination and creativity.

Because engagement is now a metrical phenomenon, tied to the anxious discourse of student success, its drivers are under pressure, because universities can be audited and ranked according to their completion statistics. To improve engagement and also to fulfil certain articles of faith about working in teams, group work is prescribed. Group work admittedly has advantages over individual work because, at least in some contexts, it is more authentic in reflecting the real world, where we might work in teams rather than on our own. The work of a group may or may not be creative and imaginative. It is possible for group work to be highly creative, as we know from films, which are the result of group activity on a large scale and which are sometimes imaginative. Structurally, however, the faculty of imagination of the individual is subordinated to a faculty of negotiation, diplomacy, compromise. The undertaking may be creative but the learning activity is much more characterized by ego management than imagination. Paradoxically, when it comes to assessment, discriminating between the effort of separate participants seems necessary. So a good check to attribute the respective contributions is the level of engagement as demonstrated by activity on the LMS. What begins in inducements to student solidarity ends up as a fracturing isolation of individuals through our need for discriminatory assessment.

If you consider the impact on creativity that these scenarios have, scenarios which are now the gold standard of global education, the outlook is baleful. There is scope for poetic moments within an LMS but not when the design is centred on engagement, on boosting levels of involvement in tasks or readings or comment, group work and forced interaction. Engagement, when understood through click counting, encourages the wholesale collapse of student autonomy. How, then, do we moderate engagement or see it in more creative terms? What could engagement be if it is not overwritten with these withering metrics? Can we look into the dark heart of this teaching trophy and discover historical reasons to redefine it for the benefit of creativity?

To be fair, engagement is sought in education in the same way that it is fetishized in other fields where, admittedly, the target audience cannot be controlled. Engagement is also a centrepiece of writing, museums, environmental science programs, theatre, television, social media, marketing, anything where enticing an audience and gaining a reaction seems to be important, the very *raison d'être* of a publishing house, a gallery, a lobby group, a production company, a network or platform. If a piece of writing is not engaging, it will have fewer readers; and those who persist in reading—perhaps because they want the information irrespective of how it is written—are less likely to be favourably disposed to the text or to develop an affectionate relationship with the content or its author.

Considered somewhere between an art and a mystery, engagement is just as hard to explain in literary, curatorial or filmic media. It lies close to rhetoric, the ancient art of persuasion, and is seldom aligned with simplicity, science, objectivity or clarity. It is more likely to be highly voiced, partisan, passionate, as Baudelaire says of criticism: it may be engineered to have suspense, to be folded with surprise, colour and exciting juxtapositions, and perhaps a touch of morbid imagery. The full aesthetic register of controlled turmoil is inexhaustible. We have art not just because there are always new things to say but because there are also new ways to say old things; and this almost convulsive energy riddles cultural production, bringing interest to dull themes and investing brilliance in mediocre ideas. Pervasive and infectious, these tropes of winning attention dominate mainstream media, with their line-up of beautiful presenters, bright teeth and colourful backdrops; and from high culture to popular culture, our encounter with information and experience is comprehensively larded with artificial strategies for achieving engagement.

There are deep questions about the fitness of such artifice when it comes to learning. By virtue of belonging to a promiscuously marketed culture, the typical learner is already inevitably steeped in a medial environment of competitive messages, each vying with the other for attention. So to gain the student's attention, it is tempting for teachers or any university video to try to adopt the same language of engagement, even if it turns out that the teacher's rhetorical ruses to secure engagement are antithetical to learning. But remembering that learning is 'what the student does', it seems more legitimate simply to compel students to demonstrate their engagement by mandating and monitoring their activity on the LMS.

Supposing that you momentarily resist this low-level fascism. How much and what kind of stimulation to enjoin to the learning experience are questions that are structurally fraught, which perhaps explains why teaching is sometimes considered an art rather than a science. Fatefully, these pedagogical agonies are prefigured and to some extent explained by the history of the very words that we use to describe the objective.

*

In the history of language, engagement is a happy mutant, a bit like rigour, which begins with a somewhat negative, severe and even aggressive meaning and becomes positive and highly sought after in the modern epoch.[1] In French, no less than English, the word 'engagement' commences as a transactional term. In the sixteenth century, one already 'engages' a mason or a painter to do work on the property.[2] Montaigne, speaking for Plato, fears our 'bitter engagement' to emotions (*nostre engagement aspre à la douleur et à la volupté*);[3] and this sense of the yoke or constraint is at times suffocating. In a genial passage, Montaigne gives reasons for discounting death: if it is a short and violent end, he says, 'we have no leisure to fear it; if it is otherwise, I forswear life in the same measure that I am engaged in the illness'.[4] 'I am engaged with'—literally 'I engage myself with'—means 'I am in the grip of', in a deadly bond, as the illness takes over my faculties. In another place, Montaigne describes feeling the soul engage with death,

---

1   Robert Nelson, 'Toward a history of rigour: an examination of the nasty side of scholarship', *Arts and Humanities in Higher Education*, vol. 10, no. 4, October 2011, pp. 374–387 (doi: 10.1177/1474022211408797).

2   'il engagea pour quinze cens.' Marguerite de Navarre, *L'Heptaméron des nouvelles* 2.15.

3   *Essais* 1.14.

4   'qu'à mesure que je m'engage dans la maladie', *Essais* 1.20.

like the body.[5] Similarly, when the Cretans wanted to damn someone, they would pray to the gods to engage him or her with some ill custom.[6] The engagement is a trap.

We search in vain for a happy connexion and there is certainly no talk of a sparkle in education that we recognize as engagement. It is more like the LMS. In one place, Montaigne laments how in France, only people of low rank engage in study, because they see in it a means of making a living.[7] But this engagement is what motivates study for base reasons, not a stimulant inside the study itself, even if active individuals might somewhat positively 'embrace everything, engage everywhere, who become passionate about everything and who give of themselves on all occasions'.[8] Nor is this readiness to *hop in* necessarily a sign of a good enthusiasm. For example, Montaigne deplores the way we see thousands of soldiers-of-fortune engaging their blood and life for money in some disagreement in which they have not the slightest interest,[9] recalling Shakespeare's somewhat nobler 'I do engage my life'.[10]

In these examples, we see the origin of the word emerging, which has to do with being bound to a contract (*gage*), which survives in our word mortgage, a debt of obligations or a vow, like Shakespeare's 'engaged by my oath' or 'To break the vow I am engaged in', always a constraint: 'O limed soul, that, struggling to be free, / Art more engaged!'[11] We also recognize the word in the military context, as when one engages with the enemy, meaning exchanging fire or doing battle, which one can also express as engaging oneself to fight for someone else.[12] On another occasion, honour engages one to fight.[13] Elsewhere, resentment can engage someone,[14] meaning something like 'move' or motivate, in the same way that sadness can 'engage' the heroine.[15]

---

5   *Essais* 2.12.

6   *Essais* 1.23.

7   'il ne reste plus ordinairement, pour s'engager tout à faict à l'estude, que les gens de basse fortune qui y questent des moyens à vivre.' *Essais* 1.25.

8   *Essais*, 1.39.

9   'engageant pour de l'argent leur sang et leur vie à des querelles où ils n'ont aucun interest.' *Essais* 2.23.

10   *As you like it* 5.4.

11   Respectively *Richard II* 1.3, *Love's labour's lost* 4.3, *Hamlet* 3.3.

12   'Je le vais engager à combattre pour vous', Racine, *Alexandre le Grand* 1.3.

13   'l'honneur m'inspire … il m'engage à sauver mon empire', *Alexandre le Grand* 1.2.

14   Racine, *Britannicus* 2.3.

15   Racine, *Iphigénie* 3.6.

Our modern usage also expresses happy ties through the word, as when people about to marry are 'engaged', meaning that both lovers make a pledge: 'the secrets of my heart: / All my engagements I will construe to thee',[16] which is echoed throughout the seventeenth century, as in Racine's line that 'you alone engage me beneath the yoke of love'.[17] It follows that if one can engage someone in love in the seventeenth century, one can already speak of 'engaging people in conversation', though this is devious in order to entertain other love affairs;[18] but still for the most part, one engages faith[19] or 'my engaging itself under under its law'.[20] While the gerund 'engaging' is used in some of these examples, it does not describe a quality of an action or conversation. It has no adjectival agency but is strictly verbal. Further, it is always transactional, never far from the pledge and the root of a tie: 'in receiving his faith at the altar, I will engage her to my son by immortal knots',[21] which explains why one also sees lines of astonishing coldness, as with 'nothing engages you to love me',[22] meaning that nothing has to compel you.

The motif of engagement has remarkably little charm and is overwritten with obligation. In this severity, as noted, it is somewhat like other words that transition to the positive in modern language when understood in an aesthetic context. One of them is 'compelling'. In legal or political contexts, the term is harsh. You could be compelled to sell your property to pay a fine or compelled to go to war. But in aesthetic discourses, the word is positive, a much sought-after quality of transporting emotion beyond one's power of moderation. It is also hard to find a positive meaning for the word in pre-industrial languages; it is always rigorous and threatening. Other horrible terms that take on a celebratory air in aesthetic discourse are the violent words 'striking', 'impact', 'a hit', 'stunning', a 'knock-out'. Nor is it a coincidence that these are all ingredients that might be considered core components of the theatrical engagement that a charismatic lecturer, for example, might achieve with a student audience.

---

16   *Julius Caesar* 2.1.

17   'Que toi seul en effet m'engageas sous ses lois', *Alexandre le Grand* 4.1.

18   'Engageant Amarante et Florame au discours', Théante in Corneille, *La suivante* 1.1.

19   'engageant notre foi', in Corneille, *Horace* 3.4, Racine, *Bajazet* 5.4.

20   'mon cœur s'engageant sous sa loi', Axiane in Racine, *Alexandre le Grand* 1.3; Racine, *Andromaque* 2.1.

21   Racine, *Andromaque* 4.1.

22   Racine, *Andromaque* 4.5.

Other terms that have swung radically from a base of certain horror toward aesthetic delight derive from the metaphor of captivity or confinement: to enthral, to capture (as in capture attention or capture the imagination), which extends to gripping, seizing or grabbing. These are deeply horrible motifs, reminiscent of the biblical peoples led into captivity and handled by the lash and the sword. But by the perversity of aesthetic discourse, the loss of freedom effected through beauty or rhetoric is an admirable property of art or human seduction. Thus, in poetic literature of the renaissance, it became fashionable to describe the completeness of love as a form of enslavement, whence the amorous courting songster would express a thrall, an emotional subservience. This poetic motif is very old and can even be traced to the *Bible* (or at least the *Apocrypha*: 'his beauty made his soul captive'[23]) which is dominated by a series of horrible captivity narratives. It has great traction in English as well: 'So is mine eye enthralled to thy shape'; 'Love hath chas'd sleep from my enthralled eyes'. Romance aside, Shakespeare uses words like 'captivate' in a fierce and resentful spirit.[24]

Even closer to the theme of engagement, the term entertainment reveals a similar pattern. One thinks of something entertaining as gorgeously cheerful, funny, diverting; but this joy is by no means the main historical motif embedded in the fabric of European language. A little like thrall and captivating, entertaining has the root of 'holding' (*tenere*), which is logical and not necessarily negative, as when we hold someone's attention or even hold someone dear. But contrary to such tenderness, entertaining in the renaissance is highly transactional and even managerial. For example, Francesco Guicciardini explains that a lord should always try to bring profit to his servants; however, they can sometimes become spoilt and begin to complain when benefits rendered in fat years are scarcer in lean years, so it is better to ration the indulgences, to err to parsimony rather than largesse, entertaining the servants more with hope than with goods (*intrattenendogli più con la speranza che con gli effetti*).[25] The verb recurs in the same passage with a similar meaning, that we might also translate as 'treat'.

Do everything that you can, Guicciardini later counsels, to have yourself entertained well (*intrattenervi bene*) among princes and the estates that they rule.[26] It is not as if the word meant something entirely different to

---

23   'pulchritudo ejus captivam fecit animam ejus', *Judith* 16.11.
24   'To triumph, like an Amazonian trull, / Upon their woes whom fortune captivates!', *III King Henry VI* 1.4; 'women have been captivate ere now.' *I King Henry VI* 5.3.
25   *Ricordi* 5.
26   *Ricordi* 174.

its current acceptation. The modernity of the conception can be witnessed in Guicciardini's century. For example, Bandello, writing to Baldassare Castiglione, describes the joyful festivities and sumptuous banquets in Milan, music and other virtuous entertainments (*onesti intrattenimenti*). One of them, a performance of a farce, held the joyful company in the greatest pleasure. The windows to the east admitted fresh air and after dancing, the *lieta brigata* turned to discourse.[27] In a later novella, Bandello also speaks of a garden where one could well entertain oneself with some decent and pleasant discourse;[28] and Giorgio Vasari, also writing in the mid sixteenth century, describes how sometimes fatigue gets the better of artists: they cannot face up to the challenge and become lazy and cowardly, indulging rather in entertainments (*si intrattengono più volentieri*) with chatter and drinking by the fire, relinquishing all vigour of soul.[29] So too, Vasari tells of the desire of the Paduans to keep Donatello in their city: in order to entertain him or keep him (*per intrattenerlo*) they commission him to make relief sculptures beneath the main altar at the Church of the Minor Friars. The term is used in a similar sense of 'retain him', 'keep him here', with Perino del Vaga. The most light-hearted entertainment arises when Vasari narrates that in his last days, the sculptor Verrocchio made a joke in hospital that he needs a bit more fever in order to remain entertained in the hospital in comfort and service;[30] but even this circumstance tellingly involves an arrangement and a privilege: to 'keep me here'. In most of Vasari, entertainment has a positive connotation but it is nevertheless transactional.

In French, the same observations hold; though occasionally, the term indicates a more autonomous humour, as when the philosopher Montaigne describes his aspiration to a contented retirement in which he can think of no greater favour to his spirit than to entertain himself in full leisure.[31] Montaigne also describes his interaction with a company of Germans who spoke no French but excellent Latin: they entertained me in nothing but Latin.[32] In French, the very word for conversation or discourse takes the same form as entertainment (*entretien*),[33] rather like the form of the German

---

27   prologue to *Novelle* 1.53.

28   'bene d'intrattenersi con alcuno onesto e piacevol ragionamento.' 3.12.

29   *Life of Luca della Robbia*.

30   'per potermi intrattenere qui agiato e servitor', *Life of Andrea del Verrocchio*.

31   Montaigne, *Essais* 1.8.

32   'ne m'entretenoient d'autre langue que Latine', 1.26.

33   *e.g.* Montaigne, *Essais* 1.39.

conversation (*Unterhaltung*), literally under-holding, where the French is inter-holding.

In sixteenth-century French we also find the meaning that we retain today of considering or contemplating: it would be better to entertain some sterling foundations of truth.[34] From there, it is highly suitable for baroque convolutions, as in Shakespeare: 'Until I know this sure uncertainty / I'll entertain the offer'd fallacy.'[35] That means: I will accept the suggestion, perhaps with an air of condescension. To entertain in premodern cultures sometimes has the reverse sense to the one prevailing today, where one entertains in the sense of granting an audience rather than having an audience and making it laugh. A good example is Shakespeare's character Rosencrantz who admonishes Hamlet over his morose disposition against humanity when the actors have turned up to perform a play: 'what lenten entertainment the players shall receive from you'.[36] We would say that the players entertain Hamlet; instead, Hamlet entertains the players. For Shakespeare, Hamlet is the patron, so it is Hamlet who entertains by virtue of indulging the players. To entertain somebody is to give your time to them and hence dispense your grace. It is Hamlet's prerogative, not the players'.

To be 'worthy your lordship's entertainment' means that his lordship will endure a meeting: the person in authority—the patron who controls time—is the one who entertains, not *vice versa*. This meaning persists in contemporary language, where we entertain visitors or dinner guests, have them over for the evening and provide an extravagant table for them. In the same economy that Derrida identifies with the gift, the guests are in some sense obligated by this generosity; and until they feel compelled to reciprocate, they are in debt.[37] To acquit this debt, they must entertain you in return; and if they do so more extravagantly than you did at the outset, you will in turn go into debt.

Perhaps to relieve the tension inherent in the relationship, entertainment could be built on a commercial basis, where it is provided for a fee. It is the structure of theatre and restaurants, elements of a happy society that accord payment for services in a free market. Throughout the periods examined for the roots of our concepts, the term entertainment was developing as a commercial cultural proposition, as one can see in a preamble to one of Goldoni's plays in the eighteenth century, where the genial playwright

---

34   Montaigne, 'entretenir des vrays fondemens de la verite', *Essais* 1.32.

35   *The comedy of errors* 2.2.

36   *Hamlet* 2.2.

37   Jacques Derrida, *Donner le temps*, Galilée, Paris, 1991.

describes the exemplary Signor Antonio Grimani who led a life of charity in his retirement after having acquitted himself of every duty as a good citizen; but after having satisfied the pious inclination of his heart, he was still keen on recreating the spirits with noble and honest entertainments (*intrattenimenti*), whence he admired Goldoni's comedies.

When a lecturer self-consciously entertains the class with jokes or harmonica or funny cartoons, however, these arrangements do not resolve themselves as paid entertainment, because there is no trade or agreement that the funny act deserves the door charge. Instead, it is gratuitous in a structural sense: the lecturer performs the joke or guitar solo as an unconditional extra, hoping that it will pay off by creating admiration or perhaps a happy mood or light relief. In this aspiration, the entertaining lecturer recedes to the position of player or clown of the early modern period: will the audience indulge him or her with their polite attention or, recognizing authority in those who judge, will the audience entertain the lecturer?

The motif is unstable and tense in a way that has nothing to do with learning. If the audience laughs, the lecturer is in credit and the students owe him or her a bit more attention and admiration. If the audience does not laugh, the lecturer must attempt to recover, a bit like a lover committing a *faux pas* and having to overcome the embarrassment and re-establish trust and innocence. For a spell, the lecturer will be in the audience's credit, anxious not to be seen as awkward or gauche, a fool or a loser. And if both lecturer and audience are concerned about these outcomes while the impressions are psychologically negotiated, it is hard to imagine much learning taking place.

Entertainment is only one strategy for achieving student engagement; and it may be unself-conscious and endearing. Some lecturers have natural charm, which should be respected, of course. If students are asked if the class or the teacher is entertaining, responses will naturally vary; and, provided that there is no inverse relationship with learning, the entertaining aspect is likely to remain popular as a means of engaging students. Lecturers with a skill for gaining comic credit are likely to be favoured with the large class; and, alas, student audiences can be quite demonstrative in their intolerance of a boring lecturer. Sadly, however, the ability to animate the content *as content* is easily collapsed with comic talents; and so the faculty of engagement is misconstrued as a theatrical condiment rather than a narrative or interlocutory aptitude proper to the content.

If this misunderstanding occurs, it fulfils the historical paradigm by which our vocabulary of engagement has slipped from negative to positive meanings under aesthetic privilege. The lecture is seen as a performance and the beam of light controlled from the lectern is the proscenium arch. The terms of the interaction are theatrical and the way that the lecturer snares the audience puts his or her rhetorical gifts to the test. If the content is animated *as content*, we have no quarrel with the lively lecture, because this process of animation is proper to the intellectual grasp of the material. But insofar as it is framed by an artful construct of entertainment, it is more likely to damage learning than enhance it.

When, on the other hand, engagement is sought though participatory strategies, there are fewer risks of an aesthetic distraction constructed around the lecturer's ego. Students are organized into collaborative groups and are asked to solve problems together, thus activating the process rather than passively—so the theory goes—attending a lecture and absorbing the content. Certainly, if that is the choice, we would not deny the greater efficacy of an active or participatory mode of learning. But the contemporary wisdom on collaborative participatory learning paradoxically invokes engagement with its ancient emphasis on the contractual.

Learning is construed as a learning task: a job is set and a convention for splitting up the contribution of participants must be established. Though this process is understood as liberal, emancipating the student from an assumed passivity in the lecture theatre, we are in fact led to a somewhat managerial paradigm. Learning through the workshop is more likely to instil process skills in teamwork, projection and leadership than content in physics or grammar. If, on the other hand, we think of learning as integral with reflexion—much the same kind of reflexion that we need for research and originality—it is less clear that collaborative forms of engagement are helpful; indeed, they may even discourage reflexion. Meanwhile, the maligned lecture may stimulate high degrees of reflexion, including when its very theatricality casts a coloured light on the content. It depends on the individual and the discipline; but nothing is more engaging than the faculty of critical deconstruction, and it is totally free of the contractual bonds and ties of archaic engagement.

To perceive the listener in the auditorium as passive is fair when the content is factual and when the communication is purely transmissive. But in many cases (as in humanities and social sciences), the lecture can be understood as a representation with selective material and an interpretation that is highly available to the student's critique. Far from passively absorbing content, the student may be furiously seeking the reasons for the lecturer's bias or misguidedness (in his or her critical estimation) and may spend time pondering the appropriate correction. This form of engagement may or may not be readily socialized—as in a Socratic tutorial—but it is nonetheless powerful, in fact research-friendly, and is free of the obligatory and contractual dimensions of engagement that we have reason to scruple about. One might argue that the prime form of engagement in study is where a person engages with his or her own thought or reading, quite possibly in solitude, which could also be called reflexion. It is what Montaigne meant in speaking of people 'who make a study of it, their work and their calling, who *engage themselves* sustainably, in all faith and with all force'.[38]

Depending on how we define it or think about it, engagement in modern language remains positive and will continue to be sought across all educational settings. But it has a tellingly shady history and, uncannily following some of the dubious motifs revealed in its philology, engagement in education sometimes returns to its roots of a pledge, a bond, a yoke. Perhaps the worst aspect of engagement is that it is very difficult to question, because no one can ever say that we should have less of it; and as a consequence, it is pursued somewhat dogmatically at the expense of things that we may not fully understand; and in fact, we do not fully understand engagement either, especially in some of its monitoring guises which are so inimical to creativity, the privacy of the imagination and student dignity. The history of the concept and its many contingencies throws helpful light on a dimension of learning and teaching that needs urgent review; because if we are to create a creative university, we will at times need emancipation from the engagement that we are mechanistically fixated on.

---

38   'qui s'engage à un registre de durée, de toute sa foy, de toute sa force.' *Essais* 2.18.

Chapter 4

BEING NICE

We enjoy the thought of teaching which is effective; that is, it delivers on the learning outcomes or, perhaps more generously, it yields learning. Effective teaching, of course, has a good effect. But does the effectiveness include creativity and, if so, what might that entail? Normally, we recognize that effective teaching is conditioned by many factors of a tangible nature. Themes such as the alignment of learning outcomes, delivery and assessment, feedback, syllabus progression, learning management systems and even learning spaces have received understandable attention in building up a picture of the necessary elements of effective educational practice. These stalwarts in the scholarship of teaching and learning have two characteristics that make them rewarding to study: first, they are to some extent measurable and second, they are manageable: you can do something about them if they are skew or untimely or contradictory.

Behind this positivistic discourse of items that are in our control lies another grid of highly subjective variables which are at times unrewarding to contemplate and perhaps even attract the suspicion of serious researchers. They too have become topics for scholarship but the outcome is harder to embrace. These include relationship issues between teacher and student, personal presentation, engagement, appearance, even fashion sense, items easily dismissed as unacademic and frivolous, and which seem unlikely to contribute to long-term benefits in learning, though they are quite likely to show up in surveys. They are harder to measure and may or may not be something that a given individual can do much about or might want to alter, and with good reason.

Among these subjective indices, however, lies a substantial group with potential credibility for the scholarship of teaching and learning. Sometimes described in survey instruments with terms like 'approachability' or 'enthusiasm', the lecturer has appeal to students according to his or her personality. But being approachable or enthusiastic is only one of the wider aspects of personality that we could describe more generally as personal characteristics of the teacher that engender delight in the learning subject (the person who learns). Vague but nevertheless compelling, these qualities can be summed up in common language with words like 'nice' or 'kind' or 'sweet' or 'lovely'. Not all teachers display these qualities, but disparate levels of educational niceness throw the issue into relief. When such differences are seen in relief, it seems likely that niceness may have an effect on learning but especially when it involves the creative. Our assumption from the outset is that the creative is easily suppressed by an unsympathetic environment and is fostered by encouragement. A part of this encouragement is the personal niceness of the teacher, whose characteristic benignity creates a safe place for imaginative expression. From personal observation for thirty-five years, I am inclined to think that the niceness of the teacher has an overwhelming effect on the confidence, empathy and productive creativity of the student.

It is difficult to broach the topic, because niceness does not fit in any learning and teaching taxonomy. Survey designers prefer adjectives like 'approachable' or 'enthusiastic', first because they are somewhat identifiable and hence measurable on a Likert scale and second because a given teacher might still be able to do something about them. You can resolve to take mechanical steps to become more approachable (more or less by insisting that you are approachable and advertising your consultation-times, even if you are fundamentally unapproachable by any individual's feeling) and you can demonstrate more enthusiasm by remembering to quicken your voice and become excited at key points in a presentation.

To the extent that these qualities may be controlled or manipulated or falsified, they are not the theme of this chapter. I mean 'nice' as in how lovely a person is, not how much he or she can become energized over his or her topic or how diligent he or she is in consistently having an open door and inviting students in. Niceness in the familiar sense that I invoke is a feeling that the teacher is well disposed to the students and enjoys time spent with them, that he or she wants the best time for each of them and warmly responds to their presence. In essence, the quality of the teacher being nice lies in the experience of the student and is not demonstrable in a strategic sense.

How nice the teacher may be is a powerful part of the student learning experience and seems especially likely to have a relationship with learning whenever the student is invited to take risks, where the challenge is bracing and the assurances are treacherous. With creative work, the student needs to feel comfortable with some degree of faith in the teacher;

and what one person calls faith another may consider niceness. We are not up to proving this link between creativity and niceness because, as will become clear, the definition of nice is obscure and warped, as are its near but inadequate synonyms like 'kind' or 'generous' or translations in other languages, like *gentil* in French. At base, these ideas are embarrassingly convoluted, bizarrely empty or full of archaic prejudice with counter-intuitive negative connotations.

From a methodological point of view, we have every reason to ignore such factors. They cannot even be defined, much less measured or controlled. At the same time, however, one might entertain reasonable suspicions that the niceness of the teacher is a powerful force (indeed the most powerful force) in most student's experience and that it would bear considerably on learning, especially in fields where the intuitive faculties of the student are drawn from the privacy of imagination to the eyes of the classroom and the rigours of assessment. Unlike charisma—that leaderly confidence that encourages belief in an illustrious authority—niceness is (a) modest and humble and (b) likely to be good for learning on an axiomatic basis. Whereas charisma, for example, could fulfil a delusional or needy motive on the part of either teacher or student, niceness is seldom part of an unwholesome power structure and has no psychopathology that annuls curiosity and criticism.

The niceness of the teacher instead contributes to the comfort of the student to learn. The student has no fears of a social barrier that might in turn symbolize an intellectual barrier. If so, the encouragement to follow the teacher can only be good: there is no down-side to niceness, unless it degenerates into indulgence; but then in a sense that is no longer nice but lazy educational practice. In this chapter, I will indeed describe the pre-conditions of niceness and the limits to niceness, which in many ways grow logically out of the troubled heart of this simple yet strangely fraught concept. Our first task, however, is to explain how and why niceness has such a crazy history that even the world's finest lexicographers are baffled by its vicissitudes.

*

The origin of 'nice' is the Latin *nescius*, to be ignorant. It is not an encouraging start. Because of its historical character, the *Oxford English Dictionary* dwells much on the legacy of this derivation, because pre-industrial usage greatly reveals its influence. When applied to a person, it meant foolish, silly, simple, ignorant.[1] When said of an action or utterance, it meant displaying foolishness or silliness, something absurd or senseless; and in relation to conduct or behaviour, it meant encouraging wantonness or lasciviousness. In relation to dress, it might be extravagant, showy or ostentatious. Perhaps hinging on the motif of costume—with many layers of sartorial accuracy as well as fashionable perversity—the word turned slowly toward the positive, sometimes describing a person as finely dressed and elegant; and so too with arrangements, where it might mean precise or particular in matters of reputation or conduct, scrupulous, punctilious. Still contrary to modern usage, the word could mean 'fastidious, fussy, difficult to please, especially with regard to food or cleanliness; of refined or dainty tastes'.[2]

Toward the end of the sixteenth century, the adjective 'nice' could mean 'refined, cultured, associated with polite society'; though as applied to persons, the development is more toward the end of the eighteenth century. The lexicographers dwell a great deal on usages that we find remote from current acceptation and describe, almost with exasperation, the unusual twist in the etymology:

> The semantic development of this word from 'foolish, silly' to 'pleasing' is unparalleled in Latin or in the Romance languages. The precise sense development in English is unclear. N.E.D. (1906) s.v. notes that 'in many examples from the 16th and 17th cent. it is difficult to say in what particular sense the writer intended it to be taken'.

While the development might be unprecedented in Latin or in the Romance languages, it is not completely unparalleled. The development was mirrored in reverse, say, in the word 'cretin'. In French, this term for imbecile arose from the most unlikely adjective, namely Christian. The descent from a good believer into a dolt seems linguistically impious but it is also not without a vein of theological probity. The children in the asylum needed to be protected, were good Christians, harmless souls who needed experienced Christian instructors to protect them and help them in the world. To appeal to the spirit of Christian charity, one might have referred to the poor delinquents as Christians in order to identify them as worthy of benevolence.

Be that as it may, the turn from foolish to lovely in the word 'nice' suggests a deep equivocation in the idea itself, as if the benign field that it now

---

1   *Oxford English Dictionary, s.v.*

2   *ibid. s.v.*

describes is structurally unstable. How much do we really know what it is to be nice? At school, children used to be taught not to use the term *nice* because it says too little and seems too general and, above all, seems too common. Worse, however, the quality of niceness seems to harbour a risk, as if by calling someone nice we lessen his or her authority; and so the unconscious, on a large public scale, folds niceness into its contrary. Fatefully, the negative origins of the word seem to persist. Even when we speak of a person being benign, there may be a subtext that he or she is 'harmless', that is, somewhat lacking in vigour, a bit weak, unable to stand up for things, powerless, incapable of causing a disturbance. It is a bit like the French expression *belle âme*, beautiful and decent soul, perhaps not very animated, without a malicious spark and perhaps therefore a bit dull and not at all sexy.

The situation is perplexing because, since early times, European languages have been rich in words that describe goodness, benignity, niceness in our terms. Ancient Greek language, for example, is laden with adjectives for mild or gentle (ἀγανός), with substantive forms (ἀγανοφροσύνη), gentleness, kindliness (ἀγαθωσύνη). So too with adjectives for kind and gentle (ἐνηής, ἤπιος, μείλιχος) with respective substantive forms (*e.g.* ἐνηείη). One spoke of kindness in the sense of courtesy (ἐπητύς) and there are many conceptions of goodwill or favour (εὔνοια) with adjectival form (εὔνοος, εὔνους) or kind and generous (εὔθυμος). There is beneficence (εὐεργεσία) as well as being of good feeling, considerate, reasonable (εὐγνώμων) with substantive form (εὐγνωμοσύνη) which also has connotations of courtesy. One could be gracious, kindly (εὐμενής) or refined, gentlemanly or kindly (κομψός) and well-disposed (εὐνοητικός, εὐνοϊκός) before we get to expressions for tender-hearted or people-friendly (φιλάνθρωπος, προπρεών, πρόφρασσα) or words like benevolence or kind-heartedness (φιλανθρωπία, our philanthropy) or the genius of friendliness (φιλοφροσύνη).

They are all impressive but not exactly what we mean by nice or niceness; they all err to the gallant or generous, slightly institutional in flavour, for which there were further vocabularies, like good-giving (εὔδωρος), readily imparting (μεταδότης, εὐμετάδοτος), liberal with resources (κοινωνατικός), high-mindedly generous (μεγαλόφρων), great of soul (μεγαλόψυχος, that magnanimity that would be used of every noble in the renaissance with any show of largesse) or rich-souled (πλουσιόψυχος). These grandiloquent conceptions are remote from the peculiar intimacy that tickles our heart when we think of a person being nice. When we speak of a person being nice, it involves a similar judgement to the spaghetti being nice or a comfortable chair being nice; it is not specific to an altruistic propensity to act magnanimously, to extending grace, to sacrifice one's interests in favour of someone else. Being nice, as noted, can equally apply to a person's appearance, where it would be translated with words like *bello* in Italian or *nett* in German. It is an extremely convenient term that slips in and out of metaphor without a trace of where it began or where it might end.

To define nice, we often resort to kind and generous, two words of the most telling structure in their derivation. Though one is Germanic and the other Latin, they both refer to class and birth, by the same metaphor of nobility or gentleness, being of noble birth and hence—by the fateful extension that chauvinism operates through language—nobility of action and thought. In its origins, 'kind' is related to kin, like the German word for child (*Kind*). Remembering that the very word for nature also has 'birth' in it, the term 'kind' indicated a type of nature, what one was innately predisposed to from birth, giving you a certain character or condition, as the *OED* suggests. Effectively, this quality makes you a certain kind of person. Your kindness signals your belonging to a class or race. You are genetically distinguished, possessing innate characteristics of a positive kind. In the same way that good birth is noble and hence gives onto psychological nobility, so—if you are of the right kind—you are well-born or well-bred; and it follows by the same principle that you are courteous, gentle, benevolent, well-disposed by nature to extending kindness.

Every sweet thought turns out to be self-flattery according to the great historical perversity of language. When we are kind, we are of the *right kind*, illustrious, privileged, better than others, higher up, from which social perch we can look down on our lessers and sometimes extend favours. The same is true of the generous. As noted, it is a Latin root (*generosus*) from stock or race (*genus*) and refers ultimately to the act of begetting (*generare*). Because of the primacy of breeding in preindustrial cultures, the word immediately turned by chauvinistic metaphor to mean noble and magnanimous. As richly documented in the *OED*, the English 'generous' long retained the value and connotation of noble birth, hence courageous and magnanimous, rather institutional forms of being not mean. The pattern in fact has its roots not just in Latin—observed by all lexicographers—but Greek, where the word for birth or breeding (γεννάδας) meant both noble and generous, as in Aristophanes' useful and generous or noble[3] or Plato's noble and meek,[4] and also highly bred, especially as applied to horses.[5]

---

3 χρηστὸς καὶ γεννάδας, *Frogs* 179.

4 γεννάδας καὶ πρᾷος, *Phaedros* 243c; *cf.* Aristotle, *Nichomachean Ethics* 1100ᵇ32.

5 ἐπὶ τῶν γεννάδων ἵππων, Polemo the Physiognomist 78.

This motif of breeding runs directly into modern languages, as with the prolific sixteenth-century writer of *novelle*, Bandello, who describes a spirited and most generous racer (*animoso e generosissimo corsiero*).[6] In a letter to Isabella da Este, he notes that if you want to nourish a good stable of horses, go look for generous mares produced by good and noble mares[7] and the same goes for dogs. Generous in this circumstance means well bred, of the right genes, as with the 'fierce and generous steeds' used in jousting[8] or 'generous horses' that one might parade upon around the Brera for leisure,[9] meaning one's thoroughbreds. In another *novella*, Bandello imputes the same quality to ferocious lions, the most generous among the beasts.[10] In no other context would the bloodlust of this zealous killer be considered generous.

In most circumstances, Bandello uses the word generous in a way that is congruent with its acceptation in modern Italian and English, like generosity of heart;[11] but peppered throughout the vast corpus of stories, one finds telling regressions to the earlier genetic usage. An example is when he refers to people's name as generous[12] meaning noble by birth. Another is when he specifically refers to people by their 'generous and most noble lineage' (*di generosa e di nobilissima schiatta*)[13] or a gentleman of noble and generous ancestry,[14] which admittedly entails liberality. Similarly, one can be of generous blood[15] which, in Bandello's narration, turns out to be no proof of good character. These usages are never completely remote from the modern idea of generosity as a preparedness to lavish kindness on others[16] but nor are they far from the archaic root of congenital privilege.

It helps to know this backdrop to the term generosity, because it discourages identifying niceness too closely with a quality whose origins and deeper associations are linked with privilege. It is a constant temptation,

---

6   Matteo Bandello, *Novelle* 1.2.
7   1.3.
8   'feroci e generosi cavalli', 2.18, and again 2.44.
9   'sovra generosi cavalli', 2.31.
10   'con la ferocitá è il piú generoso tra le bestie', 2.48.
11   'quella generositá di core', 2.35.
12   'generoso vostro nome' in a letter to Cesare Fregoso, 2.13, or to Anna di Polignac with 'quel generoso nome vostro', 2.39, signora Antonia Bauzia, 4.4, or Guglielmo Lurio, 4.26.
13   1.2.
14   'gentiluomo di nobilissima e generosa stirpe', 1.49 and again 2.27.
15   3.52.
16   2.10, 2.14, 2.19, 2.58, 3.24.

because generosity in the modern sense is impeccable, positive and universally recommended, as if—as suggested already of niceness—there is no downside. But generosity is not exactly *niceness* and contains a germ (or seed) of stress in an economy of favours, transacted among people, some of whom are superior to others and are therefore in a position to dispense favours. They thereby exercise their generosity, their privilege, in the same way that Derrida observed of giving, where the giver is at a great moral advantage over the receiver, rendering the gift a kind of diplomatic hook, akin to poison for which it shares etymologies.[17]

Generosity, alas, does have a downside. Essentialized by its roots, it resembles a gesture of the socially elevated, akin to magnanimity and liberality with which it is frequently coupled in renaissance authors;[18] but when it is practiced by ordinary people—like teachers who have few resources beyond their education and good will and an allocated amount of time—it is exhausting. As a person who cannot be a patron, you are not quite of the right kind (or social *genus*) to extend largesse in anything except your time and encouragement; but these cherished qualities are finite and depleting them to satisfy your own expectations for generosity rapidly reaches painful limits. It has to be managed as a grid of compromises, mindful of equity and fairness to all the other students to whom you have to extend equal generosity. Your generosity will soon make you anxious.

Generosity in the unconscious is indivisible, an archetypal quality of great integrity, like greatness of soul. But in practice, it is highly divisible, almost divisive, because its grace is invidiously accorded to some but not to others. One has built up this concept of generosity throughout many centuries of Christian belief, fertilized by trade and industry, in which love (ἀγάπη) turned by degrees into dearness (*caritas*) or loving kindness—as of Christ's love (*caritas Christi*)—which finally makes a touching but also a somewhat dismal mechanistic turn into institutional charity.[19] Charity as an institution is an altruistic system of giving *pro bono*, making payments with money or time or goods (in kind). It is to a large extent quantifiable, even though we might be more touched on

---

17 Jacques Derrida, *Donner le temps*, Galilée, Paris 1991.

18 as in 'generoso e magnanimo eroe', Bandello 4.12, or of Galeazzo Sforza, 'generoso e liberale prencipe', 4.13.

19 See my argument against Peter Singer's case that charity morally trumps cultural investment, 'Culture is not a luxury any more than education', *The Age* and *Sydney Morning Herald*, 29 April 2009 (www.theage.com.au/federal-politics/culture-is-not-a-luxury-any-more-than-education-20090428-am3t.html).

a sentimental level when poor people give a small amount as opposed to rich people giving a large amount.

As a model for social adjustment, sweetly mediating between rich and poor, charity is beautiful and affecting. We are moved that people, irrespective of their personal wealth, give when they do not need to, when they will be less well off as a result of helping others. The $100 given to a charity is $100 that cannot be spent on themselves or their kin; it is forgone and counts as a deficit, even though in many countries it is rewarded with the encouragement of tax deductions. For all that, the kindness once extended cannot easily be extended again, because the $100 once given cannot be claimed back in order to regenerate the same kindness. It is to some extent unsustainable; and to have enduring life, it depends upon memory. Above all, however, the $100 cannot be spent on an investment that yields further money or opportunity or comfort or security; so the giver's capacity to earn—as well as enjoy or feel secure—is also to some extent dented in the same way that the money, once given, cannot benefit anyone else in the family. Unless there are benefits of reputation, you have possibly acted outside your own interest and probably against the interest of your family; and if the generosity is paid back by return favours (even in producing goodwill), it may have been strategically calculated for the purpose and therefore not really very generous. If one might acknowledge the self-interest and still claim charity—because charity is edifying, as the apostle Paul notes: 'Knowledge puffeth up, but charity edifieth'[20]—it is in the ancient sense of love.

As in the core motif of Christian redemption, the ideal of kindness involves sacrifice. One is generous to the extent that one sacrifices something. If nothing is deleted in your capacity or wealth or opportunities, nothing is enormously generous, except perhaps words; but even they, if they mean something, cost something. For example, if you say: I love you, it is meant to be somewhat exclusive and cannot be squandered on just anyone, else your kindness will be devalued. If the words are thrown around liberally to all kinds of would-be lovers, there is a double cost, first to your credibility (because you are sounding like a slut of either sex) and second to the confused prospective lovers who will have to be disabused at some point of the illusion that you love them to the degree that only one person jealously experiences. You have cost them their hopes.

The cost of kindness may be offset by many psychological benefits; and whole books have argued that we gain much more by giving or helping

---

20   *1 Corinthians* 8.1.

than by not giving or helping[21] which is, after all, the basis of voluntary work as well as every other kind of charity. But it is not necessarily a sustainable model for education because it belongs to a single-use economy that depletes the resources of the giver with every favour. And when the dynamic is expressed with words like 'favour', one might already detect a less than professional aspect to the equation that ties it into archaic patterns of patronage.

Potentially, Christian providence allows *the believer* to transcend material welfare and absorb an infinity of God's grace through belief. Even so, the basis of receiving this grace is a sacrifice made on your behalf by God, namely the blood of Christ. This holiest death on the cross was supremely generous, because it was occasioned on our behalf against the personal interest of Jesus the man and the immortal God whose only son would die. The sentiment is echoed in countless instances where the word generous is used of sacrifice, as when Lucretia stabs herself as a kind of pagan martyr. In Bandello's narration—remembering that he was a Catholic priest— the chaste Lucretia's generous and unconquered soul gave in to be raped by Tarquin, lest he carry out his threat to kill her and an innocent servant whom he would represent as her assailant.[22] Her suicide, though clearly destructive, is also somehow generous.

'No stalwart and generous soldier', Bandello says in the next story, 'ever died in retreat'.[23] The act of generosity is in dying willingly, where there might perchance be a hope of survival by fleeing. It is everyone's nightmare in battle, where honour indicates death and one might select the generous option, as the sixteenth-century philosopher Montaigne puts it, choosing to die generously.[24] As with Christ, one's blood is generous or generously spilled. The term generous blood arises in seventeenth-century literature[25] with a poetic *frisson*: it means both generous in the sense of noble, of high-born blood, but also in the sense of giving, spilling it in sacrifice. Racine pursues the more archaic side of generosity to the point of paradox. Thus he talks about a generous scorn that promotes fury,[26] just like the 'generous disdain' of a fierce horse in the poet Tasso from the previous century.[27] It

---

21   Adam Phillips & Barbara Taylor, *On kindness*, London, Hamish Hamilton, 2009.

22   'il generoso ed invitto animo de la castissima Lucrezia si piegò', 2.21.

23   2.22.

24   'choisissant de mourir genereusement', Montaigne, *Essais* 2.3.

25   'généreux sang', Racine, *Phèdre* 5.6.

26   'un généreux dépit succède à sa fureur', *Bérénice* 5.2.

27   'generoso sdegno', *Rime* 569.59; *cf.* 723.

means that the scorn is high-born, justly arrogant, like the generous pride (*orgueil généreux*)[28] or noble or generous envy,[29] which, if you think only of modern usage, you would flatly consider a contradiction in terms. But these bizarre usages are clinched for their poetic resonance just because the word is in telling transition: the movement of generosity from haughty privilege to touching kindness involves a confluence of meanings where, as we have seen, a horse is considered generous. And of course a horse may well be generous, may risk its spindly limbs for a passionate race and display all the bravery of its heroic rider with the lance.

Even charity (ἀγάπη) shares in some of this paradox. In his famous letters in the *New testament*, Paul describes how various gifts, even when angelic, are nothing without charity; if you lack charity, both you and your offices amount to nothing, even when they are about giving, that is, when they approach the contemporary meaning of charity: 'And though I bestow all my goods to feed the poor, and though I give my body to be burned, and have not charity, it profiteth me nothing'.[30] In other words, you can do great sacrificial kindnesses and burn yourself up; but these gestures of philanthropy are not equated with charity. Charity or loving kindness (ἀγάπη) is not the gesture; it is not even the substance of relinquishing your assets for someone else. Charity, for Paul, is beyond the material world; it is an affection akin to a blessing.

A blessing is also how one might characterize someone who is nice: that person is blessed with a happy nature. But charity in anyone's definition, including Paul's, is not that kind of blessing. It carries a colossal theological sense of sharing with divinity. So close to the apex of spiritual aspirations is charity that at the end of the chapter, Paul places it above faith itself: 'And now abideth faith, hope, charity, these three; but the greatest of these is charity'.[31] Faith, we suppose, is about accepting a truth, whereas charity is about what the human subject does with it: it is not passive but activates desires in a positive way.

So keen is Paul to extol this virtue that he even personifies it as a kind of exemplary citizen: 'Charity suffereth long, and is kind (or useful χρηστεύεται ἡ ἀγάπη); charity envieth not; charity vaunteth not itself, is not puffed up, Doth not behave itself unseemly, seeketh not her own, is not easily provoked,

---

28 *Phèdre* 2.1.

29 *Athalie* 4.2.

30 *1 Corinthians* 13.1–3.

31 *1 Corinthians* 13.13.

thinketh no evil'.[32] In many ways, this vigorous rhetoric sets up the institutional brand of charity with which individuals may identify: it is saintly and admirable, long-suffering, a construct of pure goodness whose open-heart seeks no reward and has no malice. If we do as Paul exhorts—'Follow after charity (Διώκετε τὴν ἀγάπην), and desire spiritual gifts' (ζηλοῦτε δὲ τὰ πνευματικά, literally spiritual things or the spiritual)[33]—we would do so in order to prophesy, as Paul says, that is, give witness and spread the Gospel. In an ideal theological world, belief in God would make people selfless. The centrality of charity to Paul's universe makes a lot of sense. In this equation, faith is almost given; but charity, loving kindness, is the virtue that clinches everything: 'Let all your things be done with charity';[34] it is 'the bond of perfectness'.[35] One could add, for special relevance in an educational context where many chaotic impulses prevail, what Peter ingenuously confesses, namely that 'charity shall cover a multitude of sins'[36] which should also hold for the internal operations of the early church.

It is not hard to see why any spiritual leader would exhort a community to charity. Aside from the intrinsic benefits of the term, it helps build solidarity and trust, in the same way that the opposite rhetoric can foment jealousy and strife. Be well disposed to one another. Show your virtues and an open heart. Be generous. The fact that acts of charity are sometimes quantifiable (and are so exclusively from the point of view of the Tax Office) does not in any way discredit the profound and uplifting dimensions of the concept. For the same reasons, it could be commended to teachers, many of whom labour in extra hours with no paid reward in order to do the students and fellow teachers a good turn. With this giving spirit, organizations function better and enjoy a richer confidence in mutual support. It is one of the most essential, if indefinable, ingredients of a warm work environment: the opposite of a mean work culture where everyone is resentful about anyone else's gifts, opportunities or achievements.

At base, however, these concepts sit within a psychological reality and only induce their benefits in a social reality when they are genuinely harboured in personal affinities. We are most likely to do someone a good turn because we like that person; we are happy for that person to have the benefit, whatever it is, and to prosper. He or she is nice, a shade of which

32   *ibid.* 13.4–5.
33   *1 Corinthians* 14.1.
34   16.14.
35   *Colossians* 3.14.
36   *1 Peter* 4.8.

is to be found in an unusual Greek word suggesting good to talk to (εὐπροσόμιλος),[37] pleasant, nice to deal with. It is a quality of soul, according to old language, which recognizes a cluster of qualities. It is often expressed in the renaissance language examined earlier, as in Bandello, where liberality and courtesy are put together with a lovely and generous soul,[38] or generous and virile soul,[39] which is said of a young woman.

The twin appeal of the word nice, this maverick of the English language that has no decent ancestry but foolishness, is that (a) it escapes the economy of nobleness, gentility and magnanimity and (b) it is sufficiently vague to owe no debt to an image but musters several unspecified qualities in the general service of benignity. Even the term gentle, which is one of the most popular in renaissance literature from the time of the *Dolce stil novo*, is aristocratic both by derivation and usage, as in Petrarch's 'gentleness of blood'[40] or the somewhat chauvinistic 'gentle Roman blood';[41] though Petrarch does concede elsewhere that a low-life soul can be made gentle.[42] The gentleness of blood of course has no physical dimension. It is a property of genetics. The same is true of a beautiful gentle name.[43] A name cannot be gentle in its agency—even if some are hard to pronounce and others are mellifluous—because the name in this sense designates the noble family or genetic stock. Petrarch enjoyed the concept of a gentle spirit, but it might be associated with valour, astuteness and wisdom,[44] even though religious qualities may also be attached to it, like a gentle spirit of paradise,[45] or a gentle piety,[46] or lofty piety that seizes a gentle heart[47] or that is gentle beyond all others, holy, wise, graceful, honest and beautiful.[48] Like 'kind' and 'generous', a gentle spirit is also linked to 'a magnanimous undertaking'.[49]

Notwithstanding this quality attributed to the most lordly, there is already evidence in Petrarch of a modern, post-aristocratic gentleness, where

37 Phrynichus, *Sophistic preparations* 68B.
38 'animo grato e generoso', *Novelle* 3.67.
39 4.18.
40 *Canzoniere* 263.9.
41 'Latin sangue gentile', 128.73.
42 270.83.
43 'bel nome gentile', 297.13.
44 53.1–7.
45 109.12.
46 157.5.
47 158.6.
48 247.3–4.
49 'gentile spirto, / non lassar la magnanima tua impresa', Petrarch, *Canzoniere* 7.13–14.

the poet applies the term not to a person but to nature. It seems rather modern when he speaks of a tree being gentle,[50] or a gentle branch,[51] or even a gentle breeze,[52] which remains current diction today. In what sense could the breeze be considered noble? It is, at a stretch, possessed of the ease, the privilege of free movement, the liberality of gentility (or aristocracy) but it is in no sense 'lordly'. Perhaps one takes from the 'better people', gentle folk, the metaphoric adequacy, sensuality, bounty, a lack of meanness. In all events, the moment is reached for the metaphor to slide into a change of meaning, to become, in effect, a dead metaphor. But not so fast! The quality of gentle is in certain respects agonized and oxymoronic, as in your gentle scorn,[53] which anticipates Racine above, or the gentle fire whence I totally burn up,[54] a gentle longing that flares up in me.[55]

These artful tropes that depend upon ambiguities between the archaic and the modern have a long afterlife. We have 'the gentle condition of blood' in Shakespeare[56] and the telling person 'of a gentle kind and noble stock',[57] just as we have paradoxes like 'our gentle flame'[58] or 'gentle knave'.[59] And then we have the physical and natural world, as with a gentle current,[60] of livestock which is not necessarily well bred but passive as a victim: 'as gentle as a lamb'[61] or 'to worry lambs and lap their gentle blood',[62] 'The tiger now hath seiz'd the gentle hind',[63] of atmospheric behaviour 'with gentle breath, calm look',[64] 'gentle night',[65] 'the sweet infant breath of gentle sleep'[66] or 'gentle gusts'.[67] Thus 'gentle' passes from chivalry to a low state of energy without an intervening period of happiness. The condition is either

---

50   60.1–4.
51   126.4.
52   194.1 and 270.31.
53   'vostro gentile sdegno', 71.25.
54   'foco gentil ond' io tutto ardo', 72.66.
55   'd' un gentil desire avampo', 98.12; *cf.* 'gentil foco accese', 224.3.
56   *As you like it* 1.1.
57   *Pericles* 5.1.
58   *Timon of Athens* 1.1.
59   *Julius Caesar* 4.3.
60   *Two gentlemen of Verona* 2.7, later the same act 'gentle stream'.
61   *Romeo and Juliet* 2.5.
62   *Richard III* 4.4.
63   *Richard III* 2.4.
64   *Romeo and Juliet* 3.1.
65   *Romeo and Juliet* 3.2.
66   *Richard II* 1.3.
67   *2 Henry VI* 3.2.

formal or tranquillizing, a birthright or sedation; and in the former, there is no guarantee even of benignity, as when Queen Margaret calls the butcher Gloster a 'gentle villain',[68] an oxymoron calculated to express the lack of correlation between nobility and decency.

The more we look at these options, the more appeal we see in 'nice', which is ignorant of this aristocratic hang-up. It is a quality accruing to people who are decent but not just in a moral sense. There is something reassuring in their presence and they somehow radiate good will. They are not necessarily generous in the sense of self-sacrificing. It is perfectly conceivable to be nice without magnanimity, just as it is possible to be noble without being sympathetic. The peculiar radiance of people who are nice is not transactional. It is in their benign bearing, their communication of joy in your presence, their humility, their contentment with other people's pleasure.

There is no need to have other graces to be nice. A person can be awkward, unskilled in making a good impression; one can be unambitious, unsexy and lack zeal or eagerness. There is no narcissism in being nice, where there might be much in generosity; and nobility, true to its origins, will easily accommodate a swollen head. There are no conceits in niceness. There is no necessary social appeal and certainly no status, which one might assume more by arrogance; but at the same time, niceness does not equate with humility, because a person with a good opinion of himself or herself is still capable of being awfully nice. Certainly, if you are nice, you are unlikely to be arrogant, because that would clearly not be nice. To have no malice at all is perhaps unachievable; so nice people manage to be nice in spite of their occasional snicker, their peccadillo, their rude joke.

As with kindness, we cannot be nice to everyone in exactly the same way. For example, we do not like certain people; and we cannot easily be so nice to them. But then not even Christ was so nice on each occasion. Sometimes he said threatening and reproachful things: he was, after all, a teacher. If we cannot be infinitely generous to each and every comer, similar things can be said of niceness. There are limits. Niceness is not universal or consistent in the person who evinces it: niceness waxes and wanes and is produced or suppressed by responses to others. But what distinguishes niceness is that it is capable of responding to another person's presence alone, rather than responding to his or her behaviour. Its structure may be no less reciprocal than that of kindness or generosity; but by functioning on the presence of others rather than their actions, it more easily covers the multitude of sins

---

68   *Richard III* 1.3.

and is stimulated more quickly and less discriminatingly, with low stakes and little fear that it may be mistaken or poorly invested.

If you are nice to a person who proves to be a bit nasty, nothing much is lost. It was only a smile, an encouragement. Yes, it would have been better if in that moment the radiance could have been directed to someone worthier; but fate did not ordain it so. The gesture was perhaps lost but perhaps it will generate a degree of niceness in the world at some later stage and, in all events, the cost to me is negligible. In the classroom, however, there are often disruptive or inattentive students, a challenge which calls for a special balance between niceness and firmness. With this combination that all talented educators possess, a teacher can be nice, possessed of a lovely spirit, without having to be less nice to any of the students, including the unwilling and the cheeky. They can all be handled in a nice way; though many will experience maintaining this joyful disposition as taxing their patience and sometimes inviting severity. For many teachers niceness equates with patience; though if they have niceness by nature, it may cost them relatively little to sustain it.

As a rich correlate of niceness, patience also has a tellingly spiritual history. It is a quality associated with Jesus, the proverbial patience of Christ. But the theology behind this beautiful quality places patience alongside suffering. We too have to prove ourselves 'as the ministers of God, in much patience (ἐν ὑπομονῇ πολλῇ), in afflictions, in necessities, in distresses, in stripes, in imprisonments, in tumults, in labours, in watchings, in fastings'.[69] And then in the next line, Paul says how we achieve this by pureness, by knowledge, by longsuffering (ἐν μακροθυμίᾳ), by ... unfeigned loving kindness (ἐν ἀγάπῃ ἀνυποκρίτῳ).

It is fateful that the Latin word under our term patience (*patientia*) means suffering, what one undergoes by way of endurance. Teachers, it must be acknowledged, are called to suffering; but let us not recommend the condition as a route to virtue. There is no need for education to depend upon martyrdom, for the teacher to feel imprisoned or bear the stripes (ἐν πληγαῖς) of the lash, as Paul has it. The Greek word for patience (ὑπομονη) is not directly linked to suffering; but Biblical usage makes the connexion anyway, because what one is patient with is affliction.

Patience today is gratefully experienced through less stressful stimuli. It is more about putting up with people—and many teachers will say other staff rather than students—wasting our time, getting things wrong, misunderstanding us, being a bit misbehaved or rude or ungrateful and arrogant.

---

69   *2 Corinthians* 6.4–5.

No teacher is without the experience of slow or lazy or contrary pupils; and admittedly, a quality of forbearance is required to contain the reflex of reproach or even anger. University lecturers have double reason to require patience, because as well as any tedium in having to explain things tactfully and repeatedly to students who do not even show up for class, our lecturers sacrifice their precious time for research through the extra labours of kindness. Their reputation, prospects and livelihood depend on their research output. It is not a trivial problem to fit enough of it in; and most academics feel under pressure over it.

This pressure is not nice and it may well have a corrosive effect on the niceness of the lecturer. We can only imagine; but in all events, the quality of patience moves into striking relief. To maintain the niceness that makes for a pleasant learning environment, a teacher who is extensively assessed on his or her research—which is seldom without frustrations—is a considerable challenge. An anxious teacher has anxious students; and it is hard to imagine that anxiety would not harm learning, in the same way that impatience, either on the student's part or the teacher's, would also not harm learning; and both are catastrophic for creativity.

My aim in this chapter has not been to prove that niceness is more important than anything else or even that it has an absolute importance. Many students would rather be taught by a severe expert than a benign ditherer. But all things being equal, the nicer teacher will be better for my learning, especially when it intersects with creativity, because I will feel safe and encouraged in my learning and in exercising my imagination, without fearing my mistakes or premature comment. To me, a creative learning space should be a haven, so it makes no sense to install a wolf in it. But niceness, which we have discovered always has a twist in it, is not as fragile as kindness and generosity and is rather more renewable than the act of giving. In the end, the learner may not need to be given very much; because the character of learning is also ideally sustainable. The imaginative ability to see oneself in the material yet to be learned is, up to a point, self-generating; so the critical moment is to set it in motion and guide it, not so much to push it along. In this critical phase, the niceness of the teacher is crucial, though it does not require the teacher's generosity or preparedness to sacrifice hours of research time. This warm quality of fondness that we are identifying as niceness has no cost to anyone and may well be worth more to learning and creativity than all the mechanistic processes of anxious syllabus design in fussy constructivist lockdown, not nice to work within and unlikely to inspire niceness in others.

Chapter 5

TELLING

Today we enjoy the dynamic of socialized learning. We are ready to abandon the lecture theatre, because the experience of listening to a professor is considered passive; and there is no doubt that lecturers who challenge the students with lots of questions and opportunities to speak may have a superior buzz than the run-of-the-mill lecturers who labour their way through boring slides and barely acknowledge the audience. They are, in fact, the reason for the slow but certain falling from grace of the lecture theatre, where students are lined up in tiers with a single orientation, all together but alienated—at least in a bad lecture—as silent individual cells without agency.

To socialize learning, then, we love to construct classes with conversation, group work, tasks and activities where students contribute jointly, sometimes collaborating with the assistance of the teacher, interacting energetically and filling the room with conversation. As a part of 'active learning', it is a healthy change, entirely sympathetic to the student voice and student-centredness, where the energetic activity of students who are involved in a job aggregates to produce the buzz that sounds a lot like learning. It is admirable and lecturers have found the arguments in favour of active learning compelling. It is unlikely that we will go back on this trend, even if we discovered that the learning that takes place through group activities is superficial, an echo-chamber that either makes students complacent or anxious.

One possible shortfall of the active paradigm is creativity. Any individual student can still act imaginatively within a group context; and in fact the diplomatic negotiation among strong-willed students requires much imagination to transact. But for all that, there is a precondition of creative work that is compromised by a highly socialized context, because there is no intimacy with thought, no privacy, no space of contemplation where the mind can race in its own exponential registers, free of noise and contention. Paradoxically, the creative mind may be more stimulated by the so-called passivity of a lecture, where the content is delivered from one source down the front and the student in the middle of the theatre, silently ensconced in the anonymous pew, enjoys whatever intimacy in the idea is worthy or enjoins the fancy. In a world of listening, half-listening, doodling, remembering, connecting with preoccupations and projects already surging in the imagination from earlier in the morning, the student is able to entertain rhapsodic thoughts that are conducive to creative growth.

If I am in a participatory lecture with a teacher who throws out challenges to the audience at regular intervals, my imaginative safety is broken. Essentially, I have to do what the lecturer wants me to do and think what he or she has challenged me to respond to, not what I want to think. I am railroaded by busy activities and feel threatened by falling behind if my mind wanders. Instead of enjoying the liberties of speculation, I am dragooned into service. I experience the active learning as glorified drill, a cheerful bootcamp, where I am marshalled into duty, because I am no longer free to wonder but must comply with the terms that are set by the lecturer. Actually, I would much rather be passive—if that is how we are now forced to describe listening to a lecture—where I can also be sceptical, where I can entertain doubts about the validity of the discourse, the teacher's grasp of it, my own capacity to master it and any number of connexions with my imagination.

If I am allowed to enjoy time with texts and presentations in the intimacy of my imagination, I have scope to be creative. Creativity calls for the privacy of learning, where an idea can establish synapses with other ideas under no pressure beyond the rhapsodic stitching-power of the imagination itself.[1] However, education is not the romantic artist's garret, the poet in a dressing gown, the scholar in the loft, like Nietzsche at the Waldhaus Hotel in Sils-Maria or the solitary Wittgenstein who felt a need to escape from the gregarious cafés of Vienna to philosophize in a hut by a Norwegian fjord. Students are not so autonomous and need the help of teachers for their thinking, creative or otherwise; and the necessary conversations call for a social context, such as we know from tutorials, seminars, labs and studios. If a creative dimension is fostered, it requires neither active learning nor isolation in a cell but rather a voluntary oscillation between the communal and the hermitage, a ready slippage between the social and the monastic and back again. During the monastic phase, however, when reading for an extended essay, a social dimension is also necessary: we need to

---

1   Stitched together in the Greek sense of 'rhapsodized' (ῥαπτός, stitched), *Odyssey* 24.228,229, already metaphoric in Greek, as in strung together, continuous, Pindar, *Nemean odes* 2.2; hence ῥαψῳδός.

be able to tell someone about what we find so interesting. It is not enough just to write, because we might not yet know how to begin. We have to tell someone about our enthusiasm.

Around creative work, there are creative conversations. Any artist or essayist with a creative project is desperate to tell someone about it. When I have been learning something, I have gained a new identification with some wonderful material. First, it may not have been so wonderful: incomprehensible, more likely! Slowly, the obscurities lifted and I was able to peer into the unfathomable and see myself in it. My view of myself changed. I gained a dimension of myself as someone who could, say, read Portuguese or understand the inverse square law and relate it to sound as well as gravity. Ahead of my knowledge expanding, my identity grew: it began to subtend the previously unmanageable. As I grappled to understand, I was morally assisted by a burgeoning hope not just that my comprehension would extend to new realms but that my very identity would assume new entitlements. If so, I am in a mad rush to tell someone about it, because it is not just that I have learned something new but that I have become more of an Iberian or a physicist or whatever the passion involves. To tell someone is to reinforce this new identity, to confirm a status that I sense myself having arrived at. To tell someone about my learning is to consolidate the new person that I am becoming, to clinch the very ontology of learning.

The act of telling miniaturizes the social because, while a commitment to sharing, telling someone is still intimate: telling someone does not mean socializing the ideas in the sense of a seminar or a publication but a kind of personal release, a rush of happy belief in the ideas, which is also a toehold on the next stage of finding language for the project. If I am thinking and investigating, trying to make connexions within opaque domains, I benefit by being able to relay some of the thrill. It does not mean that I want to be interrogated about what I have found so interesting. That process might only introduce anxiety into the development of ideas, which is also fragile if it is genuinely creative. I just want to be able to tell someone, partly to reinforce my personal stake in the solitude but also as that first step in reaching out in order to fulfil the eventual creative destiny, which is to produce a creative outcome for an audience to engage with. Telling has the blessings of the social on the terms of the intimate.

In the act of telling, which the creative hermitage requires for relief and refreshment, I do not want to negotiate with anyone and engage with protocols in a collaborative process; I just want to tell someone spontaneously about how my thoughts have developed, to relish my new ownership of knowledge and especially the imaginative trajectory that I can now consider following further. To think creatively is to have a project; and a person in possession of a project wants to tell you about it if you are any kind of friend. In existential terms, the excitement is only as good as it can be prospectively shared; and at any point in the development of a project, the motif of the sharing ear is decisively encouraging.

But telling is also important for learning. Among the many activities that help us learn is the act of telling, telling somebody about what we have just read or learned. It may seem marginal—a condiment rather than a necessity—when compared to verifiable learning activities or tasks that require discipline and rigour, such as reading, looking up, working out, doing examples, swatting verbs, engaging in group work, learning on the job or work integrated learning, repeating mnemonics before going to sleep, writing summaries under dot points or tabulating information or ranking its importance for recall under pressure. But what appears of minor importance relative to these orthodox forms of strain and investigation may have equal importance if ever it were possible to measure the benefits, because telling someone about your learning translates those fragile and delicate imaginative projections—I would argue inherent in all learning—into the expressed reality of one's identity, rehearsed intimately to a forgiving person.

Reading and various forms of exercise belong to the canon of study methods: they are almost mechanically equated with techniques of absorption and could be recognized in pious traditions of monastic practice (ἄσκησις), in which the devout rehearse and embed the verities of faith with repetition and reverence. Telling, on the other hand, does not enjoy this venerable authority as a study method and is scarcely recognized as any kind of cornerstone or foundation of education. It is informal, often spontaneous and opportunity-based. It depends on the availability of listeners. They have to be sympathetic listeners, which means friends or prospective friends. It may also have the limitation of benefiting those with a ready propensity to communicate, who are perhaps already enthusiasts and only crave an outlet for their passion. Alternatively, the practice may be understood as cultivating enthusiasm where it is only nascent and needs to be socialized to grow. Little is known and contemporary interest and inquiry in the field are not conspicuous.

There are grounds to rethink this neglect, because academics themselves depend greatly on the act of telling which goes beyond the altruistic framework of sharing new knowledge in order that others build upon our findings. As scholars, we wither psychologically if we cannot tell someone about our research in learned forums and sometimes informal contexts as well; research graduates feel isolated and uninspired if they cannot tell their supervisors and maybe fellow research graduates—or sympathetic flatmates or partners or parents or children—about what they are reading and what ideas they are encountering. Even in informal contexts, a person reading a book may experience much more incentive to continue or to read in a more penetrating and invested spirit if he or she has someone to tell about it (which would partly explain the virtue of reading groups, given that reading itself is largely private). An undergraduate student gains greatly from the ability to tell another student about his or her learning; and likewise, school children have a huge advantage if they can tell someone in the family about the ideas that they have come up against in a class or a book. It seems as if the act of telling is a significant catalyst to depth and sustainability in the learning process.

It stands to reason and not just because the imaginative projections in learning are consolidated through a kind of intimate performance of identity. There is also the issue of language. To tell someone about some topic, you merge the language of your discipline with the language that belongs to you as an individual. It is more than just a translation exercise; it is about ownership too. A process of assimilation takes place, where language once outside your immediate familiarity becomes appropriated to the degree that you pass it on. The academic calibre of the person you tell may be less important than the fact that he or she is receptive. When young students take their learnings out of the classroom and tell some family member or carer, they own the knowledge and they are empowered by a feeling of proprietorship and generosity in sharing the knowledge with them. In fact, the motif calls for reciprocal generosity on the part of the listener, who may well have other business to attend to.

This dynamic is integral to peer learning initiatives: the more knowledgeable student benefits by operating at a higher level than just being a learner; and the less knowledgeable student also gets to learn by the assistance that is proffered for the purpose. As suggested, the motif mirrors—albeit in a naïve way—the method by which research is extended when it is transacted in a learned forum, which is so much more than merely dumping knowledge in a publication. The act of scholarship, after so many resources have been collected and subjected to scrutiny, is effectively an act of telling someone about the research. It presupposes another act, that of listening; and we as scholars might well feel flattered and encouraged that an audience welcomes our thoughts.

In higher education, we already work hard training students to do the listening when they are introduced to material through lectures or some other interface. But if we want our students one day to become scholars, our goal should be that they can tell someone about it. We have very little knowledge of the processes or benefits of educational telling and it seems counterintuitive, if not irresponsible, to engage it as an official technique when it is uncontrolled, largely independent of a teacher, unassessable and academically unreliable as a genre that has no bookish or refereed authority. Students can easily become fantastically excited about an idea that is misunderstood or mistaken; and the person whom they tell is likely to be in no position to correct the error. They deepen their illusions as they rehearse their misconceptions.

Telling, however, cannot really be blamed for reinforcing inaccuracies. It is never a substitute for learning or instruction or accurate input. Telling is something else, an instrument of enthusiasm, a method not so much for the refinement of learning or for consolidating knowledge but for establishing an identity as a scholar, a means of consolidating interest by projecting ownership. It also has a remarkable history which richly reveals the many senses in which the concept is useful and, one might argue, structurally necessary to learning. The way in which we use the word today is slightly different from that of former epochs; and in fact precise equivalents are sometimes hard to find.

In ancient Greek, from which we get words like pedagogy, logic and empathy, the act of telling is rendered by a plethora of words, which are, however, somewhat instrumental. For example, there are verbs that can sometimes be translated as to tell or to speak of (αἰνέω)[2] but the term in most instances is formal, meaning approve, advise, recommend, give counsel, sometimes even to be content with something or acquiesce in some matter. There is a group of verbs, nouns and adjectives with a root in the motif of leading (ἄγω) related to narrative[3] but the meanings range from declaration, announcement and rehearsal to betrayal. They lack the intimacy of our simple verb to tell.

A further group takes its shape from the motif of utterance or the phrase or speaking out (διαφράζω, ἐκφράζω, προφράζω) which ends up meaning proclaim or even show plainly, which has its agent in the form of a teller or

---

2   Aeschylus, *Agamemnon* 98,1482, *Libation Bearers* 192.

3   ἀφήγησις, ἀνηγέομαι ἐξαγόρευσις, ἐξαγορεύω, ἐξαγορευτικός, ἐκδιηγέομαι, εὐδιήγητος, καταγορεύω, προαγορεύω, στοιχηγορέω.

expounder (φραστήρ). Another group again can be identified with saying or speaking[4] in one form or another.[5] Insofar as they are intimate, they are the same as saying. Some of the forms also have negative counterparts with the sense of hard to tell or hard to say.[6] Some forms are highly institutional (ἐξαγγέλλω, ἐπαγγέλλω), to tell in the sense of announce, to be the messenger or to proclaim, an idea that has great biblical resonance. In ancient Greek, there are conceptions of telling that reach such cultish grandiloquence that they are sometimes hard for us to relate to, a telling unique to heroes or those worthy of fame, to celebrate (κλέω) or clarion, to tell of in the sense of make famous, just as one can declare as an oracle (ἐκχράω) or, of course, tell the stories (μυθηγορέω) that are the patrimony of myth.

In the common Greek of the *New Testament*, it is normal to use the word 'say' where the English, since the seventeenth century, have been tempted to translate the word as 'tell'. Thus the King James translators write: 'Tell us therefore, What thinkest thou? Is it lawful to give tribute unto Caesar, or not?' But the Greek text does not say 'tell us' but reads 'say then' (εἰπὲ οὖν),[7] a pattern which is repeated many times.[8] Jerome's translation into Latin accurately uses the verb 'to say' (*dicere*). However, Greek language does have other expressions for telling, which remind us that 'to tell' is slightly different from the verb 'to say'. One can say anything, like 'I am bored'. 'To tell', on the other hand, somehow registers the pre-existence of a fact or sentiment, which one then conveys to another person. For example, we would tell someone our name. We would not 'say' our name to somebody. The name already exists and for one reason or another, we want to convey this intelligence which is already known to us. So we tell that person some information which belongs to us intimately but which has not yet been shared. If you say 'I am bored', technically I could come back at you and say: 'you seem to be having a lot of fun; why did you tell me that you are bored?' In this case, the telling is a subject of interrogation. Suddenly, we are talking of bearing witness, not just saying something coincidental.

Greek has two expressions which come closer to the motif of telling and which are sometimes translated as telling. One is telling in the sense of talking (λαλεω), though this word often had connotations of idle chatter,

---

4   ἀπεῖπον, διεῖπον, ἐξεῖπον, ἔσπον, προεῖπον.
5   ἐξενέπω ἐνέπω, παρεννέπω.
6   δύσφραστος, δύσλεκτος.
7   *Matthew* 22.17.
8   24.3–4, 26.63, 28.7–10, *Mark* 7.36, 8.26, 11.29 and 33; *cf.* λέγω.

in spite of being used in some grave contexts.[9] The other brace of verbs expresses the idea of 'to convey': tell no man (παρήγγειλεν μηδενὶ) that thing[10] but more commonly 'announce', as in they kept it close, and told no man (οὐδενὶ ἀπήγγειλαν).[11] Both have the same root, which is the messenger (ἄγγελος), and is also the word angel, an emissary of god. In translating the verbs into Latin, Jerome uses a counterpart (*nuntiare*) which similarly contains the image of the messenger (*nuntius*) and is the root of our 'announce'.

These ancient forms can all be translated by our verb 'to tell' but in their original context they all lack something. The motif of the messenger reveals a mechanistic process, in which the message is transferred faithfully from one who generates it—and takes responsibility for it—and the recipient. The messenger neither generates nor owns the message but is a passive intermediary who travels. It is qualitatively different from the concept of telling, which may have a confessional dimension and may come from deep within oneself. In one form, the idea of passing on the message may indeed involve personal investment (to evangelize) which is akin to broadcasting, with propagandistic overtones, a form of proclamation which already existed in common Greek before Christ.

It is really the prehistory of telling, where we announce, proclaim, relay, convey. One bears a message but as a messenger one is not the owner or originator; otherwise why would we need an envoy? There is no necessary stage of assimilated intelligence, where the thought, by virtue of being relayed through an urge to speak, is formulated and owned by its communicator. There is no phase of interpretation or reflexion, where the utterance is intellectually fondled to yield a kind of glee for its further potential. To tell in antiquity pushes back the provenance of the thought to an anterior authority, some pre-existing stock or superintending power.

To tell in antiquity is to report; and to this, one could add the idea of explaining or narrating, which we already noted in the words with a root in leading (ἄγω). 'And the apostles, when they were returned, told him (διηγήσαντο αὐτῷ) all that they had done.[12] Again, in the *Vulgate* the verb is rendered as 'they narrated' (*narraverunt*). And because the assimilated or confessional dimension of telling is missing, it is also very far from the

---

9   *Acts* 9.6, 22.10.
10   *Luke* 9.21.
11   *Luke* 9.36.
12   *Luke* 9.10.

concept of 'revealing' against our will, as when we say that a feature or a situation is telling, meaning that it gives away information that might be construed critically. There is no similar connotation in the verb 'saying' or 'narrating', neither of which suggests a revealing element or informing or divulging significance.

The more one explores alternatives in the ancient world to our idea of telling, the more one notices two elements of our own idea that cannot be found. One is the intimacy of telling and the other is the ownership, the responsibility for the thought. If we want to convince ourselves of something, we might say: I tell myself, we tell ourselves; that is, we get into our own ear and strengthen our resolve. As fugitive as it may sound, the element of accountability sits structurally within the root of telling, and for very logical reasons. In its origins, to tell is to count. It comes from the same word as the German, to pay (*zahlen*), whence the word teller, the clerk at the bank who counts the money for you; and further, the same origins of telling take us to the German word for counting (*zählen*) or number (*Zahl*). The motif in English emerges most hauntingly in the toll, the way that the bell counts and which survives most horribly in the disaster toll, the road toll, the deaths which are told or counted.

The link between telling and counting is not coincidental and nor is the intellectual implication that the process involves the calibration of value or significance. The German word for explaining (*erzählen*) also contains the root of counting—shadowed by our idea of explanation as accounting for something—as noted above; and most notably, the Romance languages all express the idea of telling through the motif of counting, namely recounting (Italian *conto*, *racconto*, Spanish *cuento*, Portuguese *conto* and the French *conte*). In the Mediterranean lands, from Boccaccio onward, the practice of telling stories was a wonderful sign of courtly accomplishment in which the narrator would relay and adapt inherited stock to the great enjoyment of the company or *brigata*. The ritual is all about assimilating an older story, owning it and being accountable to its content, its emotional power and the effect that it has on the listeners, who are specifically mentioned as part of the genre, even till Bandello's age in the sixteenth century.

In telling a story, one is accountable for two elements: first, the truth of the narrative or some honourable substitute, like the poetic coherence or integrity of the narrative. Second, one is accountable for the importance of the story. It is a story worth telling, as the Greeks used to say (ἀξιαφήγητος).[13] To

---

13   Herodotus 1.16, 177.

express this idea of importance, we also use the verb to count. If something counts, it is important or valuable in some way. It cannot be discounted. People themselves want to count. To count in that sense does not mean to keep a tally but to have a tally kept of yourself, where the unit measures esteem or love or importance or some other admirable value: you do not do the counting yourself but someone else considers you to be—or counts you as—someone worthwhile. To count means to be influential, to have sway; your opinion is sought. If you are both competent and benign, other people will count on you, meaning that you are reliable but also responsible, in a position where others are somewhat dependent upon you and probably have expectations of you, for which you are assumed to be responsible.

It makes sense, then, that to tell or to count in modern languages also means to be considered, to be judged or to ascertain. If we do something wrong, we are called upon to account for ourselves.[14] It belongs to the psychological side of estimation that a person can be 'counted wise',[15] perhaps technically to be numbered among the wise but perhaps more practically just thought of as wise. Numeracy is a cue but more a metaphor which sits behind accounting. An activity could be considered unfortunate or 'accounted ill'[16] or 'but a trifle'. A person could be 'accounted a merciful man'[17] or a good actor[18] or a woman 'accounted beautiful'. Hermione's integrity is 'counted falsehood'[19] and Lady Macduff proposes that sometimes doing good must be 'accounted dangerous folly'.[20]

Even before Shakespeare's time, it was common to invoke counting to express the idea that some phenomena, like love, are beyond our ken. In the poetic language of early Italian verse, the idea of telling or counting is often phrased in the negative: I would not know how to tell or account for something (*non saccio contare*),[21] which persists into the sixteenth century, as in Tasso, where the poet cannot enumerate the ineffable in the same way that one cannot count the stars or the grains of sand on the beach,[22] summed

---

14   'avendo nella patria lassato tanta aspettazion di sé ed avendo ancor a rendere cunto a giudici severissimi, i quali spesso castigavano non solamente i grandi ma i piccolissimi errori', Baldassare Castiglione, *Il libro del corteggiano* 3.44.

15   Shakespeare, *Love's labours lost* 2.1.18.

16   *Love's labours lost* 4.1.25.

17   *Measure for measure* 3.2.203.

18   *Hamlet* 3.2.105.

19   *Winter's tale* 3.2.28.

20   *Macbeth* 4.2.77.

21   Guido Cavalcanti, *Rime* 1.27–21, *cf.* 4.6.

22   'contar non possiam', *Rime* 1348.52–54; *cf.* 1424.5–6.

up in Shakespeare's: 'No thought can think nor tongue of mortal tell'.[23] And this indisposition could also characterize any kind of puzzlement, as in Shakespeare: 'What I should think of this I cannot tell',[24] where telling could either be saying or knowing or judging, as in 'What then became of them I cannot tell'.[25] When things have slightly mysterious origins, it is more curious to tell. Portia cannot quite know but says: 'There's something tells me, but it is not love... '[26] So far from merely relaying information, telling is what one does in a condition of doubt, as if one tries to tell what is so and what is not. Elsewhere Portia calls upon us to interpret: 'Tell me where is fancy bred, / Or in the heart or in the head'.[27]

In no part of the early modern period, therefore, is the verb 'to tell' restricted to a passive rehearsal of a story that has been received. It is not merely transmission, as if a person is charged with a message which is dutifully delivered as if the envelope has scarcely been opened. Telling involves a whole interpretative and possessive process that goes beyond the mechanical act of relaying: it is integral to the faculty of judgement, evaluation, interpretation and assimilation. That is the reason that we say 'you can tell that someone is sad', meaning observe, divine or detect: it registers and we understand what we perceive. It is subjective. And because the act of telling lets the teller appropriate the material, the communicative process is relished.

Telling is a genre of subjective communication. The high subjectivity of telling is acknowledged by La Bruyère in the seventeenth century who notes that no amount of epithets and praises speaks as glowingly as facts and, he adds, the 'manner of telling them'.[28] Writing toward the end of the baroque, La Bruyère is a keen observer of the way people tell things to one another. It forms a large part of his subject matter. He notes, for example, how there are certain bombastic people who occupy a lot of room. They tell stories in a way that takes no account of anyone entering the room. If someone else tells a story, they feel a need to take over and tell it in their own way. They will distort certain details of a story so that they appear to be the origin of it. They abstract the content to avoid the scrutiny of the expert in the room. In short, the author depicts a game of manipulation to hold

---

23   *Love's labour's lost* 4.3.
24   *Comedy of errors* 3.2.184.
25   *Comedy of errors* 5.1.354.
26   *Merchant of Venice* 3.2.4.
27   *Merchant of Venice* 3.2.63.
28   Jean de La Bruyère, 'Des ouvrages de l'esprit', *Les caractères* 2.13.

forth.[29] La Bruyère details a great economy of self-love, the psychopathology of the know-all. He identifies a pompous lust for telling with a perverse motivation: it is not to instruct or help the listener but to gain the merit of telling it[30] and it follows that such people are often very loud.[31] One is left to imagine that perhaps La Bruyère is thinking of such presumptuous characters in a power-game. Their interest is to feel more important and powerful than anyone else in the room and, as with the leader of the pack, the other dogs have to follow.

Another scandal in the economy of telling is a failure to connect with the capacity of the listener. Thus, for example, there are people who will hold forth on the archaeology of Egypt or the battle history of Mesopotamia, who will enumerate all the kings and generals in various Babylonian wars while paying no regard to common interests among company.[32] Finally, La Bruyère gives a chilling material insight into the economic basis for these various obnoxious positions in conversation, suggesting that one occupies a lot of room if one is rich; but if one is poor, one tells things very briefly and possibly in a confused and apologetic way.[33] One has no power and is even embarrassed to open the mouth in rich and confident company. It follows that imposing people often tell you anecdotes about how much money they spend.[34] There is no sensual extravagance (*volupté*) that they have not tried out and which they have not been able to tell about (*rendre compte*).[35]

Telling can thus be helpful but also competitive and diminishing. If ever you have the feeling in talking to an incurious braggart that you have lost a pint of blood, it seems that the demoralized feeling is centuries old. But telling can also be downright malicious, as with gossip. The management of social knowledge was already a big part of the comic stage in the eighteenth century. In one of Goldoni's plays, for example, one character does not want to give another the satisfaction of boasting and 'telling his friends about my desperation, as if a triumph of his perfidy'.[36] In Goldoni's play

---

29 'De la société et de la conversation', *Les caractères* 6.8–9.

30 'c'est moins pour l'apprendre à ceux qui l'écoutent, que pour avoir le mérite de la dire', *ibid.* 6.11.

31 *Les caractères* 6.12.

32 *Les caractères* 6.74.

33 *Les caractères* 7.83.

34 *Les caractères* 8.10.

35 *Les caractères* 9.18.

36 *Gl'innamorati* 3.8.

Crazes for country holidays, a gossip is under suspicion 'lest he tell about our miseries'.[37] It matters a great deal to know the purpose and the recipient of anything that one tells. It is a very different motif if we tell a friend or we tell the Police; and even when one acts out of indignation—as Shakespeare says, 'with an outstretch'd throat, I'll tell the world / Aloud what man thou art'[38]—there is a problem in credibility, because people may not believe you. And certainly few forms of telling are without some danger and therefore adrenaline.[39] Even when benign, they tend to be full of eagerness and enjoin much energy in social participation.

Today, in a benignly self-stimulating culture, we are witnessing an epidemic of telling. Social media are largely organized around the motif of telling people. The key window in facebook says 'what's on your mind?', which implicitly says: 'tell us'. The robot facebook speaks for your friends. The implication of the phrase 'tell us' is that we are already talking to you and asking you to tell us things. However, the digital communicative structure is supremely telling-oriented in Twitter, where each of the millions of tweets represents someone telling something to his or her followers. If we read something interesting, we have an incentive to tell people through a tweet; and sending another tweet also ensures that we remain in currency, that people continue to think of us. Telling people via Twitter then gives us an incentive to learn or at least to gather more resources to tell people about. It seems marvellously self-generating, where interest in current affairs is propagated as a result of the desire for another tweet.

In relation to learning practice, there are difficult but necessary questions to be faced in this telling-rich environment. For a long time, education has assumed a structure where the teacher or lecturer tells the class, and the class-members do their best to absorb what they are told. How much this assumption needs to keep up with the times is a curious question. The proselytes of active learning assure us that students learn when they do things rather than when they are told about them. When they are told, they try hard to concentrate and grab what they can, but it requires much discipline which not everyone is up to all the time. Just the same, doing things can be impractical, as when students might be learning about Homer. But when they tell (assuming that they have cottoned onto something pertinent at

---

37   *Le smanie della villeggiatura* 1.4.

38   *Measure for measure* 2.4.153.

39   *Measure for measure* 4.3.175.

some stage), they are already highly invested in the utterance; and the ped-agogical benefit may even be greater than doing.

In the age of Twitter, telling is a sign of being stimulated. If nothing is happening, no ideas are worth telling and the person's world, if not the person himself or herself, might be considered null and boring. Rightly or wrongly, we more and more unconsciously measure interest according to telling. To have nothing to tell someone about is a sign of being under-stimulated. To tell someone something is automatically to be energized, to have access to adrenaline, to be on the point. One almost establishes through the act of telling that there is a use for the knowledge that has been so recently acquired. We like to share not necessarily to enrich others and make for progress—which would be the traditional view of research public-ations—but to build reassurance within ourselves and enrich our nascent self-perception as a scholar.

In a traditional educational context, there is a shade of resistance to the motif of telling, as suggested, at least for the sake of learning. If we are learning about a topic, we are still relatively ignorant; clearly we cannot already be an authority because we are just setting out. An urge to tell someone about this learning may seem premature, precocious, immature, embarrassing. Any quiet student in a class that is full of loquacious stu-dents, all competing to tell about their encounters with science or culture, may be put off. With classes constructed around the student voice, the more introspective student hears the tutor too little and the other students too much—given that they are still assimilating material—to be of great edu-cational use. So the humbler student may want to hear the expert rather than fellow students guessing and bluffing and scoring nods and winks and jockeying for a position of merit in the class.

The situation is delicate by the same dynamic that La Bruyère noticed in seventeenth-century conversation. Often we do not enjoy the prospect of being instructed by a relative novice on his or her new enthusiasm. If we ever had cause for anxiety in tutorials by our attention being flooded by neophytes, the risks are constantly refreshed in the digital age. Virtual classrooms are awash with chaotic disinhibited contributions from enthus-iastic but often misguided students. And in any case, real classrooms are never terribly good for the more introspective students when they are so easily dominated by socially confident students. A class can still be very good and valuable, even if the student dynamics could be more inclusive. Whether a culture of telling, either in the class or in parallel by more intimate circumstances, can achieve greater inclusivity as well as all the other benefits described remains a tricky question.

An arrangement contrived to get students to tell about their enthusiasm would fail if it lacks trust on both sides. It is a condiment to study but also a product of friendship. As often happens, the students who most take advantage of willing listeners are possibly the ones who need the benefit least. They may be the students whose private study already has a delightful intimacy which is capable of transfer through telling, relaying the content to some sympathetic friend or family member. Friendship, the precondition of authentic telling, is perhaps the 'elephant in the room', which writers on student success somewhat avoid recognizing.[40] It is a difficult theme, because it is not quite friendship in general but academic friendship. If students gain as much from telling as being told, there is a further question of how much it needs to be reciprocal (as friendships usually are). But Twitter reminds us that there is no need always to respond to telling. The need is to be able to tell, whereupon an unspecified number of people will hear or listen. Occasionally, someone might retweet or favourite your tweet; but this kindness or vote of sympathy depends to a statistical degree on the size of your followship.

Twitter reminds us of the formula that we figured out from antiquity. To tell ≠ to talk. Telling is different to conversation, where the response to the last utterance is imaginative and entertaining. When we tell, we only need to focus on our own narrative, our own reasons for fathoming, for loving, for becoming enthusiastic. We do not strictly need to gain reciprocation. Telling has an energy all of its own, which may flow in and out of a conversation of which telling is a component. The historical development of telling is far from a conclusion and one might sense that social media are not only the cause of exponentially greater participation but also fragmentation of demographics and headspace, all with greatly differing styles and assumptions. Exactly what telling is always requires a historical perspective, because it evolves and is not absolute, just like learning and teaching. In tracing its remarkable history, however, it seems clear that the educational potential of telling is far from exhausted and that it deserves to have a much larger profile in the future than it has at present. With its roots in counting

---

40   For example, George D. Kuh, Jillian Kinzie, John H Schuh, Elizabeth J. Whitt, *Student success in college: creating conditions that matter*, American Association for Higher Education, Washington, Jossey-Bass (Wiley) 2011, especially ch. 9 'Active and collaborative learning', with its sections 'Learning to learn actively' and 'Learning from peers'.

and recounting, it is a timely helpmate between imaginative projections that arise with learning foreign material and the new identification that we gain by taking it on. It uniquely includes both the zeal to socialize your learning and your desire to hold onto the privacy of your enthusiasm, which collaborative work does not afford. It is part of the necessary noise of creative thinking and it pays to hear it out.

Chapter 6

STUDENT-CENTREDNESS

Student-centredness is a beguiling catchcry of higher education, with sustained world-wide interest for many decades. A lot has been written; a lot has been promised. Each Faculty in each university likes to boast that it is student-centred; and for many, the pious wish is genuine and not just an artifice of marketing, which forces all academies to take on the rhetoric regardless of their belief in it. Which school anywhere in the world is going to say: we are not student-centred but teacher-centred or bureaucracy-centred? Once the term reached any degree of spread, it became necessary to adopt it in all publicity about learning and teaching. The suggestion by Google of 'student-centred learning' alone yields about 1,430,000 results.

Nevertheless, student-centredness is a promising concept if it does not automatically default to the empty rhetoric that every other institution uses in promoting itself as delivering student-centred education. It matters a great deal in the cultivation of creativity, where learning design often compromises the cognitive independence of the student. A student-centred approach to education could well make room for the imaginative privacy of the student in following a similar kind of curiosity-driven learning that inspires research graduates, albeit with a greater degree of scaffolding.

For many lecturers, student-centredness is the same as active learning, which is cultivated energetically in favour of greater engagement and more vigorous learning. It means running classes where the students are engaged doing exercises together, solving problems, revealing how they go about tasks and explaining methods to the group. An example would be a lecturer who uses a tablet to demonstrate ideas in physics, where the strokes of the stylus are projected on a screen. The lecturer then asks students how we might go about an analogous problem and hands the tablet to the nearest eager student, whereupon they pass the tablet among one another, each demonstrating or responding to a further aspect of the challenge. Active learning is a splendid strategy to create greater investment in learning, and requires special skills on the part of the lecturer, who must (a) propose a curious problem at the right level and with suitable scaffolding, (b) withdraw from centre-stage and let the students take over and (c) maintain an encouraging but ultimately judging presence, so as to retain control and direction of the class. It is easier to do in problem-based subjects rather than humanities where, however, the traditional Socratic tutorial model is also somewhat student-centred, even if it is not normally described as active learning.

Asking students to solve problems is nothing new and, as worthy and laudable as it is, it is far from a blueprint for student-centredness. It was the basis of studio education, for example, since time immemorial. The way you learn to draw or play oboe is to draw or play oboe. A teacher cannot lecture you how to draw in a way that then results in good drawings, in the same way that reading a book cannot by itself make you competent at oboe; you have to take the pencil in your hand in front of the motif and practice, just as you do with the oboe and a musical score. In many disciplines, this priority of students being active in their learning is deeply embedded and necessarily so. In all good programs for a long time before we were born, students have learned by doing tasks, just as you might in a maths lab or a language lab today.

But we would not call such programs student-centred if the tasks within it are alienating, obscure and pointless to the students, especially when they are compulsory and resented as such. I could be asked by a lecturer to take a lead in explaining something to the group and experience the event as humiliating, because I have misunderstood the challenge or I feel exposed next to the confident people around me. Yes, some students can shine while taking on the pyrotechnics of the lecturer and filling in his or her expectations, but it might leave a whole lot of other students feeling much more inadequate in the active group than they would in a traditional 'passive' learning situation.

Active learning is clearly a good thing, and all creative people like artists and musicians owe their genius to its timeless magic. But active learning is not necessarily student-centred, even if the higher levels of student involvement that it entails are broadly sympathetic to student-centredness. There is no necessary stage of metacognition or self-directed learning within it— though there may be—just lots of practice. The same is true of project-based learning (PBL) which champions the 'guide on the side' rather than 'sage on the stage',[1] but we would not own it as so marvellously student-centred if the students are compelled to do projects that they do not want to do.

---

1   Kimberly Overby, 'Student-Centered Learning', *ESSAI*: Vol. 9, 2011, Article 32. Available at: http://dc.cod.edu/essai/vol9/iss1/32.

In-class student learning activities have bit by bit replaced didactic teaching by lectures in other disciplines and their appeal is well-recognized. Mostly, students do not glaze over or neglect to come to class. The methods are not especially radical but resonate happily with student-centredness. Active-learning strategies could easily become part of an emphasis on student-centredness. The problem would be if student-centredness were subsumed by active learning or PBL, because student-centredness is a lot more than just active learning or PBL.

We can begin by distinguishing three perspectives of student-centredness. The first is purely operational: give students choices of subject, time and place, so that the combinations and modalities that they select are their own. The second is pedagogically dynamic, where we see learning as an activity with the student doing the learning at the centre, actively constructing their knowledge rather than passively absorbing it from an authority. The third is radical, which I would like to define as an emancipation from assessment-led education, an ability to exercise freedom of interpretation in any learning brief, so that the student cultivates intellectual autonomy and imagination.

The most popular understanding is something a bit like student-choice or study-flexibility in course architecture and delivery. It means offering lots of alternatives for the student to select from. It might not be convenient for the institution but students come first—'they're what we're here for'—and students need choice and freedom as a priority. This understanding of student-centredness is technical, operational and tangible. It might not even extend to what a student does within the classroom (though it might) but sometimes just operates between classrooms, in the sense that students may be flooded with electives and the student-centredness is defined by the decision about which subjects to take. With technologically-assisted pedagogy and clever timetabling, we can give students choices of subject, time and place, so that the path that they take is all their own. With these enlightened technical provisions, theoretically, students could direct their syllabus and opt for subjects and methods that suit them best; and in this way, they have greater ownership in the material that they choose.

You can already imagine a critique of this blueprint. Never mind that it is impossible to cater for such diversity in any given cohort, even for the majority! Assuming that we can run everything that students want, and when and how they want it, we would still have the problem that they may not enjoy the subjects that they have chosen from the formidable spread. Choice in itself is positive and honours diversity; but it is no use if you are choosing between three or four options, all of which are dreadful and are not themselves student-centred. It is the same with the timing of lessons. Here, we really can offer infinite choice, because technology allows us to run classes online, especially virtual lectures, readings and interactive quizzes; so students truly can do those parts of their study whenever and wherever they like. But the choice to attend a boring, anxious and confusing lecture at 9.00 am or 11.00 pm is still not a major pedagogical gain if both of them are of the same dull calibre. Choice is no guarantee of learning—as when our choices were misguided—and the motif only satisfies student-centredness to the extent of a mechanistic precondition of learning, not the learning itself.

We should not make a caricature of this common understanding of student-centredness, because it is tangibly beneficial in one sense, honouring diversity and choice and allowing the individual some latitude in how to study. Especially when it comes to time and place of study, the proliferation of technologies and willing lecturers who love installing their talks on YouTube and creating excellent interactive resources on learning management systems! Ultimately, after contemplating the next category, we may have little more than this practical level of student-centredness; and within its simplicity, we may discover a conceptual extension that clinches the aspiration.

Choice is mostly desirable from a student point of view, except when it brings anxiety, as when it threatens to visit the student with remorse over the bad choice. You do not want to reproach yourself later. But assuming that it is positive for the student, it is uncertain and menacing for the teacher. Student choice means individual treatment. Any one learning activity will not necessarily be congruent with another. Tailoring assessment will be especially difficult because standardization means fairness. In each circumstance student-centredness is a headache for the teacher.

For all these reasons, student autonomy is not normally what scholars mean by student-centredness. Rightly or wrongly one thinks of student-centredness as embodying certain cognitive processes and volition unique to the student. An example is the power of reflexion or metacognition necessary to deep learning or the ability of the student to direct her or his learning, that is, self-regulated learning. There is a large overlap of such concepts, broadly relating to the idea of taking responsibility for your own learning, not necessarily being an autodidact but being able to gain access to the right kind of assistance and guidance when the moment is most convenient. But because the key ingredients involve reflexion or learning about learning (let us say metacognition) it is not enough to ply student with online material with information and exercises: there has to be an invitation or cue for students to interrogate their progress, to take stock of their processes and so empower them to self-regulate their progress in a prudent way. Provided these elements are installed in the flexible formats that we are becoming accustomed to, a substantial part of student-centredness is being served.

The second understanding of student-centredness involves a dynamic narrative of classroom activity. It comprises a whole anatomy of learning, strongly associated with John Biggs, who described a scale of thinking about teaching in the contemporary academy. In the most negative learning-and-teaching cultures, says Biggs, there is an unfortunate focus on what the student is, what species, what calibre, what standard. There is often subliminal resentment over the low grade of students that we end up with in our classroom, even in an exclusive research university; lecturers may have contempt for what the students are by nature or upbringing, what intellectual mettle and stock they come along with. This level fatalistically considers learning to be simply a function of the preconditioned talent and interest of the student. If they do not learn, they are to blame. I as a teacher am not given students who are good enough. Judging by the results, they do not understand even after I have taught them; and if I were honest, I also would not be able to take credit for their learning when they have demonstrated a good grasp of the topic. This aloofness is admin-centred. The gate-keepers have to be vigilant and only allow suitable students into the course.

At a higher level, the focus is on what the teacher does. Biggs describes the archetype of teacher-centred lecturer, who is better, if vain, much less deterministic, but still far from perfect. Teacher-centred lecturers see their role as to animate the class in a performative way, perhaps jazz up the syllabus with witty language or parallels in popular culture—using jokes, allusions, inflected voice, visual pyrotechnics or music—and make students take an interest by entertaining them. Biggs, like all the universities that he has inspired, is justly suspicious of these artificial strategies to win student interest, because their theatricality is unlikely to lead to learning, though these charismatic performances might well be ingenious and might also win hearts among the student audience and produce stellar student evaluations.

Instead, Biggs commends a third level to us, where the focus is on what the student does. It is when we see learning as an activity by the student. Learning is what the student does. We need to acknowledge this fact in a model with the student doing the learning at the centre (hence student-centred) and arrange the delivery of the syllabus accordingly. When delivery, learning activities and assessment all line up with the learning outcomes, students are no longer disempowered by the caprice of incongruent elements but their learning is facilitated optimally, no longer upstaged by the performative brilliance of the lecturer. Sometimes the term is modified to 'learner-centredness' or 'learning-centred education' but it often means much the same thing.

The case is compelling and has convinced the Anglophone world to change its emphasis as best it can, diligently following the constructive alignment that Biggs himself coined. Philosophically, however, the move to constructive alignment to secure student-centredness must be interrogated, because the logic is open to question. For example, the levels that Biggs outlines are not mutually exclusive. It is possible simultaneously (1) to blame students for failing to match your own brilliance, (2) nevertheless to treat them to a grand show of your brilliance and finally (3) to organize learning activities for students that keep them busy and engaged in good alignment with learning outcomes and assessment. Professing the rigour of the third is no guarantee of abstaining from the arrogance of the first and the pleasurable conceit of the second. Teacher-centred academics might well imagine that their antics are 100% constructed around student learning, which is what the student does, only encouraged by the theatrical prowess and leadership of the lecturer. It really depends on what we mean by student-centred.

The second definition, if you like, is this: student-centredness means acknowledging that it is the student who does the learning, not the song and dance of the lecturer. It is a huge contribution and aligns with some fundamental claims about how students learn, how they achieve life-long learning when their learning is deep and reflective, not merely memorization. But in essence, student-centredness means something that happens within the classroom, putting the organic experience of the student at the centre. Much is to be located at the centre, a construct of remarkable pressure. With student-centred learning, the centre swells to subsume the syllabus, the agency of the teacher, the assessment and the learning activities.

As with the metaphor of deep and shallow in deep and surface learning, the great edifice of Anglophone academies organizes itself around an image: the image of a centre. Before proceeding to a third definition of student-centredness—which is rather on the conjectural side and is more radical than both the technical definition and the dynamic pedagogical narrative of Biggs—it is necessary to question the very term 'student-centred'. We know what a student is but what is a centre? What does 'centred' mean? In good faith, we put the two words together to mean 'focused upon students', so that students are the primary preoccupation of the educational system. The implication, as already suggested, is that this centre might formerly have been posited as the teachers (who either have clever or dull ways of conveying material or instilling ideas). More likely, this central- ity of the teacher is subsumed by the centrality of the institution itself. It could arise, for example, when a university has an enviable tradition and brand-name which it owes in large measure to its research profile and repu- tation for attracting elite students. The institution sees itself, and demands to be seen, as the epicentre of advanced thinking. The individual student within it might be felt to be not at the centre of the university but some junior periphery, whence the student might patiently aspire to a condition of greater centrality with the university's greatness, its high attainments of scholarship and intellectual advances. In Biggs' scheme, this sense of the centre as the university itself belongs to the first level of thinking about students: what the students are, not what they do.

But to use the word 'centred' means neither what they are nor what they do but *where* they are. Clearly 'centred' is a metaphor and is not intended physically; but the language is both recent and telling. Centre and centred invoke an image, a lot like a wheel, where the middle is the axle, the point at which everything turns.

'Centre' is an old Greek word (κέντρον) which, however, did not mean centre in the sense of 'middle'. It meant a point, a pin or spike, a goad such as one uses for a horse[2] which was sometimes double[3] and hence perhaps best translated as spurs. As a spike, it is what Oedipus might put his eyes out with;[4] and, as horribly, it could be an instrument of torture, mentioned together with whips.[5] It could be used metaphorically but in the sense of an impulse[6] and is never very far from its verbal form, to pierce or prick (κεντέω), which is what bees and wasps do,[7] or to even stab,[8] which is

---

2   Iliad 23.387, *cf.* 430, Aristophanes, *Clouds* 1297, Xenophon, *Cyropedia* 7.1.29 (examples from *LSJ*).

3   Sophocles, *Oedipus the King* 809.

4   Sophocles, *Oedipus the King* 1318.

5   Plato, *Laws* 777a, Herodotus 3.130.

6   Pindar, *Fragments* 124.4, 'πόθου κέντρον' in Plato, *Republic* 573a, or κέντρα καὶ ὠδῖνες', in his *Phaedrus* 251e; 'κέντρον ἐμοῦ', a desire for me, Sophocles, *Phoenecian women* 1039.

7   Aristophanes, *Wasps* 225, 407, Aristotle, *Parts of animals* 683ᵃ12.

8   Sophocles, *Antigone* 1030.

echoed through the etymological insight of our Shakespeare in his line 'Affection! thy intention stabs the centre'.[9]

Already in Greek, however, the word transitioned toward a geometric meaning through the image of the pin or peg or rivet or rowlock.[10] If you draw a circle with a compass, one point stays in the middle, the centre where the spike is, and the other describes the continuous arc that surrounds it. This stationary point at the middle is the pin (κέντρον) or centre[11] which could also be the centre of a sphere[12] or the earth which was correctly understood to be a sphere.[13] From this technical image, the idea arose that any body has a centre: a zone is centre-like (κεντροειδής) whence something may turn on a centre (περίακτος) and something that wobbles rotates in a way that is not true to its centre (ἔκκεντρος), that is, eccentric.

By the renaissance, the idea that the earth is in fact a sphere still had a degree of excitement. 'Now we know', says a poem by Agnolo Firenzuola, 'that there are people beneath us and they turn step by step by the force and virtue of the centre',[14] anticipating Shakespeare's hyperbole that 'This whole earth may be bor'd; and that the moon / May through the centre creep and so displease / Her brother's noontide with the antipodes'.[15] Elsewhere, Firenzuola describes the impenetrability of the centre of the earth.[16] Derived originally from the point of the compass, the motif of the centre has enormous prestige, as it translates to the eternally immovable, the rock-solid core surrounded by unthinkable tonnages which are the weight of the universe. So in praying to God, Vittoria Colonna contrasts herself as afflicted earth, with a centre around which divine providence gyrates.[17] So too in love, one is drawn into contrasts of a centre in an unchanging universe and the unstable wheel that spins one's fate.[18]

---

9   Shakespeare, *The winter's tale* 1.2.

10   ῥακτηρίοις κέντροισιν, of oars, Sophocles, *Fragments* 802.

11   Plato, *Timaeus* 54e, Aristotle, *APr*.41^{b}15, al.; ἡ ἐκ τοῦ κ. (sc. εὐθεῖα) radius, Euc.Opt. 34; 'ὥσπερ κύκλον κέντρῳ περιέγραψαν τὴν πόλιν', Plutarch, *Rom.* 11.

12   'τὸ κέντρον τᾶς σφαίρας', Ti.Locr.100e.

13   'τὸ κέντρον τῆς γῆς', Ptol.Tetr.52.

14   'Sappiam pur chiar che son oggi nel mondo / Uomini sotto a noi, e che, del centro / Forza e virtù si volge pianta a pianta;' Agnolo Firenzuola, *Rime* 79.92–94.

15   *A midsummer night's dream* 3.2.

16   'E come pietra, o qual sia cosa grave / Non può passare il centro della terra', Agnolo Firenzuola, *Rime* 92.164–65.

17   'Risguarda me, Ti prego, in questo centro / terrestre afflitta, e, come sempre sòle, / la Tua pietade al mio scampo proveggia', Vittoria Colonna, *Rime spirituali* 88.9–11.

18   'Dal basso segno omai non volge altrove / per me l'instabil rota, e s'affatica / tirarla al centro, e 'n Ciel stella sì amica / non sent'io che s'opponga a le sue prove,' Vittoria

The word centre is rare in literature of the renaissance. It occurs in few circumstances, perhaps because the subject matter is so seldom geometrical. The only instances where it arises are circumstances that describe geology with a certain hyperbole, referring to the centre of the earth as a sign of how deeply one might plunge into the abyss, as in Bandello: 'I should have been submerged and hurled into the chasm to the centre of the earth'.[19] In poetic language, the centre of the earth was a byword for the deepest engulfment, 'to penetrate the earth right to the centre and the infernal pits that encircle it',[20] or where the earth opens up to the very centre.[21]

Slowly, however, the word moved to mean the middle of anything, not just that unique axle of the universe. It begins in the high renaissance where, for example, Baldassare Castiglione describes the Aristotelian formula for virtue as the middle of two extremes, both of which are vices, the one for being too much of something and the other for being too little. To explain the subtlety, he uses a nice analogy: just as it is hard to find the centre of a circle, so it is hard to identify the mean between excess and deficit.[22] We see the first signs of the centre being moralized, positioned, so to speak, as the ideal. A little later in the same chapter of *The courtier*, the image is identified with goodness. 'I say that beauty is born of God but it is like a circle, of which goodness is the centre; and just as you cannot have a circle without a centre, so beauty cannot exist without goodness'.[23]

As we know from the ordeal of Galileo, it was believed that the centre of the universe is the earth, as Castiglione says, the rotund heavens adorned with so many divine lights, and the earth in the centre, surrounded by the elements and sustained by its own weight.[24] This image of planetary grandeur especially suited baroque taste, with its majestic command of extravagance in things good and negative. For Shakespeare, 'the strong base and building

---

Colonna, *Rime amorose disperse* 26.5–8.

19   'Io, io devea allor allora essere sommerso e abissato nel centro de la terra!' Matteo Bandello, *Novelle* 4.5.

20   'e penetrar la terra fin al centro, / e le bolge infernal cercare intorno.' Ludovico Ariosto, *Orlando furioso* 34.5.3–4.

21   't'apristi insino al centro', *ibid.* 43.140.7–8.

22   'perché così come è difficile nel circulo trovare il punto del centro che è il mezzo, così è difficile trovare il punto della virtù posta nel mezzo delli dui estremi, viciosi l'uno per lo troppo, l'altro per lo poco', Castiglione, *Il libro del Cortegiano* 4.40.

23   Castiglione, *Cortegiano* 4.57.

24   'l ciel rotondo, ornato di tanti divini lumi, e nel centro la terra circundata dagli elementi e dal suo peso istesso sostenuta', Castiglione, *Cortegiano* 4.58.

of my love / Is as the very centre of the earth'.[25] To discover its centre, the earth itself is enjoined to turn itself inside out: 'Turn back, dull earth, and find thy centre out.'[26] As in the earlier period, the extreme of anything deep can be figured as the centre of the earth: 'you must dig with mattock and with spade, / And pierce the inmost centre of the earth'.[27] For all that, the centre begins to lose its cosmic uniqueness as the centre of the earth and one begins to talk of other things having a centre. Thus England may be conceived as having a centre: 'even in the centre of this isle, / Near to the town of Leicester';[28] and so the town square is seen as the urban centre: 'the market-place, / The middle centre of this cursed town'.[29] Applied to geography, it is a considerable breakthrough in the history of ideas, because it means that the centre is no longer unique, in the same way that any number of circles will have the same number of centres. Every country must have a centre—its own and not that of another—and within that country every town must have a centre proper to it. The relativity of the centre is discovered.

A centre can be plural but not multitudinous. On one occasion, the centre is invoked in relation to the individual: 'Poor soul, the centre of my sinful earth,'[30] which is found in the more introspective genre of the sonnet; but even here, the metaphor is not realized without the superintendence, so to speak, of the earth. The soul is unique and it follows that there are as many unique centres as there are souls; but Shakespeare does not quite say so. The centre is still the earth's, albeit 'my earth', the earth that I belong to and that belongs to me. Tantalizingly, the relation of a centre and an individual remains hanging in the air for a very long time. The baroque period is fundamentally not very interested in individuality, a word which is used in the seventeenth century but is also only understood in the contemporary sense in the eighteenth century. Throughout the baroque, the concept of a centre remained mostly geographical one way or another, either in its ancient alignment with the centre of the earth—mostly for dramatic clout, as in Corneille's line from 1636 where one plunges live to the centre of the earth[31]—or the motif of the centre of a kingdom, as when Racine admires

25   *Troilus and Cressida* 4.2.

26   *Romeo and Juliet* 2.1.

27   *Titus Andronicus* 4.3.

28   *King Richard III* 5.2.

29   *1 King Henry VI* 2.2.

30   Shakespeare, *Sonnets* 146.1.

31   'Ou t'enfoncer tout vif au centre de la terre', Pierre Corneille, *L'Illusion comique* 3.9.

the way that Augustus spread his light to the very edge of the earth while hardly moving from the centre of the empire.[32]

Certain paradoxes of the concept emerge in this strangely elliptical history, where a tiny point somehow embodies both something intimate and cosmic. The baroque is playful with its circles and centres, and begins to emotionalize them. In an idyll, Giambattista Marino describes the noon as the day being 'in the centre of its wheel'.[33] Above all, however, the centre with the greatest prestige is the heart. In another idyll he writes 'just as you've opened the centre of your heart to love's dart, thus it is necessary for me to open the most hidden thoughts of the deepest recesses to find what secrets Destiny has written in the gloomy archive of immortal laws'.[34] This image of the innermost heart, the centre of the heart, recurs in other poets, like Scipione Errico, who also discovers that the sparks of love were locked and hidden there.[35]

A gift of a painting from another poet can touch the poet Marino to the centre of his heart.[36] In a way it is a tautology. The heart is already a centre: it is imagined as the core, which is also the Latin word for heart (cor). But the heart itself is a pumping organ that can be extracted with a knife in many gory renaissance stories. For the heart to function as a core, so to speak, one adds the slight redundancy 'the centre of' the heart. It is a bit like the colloquial 'in my heart of hearts', also illogical but well portraying the mental stress in capturing an idea of emotional centrality. It might be nonsense, too, since the things that you feel so deeply and impute to the innermost heart are tingles that are felt all over the body but perhaps least of all in the heart, which only registers a feeling by its increased pulse. For one reason or another, the centre of the heart recurs in Marino's epic many

---

32   'on n'a point vu de roi qui, à l'âge d'Alexandre, ait fait paraître la conduite d'Auguste; qui, sans s'éloigner presque du centre de son royaume, ait répandu sa lumière jusqu'au bout du monde', Racine, *Alexandre le Grand*, address *au Roi*.

33   'Era nel centro / dela sua rota il giorno', Marino, *Atteone*, Idillio 2.266–267.

34   'sì come il centro / del cor più volte dal tuo dolce figlio / saettato t'apersi, / così gli arcani interni / de' più chiusi pensier convien ch'io t'apra, / con quanto di secreto / dentro l'archivio cupo / dele leggi immortali ha scritto il Fato.' *Proserpina*, Idillio 5.37–44.

35   'Le dolci fiamme ch'a la prima etate / M'arser il sen, poi che il mio ben fu assente, / Non furon punto intepedite o spente, / Ma nel centro del cor chiuse e celate.' Scipione Errico, *Sonetti e Madrigali* 14.1–4.

36   'L'imagin tua, che 'n dono or mi concede / Claudio, affetto cortese, è quella istessa / che nel centro del core io porto impressa, / e che de' miei pensieri in cima siede.' *Ringrazia Claudio Achillini del suo ritratto mandatogli* 1–4.

times:[37] open my breast and look in my heart at the centre;[38] from the centre of the heart, one draws a sigh[39] or words that rise like fire.[40]

But Marino is also open to using the word centre to describe the middle of anything. An example is the centre of a wide and shady forest,[41] the centre of a room with a statue of Atlas[42] or even the inner penetralia of the ear[43] or a secret bath sculpted in the centre of a wood[44] or a tree of immortal green that makes a terrace of shade in the centre of the field.[45] Like a baroque garden designer, Marino loves the centre of things, especially when clinched with some landmark like a fountain[46] and which accords not just with the palatial vistas of baroque gardens but the centralizing of government in the baroque.[47]

On one occasion, Marino writes of the 'centre of my desires'[48] but even in the following century, the metaphor is not hugely advanced. Often writers of great wit and sentimental imagination like Montesquieu only use the word to apply to the centre of a circle.[49] During the enlightenment, one spoke of 'the centre of virtue, the idea of true love'.[50] In his instructions for the scene of *La fiera di Sinigaglia* Carlo Goldoni calls for a town square or the town centre with various shops[51] and in the preface to *La buona madre*, Goldoni calls the court the centre of the nation,[52] and elsewhere, one of his

---

37   'perch'al centro del cor premendo il dardo / su la cima d'un labro accoppia l'alme.' *Adone* 8.127.3–4.

38   'Aprimi il petto e cerca il cor nel centro', *Adone* 12.86.7.

39   'e dal centro del cor trasse un sospiro.' *Adone* 5.91.2.

40   'dale parole / che dal centro del cor m'escon di foco.' *Adone* 16.25.6.

41   'nel centro allor del'ampia selva ombrosa', *Adone* 4.257.7.

42   'Nel centro dela sala un vasto atlante', *Adone* 5.119.1.

43   'passando al centro / il caratter del suon vi stampa dentro.' *Adone* 7.15.7–8.

44   'un secreto bagno / che nel centro del bosco è fabricato.' *Adone* 8.26.5–6.

45   'Un Parnasetto d'immortal verdure / nel centro del pratel fa piazza ombrosa', *Adone* 9.94.1–2.

46   'Quel fonte è il centro onde la linea piglia / ciascuna dele vie che dianzi ho detto.' *Adone* 12.162.1–2.

47   'e nel centro il piantò del suo giardino / tra mille d'altri fior schiere diverse.' *Adone* 19.420.5–6.

48   'Centro de' miei desir', *Adone* 15.102.1.

49   Montesquieu, *Lettres persanes* 16, 98 centre of circle.

50   'il centro di virtude, l'idea del vero amore.' Carlo Goldoni, *Ircana in Ispaan* 3.10.

51   'Piazza o sia centro della Fiera con varie botteghe, fra le quali una bottega di caffè, una di chincaglie, una di panni e sete ecc. Da una parte locanda con finestra, dirimpetto alla bottega da caffè.' Carlo Goldoni, *La fiera di Sinigaglia*, description of opening scene.

52   'La Corte è il centro della Nazione dove l'aria usa più di cautela, ma dove si sviluppano meglio le verità.' Goldoni, *La buona madre*, preface.

characters says that 'I am yours, that which the throne represents in this centre'.[53] On the other hand, the centre can be used—as in Australia—to indicate the remoteness of a place. It occurs in a letter by Metastasio, declaring that there is no gondolier in Venice, no crook in Rome, no idiot in the furthest edge of Calabria or in the middle of Sicily (*nel centro della Sicilia*) who does not detest, condemn and deride this plague that we call eighteenth-century fashion (*secentismo*).[54]

These stories in the evolution of the concept are valuable not because we need a complete and continuous history of the word from antiquity to now but because the period to the dawn of the industrial revolution reveals a structural stress and unsustainable pomposity in the word. Centredness begins with a prick and rises by geometric metaphor to an assertion of universality—indeed that unique point which is the centre of the universe—but is fraught the moment it transcends this uniqueness. Once the centre applies itself to multifarious settings, it becomes contested and vague, at risk of banality and solipsism. Historically, it begins as a physical point and arrives at the condition of immovability, the one centre for the whole world. Then it wanders somewhat and is applied with relativity to nations, cities, gardens and hearts. Today, in spite of the untrammelled proliferation of the word, now commonly reaching into the psychological, there is no certainty that the centre is positive; and even 'centredness' is not always a virtue. Normally, when we say that someone is centred, it indicates stability, balance, lovely metaphors that also derive from physics. The lexicographers of the *Oxford English Dictionary* also acknowledge a psychological meaning of the word 'centred', which arose in the 1970s, apparently in America. It means 'emotionally well-balanced or serene, at ease with oneself, self-assured.'

Even these latter-day meanings, however, are not as stable and unequivocal as the physical image suggests; and the historical paradoxes continue with other equivocations. We can equally say that someone is 'self-centred',

---

53   'Io son per grazia vostra, per amor vostro io sono Quella che rappresenta in questo centro il trono.' Goldoni, *La donna sola* 5.8 final scene. See also 'Nel centro della terra da me non sei sicuro.' Goldoni, *Il filosofo inglese*. 4.9; 'Parte di voi coll'armi formi nel centro un forte, Altri i giardin difendano, altri le doppie porte', *Ircana in Ispaan*. 2.1; 'Favoritemi dire come formisi il centro vuoto' (a military term for entrapment) Goldoni, *L'impostore* 1.13.

54   'Ed è poi palpabile che da un mezzo secolo in qua non v'è barcaiuolo in Venezia, non *fricti ciceris* emptor in Roma, né uomo così idiota nell'ultima Calabria o nel centro della Sicilia, che non detesti, che non condanni, che non derida questa peste che si chiama fra noi secentismo.' Pietro Metastasio, *Lettere* 53, A Francesco Algarotti, Vienna, 1 August 1751.

meaning egotistical and selfish. This negative conception of centredness is extremely common and is the opposite of being 'centred' in the sense of balanced: rather it means needy, self-absorbed and probably insecure. Google finds four million instances of it. There is scarcely a stronger image of morally reprehensible narcissism, because it suggests that love of the self comes at the expense of consideration for others. Lexically, it has no natural antonym. One cannot say that a person is 'other-centred'. It makes no sense, because the address to the multiple contradicts the uniqueness of the centre.

Although relatively new in the history of ideas, the concept of centredness is archaic in atomizing people. Instead of seeing people as relational entities, it sees them as a kind of atom with a nucleus. There may be no necessary contradiction between the individual and the relational: ideally, we can be very certain of our independence and at the same time connect with our community. Ideally, communities are nodal, with each individual a kind of centre, insofar as each person provides the connection with a group.

While only a matter of emphasis, the symbolism of language is powerful. The conception is mighty in a way that highlights its own neurotic fragmentation to the very atom. Casting the emphasis on the individual with a centre as opposed to the individual partly described by his or her connexions (let us say the relational) runs counter to recent philosophy that understands human phenomena as multifocal rather than structured by binaries like centre and periphery. In particular, the work of Gilles Deleuze and Félix Guattari has challenged the positivist assumption that objects and beings can be categorized according to tree-like structures, such as Domain > Kingdom > Phylum > Class > Order > Family > Genus > Species.[55] Instead of a classification that assumes an arborific structure, Deleuze and Guattari promoted the image of the rhizome, the plant tissue which is not conscripted into channels of centrality but maintains a cellular economy without any sense of greater and lesser. It is a poststructural understanding through which human phenomena can be conceptualized by association rather than a master narrative of causation, hierarchy and centrality.

When we say student-centred, of course we do not mean to imply any kind of hierarchy. It is more the opposite, where the impulse is to offset an institutional hierarchy (or centre) and to allow for the irreducible integrity of the individuals to whom the hierarchy ministers. But what type of centrality do we expect for the decentred? At the risk of being literal, it

---

55   Gilles Deleuze et Félix Guattari, *Mille plateaux*, Minuit, Paris, 1980.

seems so odd to tie ourselves linguistically to a centre when—rightly or wrongly—contemporary understanding of the learning experience emphasizes the relational. In most cases, there are at least two foci, as with an ellipse: the student and the teacher. But then there are other students in the class, all of whom have a teaching role, just as there may be other teachers in a group-taught unit or module, all of whom have different voices and approaches, quite possibly different opinions and ideas of pedagogy. The student works it out and is intensely aware of the oddness of this class or that. The peculiarities of the lecturing staff are much likelier to be a topic of conversation among students than the syllabus.

Education is rhizomatic. It is not centred, even if we argue that the imaginative instance of learning is unique to each individual. But if the whole communicative economy of education were artificially centred, it would be mortified. It would potentially suit my case to be able to reduce the learning experience to the hermetic integrity of the individual, as the individual is the unique owner of an imaginative moment of projection, casting an identity over new subject matter and developing a self-image in the process. But education is hardly confined to that moment, which consists of legion encounters that either encourage or discourage the creative leap. Politically, we want to be able to say: in our academy, education is student-centred. But the structure, if it has any meaning related to our long history, is confusing and archaic.

The multifocality of the student learning experience is seen nowhere better than in the agency of feedback. From the student's perspective, to attend, participate and produce would be incomplete if there were no feedback. The importance of feedback is its communication of the teacher's opinion or possibly also the opinion of peers. The feedback may or may not be consonant with the learner's understanding but it structurally completes the pattern of learning-by-doing and represents the integrity of the learning experience. Even if your judgement of your own work testifies to high self-esteem, the nitpicking or approbation is a key indicator that your efforts have connected with someone. Another mind has evaluated your work, has followed where your mind has been and makes reflexions on it. It is in many ways the most outstanding element that distinguishes organized education from autodidacticism, more than assessment, because we can learn formally from a teacher without assessments. But if there is no feedback, the student is effectively self-taught. The learning experience is triangulated, as the learner, her or his effort and the teacher, are connected with an expression of reciprocal interest.

Perhaps to avoid any connotations of self-centredness, the term 'student-centred' is sometimes substituted with 'learner-centred', but the problem in logic remains. Given the classical Biggsian strategies to achieve student-centredness (which all have to do with deep learning), it would be more elegant to say 'learning-centred' rather than 'learner-centred'; because the assumption is that the process of learning is made more efficient, focusing on what it really takes to achieve deep and lifelong learning rather than shallow, opportunistic and easily-forgotten learning.

There is no absolute construct of centredness, much less student-centredness. But if we move from student-centred to learner-centred to learning-centred, the idea begins to take a more logical and tangible form, because the centre in learning is learning itself, even if this definition of centredness risks circularity (so to speak!). If student-centredness were redefined in the direction of learning-centredness, it would consist in a new freedom from assessment-led education. In learning institutions around the world, the stakes in education are competitive. Rightly or wrongly, the performance at exams and other forms of testing is foremost in the student's mind. Achieving high grades means more choices for gaining admission into other prestigious programs, preferential treatment, scholarships. I do not see how in this pressured environment—where teachers set all the terms and fill the student's mind with the travails of assessment—we can be so shameless as to invoke the term student-centred.

Under the term student-centredness we project a disingenuous promise to learners that they are at the centre of our preoccupations. But in fact our preoccupations as teachers have little in common with theirs as learners, if not anxiety. Students agonize: 'how can I pick up all the hints that I'd need to ace the assessment?' Meanwhile, educators have comparable stress in rationing the hints. They are tasked with the invidious job of telling students everything that they need to ace the assessments—making all activities and delivery line up with the stated learning outcomes—but still leaving enough traps in the assessment so that they can discriminate and produce a curve in the results. Assessment is no longer allowed to be a kind of guillotine at the end of a period of study (even when formative, like the final essay), terminating the semester with its necessary finality; rather, assessment haunts the learning experience throughout, with the ever-present reminder through learning outcomes, learning activities and delivery, all in alignment with assessment and without any scope for disinterested learning.

By disinterested learning, I mean learning that you do for no immediate advantage or without an immediate application, with the possible exception of telling someone about it or dangerously weaving it into an essay that is really meant to be about something else. Universities used to be a haven for disinterested learning, whereas now they only have room for the instructional and the prefigured. Before the doctrine of constructive alignment became universal, there was a slightly irresponsible but nevertheless liberal understanding that the noblest study involved learning that was not exactly called for but occasioned by curiosity or the sway of the syllabus. And to that extent, it was more student-centred, because the student constructed her or his own brief. Constructing the terms of learning these days is not understood in those terms. Rather, Biggs ingeniously attached the cognitive term 'constructive' to the bureaucratic term of 'alignment', with the implication that activities, delivery and assessment aligning with learning outcomes would magically put students at the centre of their learning; because, as they construct their own learning—so the assumption—they owe it to the alignment with learning outcomes. Somehow, with no embarrassment of a mixed metaphor, the line produces the circle, which produces the point.

Perhaps it is now too utopian to recall, but I remember students studying art history and spending a large part of their time reading on other forms of cultural practice, from feminist theory to poetic literature, only obliquely analogous to the syllabus. As a tutor in the early 1980s, I could see when their efforts were motivated by genuine enthusiasm and it seemed easy to detect when a student was simply piggy-backing from another subject. The spectacle of students freely exercising their imagination remains a thrill for me; and in former times, nothing constrained me from accommodating their enthusiasm, even though it stretched our idea of the syllabus. When a personal study plan was genuinely eccentric and motivated by curiosity rather than calculated for speedy expedience, it still remained risky and overambitious. Students could easily get caught up in alien subject matter and not answer the question. When they succeeded, their heterogeneous efforts were often hard to compare, because all so unalike. But it seemed important to allow students to be creative, use their initiative as individuals and forge something that they could call their own idea.

It has occurred to me to attribute some of this licence to the freedom from statements of learning outcomes. It seemed self-evident that the purpose of studying renaissance art would be to know something about renaissance art at the end of it, but especially to get to think about its history and meaning and exercise one's talents of observation, perceptive speculation and imaginative expression; whereas today we feel that it is inadequate to rely on this clairvoyance and consequently feel a need to stipulate how the knowledge should be manifest. As an intellectual exercise for us as lecturers, establishing the learning outcomes is worthwhile, as well as bracingly difficult; but what exactly is the value proposition within them for our students? I fear that it is an increase in anxious criteria-monitoring.

If as a student I had been indoctrinated to think of the learning outcomes as I planned my work for the unit or subject or module, there is little chance that I would have felt licenced to exercise my spirit of independence. It is more likely that I would have felt foolish for not following the instructions. Everything is aligned and so my learning activities would have set me up with the best chance of demonstrating the learning outcomes through the assessment process. To stray would be discouraged, because I might be demonstrating another learning outcome which is not listed. Quite likely, I would already have been made aware of the criteria used for marking the forthcoming essay, a list of bullet points which I know would be replicated on the tutor's marking rubric. I would have every assistance in being able to meet the learning outcomes and none to invent my own. In one sense, the conventions of alignment are enlightened; and we know why they have arisen. But in another sense, they are disastrously prescriptive. In observing the pedagogical machinery, I am largely constrained; my mind is owned by the task master and I would stray from the brief at my peril.

By what diabolical sleight of logic did the academies of the Anglophone world decide that this rigidity would be student-centred? To read Biggs, you would assume that constructive alignment is a precondition of student-centredness, and that only when all the elements of teaching and assessment are constructively aligned can student-centredness be achieved. Alas, the reverse seems more plausible. Sure, a constructively aligned program is student-centred insofar as it is not teacher-centred. But it does not follow that somehow students become more autonomous because the teaching methods are consistently linked with prescriptions or that students can better construct their knowledge because of the certainties of alignment.

It might be objected that the kind of autonomy suggested above is all well and good for elite humanities students—who in a sense can already be treated as research graduates—but it has no application to other disciplines that require a mastery of facts and processes. Up to a point, I cannot deny that there is a discipline-bias in the argument, since a part of it is derived from my own experience teaching and supervising in art, design and architecture for three decades. My intention in citing my own experience was to note how much pedagogical expectations have changed over the period.

In the process, however, I must acknowledge that the discipline that I have studied and taught is far from universal.

It is fine to recommend that students can be inventive with their projects when the brief is to write an essay on Titian or art nouveau architecture. The subject matter is creative and it follows that some element in the interpretation will be inflected with sympathetic imagination. If the architecture of Héctor Guimard raves and writhes and breaks convention, Nalini too can reach a high pitch of descriptive euphoria, without necessarily plunging into indulgence. Or as a literature student, say, Nalini, whom we spoke of earlier, can find a lot of licence in her essay on TS Eliot, because Eliot himself is full of imagery, evocations, ambiguities: the field invites the reader to put things together in imaginative connexions with the idiosyncrasies of the verse. Nalini cannot be as incoherent as Eliot in her essay, because she still needs to follow an expository purpose, but she can certainly exploit the moody wayward changes of Eliot's content and prosody.

This reciprocal enchantment of topic and essayist cannot be matched in maths or econometrics or physics or accounting or chemistry. Learning in most disciplines has a slightly different trajectory, which is less about creatively throwing your powers of interpretation around and more about understanding principles and techniques which then allow calculation and decisions. Even within the humanities, several disciplines are not necessarily well studied through rhapsodic personal creativity. Take German language. To fathom the grammar, vocabulary and syntax—and then to gain skills in listening and talking—might indeed involve imagination as well as memory; but the learning exercise does not afford the kind of poetic conjecture that puts me in the centre, me as the new revisionist of canonical works, charming my way to imaginative expressions that magically establish my viewpoint as the conduit of world interpretation. In my German studies, I need to build an ability to say things, for which I need a lot of knowledge and practice in conjugation and declension, word-order and of course the largest possible vocabulary. Otherwise, all my personal zeal will only lead me from blunder to blunder, and no one will find it rewarding.

There are two ways to answer this critique. First, though we definitely have technical disciplines that are understandably intolerant of eccentricity, we also have broad educational learning outcomes for all our degrees. Good universities have enlightened graduate attributes (or student capabilities) which include ethical and expressive dimensions. Monash University, for example, expects that its students will know how to communicate perceptively and effectively. It is a wonderful enlarging brief for the university as a whole. The students in maths or econometrics or physics or accounting or chemistry all need the same skill. Where will they get it? We cannot simply say that those qualities are really only proper and essential to humanities students, even though they would be admirable and desirable for all students to have.

Second, being student-centred is not really ever about the subject matter but the fact that one is learning; and learning anything, as we have argued, is a creative act, where we graft newly encountered material onto projections of an identity that we will gain as we absorb it. It may or may not be true that we learn literature by writing with an imaginative impulse; but all learning is about developing some enthusiasm for and ownership of the material because it makes sense and becomes a part of us. In learning, that is, what first seemed chaotic becomes intelligible as a set of meaningful relations; and this new perception of sense is something proper to you as a learner—delightfully so—not the subject matter itself, even though someone may be demonstrating the sense in it for you and activating the thrill of seeing it. So understanding the inverse square law or the pressures in a pipe are realities in your mind when you learn about them: they aren't abstract or remote any more than poetic literature is. Certainly the inverse square law is universal and does not harmonize with idiosyncratic interpretation; but it still exists in the imagination, is enlivened with language and metaphor: you understand it through stories and images and can explain it as an interpretation of other curiosities of physics, like gravity.

Student-centredness is not about eccentricity or flattery for students who have the confidence to indulge their imagination. Still less is it about the teacher withdrawing from a forceful narrative presence in the relationship. It is not about choices offered on a purely technical level. It may, from time to time, involve all of these qualities, but the one that is primary is the ancient motif of sympathy between teacher and student, where the teacher actively participates in the thinking of the students and enables the embrace of foreign concepts or methods toward an enlarged identity. This sympathetic form of engagement has arguably been suppressed by the very system that is represented as student-centred, namely constructive alignment.

We are not about to dismantle the established architecture of constructive alignment, even though it is so prescriptive and corrosive to intellectual autonomy. For the moment, we have to live with it, because any alternative will be construed as confusing or mystifying students; it would stand accused of not ministering sufficiently to anxiety over assessment and may be identified with the arbitrariness of older arrangements in liberal studies.

For all that, the doctrine of constructive alignment will not last forever; and of all the competing pressures on educational priorities, the claims of student-centredness are among the more exigent. Our ability to think of what student-centredness is, what learning-centredness is, could be considered undeveloped.

Beyond pointing out the somewhat contrary nature of student-centredness and constructive alignment, my contention in this chapter is to suggest that the understanding of student-centredness is advanced by thinking of the very motif of centredness, the centredness of anything, which is always relative to parameters that include other entities and other centres. Whatever else it involves in its tellingly paradoxical history, centredness in our environment involves two people: a learner and a teacher. For students to own their learning and enjoy their due margin of creativity, they need maximum licence to engage their powers of interpretation and invention; but for this autonomy to be realized, they need the support of a teacher, a person who eyeballs their attempts at speaking, their plans and their efforts, and gives them confidence in the worth and growth of their intellectual integrity. In education, the centre moves constantly and it makes little sense to pretend that it is fixed in the student any more than it might be fixed in the teacher. This mobile, dynamic perspective is at the heart of a post-constructive paradigm of learning and teaching.

Chapter 7

EXPECTATION

We wait for our students and our students wait for us. In a literal sense, we are always waiting. After the lecture or tutorial has been prepared, we nervously wait for the time when the students appear. The students themselves have been waiting for the occasion, either on-campus or coming toward the campus, waiting for public transport or traffic. These literal forms of waiting are interesting, even when sometimes resented; but they are not the motif that I have in mind as an essential part of learning. They are analogous to the tension that boxers must experience before their match, which must be almost as hard to bear as the gloves of their opponent once in the ring. Rather, the waiting that counts for our purposes is integral to cognition itself.

By convention, my purpose in writing is to communicate my research. The classical view of research is empirical and is conceptualized along stages of design, testing, proving and writing up. But if the process of the research involves thinking of new ideas—if, say, it is approached creatively in arts and humanities—the act of doing the research is intimately a part of the writing and *vice versa*. In writing, my exhaustive plans are mostly in vain, because I do not really know what I am going to write until I come to write it. In effect, as I write and I try to match several ideas that might lie in the vicinity (a process which is simultaneously entrancing and stressful) I am waiting. The ideas will not come to me without waiting, in the same way that they will not come to me without a technique of eliciting all the likely options that might relate to the theme. Sometimes we wait seconds or minutes; at other times we wait hours or days; with greater risk of frustration, we sometimes wait months or years for the ideas to gel or at least sufficiently to give us licence to sketch their nascent lineaments in writing. In all that time, we have been learning.

Waiting is subjective. Our tolerance for waiting or even our propensity to recognize a given period as waiting-time varies from individual to individual. A person on a train who is fidgeting may experience the time between departure and destination as a period of waiting, analogous to the time spent on the platform for the train to arrive. But the person nearby in the same rail coach who is reading a book or admiring the scenery in rapture does not experience the same duration as some kind of hiatus that must be waited out.[1] Rather, the time spent in travel is a useful break during which the mind allows itself to wander delightfully, unharried by pressure and stressful goals.

The phenomenology of waiting is layered with levels of engagement. First, you can be waiting in the sense of being at a loose end. Second, you can become marvellously distracted with a rhapsodic independence from the thing or event that you are waiting for. And third, you can wait for some event in a way that greatly enhances its impact or development in your mind and which conditions the way that you think. Music is the perfect example. When we are conscious of the music in the moment, the imminent notes have all been awaited. The sequences that anticipate the next development cause us to entertain certain expectations which hugely enrich our appreciation of the music. In music there are regular cycles of expectation and fulfilment: you wait for the high notes to descend or to repeat a pattern and, even as this movement is about to be achieved, you await the reciprocation; the scale will return upward or the beat will divide or lengthen, the *basso* will shudder, with its magic reverberations from below overtaking the treble voices, only to be overturned, to recede. These are patterns that you know will happen. Even if you were surprised on the first listening, you may have heard the music—or even played it yourself—scores of times, and yet the predictive duration, during which you wait for the known eventuality, thrills you: in short, it is the musical response.

This sense of waiting as expectation is particularly significant for learning, because it is assumed that when we are expecting to learn, we are ready to learn. The expectation not only heralds the learning but propitiates the learning. It is part of the logic of learning outcomes, to create a predictable and reliable schedule of what is to be learned, which is duly fulfilled by the learning activities connecting in alignment. Thanks to the flow of expectation, students can plan their learning, knowing what to await and clinching their expectation with certain realities. But with all this certainty, we have to ask: how poetic, how imaginative can expectation be?

---

1   This relativity in anxiety has been often noted, especially for different individuals while awaiting death, *e.g.* Montaigne: 'Et comme les uns l'attendent tremblans et effrayez, d'autres la supportent plus aysement que la vie.' *Essais* 1.14.

There is a subtle difference between waiting and expectation. What we wait for is always something in general, whereas what we expect is something in particular. As I wait for my ideas to find some formulation through writing, I do not have too many expectations. I am curious to see what unfolds, knowing well that patience is needed and haste is destructive. I wait on the thoughts, meaning that I attend upon them; but if I expected to think of something, I feel sure that my openness and curiosity would be compromised. To be creative is to want something but not necessarily expect it; because discovery is beyond expectations. By what we have already encountered, we might have an inkling of what we will receive and gain in the instant ahead, so that when it arrives, it is recognized and immediately finds a receptive audience in our intelligence. But in older language, the distinction is not clear. We wait or expect, as the early Italian writer Boccaccio said, with desire (*con disidero aspettando*),[2] and the high renaissance writer Baldassare Castiglione describes an intense and beautiful discussion where 'everyone awaited the proposed argument with keen attention (*con attentissima aspettazion*)' or 'most attentive expectation'.[3] Waiting is integral to ratiocination but especially the kind of ratiocination that belongs to listening.

The link between waiting and expectation is natural and is underscored by language. In Italian, Spanish and Portuguese, the word for waiting (*aspettare, esperar*) is also the word for expectation, with links to hope (*speranza, esperanza, esperança*) or aspiration, from Latin to look out for, await, wait for (*exspecto*).[4] The same Boccaccio, writing in the fourteenth century, can intend the verb to mean either waiting or expectation. The instances for which we would choose waiting are very numerous: one begins a story without waiting (*senza aspettare*) for the signal from the queen;[5] one goes to

---

2   *Decamerone* 6.10; the same motif of desire occurs with waiting for a meal: 'la sera a cena e con disidero grandissimo l'aspettava', 4.9.

3   A few sentences earlier the noun (aspettazione) is used as expectation: '"Gran peso parmi, messer Federico, che sia quello che posto è sopra le spalle vostre, e grande aspettazione quella a cui corrisponder dovete." Quivi non aspettando che messer Federico rispondesse: "E che gran peso è però questo?" disse l'Unico Aretino: "Chi è tanto sciocco, che quando sa fare una cosa non la faccia a tempo conveniente?" Così di questo parlandosi, ognuno si pose a sedere nel loco e modo usato, con attentissima aspettazion del proposto ragionamento.' *Cortegiano* 2.5.

4   In turn from *specto*, to look on, look at, behold, watch, inspect, attend.

5   'Già si tacea Filomena dalla sua novella espedita, quando Dioneo, che appresso di lei sedeva, senza aspettare dalla reina altro comandamento, conoscendo già per l'ordine cominciato che a lui toccava il dover dire, in cotal guisa cominciò a parlare', 1.4; *cf.* 'Sedeva appresso Filostrato Lauretta, la quale, poscia che udito ebbe lodare

one's room and waits till the monk departs;[6] one waits or hangs on (*ma pure aspettava*) because it would not look good to leave;[7] one waits for decorum's sake but begins to eat on seeing that the Abbot was not coming;[8] one waits for peace in England;[9] one remains waiting in melancholy circumstances.[10] In a sinister vein, one waits for the time and place to fulfil one's dastardly plans;[11] a motif which arises in the contemporaneous poet Petrarch.[12]

On the other hand, the cases where we would choose 'expect' are equally impressive. One expected the diametrically opposite conclusion (*aspettava dirittamente contraria conclusione*);[13] one expects nothing less than the arrival

---

la 'ndustria di Bergamino e sentendo a lei convenir dire alcuna cosa, senza alcuno comandamento aspettare piacevolmente così cominciò a parlare', 1.8; also 'A Elissa restava l'ultimo comandamento della reina; la quale, senza aspettarlo, tutta festevole cominciò', 1.9. The phrase 'without waiting' is common in the later Italian renaissance, *e.g.* 'e senza aspettar l'uno la risposta dell'altro, facevano instanzia alla signora Emilia che ordinasse chi gli avesse a dar principio', Castiglione, *Il libro del Corteggiano* 1.12.

6   'tornatosi alla sua camera aspettò che il monaco fuori uscisse.' 1.4; *cf.* waiting for a husband to fall asleep in order to make love to his wife: 'e tanto aspettò, che, tornati costoro e andatisene a letto, sentì il marito di lei adormentato, e là se ne andò dove veduto aveva che la Salvestra coricata s'era; e postale la sua mano sopra il petto pianamente disse: "O anima mia, dormi tu ancora?"' 4.8; also 'aspettando che da se medesima si svegliasse', 5.1.

7   'Bergamino dopo alquanti dì, non veggendosi né chiamare né richiedere a cosa che a suo mestier partenesse e oltre a ciò consumarsi nello albergo co' suoi cavalli e co' suoi fanti, incominciò a prender malinconia; ma pure aspettava, non parendogli ben far di partirsi.' 1.7.

8   'Primasso, il quale avea talento di mangiare, come colui che camminato avea e uso non era di digiunare, avendo alquanto aspettato e veggendo che l'abate non veniva, si trasse di seno l'uno de' tre pani li quali portati avea e cominciò a mangiare.' 1.7.

9   'Alessandro, il quale in Inghilterra la pace più anni aspettata avea', 2.3; 'Restava, non volendo il suo privilegio rompere a Dioneo, solamente a dire alla reina, con ciò fosse cosa che già finita fosse la novella di Lauretta; per la qual cosa essa, senza aspettare d'esser sollecitata da' suoi, così tutta vaga cominciò a parlare', 3.9.

10 'e alcuna volta con molte lagrime della sua lunga dimora si doleva e senza punto rallegrarsi sempre aspettando si stava.' basilico.

11 'E così di varie cose parlando e al lor cammin procedendo e aspettando luogo e tempo al lor malvagio proponimento, avvenne che, essendo già tardi, di là dal Castel Guiglielmo, al valicar d'un fiume questi tre, veggendo l'ora tarda e il luogo solitario e chiuso, assalitolo il rubarono, e, lui a piè e in camiscia lasciato, partendosi dissero:' 2.2; or one waits for the night: 'e aspettata la notte e di quella lasciata andar buona parte, là se ne tornò e aggrappatosi per parti che non vi si sarebbono appiccati i picchi nel giardin se n'entrò, e in quello trovata una antennetta, alla finestra dalla giovane insegnatagli l'appoggiò e per quella assai leggiermente se ne saglì.' 5.6.

12 'celatamente Amor l' arco riprese, / come huom ch' a nocer luogo et tempo aspetta.' 2.4.

13 'Giannotto, il quale aspettava dirittamente contraria conclusione a questa, come lui così udì dire, fu il più contento uomo che giammai fosse', 1.2.

of the marchese;[14] one expects nothing other than to lead a miserable life forever;[15] one expects to be seized;[16] one expects to be trounced and to drown.[17] This sense is also used in later renaissance writing, as in Castiglione.[18]

Sometimes, the word can go either way, like expecting to die or perhaps waiting to die.[19] You can also go fetch someone who is either expecting you or waiting for you.[20] Both seem valid. The poet Petrarch, a contemporary of Boccaccio, seems to relish the ambiguity, as when he describes people to the west expecting or waiting for the daylight that slips from the sky where we are;[21] and he himself awaits or hopes for the night.[22] He puts up with the present but either expects or waits for better;[23] he either expects or waits for mortality.[24] There are, however, cases where Petrarch means expect, as in his stalwart stance against love, like a man expecting war.[25] Occasionally, he means simply 'wait', as when he says that he will never again see his deceased Laura, and waiting for the reunion makes him impatient;[26] though in another poem he acknowledges that heaven yearns for (or expects) her.[27]

---

14   'e niuna altra cosa che la venuta del marchese era da lei aspettata', 2.2.

15   'più non sappiendo che aspettar si dovessono se non misera vita sempre.' 2.3.

16   'Masetto udiva tutto questo ragionamento, e disposto a ubidire niuna cosa aspettava se non l'esser preso dall'una di loro,' 3.1.

17   'Arrestatevi, calate le vele, o voi aspettate d'esser vinti e sommersi in mare,' 5.1.

18   'i modo che di così bon principio non si po se non aspettar ottima fine,' 4.43; 'Io non aspettava già che 'l nostro cortegiano avesse tanto d'onore,' 4.48.

19   'e senza dire alcuna cosa aspettava la morte. 4.1 Tancredi: cooked heart; cf. trovò che l'aspettava parimente disiderosa d'udire buone novelle del marito e di riconciliarsi pienamente col suo Tedaldo', 3.7.

20   'similmente Giosefo fu senza indugio dalla presenza del re levato, e ritrovò Melisso il quale l'aspettava e dissegli ciò che per risposta aveva avuto,' 9.9; 'Federigo, che con lei di cenar s'aspettava', 7.1.

21   'Ne la stagion che 'l ciel rapido inchina / verso occidente, et che 'l dí nostro vola / a gente che di là forse l' aspetta, / veggendosi in lontan paese sola', 50.3.

22   'tal ch' io aspetto tutto 'l dí la sera, / che 'l sol si parta et dia luogo a la luna,' 237.29–30.

23   'Del presente mi godo, et meglio aspetto, / et vo contando gli anni, et taccio et grido,' 105.78–79; cf. 'Sol un conforto a le mie pene aspetto', 348.12.

24   'per far voi certo che gli extremi morsi / di quella ch' io con tutto il mondo aspetto / mai non sentí', 120.5–7.

25   'Persequendomi Amor al luogo usato, / ristretto in guisa d' uom ch' aspetta guerra, 110.1–2; cf. 'Ma io incauto, dolente, / corro sempre al mio male, et so ben quanto / n' ò sofferto, et n' aspetto; ma l' engordo / voler ch' è cieco et sordo / sí mi trasporta', 135.39–43.

26   'perché mai veder lei / di qua non spero, et l' aspettar m' è noia,' 268.7–8.

27   'ivi s' impara, et qual è dritta via / di gir al ciel, che lei aspetta et brama,' 261.7–8.

Structuring education around expectations is not new. For example, in becoming an adept courtier, one awaited various qualities to be instilled which proceed from the goal, to direct oneself 'to the path of virtue', as Castiglione says, 'to be magnanimous, liberal, just, spirited, prudent or to have any other quality that one awaits'.[28] The result of all the discourses is to produce someone like Cesare Gonzaga who, 'for kindness, wit, spirit and knowledge, nothing is so great that you wouldn't expect it of him'.[29] In inculcating good manners, society creates expectations, that what goes around comes around in rewarding cycles of reciprocation: younger people 'expect to receive in old age the same favours that they as youths extended to their parents'.[30] At the same time, a courtier should neither seek nor wait for any praise.[31] The educational basis of courtly discourse embraces the motifs of what to expect and what not to wait for. It begins with expectations and ends with what is worth waiting for.

Renaissance learning is concerned with a set of general expectations which are broadly humanist; and ideologically it would not be hard to find the vision limited. However, the element in the project of enhancing one's development brings out a peculiarly active kind of waiting, a time spent which is demonstratively aspirational, thoughtful and productive. Throughout the period, a favourite *topos* was the contrast of the active and contemplative life; but waiting, which was so much more normal than it is today, creatively reconciles the two. It is active because thinking to a purpose—imaginatively foreshadowing the thing one waits for—is an activity. It is contemplative because impatience is put in abeyance and thinking is licenced to be unusually rhapsodic as well as attentive.

Throughout the Anglophone world, there is a movement to abandon lectures. It is perhaps especially manifest among the science disciplines, where humanities have retained a certain degree of faith in the institution of lecture followed by tutorial.[32] Bit by bit, however, academics are creating

---

28　'e non ha formato l'animo di quel modo ed indrizzato al camino della virtù, difficilmente saprà esser magnanimo, liberale, giusto, animoso, prudente, o avere alcuna altra qualità di quelle che se gli aspettano', *Cortegiano* 4.39.

29　'tal che, per la bontà, per l'ingegno, per l'animo e per lo saper suo non era cosa tanto grande, che di lui aspettar non si potesse,' 4.1.

30　'dai quali aspettano in vecchiezza ricever quello, che essendo giovani ai padri hanno prestato', 3.14.

31　'Voglio adunque che questo e tutti gli altri, dall'armeggiare in fora, faccia il nostro cortegiano come cosa che sua professione non sia e di che mostri non cercar o aspettar laude alcuna, né si conosca che molto studio o tempo vi metta, avvenga che eccellentemente lo faccia', 2.10.

32　Miya Tokumitsu, 'In defense of the lecture', *Jacobin*, 26 February 2017.

puzzles online, making videos and flipping their classes. The concept is in many ways sympathetic: to offload purely transmissive content into videos and text, supplemented with online interactive lessons. One of the perceived advantages is that we save students from waiting for us. They do not have to attend to the same extent and their waiting for a lecture can be relieved from dependency by the great convenience of media that exist outside real time. It is surely an advantage; and a further laudable point in the great pedagogical adjustment is to make the on-campus experience more about student learning, not about the academic's teaching, more about the students and their growing capabilities; the encounter for students is more conversational, less passive, more dynamic and charged with participation.

As if surreptitiously, the stigma of passivity has infiltrated educational discourse, discrediting lectures and proposing that all learning, true and authentic learning, only takes place with activity, when students try out for themselves some technique, so that their practice reinforces their learning. In many ways, this change is mighty and praiseworthy; but it is unclear that it suits discursive disciplines. An academic's style of lecturing might already serve the purpose of letting a student rehearse ideas in her or his head. Say it has an intellectually stimulating dimension, through which students work hard while attending: they are learning at a fine rate and do not experience the lecture as passive at all.

When a student is harking to something that she or he wants to understand, the experience is not passive; and beyond the fact that the student does not physically move, there is no evidence that the level of cognitive activity is lower than when the student tries to frame a similar concept for herself or himself. In listening to a lecture, my mind is active and I feel strongly that I am exercising a life-skill, which is listening, concentrating, training my powers of predictive sympathy. An element of that activity—which I think is also quite dynamic—is separating the speaker's techniques in oratory from the content that it projects. It is like deconstruction if you will. At the right pitch, a lecture makes for extremely active concentration.

It is not automatically advantageous to eliminate this great ritual, which also has plenty of festivity and occasionally ceremonializes learning in a way that is memorable and charismatic. A performance theorist, Philip Auslander, once said that even 'within our hypermediatized culture, far more symbolic capital is attached to live events than to mediatized ones'.[33] Is it prudent, then, to dismiss the symbolic capital of the lecture? Admittedly,

---

33 *Liveness: performance in a mediatized culture*, Routledge, London and New York, 1999, p. 59.

the live event will persist in flipped modes but perhaps not the same kind as one can experience in a lecture, if it is a really good lecture, that is.

Transitioning to video and online puzzles does not mean that the whole value of lectures has been replaced by newer techniques. Lectures do not necessarily belong to 'heritage media', maintained by obsolete professors just because the students in the audience do not speak. If we are inclined to have little patience with lectures, it is because, as a culture, we no longer understand the value and dynamics of listening. Listening involves a searching pregnant kind of waiting, a form of predictive engagement, a cognitive anticipation of ideas and reconcilement with what is actually said, where contentment and eagerness rock the attention gently toward a deeper understanding of the theme. There is no learning experience like it, because I get to think sympathetically with the speaker to the point that I am already rehearsing the ideas as they are spoken. Admittedly the dynamic depends upon the speaker having a communicative ethos that invites my powers of sympathy and scrutiny. It helps if the speaker is stimulating in some way, eliciting my interest through beautiful narrative, for example, or rhetorical questions. But given this level of connexion, I have great cognitive agency in listening, because my waiting is rewarded. Few activities are as intellectually intense—with its concatenated period of waiting and reception, predictive sympathy, wonder and critique—which is perhaps the underlying reason for abandoning prolonged listening as a learning technique. It is a considerable irony that the cognitive activity *par excellence* is stigmatized as passive because it is too vigorous for us any longer to sustain.

One speaks of passive learning;[34] but there is no such thing. It is a contradiction in terms. Either one is learning or not. If one is learning, the experience is an activity; one is necessarily active in learning. I do not have to speak or practice something in order to learn. I can sometimes listen and observe and take an interest from my seat; and if I am not constantly called upon to participate or babied into group work, I can enjoy relative freedom to concentrate on the expression of another intellect, always waiting for the points of contact with my own thoughts, with images and memory. For this reason I am suspicious of the dogma of participation. It is true that for some disciplines I will only learn by trying to do a manipulative act: mathematics, for instance, and a lecture will probably go over my head. But

---

34   For example Google lists 1,140,000 for its self-populating search term 'passive learning vs active learning'.

in discursive disciplines, the imaginative vigour of listening may be aborted thanks to a need prematurely to take up a view, profess, project, charm and entertain a group.

In contemporary educational settings, we literally cannot wait to participate. We cannot wait because we see no virtue in the condition, only a regrettable delay, possibly filled with the lecturer's pomposity. Waiting is not understood as part of the organic continuum which is necessary to the formulation of ideas, the refreshment of thought, the chance to come alongside another person's insights and take on their inductive potential. Actually, it is a fertile stage of learning because waiting affords imaginative projections, during which one might create identifications with a topic. In waiting to hear what one craves but does not yet understand, a certain philosophical equanimity may assist the contemplative kind of reasoning which is so active beneath the quiet of listening (passively, it seems, only from the outside). All courtly cultures have enjoyed this air of waiting. It belonged to the etiquette of the nobility and their retinue to show patience or, as Baldassare Castiglione says in *The courtier*, 'to gain favours by meriting them: the courtier has to wait till they are offered rather than presumptuously seeking them'.[35] There is virtue in waiting, like the scholar in Boccaccio who waits a long time in a courtyard for his lover, during which the infatuated pair are sustained by their intentions.[36] The length of waiting is a measure of his abiding passion and resolve.

In even more ancient cultures, the condition of waiting in general was highly valued, not just because it suited the powerful to commend patience but because there is an aspiration within it, a hope for reciprocation, where good things ensue.[37] If I wait for you, you will wait for me. If I listen to you, you will listen to me. For that reason, waiting is honoured in most systems

---

35   "Prima che più avanti passate," disse quivi Vincenzio Calmeta, "s'io ho ben inteso, parmi che dianzi abbiate detto che la miglior via per conseguir favori sia il meritargli; e che più presto dee il cortegiano aspettar che gli siano offerti, che prosuntuosamente ricercargli,'" 2.21.

36   'e messo dalla fante in una corte e dentro serratovi quivi la donna cominciò a aspettare ... che egli cominciò a sentir più freddo che voluto non avrebbe; ma aspettando di ristorarsi pur pazientemente il sosteneva.' *Decameron* 8.7; *cf.* 'era agghiacciato aspettandola.' 4.8.

37   'But if we hope for (ἐλπίζομεν) that we see not (οὐ βλέπομεν), then do we with patience wait for it (δι' ὑπομονῆς ἀπεκδεχόμεθα),' *Romans* 8.25; *cf.* 'For we through the Spirit wait for the hope of righteousness by faith (ἡμεῖς γὰρ πνεύματι ἐκ πίστεως ἐλπίδα δικαιοσύνης ἀπεκδεχόμεθα).' *Galatians* 5.5; 'And to wait for his Son from heaven (ἀναμένειν τὸν υἱὸν αὐτοῦ), whom he raised from the dead, even Jesus, which delivered us from the wrath to come.' *1 Thessalonians* 1.10; see also *2 Thessalonians* 3.5 and *James* 5.7.

of faith. In the Judaeo-Christian tradition, from Job to Christ, the virtue of waiting is repeatedly expressed. For example Joseph of Arimathaea is described as 'an honourable counsellor, which also waited (προσδεχόμενος) for the kingdom of God' and praised for his bravery.[38] Or Simeon, who was just and devout, 'waiting (προσδεχόμενος) for the consolation of Israel', has special grace.[39] Good people 'were all waiting (προσδοκῶντες) for Jesus',[40] just as we might await his return.[41] Waiting in this sense is also not passive. It has connotations of watching for, watching out for, remaining on guard[42] and performing an office of servitude.[43] Waiting itself is full of faithfulness, if not watchfulness.[44] While waiting, one may be inspired.[45] Waiting is the greatest occasion for cultivating readiness, which is especially so in cognitive activity.

The most common biblical word for somebody waiting (προσδεχόμενος) is constructed from the verb for receiving (δέχομαι) or taking in a welcome or accepting spirit (analogous to Latin to grasp (*cepo*) which is the origin of both receiving and accepting) but with the added sense of taking in warmly.[46] Waiting, by its very lexical architecture in Greek, is an act of generosity which invites reciprocity, expectations of a benign kind; and it follows,

---

38   He 'came, and went in boldly unto Pilate, and craved the body of Jesus,' *Mark* 15.43, *Luke* 23.51; *cf.* 'For the earnest expectation of the creature waiteth for the manifestation of the sons of God (ἡ γὰρ ἀποκαραδοκία τῆς κτίσεως τὴν ἀποκάλυψιν τῶν υἱῶν τοῦ θεοῦ ἀπεκδέχεται),' *Romans* 8.19; see also *Romans* 8.23.

39   'and the Holy Ghost was upon him,' *Luke* 2.25.

40   *Luke* 8.40.

41   'So that ye come behind in no gift; waiting for the coming (ἀπεκδεχομένους τὴν ἀποκάλυψιν) of our Lord Jesus Christ', *1 Corinthians* 1.7.

42   'And ye yourselves like unto men that wait for their lord (προσδεχομένοις τὸν κύριον ἑαυτῶν), when he will return from the wedding; that when he cometh and knocketh, they may open unto him immediately (εὐθέως ἀνοίξωσιν αὐτῷ). Blessed are those servants (μακάριοι οἱ δοῦλοι ἐκεῖνοι), whom the lord when he cometh shall find watching (εὑρήσει γρηγοροῦντας): verily I say unto you, that he shall gird himself, and make them to sit down to meat, and will come forth and serve them,' 12.36–37.

43   'a devout soldier of them that waited on him continually (τῶν προσκαρτερούντων αὐτῷ); *Acts* 10.7; and so Cornelius at *Acts* 10.24.

44   'And, being assembled together with them, commanded them that they should not depart from Jerusalem, but wait for the promise of the Father (περιμένειν τὴν ἐπαγγελίαν τοῦ πατρὸς), which, saith he, ye have heard of me.' *Acts* 1.4.

45   'Now while Paul waited for them (ἐκδεχομένου αὐτοὺς) at Athens, his spirit was stirred in him, when he saw the city wholly given to idolatry,' *Acts* 17.16.

46   As in receive favourably, accept (προσδέχομαι) or expect besides, wait for (προσαναδέχομαι). In subsequent traditions, waiting may be associated with receiving, *e.g.* Racine: 'Prêts à vous recevoir, mes vaisseaux vous attendent', *Mithridate* 1.3.

given a certain kind of faith, that this beautiful deferral of impatience is rewarded. Sometimes we even make ourselves wait so that we experience the reward of forbearance; so, for example, we might put off our coffee for another hour, even though we could gladly accept it right now. To wait for something of potential profit is a rewarding experience analogous to deferral of imminent pleasure, heightening the eventuality or stretching out the forecast of ecstasy, as if extending an imaginary fulfilment. It is aesthetic waiting, if you like, as with the thought of dinner both heightening and assuaging the hunger with a prospect of delight. It is something that has a climax that you work toward, like sexual *jouissance*, which is not strictly awaited so much as brought forth by expectation itself.

Although exercising discipline over pleasure is still practiced in daily ritual, our culture is broadly intolerant of waiting. One seeks to minimize it as much as possible, especially in business. If you make people wait, you lose customers and money. One can speculate on the proportion of the global economy that is dedicated to the attenuation of waiting: speedier services in post or retail, medical, telephonic, financial services, anything where there might be a queue. There are great commercial incentives that encourage immediacy, because companies are in competition with one another to offer faster satisfaction. It is not just the service sector but manufacturing as well, which has time-efficiencies at its heart. Nothing must be left waiting. Assembly is organized through just-in-time systems. We live in the age of logistics, where the management of supply chains is primarily about the reduction of waiting, and where waiting equates with a loss of money or opportunity.

The cultural impact of these economic shifts is undeniable. If you were to compare the activity in the great art of our time, film and video, with that of former ages, especially painting and sculpture, the changes are overwhelming. Film loves action, even if it is only speaking; and even if one interlocutor waits for the other to finish, the attention is on the active side of the screen. But from the renaissance to Lucian Freud, the bulk of paintings in our museums shows people waiting. Certainly there are subject pictures with action; but even these often contain people in attendance who are effectively waiting, as with the many guests in Veronese's *Christ in the house of Levi* in the Louvre. Western painting identifies well the predicament of deferred activity, where action is in abeyance. One's portrait cannot easily show action, unless a tronie; but the portrait can nevertheless show the sitter in a condition where action could be imminent, even though the sitter is actually waiting.

Because we live in time, we live in waiting. Despite the great commercial energies to negate waiting, it remains essential to the ontology of experience. We expect a long life but technically we are waiting for death.[47] And when we die, no one waits for us.[48] Waiting is one of the necessary vectors of experienced time. What we await and what awaits us comprise most of experience.[49] It seems to be the antithesis of something happening, but it is the genius of lived time, where everything that happens, short of a surprise, is to some extent awaited. Waiting means that something is yet to happen: you hope that it is in train and it activates expectation. Part of the reason that so much of experience can be described as waiting is the difficulty of identifying anything that satisfies desire for a long duration; bliss is short and the gaps between euphoric moments are always longer than hope would prefigure. We may not construe these gaps as waiting; sometimes we fill them up with work, whether necessary or not, and feel that we are earning the pleasure of many returns to the feast. There are elaborate structures to distract us from the feeling of waiting. We can represent waiting as expectation, which we can then cultivate, as with Stendhal defining beauty as the promise of happiness. Waiting is positioned between hope and frustration, between service and punishment, between attention and paralysis, between active hope and resignation.[50]

Some forms of waiting are extremely negative, like being in the stocks or in gaol or waiting for the next lash in a flogging[51] or waiting for the blade to put you to death;[52] but these forms of torture are not a reflexion

---

47 'Ancor ti può nel mondo render fama, / ch'el vive, e lunga vita ancor aspetta / se 'nnanzi tempo grazia a sé nol chiama,' *Inferno* 31.127–29; *cf.* Montaigne, 'Où que vostre vie finisse, elle y est toute. L'utilité du vivre n'est pas en l'espace, elle est en l'usage: tel a vescu long temps, qui a peu vescu: attendez vous y pendant que vous y estes. Il gist en vostre volonté, non au nombre des ans, que vous ayez assez vescu,' *Essais* 1.20. See also Racine: 'J'attendais le moment où j'allais expirer', *Phèdre* 4.6; 'Et de mes tristes jours n'attendais que la fin.' *Ester* 1.1.

48 'Madonna, ciascun vostro parente e ogni bolognese credono e hanno per certo voi esser morta, per che niuna persona è la quale più a casa v'aspetti', 10.4.

49 In Montaigne, sometimes we await death but at other times death awaits us: 'Il est incertain où la mort nous attende, attendons la par tout. La premeditation de la mort est premeditation de la liberté,' 1.20.

50 'Rebuke and dread correction wait on us', *1 King Henry IV* 5.1.

51 As in the demons with huge scourges in Dante, where no one would wait for the second stroke or the third: 'vidi demon cornuti con gran ferze, / che li battien crudelmente di retro. / Ahi come facean lor levar le berze / a le prime percosse! già nessuno / le seconde aspettava né le terze,' *Inferno* 18.34–39; *cf.* 'I' vidi, e anco il cor me n'accapriccia, / uno aspettar così, com' elli 'ncontra / ch'una rana rimane e l'altra spiccia', *Inferno* 22.29–30.

52 'Scanderberch, prince de l'Epire, suyvant un soldat des siens pour le tuer, et ce soldat ayant essayé par toute espece d'humilité et de supplication, de l'appaiser, se resolut

on waiting *per se* but extraordinary maltreatment, with the cruel intention of hurting people. Still, in behaviour without violence, waiting may also be experienced as an indignity.[53] To make people wait is an insult but also an expression of power relations: to appear, wait till my voice calls you, as Racine says.[54] In a power struggle, one may beg one person to wait for another to achieve reconciliation.[55] If you make me wait indefinitely, I eventually face a crisis. Do I persist in my patience and risk an outrageous loss of time, or do I give up, defeated by the negation, by the absence, the lack of an advent?[56] I feel disempowered by the threat of mounting disappointment but also anxiety about leaving my post, abandoning the attendance that I might have been trusted to see out. Being denied an audience when I am expected to attend leaves me indisposed. In some ways, the absence of waiting defines our independence.[57] For those reasons, I do not want to keep anyone waiting. Apart from the personal hurt, it means that my colleague is unproductive, not functioning optimally in my organization. We do not want people to be kept waiting in any circumstance; and contemporary employment arrangements are contrived to disguise the indignity of power relations, so that even junior employees are not made to feel any inferiority by having to wait for their superiors.[58]

The structure of waiting is more apparent in premodern societies in which there was a class of people—servants and even slaves—whose purpose was

---

à toute extrémité de l'attendre l'espée au poing. Cette sienne resolution arresta sus bout la furie de son maistre, qui, pour luy avoir veu prendre un si honorable party, le receut en grace,' 1.1. In the theatre of Racine, you do not wait for the fatal stroke: it waits for you: 'Du coup qui vous attend vous mourrez moins que moi,' *Iphigénie* 4.4; 'As wretches have o'ernight / That wait for execution in the morn', *Two gentlemen of Verona* 4.2.

53   'they would shame to make me / Wait else at door', *Henry VIII* 5.2; 'Was it discretion, lords, to let this man ... wait like a lousy footboy / At chamber-door?', *Henry VIII* 5.3.

54   'Pour paraître attendez que ma voix vous appelle,' *Athalie* 5.4.

55   'Mon fils, au nom des dieux, / Attendez-le plutôt,' *La Thébaïde* 3.5; *cf.* 'Pour saluer son frère attend qu'il le salue', *La Thébaïde* 4.3.

56   Waiting encourages paradox: 'Je meurs si je vous perds, mais je meurs si j'attends,' Racine, *Andromaque* 3.7; there is always a question of how long someone will wait: 'A me chercher lui-même attendrait-il si tard', *Bajazet* 3.3; and sometimes the waiting is false: 'L'ingrat qui ne m'attend que pour m'abandonner, *Iphigénie* 2.5; 'Je ne l'attends ici que pour m'en séparer,' *Iphigénie* 2.4.

57   As Don John says, 'eat when I have stomach, and wait for no man's leisure', Shakespeare, *Much ado about nothing* 1.3.

58   Unlike in the past, Racine, for example: 'Assemblé par mon ordre, attend ma volonté,' *Bajazet* 3.5; or a whole people: 'Un peuple obéissant vous attend à genoux', *Mithridate* 1.3.

to wait, a reality with traces in our own language, like lady-in-waiting or waiting woman, to wait on someone,[59] and which persists in contemporary language with terms like 'waiter'.[60] Beyond the biblical uses already observed from Roman times, the Greeks had a vast vocabulary to describe waiting. It is hard to imagine that so many terms could have been hatched by language unless the reality were both common and inflected. For instance, there is a group that takes its root fom the verb to wait for (δοκάζω), which uses many prepositions,[61] and an even larger group around the verb to stay or wait (μένω).[62] Another group has its origin in the verb to sit (ἑδριάω), which could sometimes signal dutiful attendance (παρεδρία) or a sinister lying in wait (ἐφέδρευσις) in a pattern replicated in Latin, where the root for sitting supplies waiting words of caring attendance (assiduitas, assideo, like our assiduousness) but also waylaying (insidior, insidiator, insidiatrix, like our insidious), which is waiting for an opportunity to strike.[63] There are other words in Greek that relate to waiting, the most telling of which concern watching or attendance, as in the verbs to wait for, watch for (ἀποτηρέω).[64]

Attention shares an origin with waiting, and with good reason, because attention is a special kind of waiting where we expect to learn. Leaving aside

---

59 e.g. Maria in *Twelfth Night*; 'Thy friends are fled, to wait upon thy foes', *Richard II* 2.4.

60 Also with prepositions like on or upon, as in Shakespeare: 'Cold wisdom waiting on superfluous folly', *All's well that ends well* 1.1; 'I'll wait upon your honour', *Measure for measure* 1.1; 'I must wait on myself, must I?' *Merry wives of Windsor* 1.1; 'the wealth I have waits on my consent', *ibid.* 3.2; 'I'll wait upon you instantly', *Timon of Athens* 2.2.

61 Including the sinister lie in wait for (ἀμφιδοκεύω), waiting, watching (δεδοκημένος), wait for a fair wind (πλουδοκέω), wait for the outcome of (καραδοκέω).

62 Inclined to wait, patient (μενετός), one must wait for (μενητέον), wait, stay (μιμνάζω), wait longer (ἐπαναμένω), stay on, tarry (ἐπιμένω), wait for, await (περιμένω), wait for, await (ἀναμένω), wait instead of (ἀνταναμένω), bide, wait (προσμένω), stay behind (ὑπομένω).

63 Wait, attend upon (παρεδρεύω), attendance (παρεδρία), lying in wait (ἐφέδρευσις), sitting in (ἐνέδρα), lie in wait for, lay snares for (ἐνεδρεύω) as in 'Laying wait for him (ἐνεδρεύοντες αὐτὸν), and seeking to catch something out of his mouth, that they might accuse him.' *Luke* 11.54; see also wait, attend upon (παρεδρεύω), attendance (παρεδρία), sit near, wait (προσεδρεύω), wait in reserve (συνεφεδρεύω), constantly attending (εὐπάρεδρος), lying in wait (ἐφέδρευσις), sitting in (ἐνέδρα), lie in wait for, lay snares for (ἐνεδρεύω); on the sinister side see also lie in wait for, waylay (λοχάω), lying in wait, treacherous (λοχητικός), lie in wait for (λοχίζω), lying in wait by night (νυκτιλόχος), one that waited about the altars, to beg or steal some of the meat offered thereon (βωμόλοχος), a place where one lies in wait, lurking-place (προδόκη, προδοκή), lie in wait for (προδοκάζω).

64 Or to lie in wait for continually (διαπαρατηρέομαι) but see also to serve as an attendant, tend, care for (ἀμφιπολεύω), wait and watch against (ἀντιμέλλω), serve, wait on (ἀοζέω), servant (διάκονος), take care of, provide for (κομίζω), attend to (ἐπιμελεδαίνω), wait (προσανέχω).

the Greek conceptions, the French word for waiting (*attendre*) is the same as our attend and therefore attention, which in earlier English writing could also be used as waiting, as when Anne says: 'The dinner attends you, sir', meaning not that you are waiting for dinner but the dinner is waiting for you, just as 'good digestion waits on appetite'.[65] In French, as in any language, waiting does not necessarily have positive associations, because bad things can await us.[66] In the tragedies of Racine, for example, waiting can be about cultivating patience over revenge;[67] it can be about a threat,[68] impatience over attention,[69] the great unlikeliness of a favour,[70] a delight long desired[71] and, of course, expectation,[72] and every shade between.[73]

---

65   *Merry wives of Windsor* 1.1 and *Macbeth* 3.4 or 'Le trône vous attend', *La Thébaïde* 5.3. Waiting is often attributed to inanimate things: 'Prêts à vous recevoir, mes vaisseaux vous attendent', *Mithridate* 1.3; *cf.* Shakespeare, 'For he's no man on whom perfections wait', *Pericles* 1.1; 'Tell me what fate awaits the Duke of Suffolk?' *2 Henry VI* 1.4; 'When care, mistrust, and treason wait on him.' *3 Henry VI* 2.5.

66   'J'y trouve des malheurs qui m'attendaient encore,' Racine, *Mithridate* 2.3; 'Je l'attends, cette mort, et je l'attends sans plainte', *La Thébaïde ou les frères ennemis* 2.2.

67   'Attends, Hémon, dit-il, tu vas être vengé.' *La Thébaïde* 5.3; 'J'irais attendre ailleurs une lente vengeance?', *Andromaque* 4.3; 'J'attendais en secret le retour d'un parjure', *Andromaque* 4.5.

68   'N'en attendez jamais qu'une paix sanguinaire', *Mithridate* 3.1; 'J'attendrai mon arrêt, vous pouvez commander.' *Mithridate* 4.4; 'Le roi désespéré / Lui-même n'attend plus qu'un trépas assuré,' *Mithridate* 5.1; 'Ah! du moins attendez qu'un fidèle rapport / De son malheureux frère ait confirmé la mort,' *Mithridate* 5.1; 'Sors, traître: n'attends pas qu'un père furieux / Te fasse avec opprobre arracher de ces lieux,' *Phèdre* 4.2.

69   'Elle l'attend, Seigneur, avec impatience.' *Bérénice* 3.1; 'Bérénice t'attend. Où viens-tu, téméraire?', *Bérénice* 4.4.

70   'Et quand le ciel s'apprête à nous l'abandonner, / J'attendrai qu'un tyran daigne nous pardonner?', *Alexandre* 1.2; 'J'attendrais son salut de la main d'Alexandre? / Mais quel miracle enfin n'en dois-je point attendre?', *Alexandre* 5.2.

71   'Du bruit de ses exploits mon âme importune / Attend depuis longtemps cette heureuse journée,' *Alexandre* 1.2; 'Te jure une amitié si longtemps attendue;' *Alexandre* 4.1; 'Où sont ces heureux jours que je faisais attendre?' *Bérénice* 4.4; 'Et de ce peu de jours si longtemps attendus', *Bérénice* 4.4; *cf.* 'Seigneur, l'amour toujours n'attend pas la raison,' *Britannicus* 2.2; 'Vous devez à ce jour dès longtemps vous attendre.' *Mithridate* 2.4.

72   'Ton indigne courage attend que l'on te prie?', *Alexandre* 3.2; 'Ah! n'espérez de moi que de sincères vœux, / Madame; n'attendez ni menaces ni chaînes.' *Alexandre* 3.2; 'Quel traitement, mon frère, en devons-nous attendre?', *Alexandre* 3.3; 'On attend peu d'amour d'un héros tel que vous', *Alexandre* 3.6; 'Quoi? vous en attendez quelque injure nouvelle?', *Andromaque* 2.1; 'Mon désespoir n'attend que leur indifférence:' *Andromaque* 2.2; 'N'attendît en ces lieux qu'un témoin tel que vous', *Andromaque* 2.4.

73   'Cher Pylade, crois-moi, ta pitié te séduit. / Laisse-moi des périls dont j'attends tout le fruit,' *Andromaque* 3.1; 'Enfin qu'attendez-vous? Il vous offre sa tête', *Andromaque* 4.3; 'Quels honneurs dans sa cour, quel rang pourrais-je attendre?', *Britannicus* 4.2; 'Voici le temps, Seigneur, où vous devez attendre / Le fruit de tant de sang qu'ils vous ont vu répandre.' *Bérénice* 1.3; 'Je n'attendais que vous pour témoin de ma joie,' *Bérénice* 1.4; 'Quel succès attend-on d'un amour si fidèle?'. *Bérénice* 2.2.

The French verb (*attendre*) can also mean attend, as in English, as when people attend the temple.[74] The link between waiting and attendance is so strong that Shakespeare even uses the two words together: 'wait attendance / Till you hear further from me'; and, ending *Pericles*, Gower congratulates and blesses the audience: 'So, on your patience evermore attending, / New joy wait on you!'[75] It is typical of English that we have two words, a Germanic one (to wait) and a French one (to attend). They do not mean exactly the same thing, in the same way that attending and attention do not mean exactly the same thing. If we put the three together—wait → attend → attention—a scale of interactivity is apparent. It is possible to wait but not attend, as when we wait to get in the door but find that the room is full. And on a less physical level, it is possible to attend but not to pay attention, a condition that we fear among our students in large classes, where the attendees are definitely in the room but their level of engagement with the content is low; and sometimes attendance is negative.[76] Without doubt, the most intellectual of the three terms is attention, though it could involve any level of psychological engagement and not just attention to an argument. For example, one might or might not return flirtation with erotic attention. We might disdain to notice someone, pay him or her no attention, which is a slight. These forms of psychological attention have something in common, namely that they involve different kinds of waiting on the part of the person who seeks attention and the person who pays attention. The person seeking attention—as active as she or he may be—is effectively waiting; but the person who either does or does not reciprocate with attention is not waiting in the same sense (unless he or she cannot wait to get away) but is assessing the bid and what would make the best response.

Attention has waiting in it. There is no attention without some kind of waiting; and so the three terms do not describe a hierarchy, with waiting at the bottom and attention at the top. They are necessary to one another, with attendance (real or virtual) as the precondition of attention. But attention is liable to wander, including when we attend; and, as noted, attendance is no guarantee of attention. We get distracted when we ought to be riveted

---

74   'Qu'un peuple obéissant l'attende dans le temple', *Bajazet* 3.2; 'Il attend de mes soins ce fidèle secours.' *Britannicus* 2.2; *cf.* 'Et je l'attends déjà comme un roi doit attendre', *Alexandre* 2.2; 'Vous attendez le roi: parlez, et lui montrez', *Andromaque* 1.1; 'Dans mon appartement qu'il m'attende avec vous,' *Britannicus* 4.3; 'Dans son appartement m'attend pour m'embrasser,' *Britannicus* 5.1; 'Madame, à d'autres pleurs vous devez vous attendre,' *Bérénice* 5.6.

75   *Timon of Athens* 1.1; *Pericles* 5.3.

76   Or even treacherous: 'I fear I am attended by some spies,' *Two gentlemen of Verona* 5.1.

to the theme. In a sense, however, the tendency to slip away into a different headspace, to succumb to other thoughts that race prolifically through the mind, is also a failure to wait. The precondition of attention remains waiting; because instead of generating an oneiric efflorescence of images or narratives that distract from the theme, we resign ourselves to waiting for guidance. The speaker, let us imagine the teacher in the classroom, cannot possibly keep our attention at 100% all the time. So the person who attends with patchy attention experiences a strong temptation to think of other things; and faced with this seduction, the quickest route back into attention is to construe the hiatus as a failure of concentration and to wait for the concentration to return.

The teacher cannot directly condition the degree of attention that a student pays but can nevertheless influence the likelihood beyond supplying the stimulating content that we assume but through judiciously aerating the student's expectations. It was already observed in the renaissance that strategies like humour are sometimes about deceiving expectations. Castiglione identifies humour as an aspect of conversation when the interlocutor's responses are contrary to what you expect: you take a natural delight in your own error; and when you find yourself tricked by what you are waiting for, you laugh.[77] If so, you have developed a considerable stake in the thinking and your attention is guaranteed. This level of engagement, which is afforded by surprise and where you are conscious of your own thought process, is not just a retake, not just a metacognitive triangulation of ideas but also an event in time that makes you wait, that has you expecting something in an interval that ends differently to how you imagined. We wait on our thought. As instantaneous as the joke may seem at the point of the punchline, the mistaken trajectory of your mind has been building up, during all of which you wait on thought itself, which is why when we make jokes in common speech we sometimes preface the punchline with the phrase 'wait for it'.

In some languages, the imperative tense of waiting—as in the instruction 'wait a minute'—takes a reflexive form: wait yourself (*aspettati*), as if waiting is a practice that contains or limits your impatience.[78] To wait

---

77 'Di questa sorte di motti adunque assai si ride, perché portan seco risposte contrarie a quello che l'omo aspetta d'udire, e naturalmente dilettaci in tai cose il nostro errore medesimo; dal quale quando ci trovamo ingannati di quello che aspettiamo, ridemo.' Castiglione, *Cortegiano* 2.63.

78 'aspettati, io voglio vedere se tu vi puoi andare e chiamerotti,' Boccaccio, *Decameron* 7.3; 'Che è questo, Angiulieri? vogliancene noi andare ancora? Deh aspettati un poco: egli dee venir qui testeso uno che ha pegno il mio farsetto per trentotto soldi: son certo che egli cel renderà per trentacinque pagandol testé,' *ibid.* 9.4.

yourself, then, has special bearing on wavering attention as a reflective act of discipline that you do to yourself, where you as the listener pay special attention not only to the content of the speaker but also your response to it or your control of the reception.

'The main thing', Castiglione says, 'is to fool opinion and to respond differently to how the listener expects (or what he or she waits for)'.[79] We keep people guessing, keep them amused, keep them awaiting the next thought. Though often invoked crudely and extraneously, without a compelling relationship to the argument, jokes are a sign of the necessary process or expectations which are not fulfilled by something predictable. 'It seems to me', Castiglione says, 'that a joke is nothing but a friendly trick with things that do not offend, or at least not much; and just like saying something contrary to expectation in facetious pleasantries, so in jokes the act of going against expectation induces the smile.'[80] This charm is deeply engaging. There is no likelihood that we will become bored because we are suddenly and pleasurably induced to go searching for the unlikely: that which we do not expect. Up to a point, the unexpected—what we are not awaiting—is a surprise with an impact that leaves us defenceless.[81] With some admixture of humour or lightness in an educational environment, we would rather say 'disarmed'.

Waiting is a reponse to uncertainty. It is one of the more logical strategies in the face of any indecision: rather than rush in prematurely, you 'wait and see'.[82] With an adroit exploitation of ambiguities, Shakespeare observes the link between waiting and uncertainty. Titus says: 'We wait for certain money here, sir.' And Flavius replies: 'Ay, / If money were as certain as your waiting, / 'Twere sure enough.'[83] The first 'wait' goes with a positive mission to

---

79 'la principal cosa è lo ingannar la opinione e rispondere altramente che quello che aspetta l'auditore', *Cortegiano* 2.83.

80 'E' parmi che la burla non sia altro che un inganno amichevole di cose che non offendano, o almen poco; e sì come nelle facezie il dir contra l'aspettazione, così nelle burle il far contra l'aspettazione induce il riso,' 2.85.

81 So Montaigne: 'Je ne me puis deffendre, si le bruit esclattant d'une harquebusade vient à me frapper les oreilles à l'improuveu, en lieu où je ne le deusse pas attendre, que je n'en tressaille', *Essais* 1.12.

82 It is a very common expression, with Google returning 27 million pages through "wait and see". Castiglione counsels: 'Però se 'l primo giorno, sentendo ragionare un gentilomo, non comprenderete che in lui sia quel valore che avevate prima imaginato, non così presto vi spogliarete della bona opinione come in quelle cose delle quali l'occhio sùbito è giudice, ma aspettarete di dì in dì scoprir qualche altra nascosta virtù tenendo pur ferma sempre quella impressione che v'è nata dalle parole di tanti', *Cortegiano* 2.33.

83 *Timon of Athens* 3.4; the paradoxical coupling of certainty and waiting (or impulsiveness) also occurs in Montaigne, 'Le demon de Socrates estoit à l'advanture

recover the debt, not to give up till the credit is repaid. The second 'waiting', however, reveals that the mission may fail: it is all a matter of probability and the course of events must unfold. It is the reason Castiglione had recommended not to entertain unrealistic expectations for fame, 'because our spirits often form ideas that are impossible to match, and you thus lose more than you gain'.[84]

Uncertainty is the reason that the motif of waiting arises most in literature when there is the greatest amount of action. The more happens, the more someone has to wait for the outcome or proffer attendance. With the exception of modern classics like Samuel Beckett's *Waiting for Godot*, waiting—especially the command in the imperative—is proportional to how busy we are. When everything is in a hurry, we privilege various jobs and beg others to wait till we can turn our attention to them. In the eighteenth century, there is an epidemic of waiting, because the pace of theatre, for example, is so heightened that the protagonists are always exhorting one another to wait. Take the comedies of Carlo Goldoni. His amusing dramatic turns and twists often see one person waiting (or failing to wait) for another; and then there are innumerable *peripetiae* that incite rapid resolutions, as panic and anxiety cause the actors to demand that they wait. Waiting adds greatly to the drama.[85] In *The discontents*, a young damsel says 'I don't want them to be kept waiting for me', to which Leonardo selfishly replies: 'What should that bother me? Let them wait.'[86]

It is an instructive paradox: these concentrations of noisy activity, where there is a multiple claim on limited attention, coincide with a need for

---

certaine impulsion de volonté, qui se présentoit à luy, sans attendre le conseil de son discours,' *Essais* 1.11; *cf.* Shakespeare: 'I purpose not to wait on fortune till / These wars determine', *Coriolanus* 5.3.

84 'Però non so come sia bene dar queste aspettazioni e mandar innanzi quella fama; perché gli animi nostri spesso formano cose alle quali impossibil è poi corrispondere, e così più se ne perde che non si guadagna', *Cortegiano* 2.33.

85 In *Il servitore di due padroni* alone: 'Ha detto che mi aspetterà sulla strada,' 1.5; 'Son stuffo d'aspettar, che no posso più,' 1.6; 'Aspettava proprio che io lo maltrattassi,' 1.8; 'prendetele e portatele subito, che vi aspetto,' 1.8; 'Bravissimo. Così mi aspetti? ... V'aspetto ancora ... E perchè vieni a aspettarmi qui, e non nella strada dove ti ho detto? ... sbrigati, che ti aspetto,' 1.9; 'Retirete, camerada, e aspetteme su quel canton', 1.13; 'non per questo si ha da precipitare. ... Ritirati in qualche loco, e aspettami; esci di questo cortile, non facciamo scene. Aspetterò io il signor Pantalone ... Vi aspetto dallo speziale,' 2.1; 'E sempre bisogna aspettarlo,' 2.15; 'm'aspetto qualche altra insolenza,' 3.5; 'Vi aspetterò dal signor Pantalone; di là non parto, se non venite,' 3.9.

86 *I malcontenti* 1.3; see also the same play 1.9, 2.2, 2.3, 2.4, 2.8, 2.13, 3.1, 3.13, 3.14; *Il ritorno dalla villeggiatura* 1.1, 1.3, 1.4, 2.11, 3.2, 3.5, 3.7; *Le avventure della villeggiatura* 1.3, 2.2, 3.4, 3.11; *Le smanie per la villeggiatura* 1.9, 2.2, 2.4, 2.12, 3.1, 3.9, 3.19; *La bottega del caffè* 1.8, 1.10, 2.2, 2.7, 3.18.

waiting. It is a dialectical structure which has a bearing on the internal dynamics of learning. The intellectual intensity of learning burns up attention. Thoughts contend for attention and, for every bit of stimulation that we add, more waiting is needed, more prioritizing demanded and more patience is required. You always have to wait for your thoughts to come into alignment with the ambient stimuli. Nothing makes the connexion automatically. It is a process that happens between will and imagination, a need and sympathy, urgency and freedom. In its busy narratives and satirical humour, the comic stage of the eighteenth century is a good analogy to the cognitive process of learning: we always have to wait for the next bit that makes sense of the last; and the greater the complexity, the greater the call upon the mind to wait and appreciate the wit. Like the comic genius of the eighteenth-century stage, the patience goes with vivacity. One is never dragooned into waiting but rather it is part of a happy process in which a succession of moments makes sense.

Waiting without an expectation but only curiosity is intellectual innocence. The more one witnesses the richness of these historical concepts of attention and waiting, the more one can see the impoverished understanding embodied in our educational concepts of expectation. Expectations are primary in educational design, symbolized like a cognitive entitlement in the institution of learning outcomes. Expectations are now supposedly controlled and activated as the learning outcomes in the student: the student has already been given to expect that certain things will be reached, certain capabilities will be realized and goals will be achieved. Setting the expectations and 'being absolutely clear' about what you expect from students is one of the great monitory clichés that academics are enjoined to ensure. It is part of the grand transactional anxiety, that expectations can be reasonably defined so that the student can meet them, fulfil them, possess a blueprint and act slavishly toward their realization.

Personally, I have found that the fewer expectations that I have, the more I am delighted by what students come up with. My expectations are not as important as theirs; but I do wait for the ideas to grow and surprise me, which, of course, is worth waiting for. I wait with a waiting that is neither impatience nor expectation; because it is a kind of love on my part that waits for a kind of love on their part. Expectation would kill this curious affection and turn it into a sense of entitlement which is doomed because destined to disappointment; but the process of waiting is itself autonomously energizing and integral to learning rather than an expectation that a contract will be fulfilled.

Chapter 8

SUBJECTIVITY

We can never be creative without comfort in our subjectivity. As individuals, we depend upon confidence in our own imagination; and this faith in ourselves to wage our wits in an independent spirit in turn depends upon our security with our selves. There is always some difficulty describing this core of personhood, this self-possessed seat of consciousness which we might once have bundled up with mystical language such as the person's spirit or soul. In today's institutional frameworks, such terms are embarrassing and no one is likely to invoke them in the formulation of new educational theory. But other terms circulate in contemporary discourse that are more institutionally palatable; and one of the more acceptable acknowledgements of the student's personhood is subjectivity. The student's subjectivity is the site, if you like, where learning takes place. The ability of the student warmly to approach some new learning challenge depends on building an imaginative connexion with her or his subjectivity, so that the learning enters the intimacy of the student's view of herself or himself. This ontological core of the student's self is the point at which syllabus has a toehold or not. If I cannot find the match between the material to be learned and my subjectivity, I will learn anxiously, joylessly and without ownership.

Fatefully, however, subjectivity is not easy to define, as it means both an inalienable quality of a person's being (and is consequently central to the integrity of a person's work) and a weakness in method.[1]

All forms of education put pressure on the subjective. Most evaluation methodologies are skewed toward the systematic elimination of subjectivity. For fairness' sake and also out of respect for the paradigms of science, we are intolerant of subjectivity, even if we acknowledge that it might in some way form part of the engine of invention. To accept subjectivity within

---

1   Parts of this chapter are grafted from an unrefereed conference paper, 'Toward a history of subjectivity: a call for the deconstruction of rigour', *Art.Media.Design | Writing Intersections*, Swinburne University of Technology, November 18–19, 2009 pp. 78–87.

judgements risks the arbitrary. In all forms of scholarship, it does not suffice to call upon subjective impressions but to support them with evidence; and, once the data have been assembled and a case can be argued, the subjective impressions are, to a large extent, redundant and dispensible. In research, the subjective impressions are only as good as the facts that prove them; and on their own, they do not qualify as research. My subjectivity could be antithetical to your subjectivity; and, alas, the only mediation imaginable in this clash of opinion is an appeal to objectivity or some other means of triangulation related to values that can somehow be calibrated, as if in some sense absolute. As a scholar myself, I have no polemic against this regime of verification, by which material generated with intuition is laundered of its subjectivity and somehow holds up in the cold light of objective judgement.

As if the ghost of relativity, the subjective is not naturally a welcome partner in coursework evaluation or research method. In most disciplines, the canonical proofs or tests of plausibility cleave to objective evidence, and the subjective is attenuated or marginalized as much as possible. The persuasiveness of the case is generally respected on account of objective evidence and associated logical argument dispelling interpretative chaos.

Alas, the restrictions of the objective become dysfunctional in creative fields, which then creates a problem of method. The distinguishing feature of the artistic process is its subjectivity: the unique consciousness of the person who speaks or sees or acts. As an inalienable property of perception and narrative, subjectivity is a necessary ingredient of the creative process, and perhaps representation of all kinds. In their *Thousand Plateaux*, Deleuze & Guattari describe how the projection of meaning in Western culture requires a white wall; but this is always punctured by the black hole of subjectivity.[2] Similarly embedding the concept as crucial and inevitable for individual autonomy, Nicolas Bourriaud explains how the creative allows for changes to subjectivity, so that it becomes negotiable for the individual: 'Art is the thing upon and around which subjectivity can reform itself.'[3] And Monique Roelofs has said that 'Aesthetic experience is preserved and understood as a space for authentic subjectivity.'[4] Throughout contemporary theory, no one actually denounces subjectivity as bad, even if it is unconsciously

2   Gilles Deleuze et Félix Guattari, *Mille plateaux*, Minuit, Paris 1980.

3   Nicolas Bourriaud, *Relational aesthetics*, translated by Simon Pleasance & Fronza Woods with the participation of Mathieu Copeland, original title: *Esthétique relationnelle*, Les presses du réel, 2003, p. 97.

4   Monique Roelofs, *Aesthetification as a Feminist Strategy: On Art's Relational Politics*, eds, Davies and Sukla, Westport, Praeger, 2003, p. 197.

seen as indulgent throughout the educational systems of the Anglophone world. Alas, subjectivity is sometimes banished even in arts and humanities when assessment comes into its habitual anxiety and fears of arbitrariness set in. All learning outcomes, assessment criteria and marking rubrics are subjectivity-averse.

In the same way that creative output can condition an otherwise fixed subjectivity so that subjectivity itself may develop, subjectivity as a form of centred consciousness is necessary to the growth of the individual as well as the developmental structure of any creative idea that an individual entertains. For an essay to have expressive authenticity, its ideas and voice must accord with privacy of thought, intuitions genuinely grounded in the 'me', the ego, where all things make sense and whence all expressions proceed if they are sincere.

In any discipline, students depend for their motivation on a personal impulse which should not be excessively compromised or negated by positivistic methodology. In arts and humanities, however, the most interesting aspects of student work are those which are imaginatively *sui generis*, which have their own voice and subjective integrity. The anxious pressure to square the work within referenced coordinates, policed by a canon of rigour, is an uncomfortable fit, at times misguided and anti-inspirational. The application of rigorous objective standards must be moderated in any creative undertaking to accommodate its subjective complexions. These are in many ways antithetical to what is normally considered rigorous method in conventional academic disciplines. The concept of rigour must be deconstructed,[5] but especially in its misguided zeal for research questions and epistemological structure.

To explain the paradox of subjectivity being necessary to creative output and foreign to proof of quality, it is useful to examine the concept historically. In fact the concept of subjectivity by that name is relatively new and remains fugitive, powerless and vulnerable. Further, no sooner did subjectivity emerge than it was suspected. The term may be considered disparagingly, as with Hare in 1827 impatiently decrying 'those who cannot get quit of their subjectivity, or write about objects objectively'.[6] The grim preposition 'sub' haunts this conception, as if destined to the lower zones

---

5   See my article 'Toward a history of rigour: an examination of the nasty side of scholarship', *Arts and Humanities in Higher Education*, vol. 10, no. 4, October 2011, pp. 374–387 (doi: 10.1177/1474022211408797); see also my book *The jealousy of ideas: research methods in the creative arts*, London and Melbourne, Goldsmiths (WritingPAD) and Ellikon, 2009.

6   *OED, s.v.*

of ambiguity and confusion. And even the quintessentially subjectivist philosopher Nietzsche in 1885 acknowledges a damnable self-definition or self-referentiality (*verfluchten Ipsissimosität*) in everything subjective, which you can become utterly fed up with (*bis zum Sterben satt gewesen!*). Just the same, he warns against accepting the objective spirit, which entails spiritual destruction of the self and depersonalizing (*Entselbstung und Entpersönlichung*) under the title of disinterest.[7]

My challenge in this chapter is to provide an analysis of why subjectivity—given its centrality to the motivational integrity of anyone doing anything personally meaningful—has proved so evasive, so contradictory and fragile that it seldom forms part of a syllabus unless apologetically. There is scarcely a precondition more essential to learning and creativity and scarcely a quality more abject in academia.

Subjectivity was presumably always an element in artistic production but, like creativity itself, it only began to be recognized recently. Like creativity, it has a development from a simple noun or verb (subject) to an adjective (subjective) to an abstract noun (subjectivity). The abstract word is of nineteenth-century coinage, the substantive 'subjectivity' appearing first in 1821, following a slow development of the 'subjective' from mechanical origins in the renaissance to the enlightenment, where it may describe, say, the 'Subjective certainty … in the infinite Mind'.[8] In the romantic period, the idea is installed in feeling, from 'an internal subjective discovery' to 'an internal, personal, private, subjective diorama'.[9] The peculiarity to a single person is emphasized in 1876: 'a subjective sentiment … each individual experiences it in a degree and manner peculiar to himself' or herself.[10]

To add lexical insult to artistic injury, the term 'subject matter' involves the opposite elements to subjectivity. How did the motif attract the words subject matter? The apple or jug in a still life is equally the motif for another artist who treats it differently: the vision is different, but not the apple. Thus 'subject' turns out to be invariable or absolute: in a painting, it is (bizarrely) the objective element. When we speak of the subject of a painting, alas, it means the common topic, neither the artist nor his or her receptiveness and individual treatment. The authorial confession—which in another discourse we would characterize through subjectivity—is not reflected in what we call the subject of the picture.

7   *Jenseits von Gut und Böse*, 207.
8   Oldfield 1707, *OED*, *s.v.*
9   Boston 1850, *OED*, *s.v.*
10   Groote 1876, *OED*, *s.v.*

Language was never so perverse as in this contradiction. Grammar gives a strict definition to the word subject. In any sentence, the subject is unequivocally distinguished from the object by a simple structure. The subject is the independent person or thing which exists or acts. 'The chair holds the door open.' In such a sentence, the chair is the subject because it commands the verb. The door is the object because it is acted upon. A sentence must always have a subject though not always an object. You can say, for example: I sit. There is a subject (I) but no object. The destination—where or in what do you sit?—is missing. In sentence construction, there is no need to add an object but you cannot subtract the subject, which is indispensable. The subject, always taking the nominative case, is the centre, the point of departure. So if you translate this to art and imagine the act of painting, the subject ought to be the painter who paints, the author who senses and feels and registers, the prior body who sees the object, the apple or jug, and apprehends and depicts. Sadly, however, this dynamic in the act of painting does not transfer to the picture. Of the oil-painting itself, the subject is the objects that the painter has depicted.

So when we say instead that the apple or jug is the subject, we witness the first denial of subjectivity, the treachery of language in the artist's studio which robs the artist of his or her position as the instigator and maker. By this deceptive protocol, a person can walk into the studio and describe the subject without ever having to refer to the artist. And the same thing occurs in the writer's studio too: the subject of the poem is not the poet (who possesses the receptiveness, is the origin of the response and who has wrought the evocation) but the sunset or wind tormenting the window which the poet has evoked. The first instances of the word which was later to become 'subject' in ancient Greece in fact mean subject matter.[11] This linguistic sleight of hand testifies to a great shyness over subjectivity, which is also a reluctance to recognize the agency of artistic process. If language can own the result of an artwork, it would prefer not to have to grapple with its gestation. This evasion is confusing for studio artists seeking to elaborate and advance the gestational, in which subjectivity is of maximum importance. Language itself expropriates the artist's privilege.

But if subjectivity is a nineteenth-century conception, we might ask what existed before its invention? What is the prehistory of subjectivity? In other words, what is the understanding of subjectivity—or the counterpart of subjectivity by some other name—before it was named? These questions are

---

11   Aristotle, *Nicomachean Ethics* 1094ᵇ12, 1098ᵃ28.

not answered in the major studies in the field, such as Reto Luzius Fetz, Roland Hagenbüchle and Peter Schulz, *Geschichte und Vorgeschichte der modernen Subjektivität.*

In ancient Greece for example, the nearest word for subject (ὑποκείμενον) was still used in a verbal sense and has no metaphoric dimension: it means 'that which lies before us or lies to hand'. The nearest conceptions to subjectivity relate to what we would call the soul. Each person possesses a cell of individual consciousness, which is more than the operation of thinking (νόος) but some integrity of character, feeling and being which I suppose is what we still mean by soul, though we seldom use the word in a professional context; and, perhaps because of its mystifying spiritualism, it has receded to the sub-professional. In archaic Greece, the soul (ψυχή) is not well distinguished as a locus of consciousness so much as a force that keeps people alive and without which they die, an *animus*, if you like, which leads to the Latin *anima* in a way that is not coincidental; for these conceptions of life were relatively mechanistic. In Homeric society, greater dynamism of perception and subjective response to circumstances was expressed by the seat of emotion (θυμός); but these conceptions are vague and do not have the specificity of soul much less subjectivity, as is revealed in a beautiful analysis by Bruno Snell.[12] And tellingly, the word loses potency in classical and later antiquity and is more active in the abstract compound, meaning desire (ἐπιθυμία).

It is strange, given the extraordinary sophistication and sensitivity of Greek art. As Auerbach found in his monumental study of the representation of reality,[13] immediacy of feeling is more likely to be registered among the ancient Jews than the Greeks, noting a much more subjectivist and perhaps less intellectual soul in the *Bible*. Here, a person's soul can command a sense of attachment: 'his soul clave unto Dinah';[14] or moody negotiation: 'O my soul, come not thou into their secret'.[15] In spite of such statements of passion, the soul is often a mechanical expression for naming a person, as when souls are counted like head of cattle. Compared to our romantic conceptions, however, the soul is institutional: it is the part of a person that recommends itself to God and society, by analogy to the flesh that has not

---

12   Bruno Snell, *Die Entdeckung des Geistes*, Vandenhoeck & Ruprecht, Göttingen, (originally 1975) 5th ed. 1980, pp. 18 ff.

13   Erich Auerbach, *Mimesis: dargestellte Wirklichkeit in der abendländischen Literatur*, Bern, Francke, 1967.

14   *Genesis* 34.3.

15   *Genesis* 49.6.

been ceremonially mutilated: 'the uncircumcised man child whose flesh of his foreskin is not circumcised, that soul shall be cut off from his people; he hath broken my covenant.'[16]

So too with the heart, which is prolifically invoked; and sure, there are examples where depth and passion are felt. But the heart is also very instrumental, a receptacle of ingrained determinations: 'God saw that the wickedness of man was great in the earth, and that every imagination of the thoughts of his heart was only evil continually'.[17] The heart is the organ in which thinking takes place; but it does not reveal much scope for receiving impressions. It is rather a dead metaphor. Other less profound words could be substituted and the sense would not change. For example when the patriarch-to-be is informed by God that his wife will have a baby, 'Abraham fell upon his face, and laughed, and said in his heart, Shall a child be born unto him that is an hundred years old? and shall Sarah, who is ninety years old, bear?'[18] The text goes: 'he said it in his heart'; but we could just as easily translate it as: 'he said to himself' or perhaps 'he sincerely thought'.

Because the heart is deep inside us, it is used as a metaphor for truth, as with 'the integrity of my heart'.[19] And because it argues for truth, it is called upon to bear witness, a tool to establish legal integrity. Strikingly, Jesus says 'That whosoever looketh on a woman to lust after her hath committed adultery with her already in his heart (ἐν τῇ καρδίᾳ)'.[20] This heart is an almost legal institution, a thing of personal testimonial; and generally, the Christian interest in the affairs of the heart are for the sake of control, either of behaviour or belief: 'lay up for yourselves treasures in heaven, where neither moth nor rust doth corrupt … for where your treasure is, there will your heart be also.'[21] The intention is to change desires from the material to the spiritual; and the heart can be read as commitment, routed by divine recommendation toward the pious.

We tend to think of this economy of faith as the old world, reflecting the limited consciousness of antiquity and expect that in the later ages of genius and artistic inspiration, a new force of subjectivity arose. But it is not conspicuously so. The Biblical understanding of the soul provides the keynote for the Renaissance, in which the heart is an engine, as when Vasari

---

16   *Genesis* 17.14.
17   *Genesis* 6.5.
18   *Genesis* 17.17.
19   *Genesis* 20.5.
20   *Matthew* 5.28.
21   *Matthew* 6.20–21.

in his *Life* of Brunelleschi describes how certain people born diminutive in stature nevertheless have formidable soul and an immensely awesome heart (*di sì smisurata terribilità*).[22] Similarly, those endowed with little in their bodies may have great generosity of soul and sincerity in the heart.[23] Or Perino who had a heart for rivaling or even outstripping the ancients in his work.[24] To have heart means to be emboldened. These are not terms of profound consciousness. Where, you wonder, is subjectivity?

We look to the arts and its enormous literature for signs of such qualities; but while we are always struck by the powerful evocative character of renaissance painting and sculpture—where each artist's work is fingerprinted to the point that connoisseurs can distinguish between hands and identify authorship—when you seek lexical signs of that independence of consciousness that we are describing as subjectivity, it is largely missing. The soul remains instrumental in Vasari. In his *Proemio delle vite*, he describes drawing as the fundamental element of painting and sculpture, in fact the very soul that conceives and nourishes in itself[25] all the other parts, by analogy to God's making of the earth.

With classical aesthetics grafted upon theological traditions, renaissance art theory enjoyed the conceit of the artist as demiurge, hopefully inducing the transfer of divine privilege to the artist. From this epoch, we build a heroic view of the artist, hence the artist as genius. Yet the age of Leonardo, Michelangelo, Raphael and Titian, though bringing forth geniuses such as we still classify such figures, used the word genius in an entirely different way. Their use of the word *genio*, or Latin *genius*, was impeccably classical and equivalent to the Greek *daimon*, almost an independent being who advises the soul. He is figured, tellingly, as a little boy who is external to the body and who accompanies the adult. Genius in their terms is a quality or adjunct character-giving property of a person, but not actually a person. Nobody in the renaissance said: 'he is a genius'. You, as any person, have a genius. Your genius may not be to paint rooms in the Vatican but you still have a genius, evidently to do other things.[26]

---

22   'l'animo pieno di tanta grandezza et il cuore di sì smisurata terribilità'.

23   'tanta generosità d'animo e tanta sincerità di cuore'.

24   'cuore non solo in paragonare a gli antichi le opere loro, ma forse in passarle di gran lunga'.

25   'anzi l'istessa anima che concepe e nutrisce in se medesima'.

26   Edgar Zilsel, *Die Entstehung des Geniebegriffes. Ein Beitrag zur Ideengeschichte der Antike und des Frühkapitalismus*, Tübingen, Mohr, 1926.

So potentially, genius could be considered as some kind of antecedent to subjectivity. Admittedly, when it comes to describing the genius of a great artist, the classical definition sometimes converges with the contemporary romantic view of genius, namely exceptional and stellar greatness of talent. So in setting the scene for describing the sculptor and architect Benedetto da Maiano, Vasari says that beyond those who have great gifts to do useful things there are 'those who are moved by their genius (*mossi dal genio loro*) to learn an art or science and become perfect in it, and driven and decorated by a name, fired by glory, they then rise from an imperfect to a perfect one, from a mortal one to an eternal'.

But then *genio* can also just be one's nature to be happy. Raphael who was clearly an ambitious and angelic painter of exceptional gifts, is valued for his Olympian output above all; and yet among these peculiar gifts (*fra le sue doti singulari*) the term *genio* is reserved for his sweet nature, his ability to bring people of pompous humour together to work harmoniously. This occurred, Vasari says, because the other artists were won over by his courtesy and by his art, 'but even more by the genius of his good nature'.[27]

Genius is not absolute and immutable, as we judge from the description of the painter Pellegrino da Modana, where physiological breakdown causes 'one with a genius of happy complexion to be transformed into melancholy'. And on the other side, in the introductory paragraph to Franciabigio's *Life*, we read that hard work can overcome poverty, turning bitterness into sweetness, to the point that the goodness of heaven is forced to be favourable and kind to his genius.[28] So the genius can change or suffer a good influence. It can also instruct, as in Francesco Mazzola's *Life*, which identifies the virtues which nature in painting and his genius had taught him (*la natura nel dipignere e 'l suo genio gli avevano insegnato*). Alas, Vasari notes, the artist was attracted to many bizarre practices and these damaged his life.

And finally, genius could be a limitation, as when Bandello writes in Vasari's century that two people do not get on, because the genius of the one does not match that of the other and the blood does not mix.[29] But the eloquent Bandello has few words in his vast collection of *Novelle* to describe psychological traits, much less the subjectivity of an individual. A boy, for example, might be described as a lad of good nature (*garzone di buona indole*),[30]

---

27   'ma più dal genio della sua buona natura'.
28   'essergli nel genio favorevole e benigna', *Life of Franciabigio*.
29   Bandello, *Novelle* 1.2.
30   *ibid.* 4.3.

just like the ten-year old described by Castiglione (*maravigliosa indole*),[31] but this is a weak form of characterization; and like 'good type' (*uomo da bene*), such descriptions remain essentially moral, attesting to a kind of decency and fine disposition rather than a person's calibre of receptivity and projection. The closest that Bandello comes to sensibility is in saying that I tangibly see myself (*sensibilemente mi veggio*) dying of melancholy.[32] This means, however, that the feeling is so immediate that I can perceive it with my senses. It does not have anything to do with what we would call sensibility.

In poetic literature, however, the soul could always be used to denote internal feeling, as in Tasso's line: if my heart is with you, as it wants to be, where is my soul?[33] But it is poetic gamesmanship, toying with metaphors to express the dynamism of affection, jealousy[34] and ownership, wayward-ness, 'the errant soul'[35] which, in one variant or another, is often addressed in the first line of a poem. Tasso speaks of the beautiful soul in a way which suitably also means vague (*l'anima vaga*)[36] and sometimes, as in biblical times, the soul just means the person,[37] a Petrarchan tradition that goes long into the baroque.

Slowly, such ideas of an irreducible feeling person detach themselves from the poetic institutions and enter the intimate. So when Montesquieu says that 'you like my naivety and prefer my liberal air and my sensibility for pleas-ure (*sensibilité pour les plaisirs*) to the false modesty of my companions',[38] he is making a claim for the power of the private over the conventional. In the first lines of *La religieuse* Diderot describes a person as having 'spirit, gaiety, taste for fine art and above all originality. One has praised his sensibility, his honour and probity'. In another case an eccentric and foolhardy woman is recognized for her incredible sensibility (*sensibilité incroyable*) in her sen-sual and eroticized grasp of music; and elsewhere, the greatest sensibility can suddenly give onto ferocity (*de la plus grande sensibilité jusqu'à la férocité*). With this preamble, running from the Greek psyche to the sensibility of the enlightenment, Europe is ready to invent subjectivity in the romantic period.

---

31   Castiglione, *Cortegiano* 1.3.

32   Bandello 4.5.

33   'Se 'l mio core è con voi, come desia, / dov'è l'anima mia?' Tasso, *Rime* 26.1–2.

34   'ch'al cor non geli l'anima gelosa', *ibid.* 32.6.

35   'Anima errante', Tasso, *Rime* 61.1.

36   *ibid.* 74.7.

37   '"Anima, addio," con languide parole / e l'altra: "Vita, addio" le rispondea', 379.16.

38   Montesquieu, *Lettres persanes*, lettre 53.

The powerful statements of subjectivity that you might identify with Schubert's songs, Delacroix's painting or Baudelaire's poetry were never inherent in language or culture. They had to be invented, called into being by forces that announce the emancipation of the individual from the institutional, that declare that expression is the property of the person who expresses, not the property of the people who listen. They must enter the subjectivity of the person who speaks or sings or paints. It seems no accident that the word 'subjectivity' takes root in western thinking during an epoch when its expression can be witnessed in demonstrative incarnations through art, poetry and music. In the period from romanticism to post-impressionism, the subjectivity of the artist wins unprecedented prestige, where the artwork, before it is a depiction of the street or the apple, is a record of organic experience, wrought with a confession of its process. Subjectivity has not always been recognized and has been slow to emerge from institutional conventions. It is acceptable in expressions of emotion but, like the construction of the ego inside Freud's famous triangle of potent forces in the psyche, it has no power. In the academy, subjectivity is similarly defenceless. Unless poetic parameters are generously extended, the disavowal of subjectivity persists through inappropriate syllabus design and research methodologies, where subjectivity is mishandled as a consequence. It seems strange to me that we are so keen to claim student-centredness, yet the precondition of students identifiying their own centre is so diminished.

Chapter 9

LEADERSHIP

Good learning outcomes make good followers. Fatefully, we set up student success to fulfill the motif of following as opposed to leadership. For a student to succeed, he or she must follow the syllabus and its examples, follow the content and questions, follow the marking rubric and meet the intended learning outcomes: the student follows the teacher and, if not, the endeavour seems likely to end in failure. Speaking cynically, education provides templates, whose satisfaction yields good results. If that were all there is, there would be little scope for intellectual autonomy and especially imagination. The clarity and excellence of learning outcomes could be measured by the ease with which students follow them. Nothing must be obscure or ambiguous but rather everything leads transparently and seamlessly to their fulfilment, through beautifully aligned delivery, learning activities and assessment. All that you need to do is follow the teacher's leads. It is all about following and not at all about leading, in the same way that alignment predicated on learning outcomes makes little room for genuine student-centredness.

Like student-centredness, leadership cannot easily be accommodated within the learning outcome of any unit, subject or module. Depending on the chosen definition, leadership is about taking the lead. The cornerstone of the concept is initiative, especially in a context that involves other people who may be of a different or half-hearted persuasion. We also speak of leadership in intellectual or cultural endeavours, where a scientist or scholar is a leader in the field: he or she does not just follow others but precedes or, as a Greek might have said, is ahead by leading (ἀντιπροηγέομαι) instead of following; though this has less applicability to coursework degrees, where the chance of students distinguishing themselves with new proofs or a breakthrough is not terribly high. Certainly, we cannot write such expectations into the learning outcomes. It would be unreasonable to expect that the novice should spearhead the discipline, when even the lecturer struggles to make a credible contribution.

My purpose is not in any way to diminish the importance and dignity of following. It is more the reverse, as archaic linguistic structures reveal. The link between leading and following is counterintuitive, because leading with independence is also a kind of following with independence. It means following your own instinct. As the sixteenth-century poet Torquato Tasso said, 'henceforth I will follow my style' (or seguirò mio stile)[1] and, when it comes to erotic pursuit, the same poet also sees following in determined and predatory terms: 'he tails you like a hound the woodland doe'.[2] Following, unlike waiting, was never seen as passive. As an antithesis to leadership, the word followship or followership has been used in the literature and is itself valuable.[3] If I am in the presence of a marvellous and beloved leader, it is possibly the wrong time to seek to exercise my ambitions to assume leadership, especially over her or him. I would be much better off learning by following and making a contribution as a member of a team. Further, there is a philosophical sense in which following is not only acceptable but integral and necessary to all mental process.

If I write something where each part does not follow from the previous parts, the writing will be incoherent—it will be hard to follow: the Greeks were onto it (δυσπαρακολούθητος)—and you will be confused. If I want to make myself understood, it is necessary not only for the parts to be connected as one another's analogy but for their consecutive placement to make sense in an argument: they must follow. If the one idea follows from the others, you too can follow. The greatest leaders who ever read (unless a psychopathic part of some mystifying cult) anything were all good followers in gleaning meaning from the text: they could see, just like us, the logic by which one idea follows from the last. Every syllogism, every movement from premises to propositions to conclusion depends for its credibility on following; and we, as interpreters and critics, cannot gain any toehold on the products of other intellectuals without being followers of the logic. Among the worst sins of writing is 'inconsequentiality', that is, producing lots of details that do not follow. Not only are you likely to be frustrated by the reading—because you will spend much time searching for links that are not there—but you will conclude that the writing is inconsequential, of no consequence, unimportant. These robust critical terms derive from the Latin for following closely (consequi). In both Latin and Greek, however,

---

1   Tasso, *Rime* 31.

2   'vi segua, come il can selvaggia damma', Tasso, *Rime* 121.11.

3   Google's self-populating term 'followership theory' yields 19,000 results.

the motif of following is only metaphorically linked to imaginative ratiocination from late classical times.

If we neglect Greek words that mean follow in the sense of attend (ἀμορβεύω, ἀμορβός)[4] there are two main remaining constellations. The first has its roots in following (ἕπομαι), with derivatives to pursue, follow after (μεθέπω), to follow along with, accompany (συνέπομαι) or to follow together (συνεφέπομαι) or follow behind (ὑφέπομαι).[5] The other cluster has its roots in another verb for following (ἀκολουθέω), with a very large number of derivatives, embracing most of the prepositions of the Greek language. One spoke of one who follows or attends on (ἀκόλουθος), with abstract forms (ἀκολούθησις, ἀκολουθία), verbal forms with imperative connotations: one must follow (ἀκολουθητέον, ἐπακολουθητέον, παρακολουθητέον), disposed to follow (ἀκολουθητικός), to follow (ἐξακολουθέω), following close upon (ἐπακόλουθος, ἐπακολουθέω), capable of following (ἐπακολουθητικός), easy to follow (εὐεπακολούθητος), to follow after (κατακολουθέω), readily following (φιλακόλουθος), that which follows (παρακολούθημα), following closely, interrelation (παρακολούθησις, παρακολουθέω), to follow about (περιακολουθέω), to follow constantly, attend everywhere (συνεξακολουθέω), accompany (συνεπακολουθέω), follow together (συγκατακολουθέω), follow along (συμπαρακολουθέω) or follow along with (συνακολουθέω), and to follow closely (ὑπακολουθέω). Of these, some have a sense of connexion and interrelation (like παρακολούθησις) which is not just a convenience of later grammarians but is alive already with Aristotle.[6] From then onward, it could mean following with the mind or understanding, an inference or even awareness, or consciousness. So too with the simplest form of the verb (ἀκολουθέω), which could already mean 'follow the thread of a discourse', in Plato,[7] to 'follow upon, to be consequent upon, consistent with';[8] and one also used the verb in the third person to mean it follows in the abstract (ἀκολουθεῖ).[9]

Greek sets the pattern which is expanded greatly in the renaissance. Most instances are neither positive nor negative but synonymous with 'next', as in

---

4   *cf.* to follow, accompany, attend (ὀπαδέω), a following after, attending, pursuit (ὀπήδησις), follow, accompany or attend (ὀπηδέω), follow along with, attend on (συνομαρτέω), following along with, accompanying (συνοπαδός).

5   *cf.* follower, attendant (ἐπέτης) or given to following (ἐπητικός) or the next (ἐπεχές).

6   Aristotle, *Posterior analytics* 99ᵃ30.

7   Plato, *Phaedo*107b.

8   Plato, *Republic*.400e, *cf.* 398d; follow analogy of, Aristotle, *History of animals* 499ᵃ10.

9   GA, Cat.14a31.

'the following day'. There are numerous texts in verse where the poet regrets following a lover: 'for more than seven years I have followed your pathway, O beautiful lady, and it has taken me to death'.[10] The author of these lines, Giovan Giorgio Trissino, also wrote one of the first regular tragedies, *Sofonisba* (1524), in which the term following appears in an argumentative sense.[11] It is like Shakespeare's 'How follows that?' or 'It follows not that she will love Sir Thurio'.[12] It is unusual, however, for any value to be ascribed to following, even when it is used for logical process. And often, the term following means 'to happen', again as in *Sofonisba*: 'well after that, what happened then (*ma fatto questo, che seguì dapoi*)?'[13] This meaning of follow as happening arises in other authors, such as Bandello, who speaks of a woman provoking her lover to cut the clothing, hoping that he will not call her bluff or, as he says, 'not having the intention that the outcome should follow (*che l'effetto seguisse*)'.[14] In another story, he says 'if you had withdrawn from this enterprise, the scandal that has happened (*è successo*) would not have followed (*non sarebbe seguito*)' or 'would not have occurred' or 'eventuated'.[15] The following is identified with the happening, which makes good ontological sense.

In some authors, the word for following hardly appears, whereas in others, like Bandello, there are hundreds of instances, which makes them hard to remember. Because following is such an enormously common word, it is difficult to prove; but my suspicions are that following has only ever taken on a negative connotation since the development of the word 'leadership', which took place in the industrial period. There is nothing inherently wrong with following and it is only since the time when the abstract idea of leadership took hold on the European imagination that the idea of following or followship slid in prestige. In very few cases does one feel a contrast with leading: you lead, I follow. In one gorgeous example, Shakespeare implies

---

10   'Seguito ho, bella Donna, il tuo sentiero / più di sett'anni, e me n'andava a morte', Trissino, *Rime* 51.9–10; *cf.* Trissino, *Rime* 12.9–11, or 'ma di seguirvi più non m'assicuro', Trissino, *Rime* 52.1–3.

11   'Però seguendo il ragionar di prima, / vi ripriego ad aver di me pietate', Trissino, *Sofonisba* 1.5.

12   'It follows then the cat must stay at home', *King Henry V* 1.2.

13   Trissino, *Sofonisba* 2.2.

14   'Era in quel punto montata la fantasia a la donna di far una solenne paura a l'amante, e per questo invitava il marito a voler tagliar la veste, non perciò avendo animo che l'effetto seguisse,' 1.3.

15   'averei anteposto la nostra amicizia a l'appetito mio; e forse che tu, udite le mie ragioni, ti saresti da questa impresa ritratto e non sarebbe seguito lo scandalo che è successo,' 1.21.

that following is the opposite of leadership, when he says: 'The sheep for fodder follow the shepherd; the shepherd for food follows not the sheep'.[16] But that is not just because the shepherd is a leader but because the human stomach cannot digest grass, which enhances the counterpoint with a touch of the poetically grotesque.

In European vocabulary, the abstract noun 'leadership' arose at the dawn of the industrial revolution at the end of the eighteenth century; but it had the value of 'governing people', as when we speak of the US leadership, meaning the people, collectively, who hold office and exercise power. Although this meaning is still current, if a little old-fashioned, the sense in which we use the word today has an adjectival character, proposing qualities of a psychological kind that predispose people to assume control and take initiative, be enterprising and own responsibility. These uses belong to the twentieth-century vocabulary of management psychology whose cultures have struck deep roots in the Euro-American organizational psyche, affecting education across the Anglophone world with astonishing ubiquity. A Google search discovers 90,300,000 pages for leadership qualities—which immediately pops up as a suggested term in the comprehensive engine—and 3,480,000 results for the same words in double inverted commas, that is "leadership qualities". The term "student leadership qualities" alone yields 2,040,000 hits. Nobody has looked at them all, much less their counterparts with terms such as leadership traits.

In the same way that there are courses on management, there are units, subjects and modules on leadership. But because leadership has enjoyed such an exponential rise in popularity, it is close to a graduate attribute in universities (and often a motto in secondary schools) and cannot therefore be confined to students in the Commerce or Business schools. Medical students, architects, humanities students, engineers and every complexion of scientist, must all have access to the wisdom and know what leadership is and how to practice it. So there is a corresponding growth in extra-curricular leadership programs, which in many ways suit everyone, because the choice to engage with such peripheral studies in a committed way is itself taken as a good predictor of leadership in industry. The only problem is that the definition of leadership is sometimes vague and possibly not linked to the academic program in which the student is enrolled. Leadership could mean anything from helping more junior students to doing charity work in the community.

---

16   *Two gentlemen of Verona* 1.1.

Whom does the leader lead? When we speak of leadership, we unwittingly allow a slide in terms to occur. To lead always carries connotations of inducing other people to follow. So even when no-one follows (and in all honesty, we are not leading anyone) the term leadership is still enjoined to inflate the charity work, for example, with the quality of influence. It is valuable and clearly much to be encouraged; but the extent to which it really constitutes leadership is dubious. Various forms of volunteering, laudable in themselves, are structurally often more an expression of privilege than leadership, because they may be undertaken by people with support and time on their hands, as opposed to struggling people who study while looking after younger siblings or sick unemployed parents. To build leadership around privilege is retrograde, because it excludes from recognition the large group of battlers who cannot afford the distinction.

So when we ask: whom does the leader lead? we must further ask: does it have to be a follower? Or indeed does it have to be some plurality of followers? At what point does the credibility of the term leadership become shaky? If I am an independent soul, I have achieved a kind of leadership of myself, but not necessarily of anyone else. In whose name does the leader lead?[17] I might achieve a platform from which I can project my independence or champion a cause; but that privileged position might still only make me an evangelist rather than a leader, because it does not necessarily entail winning people's trust so that they follow.

To lead and to follow are a curious dichotomy, apparently mutually dependent and necessary to one another. They propose a linear model of human relations where people are implicitly marching in solidarity, with one person in the front who—by dint of charisma or wisdom or power or energy or initiative—determines the direction of the trek. In many circumstances, of course, the selection is not democratic. In employment, for example, there is always a boss whose superior station has been established by power structures that we are unlikely to change. Even when we get to vote or help make the decision as staff representative on a selection panel, the elected end up having power over the electors, as if there were no staff participation at all. The boss is charged with responsibilities and instated with authority over us, for which the term leadership is often invoked as both sweeter and more compelling than power. If the boss has talent and

---

17   'though the devil lead the measure, such are to be followed', Shakespeare, *All's well that ends well* 2.1.

a good nature, we experience her or his authority as leadership, because we view sympathetically the objectives that she or he has asked us to fulfill.

Translated into education, leadership may be artificial by contrast, because all students are to be treated equally and none has authority over any other, even if they help more junior students in a peer mentoring program. As leadership programs of all complexions are voluntary, the prospective leaders self-identify and assume the distinction through a positive view of themselves. They may already nurture an ambition to excel in future employment applications and a fortunate career, where leadership experience will give them a competitive advantage. There is nothing wrong with these strategies, even if they have admixtures of expedience and conceit; and ideally our students would achieve great success beyond the walls thanks to the preparation that we have been able to hatch for them.

Just the same, unless our students can all be leaders, which is perhaps hyperbole, there is something uncomfortable about supporting the dichotomy which divides the world into leaders and followers, which could easily be construed as an indicator and predictor of rank. It is as if the implicit demotion of the non-leaders might never end, as the followers have followers, always a next who follows (ὑστεραῖος, as the Greeks said), until you arrive at the least assertive, the least worthy and the most motivationally abject. However distasteful this implicit ladder of assertion, it is also illogical, because whenever we act productively, we tend to toggle between leading and following. Unless psychopathic, we do not just assume that we are the boss, in possession of the necessary wisdom and therefore viewing our followers instrumentally as the tools by which our designs are fulfilled. Rather, we exercise yet wiser powers of listening and thus encourage richer ideas and more energetic participation. That is to say, we take the lead from our followers and follow them with mutual satisfaction.[18]

This organicity of responsiveness and self-assurance is a social grace that reflects a personal reciprocity between curiosity and telling, reading and writing, learning and teaching. It is the genius of research, where our aspirations to intellectual leadership are intimately cocooned by study, absorption in the work of other scholars or primary sources, all parts of the library from which we gain a certain pregnancy in our own ideas. We lead by following and have to have followed in order to lead. As an intellectual leader, your ability to lead derives from your credibility; and that in turn derives from your ability to follow. As if signalling this relationship of

---

18 'Rendez service à ceux qui dépendent de vous: vous le serez davantage par cette conduite que par ne vous pas laisser voir.' La Bruyère, *Les caractères* 7.12 ; Des Biens de fortune.

leadership and learning, the more archaic epoch of Greek identifies a leader as also a beginner (ἔξαρχος),[19] commencing with the idea of being first. It is a little like English, where 'prime' can mean top—as in prime minister—but 'primer' or 'primary' is associated with early development; or 'first', which is both the person ahead and the beginner's level.[20] The two concepts are fatefully linked with the idea of originality, of beginning things, initiating, as we can also check through Greek with the verb to begin, take the lead in, initiate (ἐξάρχω), which could even mean teach in the classical period.[21]

Leadership is never absolute, as authority may be; and it prospers best when power and influence can be contested. Historically, a king had enormous authority but could be a terrible leader. Meanwhile, when offices are determined by that inscrutable mixture of assertion and merit, the need to show leadership as a worthy trait—neither inherited nor wangled by nepotism—the stakes rise and the claim to be a leader becomes more intense and meaningful. It is the historical dialectical paradigm of ancient Greece, where potentially any male from the voting class could put himself forward in competition with other eligible citizens. Perhaps this socially labile character of Hellenic culture explains the efflorescence of intuitions and words for leading and leadership in the Greek language. As if the bountiful expressions for following were not prolific enough, leadership is like an epidemic. As with following, leading in Greek is mostly conceptualized around two roots, though there are numerous terms beyond them which mean leadership by virtue of rank, like captain or commander or general in English. An example in Greek is commander, ruler, chief (ταγός), leader as general (στρατηγός) or leader of an army, general, commander (στρατηλάτης), a head man, chief, leader (κορυφαῖος) or one who marshals an army, commander, leader (κοσμήτωρ).[22]

---

19   *Iliad* 24.721.

20   *cf.* the word 'prince' (principal among nobility) and the German for prince (*Fürst*), uncannily the first, allied to leader (*Führer*), as in duke, from *duce*, *ducare*, to lead.

21   Plato, *Laws* 891d, Euripides, *Iphigeneia in Tauris* 743, like διδάσκω at 111, Aristotle, *Poetics* 1449ª11. See also *Iliad* 18.51, 18.606, *Odyssey* 4.19.

22   commander, ruler, chief (ταγός), leader of a countless host (μυριοταγός), join in leading the revels (συνθιασεύω), leader (στρατηγός), leader of an army, general, commander (στρατηλάτης), lead an army into the field (στρατηλατέω), to be on a campaign, in the field (στρατόω), leading forward, advancing (προβίβασις), cause to step forward, lead on (προβιβάζω), leading in procession, solemn procession (πομπεία), conduct a procession (πομποστολέω), head man, chief, leader (κορυφαῖος), one who marshals an army, commander, leader (κοσμήτωρ), lead by the right way (ὁδόω), leader, chief (ὄρχαμος), without a leader (ἀπροστάτευτος), one who gives a signal, leader, commander (σημάντωρ), without leader (ἀσήμαντος), lead in (εἰσπορεύω).

By far the greatest number of conceptions arises through the root of leading itself, the verb to lead (ἄγω) which could also have connotations of carry, fetch and bring. This root has great resonance for us as the basis of 'pedagogy', which is technically the leading of children, mirrored by the Latin root in the word 'education', which is to lead (*ducare*). Similarly, our word in English 'demagogue' contains the leading root and has a presence in Greek with more positive meaning than in English: the verb to be a leader of the people (δημαγωγέω), the popular who leads (δημαγωγός) and the abstract noun for leadership of the people (δημαγωγία). We can also recognize our word hegemony, again with largely positive associations from the verb, to go before, lead the way (ἡγέομαι, ἡγεμονεύω), leader (ἡγέτης, ἡγεμών, ἡγήτωρ), and the more abstract leading (ἡγεμόνευμα) or leading the way, going first (ἡγεμονία). There is no sense of dictatorship in this conception, for which there were other words, like tyrant. In general, Greek language has a positive view of leadership and contained a term to express it: good leadership (εὐηγεσία). Even leading dogs or goats has a noble air in the very large collection of words on leadership with the ἄγω root.[23]

23 Leader (Ἀγήτωρ), as noted to be a leader of the people (δημαγωγέω), popular leader (δημαγωγός), lead the way (ἀγεμονεύω), leader, lord (ἀγεμών), leading off the dancing (ἀγησίχορος), leader, lord (ἀγητήρ), lead, carry, fetch, bring (ἄγω), leader (ἄκτωρ), lead the way from (ἀφηγέομαι), leading the procession (ἀγαῖος), host-leading (ἀγέστρατος), leader of the people (ἀγησίλαος), leading the chorus (ἀγησίχορος), lead, bring (ἀγινέω), leader, chief (ἀγός), fit for leading by (ἀγωγαῖος), leading, guiding (ἀγωγός), one must lead (ἀκτέον), one must lead (ἀκτέος), lead up (ἀνάγω), leading up (ἀναγωγή), without leader, unguided (ἀνηγεμόνευτος), lead up against (ἀντανάγω), lead against (ἀντεπάγω), shift in order to meet attacks (ἀντιπαράγω), lead on against (ἀντιπαρεξάγω), lead away, carry off (ἀπάγω), lead the way (ἀπάρχω), leading away (ἀπαγωγή), leading away, diverting (ἀπαγωγός), one must lead away (ἀπακτέον), leader of a (βουαγετόν), to be a leader of mercenaries (ξεναγέω), to lead the people (δημαγωγέω), leadership of the people (δημαγωγία), a popular leader (δημαγωγός), lead through (διεξάγω), lead out, lead away (ἐξάγω), lead forth (ἐξαγινέω), one who leads out (ἐξαγωγεύς), a leading out (ἐξαγωγή), to be leader of (ἐξηγέομαι), one who leads on, adviser (ἐξηγητής), to lead the way (ἐξυφηγέομαι), lead to (ἐφηγέομαι), leading the dance (ἐγερσίχορος), lead out round (ἐκπεριάγω), lead in (ἐνάγω), bring on (ἐπάγω), leading on (ἐπακτικός), leader of Bacchanals (Ληναγέτας), lead out (ἐπεξάγω), lead (ἐπιβάσκω), lead in (εἰσάγω), lead up into (εἰσανάγω), lead in (εἰσηγέομαι), easily led, ductile (εὐάγωγος), easy to lead on (εὐεπάγωγος), good leadership (εὐηγεσία), easy to bring into place (εὐπαράγωγος), go before, lead the way (ἡγέομαι), leader (ἡγέτης), leading (ἡγεμόνευμα), lead the way (ἡγεμονεύω), leading the way, going first (ἡγεμονία) ἡγεμονικός), one who leads (ἡγεμών ἡγήτωρ), guide, lead (ἡγηλάζω), leader of the state (ἡγησίπολις), one must lead (ἡγητέον), authoritative, leading (ἡγητικός), act as guide, lead the way (καθηγέομαι), leader, guide (καθηγεμών), lead down (κατάγω), hound-leader (κυναγός), leader of hounds, huntsman (κυναγωγός), huntsman (κυνηγέτης), leader of a (κωμηγέτης), leader of the people (λαγέτας, λαγέτης), lead an armed band (λοχαγέω) or leader thereof (λοχαγός), leader of the Muses (Μουσαγέτας Μουσαγέτης), lead another way (μεθοδηγέω), leader of the Nymphs (νυμφαγέτς), lead the bride to the

It is also no accident that we first see in Greek a link between leadership and interpretation and even explanation. The verb 'to be leader' of something or govern (ἐξηγέομαι), designates the exercise of a position but the same verb in the classical period could mean to expound or interpret.[24] The noun for one who leads on or is an adviser (ἐξηγητής) is also the root of the word now in common use in the creative arts—adapted via biblical usage—namely 'exegesis', that is an explanatory body of writing which elaborates the creative work in whatever genre. As well as meaning one who leads on, or an adviser, an exegete (ἐξηγητής) means an 'expounder, interpreter, especially of oracles, dreams, or omens'.[25] The development of such intellectual and clairvoyant meanings around the simple stem 'to lead' makes a lot of sense. First the interpreter is led to the meaning by virtue of special insight but second, the interpreter leads us to the meaning thanks to a process which could be likened to teaching: a text, a discussion or a pronouncement which

---

bridegroom's house (νυμφαγωγέω) or the person doing it (νυμφαγωγός), lead (ὁδηγέω), mountebank, charlatan, quack (ὀχλαγωγός), leader of the rearguard (οὐραγός), lead by (παράγω), leading by (παραγωγή), lead past (παρεξάγω), lead in by one's side, bring forward, introduce (παρεισάγω), lead (περιάγω), leading round and explaining (περιήγησις), lead round (περιηγέομαι), leader, guide (ποδηγέτης), lead, guide (ποδηγέω), leading, guiding (ποδηγία), lead forward (προάγω), leading on, promotion (προαγωγή), leading on (προαγωγός), lead up before (προανάγω), lead (προεξάγω), going before, leading (προήγησις), go first and lead the way (προηγέομαι), one who goes before as a guide (προηγεμών), leader (προηγήτωρ), leader (προκαθηγέτης), leader (προκαθηγητής), lead off to prison (προσαπάγω), lead on (προϋπάγομαι), leader of dogs (σκυλακαγέτις), lead about whelps (σκυμναγωγέω), carry off as booty, lead captive (συλαγωγέω), lead forward together (συμπροάγω), bring together, gather together (συνάγω), lead away with (συναπάγω), lead out together (συνεξάγω), lead an expedition (στολαγωγέω), lead together against (συνεπάγω), leading, guidance (ὑφήγησις), go just before, guide, lead (ὑφηγέομαι), guide, leader (ὑφηγητής), leader of a hymn (ὑμναγωγός), lead or leading on gradually (ὑπάγω, ὑπαγωγή), leading by the hand (χειραγώγημα), lead by the hand (χειραγωγέω), leading, guiding (χειραγωγός), lead a chorus (χορηγέω), chorus-leader (χορηγός), lead departed souls to the nether world (ψυχαγωγέω), or the person doing it (ψυχαγωγός).

24   Herodotus 2.49, Plato *Cratylus* and *Ion* 531a, *Demosthenes* 47.69; see also Lysias, *Against Andocides* 6.10, and Andocides, *On the mysteries* 1.116. It could also mean 'tell at length, relate in full', Herodotus 2.3 (*cf.* 3.4, 7.6, 3.72), Aeschylus, *Prometheus bound* 216, 702, Thucydides 5.26 and 1.138; set forth, explain, Plato, *Laws* 802c, *cf. Republic* 474c, explain, Sophocles, *Ajax* 320, Xenophon, *Constitution of the Lacedaimonians* 2.1.

25   *LSJ*, who give the examples of Herodotus 5.31, Demosthenes 35.17, and then for interpreter, Herodotus 1.78, spiritual director, Plato, *Euthyphro* 4d, 9a, *Laws* 759c, 759e, 775a, Demosthenes 47.68, Isaeus, *Ciron* 8.39, Plato, *Republic* 427c, the pontifices in Rome, Dionysius of Halicarnassus, *Antiquities of Rome* 2.73. In the most modern sense, it could even mean a guide or Cicerone to notable sights, *e.g.* Pausanius 5.15.10, and an inscription found at Olympia, *Collection of Greek inscriptions* (SIG)1021.20.

leads us to the imagined truth. Without being led there, we would not gain the insight. We are led by the exegete so that we understand.

In English and romance languages, thanks to a familiar Latin root (*ducare*), the motif of leading is also intellectual and behavioural. Education is not the only word to draw from the root. We also have induction, deduction, reduction, introduction, production, all of which have a necessary place in the philosophical lexicon, which is why to traduce or mislead or betray is so extremely negative. In addition, the word conduct has a place both in physics or music and morality, method or psychology. A wire conducts electricity in the same way that we conduct an investigation. They both lead, like the person with the baton in front of the orchestra. For a long time, we have spoken of conduct as both noun and verb meaning behaviour. In the seventeenth-century *Caractères* of La Bruyère, for example, conduct can be purely 'lead', as when the beautiful new simplicity in writing style leads imperceptibly (*conduit insensiblement*) to witty or spirited prose.[26] Similarly, excellent artists ennoble their genre and toss out the rules if they do not lead (*s'écartent des règles si elles ne les conduisent pas*) to the grand and sublime.[27] At the same time, La Bruyère uses the noun as behaviour when he talks about women who want to hide their conduct (*cacher leur conduite*) behind layers of modesty with continual affectation.[28] He also says that with virtue, capability and good conduct (*bonne conduite*) one can still be unbearable.[29]

In the archaic recesses of Greek language, a whole extra layer of leading perhaps explains this ambiguity. The other impressive collection of Greek words about leading derives from the motif of being first (ἄρχω), with implications of initiating or beginning something but also with the

---

26 'L'on écrit régulièrement depuis vingt années; l'on est esclave de la construction; l'on a enrichi la langue de nouveaux mots, secoué le joug du latinisme, et réduit le style à la phrase purement française; l'on a presque retrouvé le nombre que Malherbe et Balzac avaient les premiers rencontré, et que tant d'auteurs depuis eux ont laissé perdre; l'on a mis enfin dans le discours tout l'ordre et toute la netteté dont il est capable: cela conduit insensiblement à y mettre de l'esprit,' *Les caractères* 2.60.

27 'Il y a des artisans ou des habiles dont l'esprit est aussi vaste que l'art et la science qu'ils professent; ils lui rendent avec avantage, par le génie et par l'invention, ce qu'ils tiennent d'elle et de ses principes; ils sortent de l'art pour l'ennoblir, s'écartent des règles si elles ne les conduisent pas au grand et au sublime; ils marchent seuls et sans compagnie, mais ils vont fort haut et pénètrent fort loin, toujours sûrs et confirmés par le succès des avantages que l'on tire quelquefois de l'irrégularité,' 2.61.

28 'Quelques femmes ont voulu cacher leur conduite sous les dehors de la modestie; et tout ce que chacune a pu gagner par une continuelle affectation, et qui ne s'est jamais démentie, a été de faire dire de soi: On l'aurait prise pour une vestale,' 4.46.

29 'Avec de la vertu, de la capacité, et une bonne conduite, l'on peut être insupportable.' 6.31 De la Société et de la Conversation.

meaning to lead, in the sense of rule, govern or command. It is therefore a slightly more bossy conception, which we can recognize through certain derivatives which are more about the exercise of power than leadership. An example is patriarchy or oligarchy or monarchy. European culture was always more concerned about a lack of leadership or rule, whence the term anarchy, lack of a leader (ἀναρχία), was—and is still seen as—a negative social condition that makes all uncoordinated members of a community vulnerable. One feared this predicament with the same unease as one witnesses the unstable suitors jockeying around Penelope and hoping each to be Odysseus' successor as King of Ithaca. Of course even established leadership could be challenged through revolt or insurrection which, however, still requires leadership in sedition (στασιαρχία). Though sometimes stern and mixed with harsh command, leading by this root (ἄρχω) is also fundamentally benign and belongs to the world of the goatherd as much as civil council or army. It draws to it a large number of prepositions and other nouns to make up a formidable list.[30]

In its structure of being first, the prince, the principle or principal thing or person, the Greek conception of leading (ἄρχω) also draws us to an analogous idea in authority. The word authority, about which we might feel a little uncomfortable, has benign roots with the Latin for author or originator (*auctor*). The power of inaugurating anything is also a claim to lead or have authority (*auctoritas*). If you are the author or originator, you are the first at something. It might not amount to very much but, insofar as it does mean something, you have the title: you have to be respected or at least acknowledged for having been the author and originator. This motif of being first is implicitly followed by the learning journey of the students who absorb or fathom the material.

---

30   lead a herd (ἀγελαρχέω), without head (ἄναρχος), to be first (ἄρχω), leader of a flock (ἀγελάρχης), lack of a leader (ἀναρχία), lead away (ἀποπαιδαγωγέω), leader of a political party (ἀρχαιρεσιάρχης), leader of revels or Dionysos himself (ἀρχέβακχος), leading the people, chief (ἀρχέλαος), leader, prince (ἀρχέτας), a leader, prince (ἀρχέτης), leading the chorus (ἀρχέχορος), first leader, author (ἀρχηγέτης), to be chief leader (ἀρχηγετεύω), leader of chorus (ἀρχίχορος), leader of Bacchanals (ἀρχιβασσάρα), leader of a Bacchic revel or rout (ἀρχιθιασίτης, θιασάρχης), leader, chief (ἀρχός), leader of a (διφαλαγγάρχης), leader of twelve (δωδεκάδαρχος), leader of a body of six (ἑξάδαρχος), leader of a hundred (ἑκατοντάρχης), leader, beginner (ἔξαρχος), begin, take the lead in, initiate (ἐξάρχω), leader of an (ἐνωμοτάρχης), to be leader of a carousal (θιασαρχέω), leader of a line of horsemen (ζυγάρχης), leader of a revel (κώμαρχος), leader of the Muses (Μούσαρχος), leader of infantry (πέζαρχος), to be leader (προεξάρχω), chief scout, leader of a reconnoitring party (σκοπάρχης), leader of a (σπειράρχης), leadership in sedition (στασιαρχία), join in leading (συνεξάρχω), leader of a (συνταγματάρχης), leader of a (ταγματάρχης), goat-leader (χιμάραρχος).

Although we first have to have followed in order to lead, to lead is assuredly not to follow. Its distinguishing features of initiative and persuasion concern originality. It is not necessary for the leader's thought to be original, because it is undoubtedly derived from much following in the past. But the leader is the originator of the suggestion: let us embark upon the project now and all of us get behind it! It is original in the same way that an undergraduate essay may be original. The ideas may have been in circulation long since but the way of drawing them together for the application in point has an integrity that reflects the unique mind of the student, which judiciously matches received wisdom with current needs. So with leadership: the originality does not necessarily have anything to do with the power of invention but rather originating a coordinating and persuasive influence which the singular vision affords.

By a similar logic, one could argue that scholarship is unlikely to yield benefits to leadership because scholarship—unless infused with creativity—is itself structurally more inclined to following. In the scholarship of learning and teaching we become leaders insofar as we are good followers: we follow the trends, good trends, like flipped paradigms, active learning or formative assessment, most of which have become a kind of orthodoxy by the time they are considered fit for leadership. At best, a scholar can lead by giving instances of technique and spirit in how to do something which is known rather than envisaging something which is not yet known.

Leadership and scholarship of learning and teaching therefore risk becoming mutually conflated, especially since, as suggested earlier, both leadership and student-centredness sit unhappily in an educational framework which is structured around competition for high grades. The competitive economy of student success, with its reassuring grid of constructive alignment, struggles to encourage student independence and intellectual initiative. Apart from unusual areas, like art, design, musical composition and architecture, the originality of the student is not greatly accommodated. It is the main reason that leadership is exported to co-curricular programs, which often have an equivocal character and uncertain relations both with study and leadership. If, on the other hand, the field of leadership is returned to the core business of syllabus—where leadership is understood more in terms of intellectual initiative—it will require a new accommodation of creativity and imagination, where the independence of the student is cultivated rather than suffocated by the restrictive closeness of learning outcomes and assessment.

Chapter 10

WASTE

We waste so much time and potential in education. From childhood, many thousands of hours have been spent attending school and university; and a great deal of that time—and especially the hopes and talents that filled it—goes to waste. We often seem to learn little and, largely discouraged from using our imagination, we forget what we learn because it has no part in anything else that we need to know or imagine doing. The knowledge sits in limbo for a while and then slowly dissolves into cognitive entropy. Fear of this waste is part of the reason for our enthusiasm for constructive alignment: it promises to stop the waste, because when we are asked to learn something, we are assured that it has a purpose and is assessed in agreement with the delivery, activities and learning outcomes. Learning and teaching become efficient: we know what we are expected to learn, we learn it and are assured at the end of it, via assessment, that we have met the learning outcomes. The problem is that the very constructive alignment that promises to attenuate the waste also stifles the creative development that would provide imaginative ownership of the material on offer.

Of course, we cannot stop the waste, because not all learning outcomes are matters of personal sympathy and, if we gather no love for them in the course of the program, it makes no difference to identify them and organize all the activities and assessment around them. There will still be waste because, without affection for the material that grows around our imaginative potential, we will still have difficulty retaining anything instructive and we will have no chance of building it into lifelong learning. So it turns out that the extra layer of fuss over learning outcomes is yet another instrument of waste, a whole administrative palaver that only constructs learning as a kind of drill, where we get told things that we do not really want to learn and are given no real chance to divert the commitment from its rigid course into our individual imagination, where it nourishes our sense of personal potential.

It would suit my case to describe the compromised position of creativity in our educational systems as chronic waste, indeed the worst kind of waste because it is the waste of potential. How many Nalinis does it take to figure out that the cost of discouragement is high and unnecessary? So many lively minds that could be encouraged to find new energies, new pathways and generate ideas and images are suppressed. It is a sad waste. But while deploring this waste, it is also necessary to scrutinize the structure of waste itself as a theme, in fact to deconstruct waste, because the spectre of waste haunts us in everything we do; and creative endeavour is inherently vulnerable to its menace. In a world that has many pressing problems, creative things never seem, strictly speaking, necessary. They are also extremely precarious, because, as Nalini discovers with a humanities essay, your best efforts go to waste. When the field is directly creative, the risks of waste escalate. Art students, for example, can spend all the years of an honours degree diligently applying themselves with long hours to arduous projects, involving expensive equipment, studio and materials; upon graduation, however, the whole creative endeavour is slowly seen to be unsustainable, because very few aspiring artists become professional artists. For me, this investment is not waste—because the failed artist can add to cultural capital in other ways and, on a personal level, nothing goes to waste if it adds creative potential—but it is easy to imagine how the frustration could be construed that way. When enthusiastic students become discouraged, that could also be considered a case of waste, a waste of energy, hope and potential. Of course, we have to countenance the ups and downs of opportunity; and it could be argued that a core part of being an artist is the ability to withstand discouragement. Further, we cannot always insulate everyone from disappointment because everyone would otherwise be encouraged to have unrealistic ambitions. It was ever thus: hope sits in an economy of rejection and with the mismatch of aspirations and opportunities comes much waste.

We feel bad about this write-off but creativity is intransigently wasteful, especially as we educate ourselves. As a poet, you could expect to spend ten years of writing high-minded rubbish before you find resonant subject matter that accords with your techniques and so becomes publishable. It is stressful but who is so blessed that a beautiful poetic idiom emerges immediately from high school and all those desperate hours can be saved? Waste is intrinsic to discovery and while we resent misspent time—remembering that we may never be the poet that we had hoped to become—we have to make our peace with waste. In ancient times, poetry itself was positively identified with a form of waste, celebrated as idleness (*otia nostra*) in Latin and Italian humanism.

In contemporary culture, when we think that one person's waste is another person's starvation, waste seems immoral and we are always uncomfortable with the thought of it. Even when successful, there is a strong sense that the arts are a luxury. It lies deeply within Western tradition to despise waste and to circumvent this antipathy. We always have to defend the arts and humanities as not a luxury but a necessity.[1] But if we disavow luxury and capitulate to the pressure always to eliminate waste, the arts and humanities are reduced to agitprop and we would have an uncreative culture. It seems necessary to wrestle with the idea of waste to accommodate creativity, especially when it enters the university under the banner of the graduate attributes. It is highly dialectical, almost the mirror of production, that production which Marx identified as dialectical and not merely mechanical. We must come to terms with waste in its stressful history before being able to manage its effects in a delicately creative university.

Waste is a difficult term with a difficult history. The greatest things that humanity has wrought can all be deemed wasteful if we do not identify with the purpose. The Pyramids, as grand as they are, can easily be seen as superstitious folly; and the labour and lives that were spent upon their construction could be considered a moral scandal. But a broad demographic still today admires them, rightly or wrongly, and finds them inspiring; and similar thrills and chills attend the prospect of stately palaces in Europe, analogous to the way that big-budget films or large sporting spectacles such as the Olympic Games are specifically engineered to secure wow-factor, only with the serene air of permanence and a lofty claim on eternity. So, on the one hand, we are mightily impressed by the grand design, as the architects and patrons intended; but on the other hand, if we thought of the thousands of dispossessed peasants who starved because funds were directed to the royal estate rather than their urgent need, we might scruple over our enthusiasm. Could the vanity of princes, even though resulting in such a lasting contribution to culture and promoting tourism ever since, be considered a kind of waste?

There is seldom agreement about what is waste and what is a brilliant investment, because waste is an inherently unstable term, rooted in the material world but expressing moral values. Depending on what we value,

---

1   *e.g.* Martha Nussbaum, *Not for profit: why democracy needs the humanities*, Princeton University Press, 2010.

we might either applaud or deplore a large expenditure; so much depends on the premises—your point of view and subjective esteem for a project—that the judgement is not always shared by those who begin with different premises. Waste is simultaneously a discourse about resources and efficiency and a discourse about priorities, things that do not exist because they represent potential.

Without doubt, the worst form of waste is war. Millions of lives—and with them their hopes and the love that they shared with family—are squandered in a terrible disagreement which could undoubtedly have been avoided with better will on both sides. But the belligerents believe passionately in the war. They do not see the war effort as a waste but a necessity, an absolute priority, precisely a matter of life and death. In the framework of a war, good patriots will also believe that the greatest efficiency in despatching the enemy means the least waste of their own resources; so the hideous perversity prevails within the antagonistic mindset that a great efficiency on one side is produced by maximum waste on the other.

The motif of war and destruction is not introduced for dramatic colour and effect. War and destruction are intrinsic to the very development of waste as a word in European languages. The closest that we come to waste in ancient Greek, for example, is a form of destruction (ἀπώλεια, like ὄλεθρος or φθορά, the verbs πορθέω, πέρθω)[2] which, like the Latin root of perdition, could also mean loss[3] or doom.[4] Our own word waste is derived from a similar motif, incorporating the desert (waste or wasteland), as in the Latin *uastus*—whence we get our vast—but more pressingly in devastation, de-vastate (*peruastare*), which also has an equivalent in Greek where the desert itself is in the verb (ἐρημόω). Our language leaves a trace of this military violence in the term 'to lay something to waste', meaning to destroy it, typically a city, to turn it into rubble, waste in the sense of wreckage, debris to be raked up and dumped somewhere; and in poetic literature, the image of destruction is, as Shakespeare would say, 'enlink'd to waste and desolation'[5] or 'waste ground'.[6] The motif of a deserted place suggests that

---

2   Aristotle, *Nichomachean ethics* 120ᵃ2, *Meteorology* 351ᵇ11.

3   Aristotle Problems 952ᵇ26 (opposite to guarding or watching over or keeping safe (τηρησις).

4   *Romans* 9.22, *2 Thessalonians* 2.3, of a thing lost *Septuagint, Laws* 6.3 (5.22).

5   *Henry V* 3.3.18.

6   *Measure for measure* 2.2.170. Having waste ground enough, / Shall we desire to raze the sanctuary ... ?' *Measure for measure* 2.2.170; cf. the 'wasted building' of the Second Goth, 'a ruinous monastery' *Titus Andronicus* 5.1.

nothing fertile strikes root, which presses upon the metaphor, as in 'the wild and wasteful ocean'.[7]

For all humanity in all epochs, one experienced different kinds of waste. Your olives could be wasted in the sense of the trees being razed by the Spartans; but the olives could also be wasted by poor husbandry or disorganization or irresponsible priorities or even cold commercial sense. For example, someone in a London office might decide that the profit from processing the olives is not worth the cost of the harvest, treatment and storage. Nobody wrecks the groves by axe or bulldozer but the good fruit go to waste just as certainly as if someone hacked the boughs down. Of the two motifs, the Greeks really only knew the first, or at least under the term of waste (ἀπώλεια) they only contemplated active destruction.

In the fascinating overlap between Greek and Hebraic culture, however, the word in question (ἀπώλεια) is used at least once in its modern sense. The instance is a famous passage from the *New Testament* when Mary Magdalen anoints Christ with expensive unguents. The disciples stridently object: 'they had indignation, saying, To what purpose is this waste (ἀπώλεια)? For this ointment might have been sold for much, and given to the poor.' Jesus however answers them: 'Why trouble ye the woman? for she hath wrought a good work upon me. For ye have the poor always with you; but me ye have not always. For in that she hath poured this ointment on my body, she did it for my burial.'[8] Nevertheless, the modernity of this use of the word waste (ἀπώλεια) is perhaps deceptive. One might also translate the term as 'consumption', simply using something up. The very word waste in English was frequently used in the sense of something being devoured or spent, without any necessary moral fault, as when the bard says that 'March is wasted fourteen days',[9] meaning that half the month has gone by.

Technically, the disciples are right: the perfume could be sold and the takings distributed to those in need. In what remains a great paradox of economics, the translation of a precious object into money is rational but the price achieved bears only an oblique relation to the value that a person may experience as the beneficiary. The disciples only see the material value of the myrrh but Christ sees its symbolic value as oblation, which turns out to be necessary in honouring his divine mission. Maybe this is not a good example if you consider the higher religious purpose an irrational superstition;

---

7   *Henry V* 3.1.14.

8   *Matthew* 26.8–12, famous because sung in Bach's *Matthew Passion*.

9   *Julius Caesar* 2.1.59; *cf.* 'some nine moons wasted', *Othello* 1.3.84.

nevertheless, the point is made that definitions of luxury are relative. What is a luxury? The criteria are never absolute. What looks like money-down-the-drain for one purpose is essential for another. Anything prestigious could be deemed a luxury and condemned accordingly. It is a puritanical foolishness which Jesus himself considers shortsighted.

Even without those symbolic associations, and whether they are sacramental or not, luxury is in the eye of the beholder and so is waste. Wherever we talk of luxury, we can talk of waste, and to speak thus is also ancient. The Greeks certainly recognized outlandish spending (καταναλίσκω)[10] or at least imprudent allocation of resources, as when Epimetheus is accused by Socrates of squandering his resources on horses.[11] In all epochs, thrift was recommended, else we should be destitute in lean times. In epochs that were more materially straitened than our own, there was always consciousness of thrift, which the ancient Greeks respected alongside simplicity of living (λιτότης) and the Romans also recognized in the value of saving (*parsimonia*), which remained an element of the renaissance development of household capital (*masserizia*) and is also a cornerstone of the prolific investment in the industrial age, where capital would cease to be localized but would spread from the holdings of small and frugal savers to large manufacturing ventures wherever credit was extended.

Against these ingredients of good domestic management and the aggregated wealth of communities, waste is pernicious. It represents everything that would weaken a community, from the moral to the material. Through waste, one would have fewer resources to contribute toward productive ends and defence; and through its luxurious corollaries, one would also have a soft and derelict population, used to being feather-bedded and spoilt rather than disciplined and motivated, courageous and self-sacrificing, altruistic and hard-working. This decadence is already captured in the Greek term for living softly or in excessive comfort or indulgence (σπαταλάω),[12] which was also associated, arguably especially through Hebraic culture, with wantonness and luxury.[13] In pagan sources of a later date, the word turns up

---

10   Plato, *Timaeus* 36b, *Phaedo* 72d; use up spend lavish money, Xenophon 1.2.22.

11   τας δυναμεις εις τα αλογα Plato, *Protagoras* 321C; Plato, *Timaeus* 1C; consume Aristotle, *Generation of animals* 763ᵃ13, Plutarch 2.160b; one must expend (with the verbal suffix -ωτεον) (την σπουδην εις τα μηδενος αξια) Aristotle, *Rhetoric for Alexander* 1420ᵇ22.

12   Polybios 36, 17.7 (second century BC), *Inscriptiones græcæ* 14.2002 in Rome, *Ecclesiastes* 21.115.

13   *Ecclesiastes* 27.13, *1 Timothy* 5.6, *James* 5.5, but also in pagan sources, *e.g.* Greek anthology 11.17, Nicharchos, 5.301.2 (Agathon).

designating a certain kind of wasteful person who luxuriates wantonly (σπάταλος) and is lascivious as well as prodigal.[14]

Reaching into the renaissance, Stoic philosophy recommended modesty irrespective of wealth, which reflects a psychological distaste for wasteful habits. The families who built the wealth of the renaissance, no matter what their personal fortunes, seem to have tussled over correct and decorous expenditure and often favoured frugality. The very family unit resembled a contemporary corporation, with a rich management structure looking after numerous stakeholders in many ventures, which included banking and finance. Increasingly dedicated to the theme of magnificence, the large families remained cautious about extravagance and were fond of savings.

An example is the aristocratic Alberti family. In the third book in Leon Battista Alberti's treatise *On the family*,[15] Giannozzo and Lionardo agree that the whole family, irrespective of its size, should live under the one roof for economy's sake, and for the family members to gather rather than spread out within the house, so that only a single fire needs to be lit in order to heat so many souls, rather than three fires. Typically, the treatise does not use a word for waste but the argument is clear.

In the fourth book of the same treatise, Giannozzo identifies the wickedness of certain priests whose habits are wasteful. The priests are extremely avid (*cupidissimi*) and vie with one another not on proper virtues or reading but who can outdo the others (*soprastare*) in pomp and ostentation. They want the largest number of plump and liveried cavalcades; they want to go out in public with a great army of parasites; and together they cultivate desires by too much idleness (*per troppo ozio*), that are lascivious, audacious and rash (*inconsulte*). They are without boundaries (*incontinentissimi*) and, with neither saving nor accumulation (*risparmio o masserizia*), they only care about satisfying their stimulated appetites (*incitati apetiti*). To feed their lust and vice (*libidine e vizio*) they burn with a marvellous malice and have perpetual competition and division in the house. In their obscene and dishonest life, besieged by wasters and wicked sycophants (*perditissimi e sceleratissimi assentatori*), the expenses are greater than the income (*più sono le spese che l'ordinarie sue ricchezze*). Thus, it seems befitting to them to be rapacious elsewhere; but when it comes to decent spending (*onestissime spese*) for the assistance of the family or friends and to bring relatives to a fair and honourable state, they are inhuman, tight (*tenacissimi*), late and miserly.

---

14   *Greek anthology* 5.17 (Rufinus), 5.26 σπαταλώδης soft, self-indulgent Soranus medicus 2.54.
15   *I libri della famiglia* 3.

The shameless practices are beneath contempt. Curiously, Alberti has no time for the rich priests even when their spending sustains the lesser folk who are their retinue. These hangers-on are described as a great army of eaters (*mangiatori*), that is, parasites, people who get into the confidence of the powerful and consume without yielding any profit to anyone but themselves. This archetype of the ingratiating good-for-nothing was observed in ancient Greece and finds its way onto the comic stage still in the eighteenth century, where they were known as urbane scroungers (*scrocchi*).[16] Though we all need to eat, we ought to earn our place at the table; and the people who merely wangle their way into the banquet with a subtle understanding of favours could be described as wasters, whence Alberti—like Goldoni centuries later—has sympathy neither for them nor their indulgent patrons. A century later again, Nietzsche would consider hospitality to be partly a negative virtue, 'the danger of dangers among cultured and rich souls who handle themselves wastefully, almost indifferently and drive the virtue of liberality to the point of being a burden'.[17]

In the Italian invectives against various shades of waste, however, a direct word for waste is seldom used. The Italian language provides plenty of verbs and nouns (*sprecare, sciupare, spreco, sperperare, scialacquare*) but they hardly ever feature in poetic or satirical literature, including by moral authors like Dante and Machiavelli, narrators like Boccaccio and Bandello, or even ostentatiously lavish baroque authors like Marino. In an amusing line in a long poem, Goldoni explains that a narrative is comprehensible even if it contains esoteric words. Wasting (*sperperare*) is one of the three words that he chooses, suggesting that the term was uncommon in popular speech.[18]

Similar points can be made of French, where plenty of words exist to describe wasting (like *gaspiller*) or wasteful (*gâcheur*) but none is used in moral authors like Montaigne in the sixteenth century or La Rochefault or La Bruyère or their contemporaneous tragedians in the *grand siècle*; and such terms have to wait to the nineteenth century before they are much exploited in poetic literature, as in Baudelaire (once), where in any case

---

16   Goldoni describes Ferdinando thus in *Le smanie per la villeggiatura, passim.*

17   'zum Beispiel unsrer „Gastfreundschaft": wie es die Gefahr der Gefahren bei hochgearteten und reichen Seelen ist, welche verschwenderisch, fast gleichgültig mit sich selbst umgehn und die Tugend der Liberalität bis zum Laster treiben. Man muss wissen, sich zu bewahren: stärkste Probe der Unabhängigkeit', Friedrich Nietzsche, *Jenseits von Gut und Böse* 41.

18   *Esopo alla grata* 3.41–51.

gaspiller could be translated as spill.[19] Occasionally, one finds the term *dépense* used to mean waste, as in La Bruyère, who speaks of a waste of time,[20] or Racine who says that three quarters of your fortune is wasted or spent;[21] but mostly the term simply means expense. Derived from the Latin *dispendium*, like the Italian *dispendio*, the French shares its root with our 'spend', and is not structurally burdened with an evil or damaging principle, like our 'waste'.

Between the renaissance and the enlightenment, baroque feeling on waste is powerfully expressed in English, where the word grew with colour and curiosity. In Shakespeare, waste is gorgeously convoluted and paradoxical, as in Romeo's ingenious counterpoint 'that sparing makes huge waste',[22] which also acknowledges that the antonym of waste is sparing or saving, rather than preservation. Although in Shakespeare waste retains the physicality of something lessening, it gains a great sense of the unnecessary, which is a key quality in our contemporary understanding of waste. As Mercutio says: 'in delay / We waste our lights in vain, like lamps by day.'[23] There is no point using artificial light when the sun provides brightness enough. This superfluity is waste in the contemporary sense, though it must be admitted that the image of the candle still supports the idea of waste as 'getting less' or 'becoming thinner' as it burns.[24] The motif of diminishing is integral to waste in other languages, as in the etymology of the German verb for waste (*verschwenden*, from *schwinden*, to wane, to shrink, dwindle or fade).

Shakespeare often contemplates the superfluous, the preposterously unnecessary and even counterproductive, which his Salisbury characterizes as being 'possess'd with double pomp' and as 'wasteful and ridiculous excess'.[25] Shakespearean language lets us witness the transition of waste

---

19   'Sur des fronts ténébreux de poètes illustres / Qui viennent gaspiller leurs sanglantes sueurs', *Le jeu* in *Les fleurs du mal* 96.9–12.

20   'la plus forte dépense que l'on puisse faire est celle du temps', La Bruyère, 'Discours sur Théophraste', *Les caractères*, preface.

21   'Les trois quarts de vos biens sont déjà dépensés', *Les plaideurs* 3.1.

22   *Romeo and Juliet* 1.1.224.

23   *Romeo and Juliet* 1.4.45.

24   as in Hero's wish to 'let Benedick, like cover'd fire, Consume away in sighs, waste inwardly', *Much ado about nothing* 3.1.78. It explains Puck's 'wasted brands', that is a torch that burns itself out.

25   *cf.* Goethe's line where the Direktor defends the Spartan character of the stagecraft: 'Gebraucht das groß, und kleine Himmelslicht, / Die Sterne dürfet ihr verschwenden', *Faust*.

from a physical decrease to a moral concept. You can sense the movement in Shylock's line 'to waste his borrow'd purse',[26] meaning to make the purse thinner by consuming the money therein, already morally dubious by virtue of the fact that the contents are on loan. Similar tensions of significance arise in King Richard's line confessing that 'I wasted time, and now doth time waste me',[27] meaning that I passed time up without profit and now time shrinks my fibre and prospects in revenge. Likewise in Falstaff's witticisms confusing the two meanings of the one phoneme, waste and waist, where the Chief Justice says: 'Your means are very slender, and your waste is great', to which Falstaff replies that 'I would my means were greater, and my waist slenderer.'[28] Even when we speak of time, the waste is not necessarily frowned upon, as in Puck's happy line that 'A merrier hour was never wasted there.'[29] In moral terms, the waste is neutral.[30] This neutrality explains the apparent contradiction in Rosalind's line: 'the burden of lean and wasteful learning'.[31] The learning is not wasteful in the sense of pointless but in the sense of consuming your hours without muscular engagement, which causes the body and the candle to become weaker, what we might still call wasting away.

The pointlessness of an action, however, does attract the word waste, especially over words spoken in vain, as in Angelo's 'you but waste your words'[32] or Portia's 'Waste no time in words'.[33] And in fact, the prime commodity that attracts fear of waste is time, the cause of moral reproach, as in Olivia's feeling that 'The clock upbraids me with the waste of time.'[34] While sometimes this waste of time is also neutral, like the whiling of time,[35] there are good reasons for the preoccupation. Of all the resources that are available to us, time is the one that measures us, that is our life, our

---

26 *Merchant of Venice* 2.5.50.

27 *Richard II* 5.5.49.

28 2 Henry IV 1.2.160; cf. Falstaff's 'Indeed, I am in the waist two yards about; but I am now about no waste; I am about thrift', *Merry wives of Windsor* 1.3.47.

29 *Mid summer night's dream* 2.1.57.

30 'To have the expense and waste of his revenues', *Lear* 2.1.102.

31 *As you like it* 3.2.341.

32 *Measure for measure* 2.2.72.

33 *Merchant of Venice* 3.4.54.

34 *Twelfth night* 3.1.141.

35 As Gower says, 'Thus time we waste, and longest leagues make short', *Pericles* 4.4.1, meaning that the passing of time does not need to be so boring. See also Prospero's charming lines: 'Sir, I invite your Highness and your train / To my poor cell, where you shall take your rest / For this one night; which—part of it—I'll waste / With such discourse as, I not doubt, shall make it / Go quick away', *Tempest* 5.1.

youth or whatever remaining age we have. In an age that sought constantly to remember that we die (*memento mori*) any waste of time was felt acutely, much resented with someone unworthy,[36] even if wasting other people's time was a privilege that the powerless had to put up with.[37] The idea of something being inherently a waste of time is not so much in evidence, or nothing to compare with Büchner's dismissive 'what a total waste of time!' (*Was 'n Zeitverschwendung!*) in the nineteenth century.[38] Nevertheless, sometimes strong feelings are associated with waste in the baroque, as when a dagger wound wastes the blood of McDuff, 'ruin's wasteful entrance';[39] and Shakespeare even associates waste with a personality type, 'a wasteful king',[40] and speaks 'of raging waste'[41] when it comes to money.

The history of ideas allows us to triangulate the concept of waste in a zone bordered on the one side by destruction or physical diminishing and on the other side as the opposite of thrift. But at the base of the triangle is another concept again, which creates the foundation of moral opinions on waste, which is plenty, bounty or luxury, themselves both good and bad according to cultural estimation.

Still today, we have much ambivalence over luxury. Few concepts are so fraught with moral and aesthetic contradictions. Luxury, though sought with envy and cultivated competitively by all the advanced economies, has long attracted criticism. The equivocation is so deeply a part of European culture that it finds an expression in the very language by which the idea is communicated. Our word luxury derives from the Latin for plenty (*luxus*) which spawned a derivative (*luxuria*) that already indicates a kind of rank superabundance, a sense retained in the English term luxuriant, as in describing thick undergrowth or a prolific pot of basil. In the renaissance, however, the somewhat wanton and overgrown associations of the Latin overtook the root, so to speak, to express an outrageous libidinous energy, impulsively lusty and expressing lack of control. The Italian term *lussuria*

---

36   As Malvolio says 'you waste the treasure of your time with a foolish knight'.

37   As Arviragus says, 'That they will waste their time upon our note', *Cymbeline* 4.4.20.

38   Georg Büchner, *Woyzeck* beginning lines, spoken by the Captain.

39   *Macbeth* 2.3.

40   As the Gardener says, 'Bolingbroke / Hath seiz'd the wasteful King. O! what pity is it / That he had not so trimm'd and dress'd his land / As we this garden!' *King Richard II* 3.4.

41   'to Varro and to Isidore He owes nine thousand; besides my former sum, / Which makes it five-and-twenty. Still in motion / Of raging waste! It cannot hold; it will not.' *Timon of Athens* 2.1.4; *cf.* Roderigo 'With nought but truth. I have wasted myself out of my means.' *Othello* 4.2.

expressed lust or 'illegitimate lewdness', as Cesare Ripa says in his book of emblems from the early seventeenth century, which became a famous source-book for artists.[42]

Our age does not look upon hedonism so reproachfully and it is much encouraged by commerce. Is luxury good or bad? You can almost see the development of language neurotically hedging its bets over this dilemma. To get around the embarrassment that we do not know, that we simultaneously want to admire luxury (and to possess it) but also to abhor and stigmatize it, the European psyche hatched two terms which might take care of the equivocation. Let *lussuria* be disgusting and lewd; let it go wild and convulse, whence it indicates moral abandon and fornication alongside the randy appetites of goats and rats. Meanwhile, let us—as people of culture and aspiration—have the luxury of things, *lusso*, grand halls bedight with pictures and stucco and replete with tables bearing unaffordable sweetmeats.

Although the idea of luxury as a purely material superfluity—untainted by erotic excess—retained a separate term (*lusso*), in fact this form of privilege was also not without anxious suspicions and concerns for social control. Anything good, by the neurosis of western culture is also something bad, because it might be owned by the wrong people or put to the wrong effect. In the fourth book of his influential treatise *The courtier*, from the early sixteenth century, Baldassare Castiglione implores us to 'temper all superfluity' for economic reasons, because wasting resources lays cities to ruin.[43] Around *lusso*, he includes over-sumptuous private buildings, banquets, excessive dowries and pomp in jewelry and clothes. Productive capital would be tied up in aesthetic nonsense or vanity.

In the exorbitant decorative century that followed, *lusso* would remain under suspicion, even with such a flamboyant poet as Marino, who saw 'soft luxury and barbarous ornament' as a phantasm that seductively gets into his hero's nostrils;[44] though Marino is not such a hypocrite that he does not also express his fondness for 'superb luxury' elsewhere[45] because he flagrantly demonstrates his liking for it. Whatever one decries as unnecessary one can equally extol as superlative. It depends on your expectations and values, which are likely to be in contention in all epochs.

---

42   'concupiscenze illecite', Ripa, Iconologia, 1610 s.v.

43   Il cortegiano 4.42.

44   'il Lusso molle e 'l barbaro ornamento', Adone 6.151.8.

45   'lusso superbo', 8.91.7; cf. 12.182.3.

This ambivalence explains why Shakespeare, whose language is at least as luxuriant as Marino's, sings: 'Fie on sinful fantasy! / Fie on lust and luxury!' or complains of 'hateful luxury, / And bestial appetite in change of lust',[46] always associating luxury with libido. As if remembering the etymological link with lust, Shakespeare associates 'the devil Luxury, with his fat rump and potato finger' with lechery.[47] It is why old King Hamlet's ghost associates luxury with erotic vice in the lines: 'Let not the royal bed of Denmark be / a couch for luxury and damned incest.'[48] And it is also why Lear makes an apology for lechery and 'luxury, pell-mell', because adultery could not produce worse offspring than his own treacherous surviving daughters, who were nevertheless 'Got 'tween the lawful sheets.'[49]

The uncanny sexual stress inside the concept is not just a quirk of philology and, up to a point, the archaic confusion of luxury and lust persists. Infuriatingly, in fact, expensive consumer goods or services for the socially aspirational are associated with sex through advertising. One capriciously represents the desired product or service with the vector of naked legs or youthful cleavage. So strong is this appeal that decades of feminism and rational reflexion are to no avail. Wealth and power are popularly considered to have aphrodisiac properties, so the archaic link between luxury and lust is not likely to disappear any time soon, no matter how much we recognize that the connexion is illogical.

The ancient critique of luxury as an inappropriate way of spending resources also has a contemporary counterpart. We are wary of many luxuries for reasons of sustainability. The more luxury we desire, the more luxury is produced, the more energy is consumed and emissions are produced. One is anxious about the exponential global consumption of goods and services, which is now reckoned to be unsustainable and also impossible to arrest. Luxury is extensively subjective and dependent upon prior values. In a comedy by the eighteenth-century playwright Carlo Goldoni, a shrewd English noble, Milord Wambert, says to his sceptical creative compatriots: 'Friends, if you so detest fashion and luxury, if you so love the common good and reformed custom, why do you yourselves make such rich works which wreak such waste (*recano dispendio*) and cause damage? You earn your bread with silver and gold. You study unusual ways of shaping shoes.

---

46   *The Merry Wives of Windsor* 5.5.98.
47   *Troilus and Cressida* 5.2.55.
48   *Hamlet* 1.5.83.
49   *Lear* 4.6.119.

Therefore, O wise and prudent heroes, luxury is only harmful when buyers don't spend on you!'[50]

The accusation was that costly foreign trends are wasteful and therefore bad for the prudent management of the economy. But if you succeed in achieving profits by producing very similar artefacts to the ones that you condemn, all of a sudden you no longer need to be so critical. A case of hypocrisy, then, that translates to various degrees of sanctimony today: you deplore luxuries that you do not have or that you have no interest in; meanwhile, you forget all the luxuries that you have accrued and continue to invest in almost unawares.

Goldoni was acutely aware of this hidden devotion to luxury in his countrymen. Italians, he considered, were ridiculous spendthrifts both on unnecessary fashions but also on ways of spending time. In four of his comedies, the Venetian humourist reserves particular scorn for holiday houses. These vacationers are pure indulgence, which cause families to forget their business in town, seek abandon in unproductive sports, gambling and consuming prodigious amounts of wine, meat and chocolate, plus the sequestered capital on the property. Today, he says in the preamble to *The malcontents*, 'holidaying has arrived at an excess of luxury, waste and liability'.[51] Echoing ideas that he would express in his play *Crazes for the country holiday*,[52] he indicates that it might have been fine for the idle aristocracy to enjoy such indulgences but for the aspirational productive community to consume its scarce resources in this frivolity is a recipe for calamity.

Paradoxically, the very economic vigour that Goldoni recommended ended up generating more luxuries, especially in the burgeoning industries of the British Isles that he so admired. The industrial revolution which began in the north at the time of Goldoni's late plays promoted the very motif that he despised in middle-class Italian communities, namely, as Nardo says in *The country philosopher*, that country folk are content to remain as they always were, whereas city people always want to be something else, something more, something different, 'oppressed by luxury, ambition and appetite'.[53]

We could therefore answer Goldoni with an existential question: why be so industrious and parsimonious if it is not ultimately to win some greater comfort, welfare, amenity and enjoyment for ourselves and community which

---

50   *Il filosofo inglese* 2.3.

51   'è arrivato oggidì all'eccesso del lusso, del dispendio e dell'incomoda soggezione', *I malcontenti*, foreword.

52   *Le smanie per la villeggiatura*, preface.

53   *Il filosofo di campagna* 1.5.

may also be a kind of luxury? We can add the principle: luxury is justified if it makes us think and feel, if it adds curiosity and vision, like philosophy itself, which contributes insight and wisdom to culture and is therefore not a luxury in any dispensable sense.

Alas, Goldoni's own characters answer him in more pragmatic terms. In *Crazes for the country holiday*, scene after scene shows the gentry over-spending, living beyond their means in trying to sustain ostentatious holidays involving new outfits, coach trips, banquets, hangers-on, expensive choco-lates and coffee, above all, countless idle hours which mean income foregone, plus the dormant capital tied up in the property. From time to time, some-times by the prudent and redemptive figure of Fulgenzio, they are caused to scruple. If it is a case of not being able to afford a new dress for the holiday or a holiday at all, the justifications for proceeding with the extravagance are passionate. The dear old figure of Filippo is persuaded to reconsider the promise of the holiday, which he personally hangs out for; but, resolved as he is to exercise restraint, he cannot deny his daughter, Giacinta, who comes back at him with a powerful argument:

> what will the good tongues of Montenero say about us? Signor Filippo
> no longer holidays; he's finished, no longer has the means. His daughter,
> poor thing! Her dowry is frittered; who will take her? Who would
> want to have her? They must eat little and go out less. What we saw
> was smoke, not roast. I can hear them. I feel a cold sweat coming on.[54]

While the hedonism of the holidays is the superintending motif, Giacinta thinks of her marriage prospects. Not to show off (*fare la figura*) means accepting lower stakes in the neighbourhood, less prestige, less social mobility. For a nubile person, the case, in its own terms, follows reasonable and natural Darwinian logic. It is a strategy of finding the best opportuni-ties for perpetuating your gene-stock: in your social milieu, you have to be able to project the air of privilege, else you will not attract a partner with the privileges and best opportunities for your future. You want to marry up.

If it is really reasonable and natural, why does Goldoni make fun of it and bring his personages to the brink of ruin in order to illustrate the vanity

---

54 'Figurarsi! quelle buone lingue di Montenero che cosa direbbono de' fatti nostri!
Il signor Filippo non villeggia più, ha finito, non ha più il modo. La sua figliuola,
poveraccia! ha terminato presto di figurare. La dote è fritta; chi l'ha da prendere?
chi l'ha da volere? Dovevano mangiar meno, dovevano trattar meno. Quello che si
vedeva, era fumo, non era arrosto. Mi par di sentirle; mi vengono i sudori freddi.'
Le smanie per la villeggiatura 2.10.

of their aspirations? He considers the holidays a waste because the reasons that Giacinta provides, though internally consistent, are also mad. At what point would the pretence end in order to bid higher in the market for eligible men? Why not use smoke and mirrors in order to secure a count or a prince? At a certain point, we need to make a moral judgement about the probity and wisdom of whatever luxury and call it waste or folly. Goldoni is sanguine in his aversion to the folly and in no doubt about satirizing it.

Despite the sharp consciousness that the eighteenth century brought to the theme, the history of waste is not linear. Through metaphor, the word changes its meaning from physical lessening to the supply-side of economic failure; but there is no pattern of wasteful behaviour that accompanies this shift. Culture does not begin with an archaic love of luxury and somehow end with the parsimony of the nineteenth century, often stereotyped through puritanical values, an abstemious century of wowsers, keen on engineering and social machinery. If anything, the prolific ornament of the great nineteenth-century cities of Europe and America—like Paris and New York, reaching into the 1920s—testifies to the 'double pomp' of capital, effortlessly erecting stately buildings of fabulous dimensions and then filling them with rich commodities for sale, endlessly aspirational, with promotional organization and distribution networks.

The age of the middle class or the industrial revolution—which we are still a part of—was not so hostile to waste. The very motor of industrial progress was based on what Marx famously termed surplus value, the margin of superabundance that makes capital; and while Marx himself would condemn the non-use value of marketed objects as fetish, the very basis for economic development was a margin identified as unnecessary. The word waste is not even always used in a pejorative sense, especially in German, where the noun (*Verschwendung*) also has benign connotations of lavishness and extravagance, which can easily be used in positive senses. Authors use the adjective (*verschwenderisch*) in admiration, say, over heavenly bounty. So in the second part of Goethe's *Faust*, a youthful driver allegorically describes himself as 'Waste (or Lavishness): I am poetry', explaining that as a poet he is fulfilled when he throws away his property; but he is immeasurably rich, comparable to Pluto, whom he enlivens with ornament, dance and banquet, dispensing to him whatever he lacks.[55]

---

55   Knabe Lenker: 'Bin die Verschwendung, bin die Poesie; / Bin der Poet, der sich vollendet, / Wenn er sein eigenst Gut verschwendet. / Auch ich bin unermeßlich reich / Und schätze mich dem Plutus gleich, / Beleb' und schmück' ihm Tanz und Schmaus, / Das, was ihm fehlt, das teil' ich aus.' *2 Faust* 1.

Sensitivity to the harmful effects of waste is not universal. Around 1800, it rather belongs to the passion and fury of *Sturm und Drang* to throw caution to the winds and see waste as a sign of integrity and strength of feeling rather than the suppression of instinct that reason might otherwise insist upon. Thus Werther scorns the philistines who counsel the rationing of time spent with a girlfriend when passion excites a young heart to become totally dependent on her, to be with her at all times, to lavish (or waste, *verschwenden*) all of his powers and fortune and to express his devotion at all moments,[56] while the unimaginative advises the young man to divide his attention between love and work. To follow this advice would be less than love.

In various metaphoric ways, overspending or lavishness or waste is celebrated in poetic literature: 'don't waste the darts of your eyes';[57] or, in Kleist, the delirious enchantment of the mob lavishes itself (*sich verschwendet*) upon your great name.[58] For Goethe, there is something marvellous about the nature of passion that heeds waste not at all; and toward the end of the nineteenth century, Nietzsche would identify the special quality of nature with superabundance, excess and waste: 'strong contrasts, harsh changes from day and night, brightness and colour, the glory of everything sudden, secret, terrible, the speed of disruptive storms, everywhere the lavish spilling over of Nature's cornucopia', against which our culture is clean and cold.[59] A similar estimation arises with respect to reality, which 'reveals an enchanting wealth of types, the lushness of a lavish play of form and change'.[60] Even the proud powers of the German people can be described thus.[61]

---

56   *Werther*, 26 May (à propos rules in art); the more conventional use of the word can be found *ibid.* 1 July and 11 July.

57   Goethe, *Torquato Tasso* 2.3.

58   Alkmene in Heinrich von Kleist, *Amphitryon* 1.4.

59   'Gewaltsame Gegensätze, schroffer Wechsel von Tag und Nacht, Gluth und Farbenpracht, die Verehrung alles Plötzlichen, Geheimnissvollen, Schrecklichen, die Schnelligkeit der hereinbrechenden Unwetter, überall das verschwenderische Ueberströmen der Füllhörner der Natur: und dagegen, in unserer Cultur, ein heller, doch nicht leuchtender Himmel, reine, ziemlich gleich verbleibende Luft, Schärfe, ja Kälte gelegentlich: so heben sich beide Zonen gegen einander ab.' Nietzsche, *Menschliches, Allzumenschliches* 236.

60   'Die Wirklichkeit zeigt uns einen entzückenden Reichthum der Typen, die Üppigkeit eines verschwenderischen Formenspiels und -Wechsels', Nietzsche, *Götzen-Dämmerung*, Moral als Widernatur 6.

61   'dass es den aufgehäuften Schatz von Kraft eine Zeit lang selbst verschwenderisch ausgeben darf', Nietzsche, *Götzen-Dämmerung*, Was den Deutschen abgeht, 1.

The case cannot be overstated because elsewhere Nietzsche uses the word to mean wasteful in a negative sense, as when art goes to waste.[62] The interesting element is again that language inherently equivocates; sometimes the word condemns and sometimes it celebrates. For Nietzsche, the equivocation is almost essential, because it expresses a deeper uncertainty in the very point of existence. The existential dilemma can be explored in other words, as when Nietzsche looks into the ultimate pointlessness of humankind and one sees one's effect on the world as waste (*Vergeudung*). But even this despair is somehow noble, and it belongs specifically to poets to extrapolate from the individual and to see the same waste in the flowering of nature.[63] Normally, this word (*Vergeudung*) is unequivocally pejorative, a frittering away, a squandering which attracts no redemption, right down to the 'noble' waste of Greek life in war.[64] But when it comes to the chaotic profusion of nature, the word ends up being positive.

The reasons are existential. It seems silly to Nietzsche that the Stoics ever wanted to live according to nature, because 'nature is wasteful beyond measure (*verschwenderisch ohne Maass*), indifferent without measure, without intention, reflexion, without clemency and justice, fertile and barren and uncertain all at the same time'.[65] One should not look to nature to fill in existential gaps because, as he notes elsewhere, one should see nature in its whole wasteful and indifferent grandeur.[66] Nor should one look to artificial

---

62   '... wird es Niemanden geben, der die Kunst, die hier verschwendet worden ist, begreift: es hat nie jemand mehr von neuen, von unerhörten, von wirklich erst dazu geschaffnen Kunstmitteln zu verschwenden gehabt', Nietzsche, *Ecce homo*, Warum ich so gute Bücher schreibe. 4; *cf.* 'eine zu negativen Zwecken verschwendete Kraft', *ibid.* 8; cf. also 'die feinste Künstlerschaft ist wie vor Tauben verschwendet', Nietzsche, *Jenseits von Gut und Böse* 246.

63   Sieht er bei Allem, was er thut, auf die letzte Ziellosigkeit der Menschen, so bekommt sein eigenes Wirken in seinen Augen den Charakter der Vergeudung. Sich aber als Menschheit (und nicht nur als Individuum) ebenso vergeudet zu fühlen, wie wir die einzelne Blüthe von der Natur vergeudet sehen, ist ein Gefühl über alle Gefühle. – Wer ist aber desselben fähig? Gewiss nur ein Dichter: und Dichter wissen sich immer zu trösten.' *Menschliches, Allzumenschliches* 33.

64   'Der grösste Nachtheil der jetzt so verherrlichten Volksheere besteht in der Vergeudung von Menschen der höchsten Civilisation', *Menschliches, Allzumenschliches* 442.

65   '"Gemäss der Natur" wollt ihr leben? Oh ihr edlen Stoiker, welche Betrügerei der Worte! Denkt euch ein Wesen, wie es die Natur ist, verschwenderisch ohne Maass, gleichgültig ohne Maass, ohne Absichten und Rücksichten, ohne Erbarmen und Gerechtigkeit, fruchtbar und öde und ungewiss zugleich, denkt euch die Indifferenz selbst als Macht – wie könntet ihr gemäss dieser Indifferenz leben? Nietzsche', *Jenseits von Gut und Böse* 9.

66   'denn hier wie überall zeigt sich „die Natur", wie sie ist, in ihrer ganzen verschwenderischen und gleichgültigen Grossartigkeit, welche empört, aber vornehm ist', Nietzsche, *Jenseits von Gut und Böse* 188.

purposes. Nietzsche finds, for example, that he wasted ten years as philologist: how useless, how arbitrary! He is ashamed of his false modesty.[67]

These agonies prefigure contemporary consciousness, where waste is simultaneously anathematized as wanton[68] and yet spooks our economy in our dependency on consumerism (or spending) and growth, as if a necessity of thriving nations as well as an ideal of ambitious individuals. The condemnation of waste arises on the political right as much as the left. Conservative parties are quick to identify waste in any form of spending by the left, especially if it relates to welfare, which is always a cheap electoral issue. Meanwhile, the left is understandably concerned with the waste of the world's natural resources and the damage that over-consumption wreaks on natural systems.

The history of waste tells us that these ideas in contention are not new. There are structural reasons revealed in the very language that we use, sometimes destructive and sometimes winsomely lavish, where even nature is suspected as the archetype of pointless overproduction and wasteful superabundance, against which moral resistance is a kind of reciprocal perversity. But at the same time, there is no escaping the discourse: one has to worry about waste. Our time is running out, as in Simonides' exhortation in Shakespeare: 'we sit too long on trifles / And waste the time, which looks for other revels'.[69] As individuals, we always have to evaluate our personal time, else the prime chance slips by. It is part of the neurosis of living in a competitive society, where our every moment is potentially agonized as either yielding profit or waste.

Up to a point, we require insulation from this reality; otherwise, we might well go mad with the preoccupation, and our personal teleology would crush us. It would be like an overactive superego, menacing the ego in the famous Freudian economy of a threatening voice inside us that compounds with libido and the challenges of the outside world to produce neurosis. To handle this psychological embarrassment, society produces prolific narcotics, which are also very marketable, that enable us to forget any exigence in decisions over time and other resources. Leaving aside the

---

67 'Eine Ungeduld mit mir überfiel mich; ich sah ein, dass es die höchste Zeit war, mich auf mich zurückzubesinnen. Mit Einem Male war mir auf eine schreckliche Weise klar, wie viel Zeit bereits verschwendet sei, – wie nutzlos, wie willkürlich sich meine ganze Philologen-Existenz an meiner Aufgabe ausnehme. Ich schämte mich dieser falschen Bescheidenheit ... Zehn Jahre hinter mir', Nietzsche, *Ecce homo*, Mit zwei Fortsetzungen 3.

68 Google finds 200,000 instances of 'wanton waste' alone.

69 *Pericles of Athens* 2.3.93.

literal social drugs, like alcohol, or medical drugs to make us feel more relaxed, we have television which constantly gives licence for the relief of worry. You do not need to feel that you are wasting time watching a ball game when apparently the whole nation—so you would imagine from the media—is hysterically involved to an equal degree. With such public momentum driving the interest, you quite forget that devoting hours to the idle spectacle is a waste; instead, it is valorized as valuable recreation with representations of fervour, bonding, passion, goals, ambition, heartbreak and glory.

These medialized drugs are a linear extension of the economy that Goldoni satirized in the eighteenth century. No less than in old Italy, middle-class Anglophone people today also have holiday houses and spend—in his terms squander—large amounts of time and money that could be directed to productive ends, such as enhancing cultural capital. But once a market develops around a behaviour, every incentive is brought to bear to support the wasteful interest, to normalize its extravagance as something that everyone would want. Thanks to a combination of advertising and the contagious enthusiasm that is culture in the wider sense, people begin to tell themselves that their desires are normal, even though they are historically confined and as stupid as Goldoni's shrewd maids and butlers recognize.[70]

There are strong reasons to talk about waste to offset equal and opposite incentives not to. To talk of waste in one's personal life is often to bump up against an ontological barrier that seems to protect us from peering into a chasm. Further, as history indicates, there is much vanity tied up in our view of ourselves; and any identification of waste is likely to be experienced as a criticism of ourselves. The topic has risks of great offence, looking down on people's tastes, national conventions and private fun. Consequently it has risks of disenfranchising the very people whose cooperation you will need. It was the invidious job of Fulgenzio in Goldoni's plays; and only the financial collapse of two families forced others to listen to him.

In our own age, as noted à propos luxury, there are pressing needs in relation to sustainability to identify waste and stop it. If we do not really need to meet someone interstate or overseas but can use telecommunication instead, we must save the jet fuel and desist from travel. There is a moral incumbency that induces us to come back to the theme of waste with a vengeance, where all forms of waste have to be scrutinized, as they are all somewhat interrelated. The task has never been so urgent; and, though

---

70   It is the argument in my 'Holiday house', *The space wasters: the architecture of Australian misanthropy*, Planning Institute of Australia, Carlton 2011, ch. 6, pp. 62–68.

history reveals that we are not particularly well prepared for the challenge, the need to examine waste in education is pressing in counterintuitive ways, facing a deep ambivalence about the values around creativity.

In the deconstruction of waste, it appears that we cannot simply label as waste anything that we do not like. To cast the term waste at any target might only be a cheap form of deprecation because, alas, there is waste in everything that we cherish. Even with the waste of potential there is much uncertainty that anything can be done. For example, students might have enormous potential in science but, in the course of their studies, they are drawn to the humanities. Up to a point, the potential to do science is never realized and therefore in a sense goes to waste. We acknowledge this limit to opportunity without lamentation, because there are necessary choices; and although five years spent learning calculus may end in very little, it is no scandal. It took five years to figure out that the humanities are a better option and, speaking materialistically, less waste will occur with the change of direction; besides, we always feel that no science ever goes to waste.

It is true that waste may be especially inherent in creative endeavour but the same economic rule applies as with any discipline: in describing the overstrike of study in any area in which it turns out our efforts are relatively forlorn, we are talking about a necessary cost rather than waste *per se*. In that sense, much that looks wasteful can be justified; but haggling over these margins is not our concern. The concern is systematic discouragement of creative impulses in any discipline, irrespective of choice and aptitude. When all is said and done, there is no excuse for discouragement; and education, which should be a furthering experience, is full of disheartening strictures and judgements. We have an educational system which is mostly structured on knocking people back, putting them down in stakes that they did not necessarily agree to. Fatefully, the effect of our negative counsel, in impeccable alignment with learning outcomes, is waste in the ancient sense of devastation (ἀπώλεια), as if the word is destined to return to its archaic violence.

Chapter 11

FLUX

Among the best known and the most intractable problems of teaching is the diversity of the student cohort. On average, half the students are less sophisticated than the other half. If the students are all close to the baseline, let us say the level that you aim at in your delivery, you will have no difficulty stimulating your audience in any presentation or tutorial. If, however, they are disparate in ability and vary hugely in their background knowledge and sophistication, you are likely either to bore the advanced students or bamboozle the beginners.

Confronting this agony is one of the larger challenges of the contemporary academic or teacher. It is part of the reason for the constructivist system of John Biggs, and his allegory of 'academic Susan' and 'non-academic Robert'; because Biggs imagined that the mass education that universities now serve is flooded with unacademic Roberts. Differences in the student cohort may even go beyond the Susan–Robert dichotomy; because there are substantial disparities among students which have little to do with how academically-oriented they are from the outset. 'I have students in my information technology class', one lecturer told me:

> who barely know basic commands on a computer and I have others who are already programming. How can I satisfy them all? I do not want to abandon the students with difficulties by assuming that they can all already do programming, and I also do not want to disappoint the advanced and eager students, who are well prepared and looking for challenges by teaching them things that are below their competence. I either break up the group—like old style streaming, which seems somehow repugnant—or throw my hands up in despair. If I devote special attention to both groups or even individuals, my workload escalates and I not only become tired with the extra consultations but confused about the standards that I expect of all students. It is a structural mess and my classes lose integrity; they become messier as

a result of handling the mess. Instead of a beautiful narrative line, my classes are clogged with incidental explanations as I cater for radically diverse levels of advantage.

This horror of extreme diversity in a cohort has contributed to the disfavour of single-discourse classes. Lectures and tutorials, where everyone in the room listens to just one person at a time, are under a planning siege: we are especially closing in on lectures, because the person speaking is bound either to underestimate or overshoot the capacity of some proportion of the audience. Better, so says contemporary educational orthodoxy, to get the students to teach one another, so that the advanced students (like those who can already program) have new challenges in communicating their knowledge and passing on capabilities, and can therefore take on a leadership role. The more uninformed students get the benefit of special attention and the more advanced students get the benefit of consolidating their knowledge and acquiring new soft skills in teaching, intellectual sympathy and leadership. Assuming that they are successful in sacrificially cultivating their own good will among their potential competitors, the advanced students do indeed have something to gain—because teaching is a great way to learn more—and so everyone is a winner.

Nevertheless, while advanced students now have an altruistic role in ministering to the less advanced, it is unclear that they are being stimulated by the learning that they thought they hoped for in taking the study. As *de facto* teaching assistants, they will gain much reward and wisdom; but who is serving them in their depth of learning? Who is challenging them with an expansion in their subject knowledge and vision? For students who need to catch up, on the other hand, the idea of being taught by other students may seem a questionable practice, since the reliability of other students relative to the internet is unknown; worse, the substitution of a lecturer by a student seems mildly discrediting. Either the leading student can do what the lecturer does (in which case are the lecturer and university effective and necessary?) or there is a difference in quality and relatively unsophisticated students need to be contented with less quality. Although the arrangement has the appearance of great student-centredness and leadership, it is structurally uncomfortable. Mixing students so that they share their expertise is a mechanical solution, as if the genre of the lecture is at fault and new active learning environments make an automatic and convenient fix, where the speed of one student makes up for the tardiness of another.

Much tension surrounds this problem, and each fix may be suspected of dubious credibility. Because of the embarrassment of both underperforming students and under-challenged students making unhappy company, there is an understandable impulse to blame the student or at least the selection process that seems not to respect the prerequisites. If I teach German on the basis that students have matriculated in German, I should be able to assume that the students read, speak and write German. But it is also unteacherly or educationally ugly to blame students for their shortcomings, because the institution has accepted them and they undoubtedly have enormous potential to become fluent in German as well as having good faith in seeking a knowledge of German in the first place. Thanks to this feeling of embarrassment, neither wanting to blame students nor ourselves, we experience an impulse to blame our tools. It must be the fault of the lecture as a genre. It takes no account of difference. It treats all students as if they are the same, symbolized by the architectural sameness of the seats bolted onto the angled floor. Even the ancient Socratic tutorial has been suspected of the same deficit, because there is only one conversation in the room and if it is pitched at a high level, too many students will struggle and become disengaged, especially finding that the 'bright' students who hog all the conversation are daunting and show-offy. Meanwhile, if that single conversation is pitched at too low a level, the advanced students will get bored and fear that they have come to the wrong university. Our reflex is to look around at a mechanistic motif to blame. It is the room. It is the genre. Change them toward active learning and let the students sort out their level with group work.

Against these mechanistic strategies, some of which do not promote creative growth, there is a more imaginative solution which does not entail the abolition of lectures and single-conversation tutorials. They must be structured with a mobile register of intensity, where everyone in the room can find his or her level. In essence, the lecturer or tutor must imaginatively *crib the complex*, that is, break down complicated things into simple things, but not too simple for the ambitious and well-prepared students, who would feel patronized by material being over-explained. The method used since literature began is to provide constant movement between the tangible and the abstract.

Imagine the typical trajectory of a conference paper or learned seminar among us academics. We present our research by situating ideas among recognizable realities but then move rapidly into theory, either escalating the whole way until the climactic end or perhaps maintaining a kind of plateau of concentrated language of great reward to the audience. We transcend our tangible point of departure, the 'situated' field that everyone knows and recognizes, and enter a kind of academic sublime, where we stimulate our audience with new ideas, new levels of synthesis, new abstractions, new interpretations or critiques. We hold this magical intensity for as long as we can, as much of the 20 minutes that we are given at a conference or seminar. The intensity of abstract thought does not waver and, as an audience, we experience limbic comfort in the very motif that the beautiful complex development of ideas can be maintained.

You could represent this as a graph, with time on the X axis and theoretical sophistication or intensity of abstraction on the Y axis. You start by grounding the ideas but ascend upward, bringing the scholars in the room to new insights. The curve that we plot rises constantly, perhaps reaching a plateau but never dipping. There is no need to drop the level of sophistication or intensity of abstract thought. You will not lose your audience in this upward flight, because they are all learned like you; and, given that you only have 20 minutes to seduce the audience, you would not risk a departure from the plateau, lest you disappoint the lofty agreement of minds—all Susans to a fault—who relish the same kind of academic vigour that you do, equally devoted to the quest for ideas pursued at their greatest extension. But that same shape will not work with our students. Across many cohorts, they need to touch base with the grounded level at rapid intervals. You must still lift the language into the abstract and can ascend to heights of theory; but not for too long. You cannot remain at the peak for more than a spell, oblivious to the fact that some students are fatiguing and becoming confused. If you remain too long in abstractions, you will lose a large proportion of the audience.

If, however, you structure your presentation with a dynamic rocking from the tangible to the abstract, you maximize the traction with both demographics: the ones who are hungry to make contact with theory and those who are unprepared and apprehensive about it. The teacher's knack, if you like, is to oscillate between the tangible and the abstract, on each swing lifting up the level of intellectual ambition but just as certainly returning the focus to the bedrock that it sprang from. This motif of flux does not compromise the integrity of the presentation. It is the intimate structure that also explains how Shakespeare's plays work or how the *Bible* works, always oscillating between the basic and the sublime, the prosaic and the exalted. In fact, even as sophisticated readers, we become fatigued if the level stays constantly at one pitch for too many pages. We too require the refreshment of an imaginative flux, pulsing between the abstract and the concrete and frequently traversing the imaginary barrier between them.

Admittedly, it requires imagination to install in a teaching practice, in writing, in conversation. To flux, to respond to a thought that someone will be lost unless the idea is grounded again, like an electric charge that needs to be earthed: this intellectual habit is a simultaneous thinking process, a way of imagining the concrete in terms of the abstract and *vice versa* so that the two produce an experiential synergy which is also highly pleasurable. One of the loveliest cues that we have for this process is installed in language itself, because language at its most abstract is still only an aggregation of concrete particles, things and actions that have come into contact with prepositions and themselves have crossed over into the immaterial, the abstract, the purely intellectual. Words, too, have traversed the remarkable distance between the here-and-now and the pure, the idea, the Platonic; they slip unbeknown to most speakers between the fact and the notion, between the tangible and the ethereal, the simple and the sophisticated. Every word with the most astonishing argumentative complexity around it has a palpable root in basic verbs or nouns, coupled with some hint of a direction, a relation or a qualification, that is, the system of prefixes which are prepositional in nature. In this way, the introduction of flux between the palpable and the immaterial is not artificial. Yes, it requires imagination to construct, in the same way that thinking of a beautiful sentence requires imagination; but it is inherent to lexical thinking, embedded in language itself, and is by no means foreign to the way we conceptualize anything vaguely ambitious, and especially if we aim to cultivate the imagination.

To flux, to go in and out of a condition, to bend and return in waves, is a crucial aspect of imaginative cognition. There are undoubtedly aspects of thinking that are linear and follow a regular logical process, as with the more unambiguous aspects of accounting. Linear thought is what we seek when we cajole ourselves to remain focused. Goal-oriented thinking is not normally subject to flux and its straight-forwardness would indeed be damaged by distraction. When we seek to eliminate distraction, it is to protect the logical integrity of linear learning, focused study, concerted and methodical concentration. Other aspects of thinking, however, depend on ideas in flux, the fertility of one idea engendering another in parallel or even in contrast, the so-called left-field, the unpredicted combination, the insight from elsewhere that makes an unforeseen match with material already pondered. It is the principal reason why imagination cannot be forced. We do not become more creative through an attempt to think harder, by putting in more effort with the doggedly linear thoughts that we already concentrate upon. It is more likely that we become creative by thinking more widely, with a greater provision of links and a greater distribution of destinations for any given thought.

Creativity enjoys cross-pollination; but florid interference is not necessary to the purpose. The issue is not so much to have infusion from another field of thought or another practice but to gain refreshment from within the same field—with the same discourse—by experiencing it with different levels of intensity. Rather than experiencing the discourse as a simple flow, our imagination prospers through flux.

As often happens in English, we have two words, one Germanic (flow) and the other Latin (flux) that express a somewhat similar idea of fluidity. Both words at various times would have been translated by a single term in other languages and there is a certain overlap with other words in English like 'current'. However, 'flux' is different from flow and, in our context, the distinction is valuable. To flow is to proceed in an uninterrupted channel, to join a constant stream, to be borne along in a continuous tug or force of absorption. To flux is almost the opposite: to change, to move in and out of true, to wobble, to waver somewhat, to let attention slip and return on any given topic, to vary in degrees of intensity among moments of concentration.

The concept of flow has achieved great metaphoric prestige, thanks largely to a book by Mihaly Csikszentmihalyi, who described an optimal zone of absorption, where you engage deeply in an activity of autotelic nature and can forget about time and noise and even your own ego, your own investments, because the activity is pursued self-generatingly for its own sake.[1] It is an antidote to apathy, boredom and anxiety, where skill and challenge are in perfect harmony at a high level. It is likely that the brilliant lecturer experiences flow in the course of the allocated 50 minutes, engaging the mind with great intensity toward a beautiful narrative, where the words percolate freely in pursuit of constantly regenerating elaborations. For the audience, too, the state of flow may induce similar charms, perhaps a little rhapsodic, possibly affording a degree of mental wandering and undoubtedly lacking the focus of the lecturer who actively composes the flow. It is psychologically a desirable stimulus: to be borne along by a kind of flow which is rich in subtlety and yields considerable contentment.

Flux, on the other hand, is full of change. You could argue that it is inherent in flow that various currents move simultaneously, slipping past

---

1   Mihaly Csikszentmihalyi, *Beyond boredom and anxiety: Experiencing flow in work and play*, San Francisco, Jossey-Bass, 1975.

one another, which you can notice in any creek or drain where water gushes along. The water in the middle seems to slip more quickly than the water at the sides, not so much because retarded by the banks but because the water has a tendency to ride upon itself. So if one current moves forward more rapidly than another, it provides a kind of vehicle for another, which can flow yet more rapidly till it encounters greater resistance. The water takes on an almost sinuous quality, dividing into separate streams that continuously redefine one another, as if it is not one continuous substance—which in reality it is, all undifferentiated H2O—but an almost grainy material induced by the flow itself, where different currents take on heightened energy and move more rapidly with greater momentum than others. It is tempting to see a parallel with thought, which might proceed at any speed but accelerates to greater consciousness not because something pushes harder but because thoughts underneath or to the side are also moving and the more energized thought can race ahead with greater vigour.

If it is a useful analogy to thought, the inconsistent flow of water is well described by the word flux. Water responds to pressure in chaotic ways because it slips; liquid is the genius of slipperiness, where 'parts' of the volume yield to impulses in dynamically folded pathways. Each part in its turn gives way to the pressure in uneven patterns, becoming mobile where other parts remain inert; and so the liquid slips, passes itself in currents and eddies, with turbulence of a chaotic kind because it is impossible to predict. Your thoughts are always flowing—you cannot stop them—but they seldom flow in a totally linear fashion, as if constrained by the walls of a pipe; and even in the tightest cylinder, those same currents and convulsively exchanging streams exist in miniature. Your thoughts flow according to laws of flux, anarchic laws, where an idea spins off the opportunity of another that advances beside it. This concatenation of unforeseen openings that race and rally through time is the precondition of imagination, where the elastic quality of thought, the ability to stretch upon the instant when copious strands surge in the vicinity, is seized as a runaway idea, a maverick impulse that glides into breakaway, running faster to reach consciousness than the other thoughts that support it.

As in water, thoughts are never discrete particles nor even some slithery plasma but are properly liquid in that the streams that carry a peculiar momentum not only run forward but run out of continuity, tumbling over one another's course in flowing exchange that we call flux. Each stream has an impact on every other; they are never independent like the electromagnets in a motor but organically pass energy to one another; and as they transfer their momentum, they redefine themselves, shift shape, as one pool revolves to become a part of another. The notion of flow as flux (*flusso*) is entangled with a process of induction, revealed in words like 'influx' and 'influence', already used often in the renaissance to describe both disease (*influenza*) and joy, as with Castiglione's description of corporal love, which 'is an influence of divine goodness'.[2]

If the metaphor holds water, so to speak, life itself may be considered a kind of flow, where no moment is without influence from every other and experience is nothing but the sum of its contingencies. Time, after all, flows; but it is not experienced with the same consistency as the steady revolutions by the hands of the clock; rather, it is experienced through our thoughts as a suite of lulls, and surges, jerks and rhapsodies, calm and inter-ruptions, panic, bliss, seduction, alarm and hope. Time is thus also a kind of current, but in the etymological sense of running (from the Latin *currere*). Sometimes the word current would simply mean running, as in Petrarch's line from the fourteenth century that 'my days run faster than the arrow'.[3] Deriving from the image of running, the word current retains its image of running even in describing water. It was used adjectivally, as in running waters;[4] but even adjectivally, the current can be seen as a vein, as when the baroque poet Marino speaks metaphorically of inspiration or the running vein of immortal happiness.[5] But it is also used as a noun, as in the current of the sea that might carry a boat.[6]

Thinking surges in currents. It is not flow in the sense of a consistent continuum. We know that for certain types of thinking, it is difficult to experience consistency of concentration over prolonged periods. The reason is not so much that one needs distraction but movement within the material to hand. Thinking of one kind needs thinking of another kind beside it, in the same way that two currents buoy one another along. One of the curr-ents, as it were, is sacrificial. But perhaps not for long. Currents overtake one another with astonishing rapidity. There is always another one that rolls

---

2   'Ma parlando della bellezza che noi intendemo, che è quella solamente che appar nei corpi e massimamente nei volti umani e move questo ardente desiderio che noi chiamiamo amore, diremo che è un influsso della bontà divina', Castiglione, *Cortegiano* 4.52.

3   'I dí miei piú correnti che saetta', Petrarch, *Canzoniere* 366.91.

4   'un ruscel corrente', Petrarch 129.68, 'corrente et chiaro gorgo', 227.13, 'correnti fiumi', Bembo, *Asolani* 3.1.

5   'Lungo il suo piè con limpid'onda e viva / mormorando sen va soavemente / il destro fiumicel, da cui deriva / di letizia immortal vena corrente.' *Adone* 10.71.3–4.

6   'Corre la navicella e ratta e lieve / la corrente del mar seco la porta', *Adone* 1.124.2.

over it; and the most current, in a short while, will also roll under. This condition can be described as flux which, in romance languages, also meant flow, a flow that has rushing perturbations within it. How to translate so many wonderful poetic lines, like the great flux of the sea?[7] Or should that be the great flow or flood of the sea? Or perhaps even tide?[8]

The prestige of flow in the history of ideas is owing in large part to the overlap with flux, remembering there is no distinction made between the two in romance languages. Since ancient times, philosophers warned against faith in fixity. In Heraclitan thinking, everything flows (πάντα ῥεῖ) and everything is subject to flux. You cannot step into the same river twice because it is always different water at each moment: all entities move and nothing stays still.[9] This esteem for flux in all things is romantic before the letter, deconstructing the conceit that human monuments outlive us and abide forever. The reality check from antiquity would have special appeal in the Christian epoch, when absolute and eternal immutability was imputed only to God (as opposed to the fickle fluxing gods of Greece) and everything that is not God is in a state of change, in a development where growth ends in decay and rebirth. Only god abides, from the *Old Testament* to the renaissance. This motif, as the epic poet Ariosto says, 'made her see that no one, unless in God, is truly contented; because all the other human hopes were transitory and flowing (or in flux)'.[10]

Although we sometimes associate the renaissance with rigid systems of one-point perspective and Aristotelian definitions of the golden mean, in fact there is a strong undercurrent of organic feeling in writers like Macchiavelli and Guicciardini, a recognition of change as the only constant in life, a sense of the momentary, the unsettled caprice of fortune, in effect the condition of flux. Convergence with Christian belief encouraged a delight in pre-Socratic philosophy; and the sober Montaigne observes that Greek philosophy retained its enthusiasm for flux even in the classical period:

> Homer made the Ocean father of the gods and Thetis the mother in order to show us that all things are in flux (*en fluxion*), nuance and perpetual variation, an opinion common to all the philosophers

---

7   e.g. 'del gran flusso marino', Torquato Tasso, *Gerusalemme liberata* 17.25.6.

8   'Col gran flusso del mar quindi condutti / i naviganti per camin sicuro / a vela e remi insino a Londra furo,' Ludovico Ariosto, *Orlando furioso* 8.26.6–8.

9   'τὰ ὄντα ἰέναι τε πάντα καὶ μένειν οὐδέν', Plato, *Cratylus* 401d.

10   'Poi le fece veder, come non fusse / alcun, se non in Dio, vero contento, / e ch'eran l'altre transitorie e flusse / speranze umane, e di poco momento;' Ludovico Ariosto, *Orlando furioso* 24.89.1–4.

before his age, as he said—except Parmenides alone who rejected the movement of things, the force of which he made much of—: Pythagoras, that all matter is running and labile (*coulante et labile*); the stoics, that there is no present time and that what we call the present is only the join and match of future and past; Heraclitus, that a man never stood twice in the same river; Epicharmus ... one can never find one mortal substance twice in the same condition, because by the suddenness and ease of change, now it dissipates, now it regroups, it comes and then goes. In this manner everything that grows never arrives at its perfection of being, insofar as its birth is never fulfilled (*e naistre n'acheve jamais*) nor ever stops as if at an end. Thus, since the egg (*depuis la semence*), each always changes and mutates into the other (*va tousjours se changeant et muant d'un à autre*) ... always unmaking and destroying (*tousjours desfaisant et gastant*) the preceding thing.[11]

Having run through this synopsis of organic philosophy Montaigne concludes with lines by Lucretius, that time totally changes the nature of the world, where everything gives way to the condition of something else; no thing remains in its similar condition; all things migrate and nature commits everything to change and compels everything to turn.[12]

If the ancients were so sanguine about the disruptive force of fortune, the renaissance intellect could hardly default on classical soberness, disappoint the expected intellectual bravery and recede to an eternal illusion, a fib of stability. Patently the world is in flux and only God, let us say, is constant and abiding. But just because we recognize flux, it does not mean that we love it. On the contrary, it is seen as a danger, a disruption, a risk to be attenuated. There is an inherited reflex suggesting that flux is random and uncontrolled and therefore undesirable, good for nothing or ridiculous[13] unless flattened out; and frequently flux is associated with invasion, like our word influx, a condition of migration that nations still fear today.[14] If the

---

11 *Essais* 2.12.

12 'Mutat enim mundi naturam totius aetas, / Ex alioque alius status excipere omnia debet, / Nec manet ulla sui similis res: omnia migrant, / Omnia commutat natura et vertere cogit.' Lucretius, *On the nature of things* 5.828–31.

13 'Ce grand flux de raisons dont tu viens m'attaquer / Est bon à faire rire, et non à pratiquer.' Pierre Corneille, *La place royale* 1.1.

14 'La flotte qu'on craignait, dans ce grand fleuve entrée, / Croit surprendre la ville et piller la contrée. / Les Maures vont descendre, et le flux et la nuit / Dans une heure à nos murs les amènent sans bruit.' Corneille *Le Cid* 3.6.

flux of the ocean is benign, it is just good luck, where it could just as easily have been catastrophic.[15]

Well into the eighteenth century, flux was associated with caprice, as in a beautiful passage of Montesquieu detailing the mad folly that arises between power and servitude (*un flux et un reflux d'empire et de soumission*), where your masters hatch the most humiliating labours for you all day long, regardless of your health or age, for the most minor bagatelle or fantasy.[16] The phrase flux and reflux is quite old, appearing already in the renaissance Italian of Bandello[17] and used often in the theatre of Goldoni, where the coming and going of people is considered mad in a comic vein.[18] But in Montesquieu this condition of coming and going (*flux et reflux*) reflects upon attitudes and beliefs rather than foot-traffic; and because you might expect that attitudes and beliefs might have some moral constancy, the flux is whimful, intellectual disarray. It arises over religion. People are, he says, 'no firmer in their incredulity than in their faith: they live in coming and going (*flux et reflux*) that carries them from the one to the other'.[19]

This fickleness is not the final definition of our concept, which has travelled richly and deeply from the innate organic mutations of nature in pre-Socratic philosophy to baroque aesthetics. The history of flux reached a high point in the seventeenth century in ornaments and architecture which, alas, lie well beyond the scope of this chapter, with beguiling heady spaces where whole buildings—as in the façade and interior of Borromini's *San Carlo alle quattro fontane* in Rome—are in flux, convulsively swaying in positive and negative sinusoidal curves. Later again, flux would also be charged with the grand sway of history, the inexorable flow of change that underlies a shift in the psyche, in the very make-up of one generation that distinguishes it from another. So Nietzsche describes the wave

---

15 'Et vous n'ignorez pas qu'avec fort peu de peine / Un flux de pleine mer jusqu'ici les amène.' Corneille, *Le Cid* 2.6.

16 'Il y a entre nous comme un flux et un reflux d'empire et de soumission: elles font toujours tomber sur moi les emplois les plus humiliants; elles affectent un mépris qui n'a point d'exemple; et, sans égard pour ma vieillesse, elles me font lever, la nuit, dix fois pour la moindre bagatelle; je suis accablé sans cesse d'ordres, de commandements, d'emplois, de caprices; il semble qu'elles se relayent pour m'exercer, et que leurs fantaisies se succèdent.' Montesquieu, *Lettres persanes* 9.

17 'Aveva egli in consuetudine ogni sabato, per via del flusso e reflusso de l'Oceano, navigare a Bruscelles e, veduti li conti del suo fattore, tornarsene la domenica a buona ora in Anversa.' Bandello, *Novelle* 4.7.

18 'Ha la porta di dietro; pazzo, pazzo! Sempre flusso e riflusso. Ha la porta di dietro, pazzo!' Carlo Goldoni, *La bottega del caffè* 1.5, 1.9, 1.13 or *Le donne gelose* 3.4.

19 Montesquieu, *Lettres persanes* 75.

of industrial civilization or humanization of European progress in terms of a huge moral and political process that ever more sets itself in flow (*der immer mehr in Fluss geräth*): this current, if you like, is more uni-directional but nevertheless indicates flux in the sense of change. For Nietzsche, the major sweeping change includes the process of assimilation (*Anähnlichung*) among Europeans, the growing dissolution from local conditions (*ihre wachsende Loslösung von den Bedingungen*) that both frees the middle-class and enslaves it to a kind of globalization before the letter.[20] For Nietzsche, the flux of history is like a tide, a great swell that brings different opportunities, different thinking, different people. The wave of development, which today we would call a movement, rolls over humanity, redefining aspirations, standards, behaviour, expectations, ambitions.

Nothing that ever unfolds can explain itself in a linear fashion, because it hits up against things that are still, that have inertia, like tranquil pools of water channelled into the torrent. Their flow necessarily forms streams in manifold rhythms of exchange; and this dynamic is essentially what happens when we encounter new ideas. They might initially make a splash, so to speak, but strike the resistance of thoughts and ideas that are already there. There is no empty vessel, where new lessons fill the void; rather material is already there which accommodates the new as an interruption, coping with its impact in a condition of flux. Then because all thinking is also the result of stimuli—either external or generated from within—it always represents flux: it is always that drama like fresh water striking stagnant water or water already induced to move in a similar direction but at a different rate.

Understanding this dynamic must form one of the first principles of pedagogy. Cognition is rhapsodic; and when we seek to introduce new material into someone else's mind, the intervention delves into consciousness in flux, in disparate degrees of sympathy with the matter, in highs and lows of receptivity, in rushing intensity and serene relaxation. Our best cue for communicating among the eddies and swell of cognitive energy is the imaginative work of writers who handle the abstract by means of the tangible, because their poetic operation is metaphorical, inherently relating the physical to the intellectual or psychological. Some writers directly invite a peculiar intimacy with their thoughts as they come in waves, faithfully representing their dreamlike concatenation, even at the risk of incoherence. Virginia Woolf is a beautiful example, where the slightly disjointed flow

---

20   Friedrich Nietzsche, *Jenseits von Gut und Böse* 242.

of thinking—what I am calling flux—is echoed in the very fabric of the writing, as throughout *Mrs Dalloway*:

> Quiet descended on her, calm, content, as her needle, drawing the silk smoothly to its gentle pause, collected the green folds together and attached them, very lightly, to the belt. So on a summer's day waves collect, overbalance, and fall; collect and fall; and the whole world seems to be saying 'that is all' more and more ponderously, until even the heart in the body which lies in the sun on the beach says too, That is all. Fear no more, says the heart. Fear no more, says the heart, committing its burden to some sea, which sighs collectively for all sorrows, and renews, begins, collects, lets fall. And the body alone listens to the passing bee; the wave breaking; the dog barking, far away barking and barking.

So often in Woolf's *Mrs Dalloway* the image of waves is invoked, concussing and unravelling and recurring. The texture of her prose imitates the folded character of thinking itself, that process of inscrutable sequences and blending, separations and appropriations which becomes creative when it is properly reconciled with its own flux.

For richly communicative and creative teaching, it would be calamitous to lose confidence in this economy of rolling transfers. The two conclusions that we can reach from this discussion are first, that a flux or pulse between the abstract and the concrete is necessary to inclusive communication; and second that the habit, when cultivated, has a higher imaginative purpose. When we communicate in order to teach, it is no scandal that our delivery is in flux; on the contrary, it is more congruent with creative thought, because some flux in the delivery of the teacher can immediately agitate an analogous fluxing condition in the minds of the students; and thus the precondition of imaginative activity is shared in the room. Today, however, the dominant pedagogical forces are hostile to the poetic latitude that we have identified through flux. As the emphasis swings darkly in the direction of learning outcomes and constructive alignment, the likelihood of any appreciation, much less legitimacy, of this fundamental creative condition becomes ever fainter; and meanwhile, great walls of verifiable consistencies, arising from a culture of compliance, make creativity in learning more remote.

Chapter 12

OWNERSHIP

Learning is difficult to define. Following behaviourist models, psychology describes learning not by what we know or feel or think but how we behave: 'Learning is a relatively permanent change in behavior brought about by practice or experience.'[1] The definition has the advantage that it is not exclusive to humans who can read and write and think abstractly but all creatures, possibly even plants, as when they are conditioned to grow sideways in search of the sunlight; and certainly mice and rats undergo a kind of learning which is reflected in their behaviour rather than thinking, in that they can be conditioned or trained to respond to certain stimuli; and in any case, it is hard to know what they think.

Among humans, learning seems to indicate a subtler definition, because learning does not demonstrably modify behaviour. If I learn about music, I do not necessarily alter my behaviour but only my sensibility. As a result of learning, I can identify Berlioz or distinguish Dvořák from Brahms; but, unless I brag about it, my behaviour is the same: I still sit in the chair or concert hall and delight in the music. You would not be able to detect a change of behaviour because my improved analytical ratiocination in absorbing the music is not accessible as behaviour. The crude mechanistic paradigms of psychology are especially unrewarding as we approach the imaginative and the creative; because the mouse or rat may exercise no imagination in learning to seek the cheese on the sound of the bell. The changes to behaviour that are supposed to define learning do not contemplate creativity. Psychology is possibly not the ideal discipline in which to investigate imagination.

But still, psychology can shed light on learning. Sticking to the templates of behaviourism, it might make more sense to conceive learning in terms of memory. To learn is to commit to memory. There are different degrees

---

1   Sheldon J. Lachman, 'Learning is a Process: Toward an Improved Definition of Learning', *The Journal of Psychology*, vol. 131, issue 5, 1997, pp. 477–480.

of both learning and memory; and the two phenomena broadly align. To learn superficially is to hold knowledge in short-term memory, whereas to learn deeply is to affect longterm memory. In a tangible way, the definition equating learning and memory seems obvious. If I learn words in Korean, it more or less means that I remember them. If I fail to remember them, I consider that I have not really learned them or not learned them well. It is the reason that in education we so often assess learning by means of memory tests, especially in fields that are rich in facts, where the learner is an absorber of knowledge.

These are cumbersome wooden frameworks for a lively and curious process, because they either have little to do with conditioning or define conditioning to beg the question, making it synonymous with learning. As autonomous students, we learn to a large extent either by perceiving a need to learn or taking a personal imaginative delight in the subject matter; and we often learn by identifying with the discipline or the person who embodies what we want to become, let us say the doctor or the philosopher or the architect or the scientist. We may be conditioned in the process; but the more motivated and self-directed we are, the more we condition ourselves—which somewhat stretches the definition of conditioning. Conditioning seems a very passive expression, as if we are being manipulated by someone who wants to control us. You cannot really do it to yourself: the idea of self-conditioning seems a contradiction in terms. Yet the process, if we abandon the ugly word, is largely what we mean by self-regulated learning, that is, learning at the happiest extreme, which is autonomous and self-directed. We consciously and purposefully take a hand in the learning, which is radically different from the way a mouse is conditioned to look for cheese when a bell rings. In learning, we handle ourselves with growth-consciousness, recognizing our psychological plasticity—the way we can shape or mould ourselves—and our potential to reach out to gain knowledge, competencies and capabilities that we previously lacked.

Consciousness is, if you like, a ghost in the machine. It consists of awareness of what the mind is doing to itself—metacognition—a process of reflexion which is remote from conditioning, as conditioning causes the mind to submit to the terms of regular rewards and punishments. Like all organic and ghostly processes, learning is distorted when conceived along mechanistic lines. It is more helpfully conceived through a cyclical narrative structure that involves imagination, where there is a quest or exploration and an acquisition, an acquisition that providently suggests further exploration, an enlarged and infinite quest and of course further fulfilment in acquisition at each stage. Regrettably, this cyclical narrative structure is coopted by gamification, where the cycle of quest and acquisition of tokens or virtual property is embedded in game design from early days. I think regrettably because gamification reinforces the mechanistic dimensions of acquisition in a routine of rewards and punishments, gains and losses, according to how well one plays. The gains are seldom very meaningful in their own right but only because they represent an advantage or privilege, a higher score that enables an arbitrary form of advancement in the game itself and which is not transferable beyond the game.

Though exploited in clumsy technological ways, the idea that learning involves acquisition is deeply embedded in common speech, both in relation to facts and skills. We readily agree that the student tangibly gains something through study, almost like personal property, the most schematic form of which is the list of learning outcomes. On successful completion of the study, you will be able to solve differential equations, recognize the application of differential equations to physical problems; over here, you will speak rudimentary Korean or recognize the centrality of certain Korean terms to aesthetic intuitions, philosophy and national traditions. Before the study, the student might have had no Korean or only intermediate maths whereas, at the end, the student has a swelling kitty of mathematical methods or words, grammar and cultural insights that can be built upon with study at a higher level.

Within this common perception of knowledge acquisition or skill acquisition lies a powerful cue to the way that learning can be understood as psychologically meaningful and enriching. When I learn a new word, say in a foreign language, I have gained something a little more than the word itself. With the word comes not only an enhanced scheme of connexions but also a reinforcement of my synaptic powers and consequently my very sense of identify. The word becomes mine, not just in the sense of a unit of stock that I can add to my tally but as something that I embrace. I already began to embrace it in my imagination before I even understood it properly. Once I have had the imaginative handle on the foreignness of it, the idea becomes my own. It is mine insofar as I can use it in my own way and at my own choosing, whereupon I cherish it. I enjoy its presence. This new word is a joy to think about. It is mine, even if it simultaneously belongs to millions of people whom I will never meet and millions more who have died or who are yet to be born. For the moments that I relish the thought of it, the word is completely mine because I have learned it and can freely weave it through my thoughts, even if no one ever hears it, as when you learn a word in a dead language. My possession of the word in a living language is not diminished by the millions who also possess it. On the contrary, it becomes even more prestigious in my imagination, because I have been granted a peculiar access to their cultural property. When I hear the word spoken by a native speaker, it excites me that I already have the word: I own it and fondly repeat the word as it is pronounced so perfectly by that native speaker.

To own knowledge is to experience pride in possession, to feel a great connectedness either with other people or bodies of knowledge or areas of sense and feeling that I have within myself. It points to an imaginative covetousness in learning, a perpetually satisfied greed which is happily conjugated with inexhaustible supply and delight. The ownership that it indicates is material to the extent that it consists of tangible elements—like words or formulae or methods, models or images—but also immaterial to the extent that it is about me. Ownership is self-defining in the sense that it adds to your sense of yourself.

This intuition is supported philologically. The verb to own is intimately related to the self. It derives from a Germanic root for possessing (*agen*) a variant of which remains in circulation in modern German to describe your own (*eigen*), a morpheme which also yields telling abstract nouns like property (*Eigentum*) and quality in the sense of property (*Eigenschaft*). Property also has at its Latin root the expression of the self (*proprius*), what is yours and yours alone, what is proper to you, what is appropriate to you. The pattern is seen already in Greek, where conceptions of the self underlie two clusters of words that mean ownership, the self as a preposition (αὐτό), as in autonomous (αὐτόνομος), living under one's own laws, independent, and the self as what is peculiar to oneself (ἴδιος), one's own (ἰδικός)—pertaining to oneself or what belongs to us, as in our 'idiomatic' language—for which there was also a verbal derivative (ἰδιόομαι), to make one's own or appropriate. Finally, there is another particle used extensively in the ancient language (σφός) meaning theirs, their own, belonging to them. There are beautiful conceptions for our purposes, like determining things with your own judgement or at your own discretion (αὐτογνώμων) or the verb to act on the basis of your own judgement (αὐτογνωμονέω). The Greeks had a strong desire to speak of independence, feeling your own experience (αὐτοπάθεια, or speaking from your own feeling αὐτοπαθής), or being your own person (αὐτοπρόσωπος), that is, donning your own mask. To follow your own counsel or to make your own way in decisions (ἰδιοβουλέω) was respected, to hold your own opinions (ἰδιογνώμων, ἰδιογνωμονέω) or to develop your own ideas (ἰδιολογέω). The roots for owning are thus not only very old but metaphorically enriched, not just with concepts of property, the material that belongs to you, but with an understanding for the privacy and independence of a person's claim to knowledge, experience and opinion.

Ownership as an abstract noun, however, is harder to find. A substantive describing abstractly the condition of having possession—as opposed to the thing that is possessed—is scarce in Western languages. Apart from technical words (like παγκτησία, full ownership, or πρόκτησις, a title-deed showing previous ownership), the concept is not greatly diffused. In the modern languages of western Europe, the word ownership is difficult to translate; but even in English, ownership is quite rare in major historical epochs. There is no ownership in Shakespeare, for example, either tangible or metaphorical, though Shakespeare was among the earliest to use the verb 'to own' to describe a responsibility.[2] Lack of the abstract word is no great impediment to expressing concepts of ownership, given that the verb has long existed and analogous terms exist in parallel, like possession. But even possession—which is the nearest romance synonym for ownership— tends to refer to the thing that is possessed rather than the verbal action of holding it. When possession is used in that verbal sense, it is political in nature, as in Boccaccio: 'suddenly, he and other friends and servants of King Manfred were cast into the gaol of King Charles and after that the possession of the island of Sicily'.[3] But normally in Boccaccio, possession means real estate or material that you can sell.[4] This pattern is seen in literature right down to the age of Goldoni, where ownership is transactional and bureaucratically defined in a deeds office.[5]

Witnessing the decadence of inherited wealth and the simultaneous growth of the middle class in the eighteenth century, Goldoni is among the earlier champions of a benign capitalist spirit, recommending savings and prudent management of assets; he frequently condemns uncontrolled spending, especially for the wasteful experience of country holidays. It could be argued that the nature of possession was changing and that property relations were slowly redefined as a consequence of management rather

---

2   'I wish ... that you might ever do nothing but that ... and own no other function.' *The winter's tale* 4.4.143.

3   'subitamente egli e molti altri amici e servidori del re Manfredi furono per prigioni dati al re Carlo e la possessione dell'isola appresso', *Decameron* 2.6.

4   *e.g.* 'vendute alcune possessioni le quali avevano' 4.3; for real estate at 2.9.

5   'Sia ringraziato il cielo! Ritornerà la possessione in potere di mio fratello?' *Il prodigo* 4.5; 'Se marito la mia figliuola, vo' appigionare la casa e la possessione, e non voglio altra villeggiatura,' *Le avventure della villeggiatura* 1.5.

than patrimony. Possession could thus be creatively generated, without necessarily implying that you take it from someone else, as in Boccaccio's King Charles seizing the land and assets of King Manfred; and this exclusivity of possession, where you own something by virtue of the fact that I do not own it—'*voi possedete et io piango*' (you possess and I cry)[6]—is the material nastiness of natural capitalism. Up to a point, so is the theory in Marxism: the accumulation of wealth is achieved by not distributing profits according to the labour that generated it. Instead, Goldoni's implicit ideal is that you live well, sensibly and creatively simply by refraining from waste; so your retention of ownership is implicitly a statement of your virtue.

The way we think of ownership today is more inflected, as befits the greater development of the word in the industrial period. The romance word 'possession' is by derivation a highly materialistic term, having no 'self' at the centre but rather a power to sit upon, (*potere* + *sedere*), the right or ability to occupy. In its origins, it did not contemplate an original integrity between you yourself and some other term. It was just the holding; and as a form of holding, it specifically refers to the power of occupation, almost your right to exclude, arguably an intrinsically arrogant conception that is military and legalistic to the core. In our conception of ownership, on the other hand, we are drawn to what is morally and psychologically proper to you (your own) in some tight relationship with who you are and your potential to lead a creative life.

As applied to learning, the metaphor of ownership is suggestive, because it presents overlap with student-centredness as well as imagination. Students who own their topic, their study, their performance, and who own a sense of where the discipline might take them, are more self-motivated, in possession of an image of themselves. Thus, educational ownership is about the student's identity, an acquisition of potential, realizing an ability to gather intellectual assets in accord with the self, and to build the self in a way that ideally never diminishes anyone else's sense of self or moral claims to the same knowledge insofar as knowledge is universal. When knowledge is not universal but proper to the culture and tradition of a minority (like the Australian Aboriginal Dreaming, for example), it ceases to be infinitely transferable; and one cannot own the material in the same way as the original owners can, who have complicated rights to the stock by initiation and ancestral transmission. When we purport to seize their glamour, say by using ancient spiritual motifs in marketed fashion items, we need special

---

6   Petrarch, *Canzoniere* 226.14.

permission, else the claim lacks legitimacy. We describe this arrogation of someone else's cultural property as 'appropriation'—seizing for yourself what is not really yours to take—which effectively means 'misappropriation'. You are in effect annexing someone else's identity; and the act is neither sympathetic nor creative.

In this close relationship with the identity of the student, the student's creative sense of self, we see the stark difference with the concept of responsibility. Universities throughout the Anglophone world seem united in publishing statements of the responsibilities of the student, often coupled with rights, hence rights and responsibilities of the student. But responsibility is a triggering word with a somewhat odious contractual overtone, suggesting an external burden of obligations placed upon the individual, a quasi legal expectation which is now apparently an imposition, a runaway duty in whose service failure may be punishable. Responsibilities exist in the world aplenty; but when I seek to be creative, I do not want to know about them. I feel in good faith that my endeavours will ultimately be reconciled with the good intentions of others; but right at this moment, the very word 'responsibilities' takes on a threatening value, because I might very well be in default of what is expected of me. Learning requires a safe place where responsibilities are not mentioned and ownership can flourish.

Responsibilities are highly contractual, as the origin of the word itself confesses. It is derived from a Latin verb (*respondere*) which has its key image in pledging (*spondere*), a pledge which is also at the origin of the English noun spouse—that is, one who has been pledged or been through a betrothal— and the verb to espouse. Western vocabularies were free of the concept until the late baroque; but even when 'responsibility' appears in English in the mid seventeenth century, it is bureaucratic and instances are rare until the eighteenth century. French and Italian poetic literatures show no trace of the word 'responsibility' until modern times; it is an unfriendly and unpoetic word which spells out transactional terms in an uncreative way that seems too bureaucratically threatening to have an encouraging, much less poetic, dimension. If I assert my responsibilities, I make a claim for my power. If someone else tells me about my responsibilities, unless I can construe the message as a transfer of power, I am being tasked with something onerous, something of weighty consequence which I will possibly experience as oppressive; so I feel (a) that the responsibilities are imposed upon me and (b) that they come with a certain menace. If I do not live up to my responsibilities, I will fear a loss of esteem and people might berate me for disappointing their expectations in me. It is a common instinct to avoid responsibilities and we readily declare that we are not responsible for some-one else's behaviour.[7]

Why do universities adopt such chilly language when they insist on student responsibilities when they should so clearly be cultivating student ownership? Ownership is in all cases the positive way of describing what a person can embrace and it ideally subsumes responsibility. If I own certain responsibilities, I do not mind them at all; in fact there is room to be proud of them. I feel a more admirable citizen for owning and discharging my responsibilities. As an author, I feel a responsibility in writing these sentences to make sense, to convey something useful and argue an intuition so that it communicates well to the reader; but because I so intimately own the ambition to scribble my thoughts—which entails owning the content and the apparatus and the burden of proof—I do not experience the responsibilities as untoward or confronting. On the contrary, this charge is borne lightly because it is happily congruent with my sense of self. It is not just that the charge pertains to a task that I want to do. It is not just a discourse of desire, as if a circular argument that I like to do the things that I want to do. Rather, I own the task of doing it because it has become something that is about me. It is a moralized sense of belonging that subsequently generates a wish but is not the wish itself. To own something is not merely to experience volition but to understand something as belonging intimately to your view of yourself.

To own is to possess in a special way, to possess with a sense of belonging rather than entitlement. It is an identification of a personal nature that immediately socializes an ambition in an ethical framework. It is no coincidence that ownership marries the self (*agen, eigen*) with the moral which, as noted, we see in the Latin counterpart of ownership, property, proper (*proprius*) and our propriety, what is appropriate. If there are barriers to the understanding of ownership, they arise over shyness, a reluctance to embrace a materialistic view of education that aligns knowledge and skills with capital. The website for heutagogy community of practice proudly champions "'knowledge sharing' rather than 'knowledge hoarding'",[8] as if there is a reactionary taint in accumulation, a kind of shame that a person cultivates the meanness of amassing and sits smugly on the scandal of a stockpile rather than distributing the goods.

---

7   'Des froideurs de Titus je serai responsable?' Racine, *Bérénice* 3.4.

8   https://heutagogycop.wordpress.com/history-of-heutagogy, sighted December 2016.

As for me, I can totally see the value in hoarding if the practice allows me to share more effectively the material that I have gathered. I do not want to share every piece of knowledge or suggestion in a haphazard way, however nicely synergized with the interests of others. I want to stay with my sources for as long as I can to exhaust their relevance to my thoughts; and if I lack an intimacy with my own learning, I feel uncreative, trapped in common experience, trammelled by social relations which inhibit the peculiarity of my conjecture. My ideas when I read and write and think are often bizarre, full of false connexions that my mind throws up in its preposterous latitude, richly distracted and driven by wayward hopes for a novel insight. It is inappropriate to share my thoughts at the wrong time; and it follows that I want to be the person who decides when the right time is.

Collaboration is now rated among the highest forms of learning. It clearly has many benefits and especially earns its reputation in fields that lend themselves to group work; however, the opposite condition has the opposite virtues. Private study, as it used to be called, puts you in better contact with the intimacy of your thinking but especially the connectedness with your own identity. Theoretically, nothing prevents ownership from being collective; and indeed it may seem anachronistic to emphasize the individual at the implicit demotion of the collective. Teamwork involves a group identity, potentially more powerful than the individual identities that it subtends. We see it particularly in sports, where a side of average but well-coordinated players is stronger than a side of highly skilled but ill-coordinated mavericks. Nor can we say that group work is uncreative, because for every masterpiece in the Louvre or symphony created by an individual genius, there are films created by pools of people with complicated working relations with diffusely distributed ownership. The desire to embrace this collective energy and to cultivate a beautiful cooperative spirit among fellow workers is admirable, as is the principle of authentic learning activities and assessments. Nevertheless, there are many forms of imaginative activity that are naturally suppressed by group work; and just because films are made with formidable layers of management it does not mean that cinematic production represents the height of creative imagination, especially for a person who only thinks imaginatively in tranquil collectedness.

Undoubtedly there is a need for all learners to communicate their learning and not just for the sake of assessment. So even when students confine themselves for days on end while reading a valuable and stimulating book, they profit greatly from passing on their stimulation in the way that we have described in the chapter on 'Telling'. The excitement of reading a text produces a desire to tell which, however, may be deferred because one needs to keep reading. Finally, there comes a point—maybe well before the end of the book—where you need to tell someone about the contents of the text. So telling is normally the outcome of private study, where a longing to explain what transpired in the thoughts between the reader and the text is satisfied. Rather than a study group, where a student's interpretations may be challenged and criticized, a listener is all that is needed to create a safe place for extended ownership. The student really only needs to communicate the ownership of things gathered in hermitage. By this gesture, there is an invitation to share the ownership, to relish its magic and pass on the profit taken in it. So long as one is absorbed in private study, one takes on ideas hungrily or warily. To tell someone about your ownership of the subject means that you no longer experience the jealousy of an idea nurtured in guarded isolation. The telling makes you feel generous about ownership, because your ownership is not normally diminished by anyone else's ownership.

There is no down-side to ownership. Sometimes, perhaps, a scholar or scientist could be suspected of owning a theory too much, developing too much fondness for an idea. A researcher should be disinterested; and the affection for a favourite hypothesis dissuades the scholar from assaying the theory with appropriate challenges; because once there are sufficient grounds for doubt, the theory must be disowned. But that concern only applies to details of a theory. In broad terms, the ownership of the discipline itself—or the resources or facts that a scholar works from—is unimpeachable.

Then what do we own when we achieve ownership in some discipline? It is not the facts themselves nor even the theories; it cannot even be the method, though all three play a part. It is the images, the imaginative life that the discipline licences, the intellectual autonomy that an investigative reading proposes. To become curious is to own one's wonder, to delve into a set of questions or circumstances or pictures or melodies or exchange relations and to marvel at how they function or fail, how they are glorious or abject and grizzly, how you could be among them yourself. We own the image even if we are an incomplete expositor, a dud scholar, a partial thinker. We own our enthusiasm, our zeal, our ambition, under an image of the person that we think we could be.

If I have not sufficiently separated ownership from responsibility, the distinction emerges in nothing so much as the relation with creativity. Imaginative work is not necessarily furthered by a sense of responsibility—

though taking responsibility for work of any kind is necessary and taking responsibility for important themes is noble—because responsibility calls for due care, sympathy, moral uprightness, justification and scrupulosity. Imagination, on the other hand, while happily a partner to all things responsible, may be errant, bizarre, at least in the first instance, irresponsible. In the first instance, I do not want to control my imagination because I want to see what it will come up with. I feel that I can control it later; but if I exercise editorial sanctions in the early stages of any creative undertaking, I will stymie its growth, cut the potential and foreclose on the development of what may have become marvellous. Being responsible with imagination paradoxically means suppressing the urge to be responsible; you must let it run loose, for the mind to have momentary ownership of its caprice.

Students in my experience are seldom encouraged to take ownership of their ideas and imagination. They are told to be academically responsible and to own their responsibilities in a reactive spirit: do not blame others for your failure. The language of responsibilities is shrouded in legalistic liabilities, fear of reproach, a paranoiac view of student success. If, on the other hand, we were sincere in wanting our students to take ownership of their ideas and imagination, we would encourage them to suspend the menace and burden of responsibilities that will suppress their growth.

To enter into the richer field of creative growth, students need to cultivate a kind of jealousy with their thoughts, a form of ownership which is reluctant to share everything all at once.[9] Their imaginative ownership means taking charge of when they release the expression of their encounters. It could be before an assessment is due, either with friends or family or with a tutor; but it could equally be never, beyond the assessment submission, that is. The discretion either to chat or withhold is a necessary kind of latitude for the student to feel comfortable managing the creative impetus. Forcing students into interactive patterns is therefore not conducive in all cases to a creative trajectory, because it strips the student of ownership when ownership still depends on a discretionary intimacy with the study material. It is not just a case of owning the substance of the essay or whatever but owning the moment of telling that is judged most propitious either for the development of the material or its impact.

When learning happily and sustainably, we own material by the images that creatively spring up alongside it and therefore resonate with ourselves.

---

9   I argue this case in relation to research graduate studies in *The jealousy of ideas: research method in the creative arts*, Ellikon, Melbourne 2009 and internationally via WritingPAD, Goldsmiths, University of London, at writing-pad.org/dl123.

We learn most creatively when we own decisions about time and we control the degree of interactivity in our learning. We learn most comfortably when we own our place in the world—albeit momentarily—that is, the space that we temporarily occupy. Here too, in a deep chair at home or a squat stool in an informal learning space or a corner in a café, we can experience the intimacy of study, that condition that I think of as ownership. In recent times the various ways that our academic attention can be disposed has multiplied, thanks to digital technology. We barely even use the word classroom but prefer terms like 'learning space' in order to think about different modes of students occupying space, not just lined up in ranks of benches facing the front. It is well and good, even if often predicated on the doctrine of interactivity. But new developments are especially intriguing in the digital realm, where there is great variety in the encounter. The term 'personal learning environment' has sprung up,[10] quite usefully, even if there is no agreed definition. I sense that my own personal learning environment is not very far from the personal library that any scholar has been using in the past, as Montaigne described, with his books encircling him, all set at 5° elevation,[11] with the exception that my books are not arrayed in a physical arc around me but rather the bibliographic panopticon exists on the computer. Above all, however, the personal learning environment for me is a rather large clutch of images and melodies and lines that are in my head, accessed randomly or in waves, the music, architecture, art and poetic literature that thrill me and form a large part of my identity.

The term 'personal learning environment' is excellent if only because it has 'personal' in it. In any creative education, we must always chase the gifts of autonomy, that space of individual safety that produces creative comfort, illusion, indulgence, fantasy, exploration, but equally exposes the learner to doubt, the need for evidence, the challenge to prejudice, jealous negative impulses that also need to be owned. If these almost irreconcilable impulses are cultivated in private, we maximize the chances of internalizing volatile

---

10   Sebastian Fiedler and Terje Väljataga, 'Personal learning environments: concept or technology?'. *International journal of virtual and personal learning environments*, vol. 2, issue 4, 2011, pp. 1–11; Alfie Kohn, 'Four reasons to worry about "Personalized learning"'. *Psychology today*, Feb 24, 2015.

11   'La figure en est ronde et n'a de plat que ce qu'il faut à ma table et à mon siege, et vient m'offrant en se courbant, d'une veue, tous mes livres, rengez à cinq degrez tout à l'environ. Elle a trois veues de riche et libre prospect, et seize pas de vuide en diametre. En hyver, j'y suis moins continuellement: car ma maison est juchée sur un tertre, comme dict son nom, et n'a point de piece plus esventée que cette cy; qui me plaist d'estre un peu penible et à l'esquart, tant pour le fruit de l'exercice que pour reculer de moy la presse. C'est là mon siege.' *Essais* 3.3.

imaginative forces at variance with one another. As fragile and ratty as it is, there is no other route to creative independence.

Once we have established the learner's creative access to a domain of intimacy, where knowledge may be acquired for the private cultivation of vision, we automatically have a problem in socializing the process. Contemporary education is organized around batches of students and we have a structural urge to bump the individual into dynamic exchange with fellow students. Sometimes this reflex to get students to talk and collaborate works effectively but sometimes it also works at the expense of creativity, which is the ownership of imaginative processes proper to the individual. Ownership depends a great deal on the extent of self-determination. It is hard to own something that you yourself have not fashioned or adapted in your mind; and those items of group-enthusiasm that are enculturated to lodge in your definition of yourself are somewhat kitschy, like the *ra-ra* of football teams or patriotism, around which the levels of identification are unseasonable and scary. Structurally, the individual preconditions of ownership and the collective culture of group endeavour are hard to reconcile. We seek an artificial overlap between the public and the personal, which is difficult to manage; and more often than not, the chosen solution does not favour creativity.

Finally, ownership is not encouraged by the pre-determined. The same reasons apply. If something has been set up for me to follow in great detail, I am less likely to feel ownership than if I can determine some part of it that I could reasonably direct with whatever wisdom and knowledge I have, often thanks to the influence of my teachers. And so a question of ownership arises over learning outcomes. How much can one actually own these formulations of what you will be able to do? In truth, it depends on the degree of identification that the learning outcome suggests. If the learning outcome is a skill, there is a good chance that it will attract personal identification. For example, if I am studying health sciences and I read in the learning outcomes that by the end of a module, I will know how to give someone an injection, I will be warmly excited at the prospect: I will possess an essential skill that identifies me as a health professional, among which are the marvellous attributes of good form in doing something that fills an already apprehensive patient with dread. But if the learning outcome in any sense approaches the gifts of autonomy—even the knowledge which is the precondition of imaginative or creative work in some field—I sense that I may be embarrassed by the prediction, which outlines a process that I have to follow. If it concerns my headspace, I do not necessarily welcome the intrusion. It may in the long run be very beneficial for me to have known various things that are predicted as my new capabilities as stated in the learning outcomes; but because I have had no role in establishing what they are and they have arisen in no organic relation with my experience, I fear that they will be obscure or redundant, a pompous distraction, mouldy old fussy stuff that is not worthwhile, almost a nuisance. Even if the learning outcomes are beautifully crafted in sympathy with all the likely needs of a poet or a painter or a composer, they do not gain in love by declaring their exigence before I have begun.

Creative projects involve intuition and need to be nurtured in concert with a developing vision, an ability to see things that could not have been foreseen before the experience of trying or committing mistakes and reflecting allows. The process is organic and is difficult to prefigure and construct as learning outcomes. You could imagine a great number of steps that would be useful to know, say, in the process of painting. They would range over the whole of art history, techniques and criticism. But for intercepting the creative trajectory of an art student, these items have to float in the background. You cannot say which will be necessary or tangential or even contrary. It is for the art student to decide. Their use is contingent on the student's ownership of them. Some that are inspiring to me are disowned by others; and some that I greet with impatience are darling concepts for artists and art lovers whom I also admire. It is not as if we deal in antithetical values. Rather, the degree of ownership in any material on offer varies as much as our several personalities, backgrounds, our impetus for making something new and our hope to get something out of it. The more freedom that a student has in deflecting the incumbency of learning outcomes, the likelier it is that ownership in a creative undertaking will arise; and, given that a similar economy of opportunity guides study in humanities or education, I can only imagine that it is equally true of any scientific discipline that has creativity in it.

Chapter 13

REFLEXION

For many years, reflexion has assumed a position at the top of the canon-ical educational taxonomy. The historical fortunes of reflexion took off when John Dewey, no less, opined that 'We do not learn from experience. We learn from reflection on experience.'[1] In the next sentence of an influ-ential book, Dewey gives a working definition of reflexion by explaining its educational agency: 'Reliving of an experience leads to making connections between information and feelings produced by the experience'. Without reflexion, then, you do not learn. It is a necessary element of learning and it works by allowing a replay—'reliving' in Dewey's text—of an earlier experience. Reflexion presupposes two moments, one which is a kind of virgin encounter and the other a review of it.[2] The subsequent moment of revisiting the anterior moment (even if they follow hard upon one another) yields a complementary benefit, as the consecutive poles of learning enhance the cognitive pregnancy of an otherwise incomplete encounter. Further, in the aphoristic quote, Dewey suggests how the complementary ben-efit arises. Fact and emotion ('feelings produced by the experience') are somehow drawn together: we link information and feeling, as if data are somehow energized with emotional attachments or reason to be meaningful and hence lodge in memory.

Once this separation of encounter and review had occurred under the seductive name of reflexion, it would become impossible to theorize edu-cational process without it. There is no going back: it is the *sine qua non* of learning and teaching, as necessary to education as any technique of

---

1   J. Dewey, *How we think: A restatement of the relation of reflective thinking to the educative process*, Chicago, Henry Regnery, 1933, p. 78.

2   Donald Schön has attempted to divide reflexion into two phases, one during an experience and one after the event (*The reflective practitioner: How professionals think in action*, Basic Books, New York, 1983) but this distinction in timing frames the discourse in terms of functional process, which is not necessarily helpful in probing what reflexion is.

presentation or explanation. The exigence of reflexion in the learning process would, in time, lead to a theory of student-centredness, where the emphasis in learning and teaching is not on the teacher but the student and her or his interest in the material. The student is the one who reflects, which might be another way of saying what John Biggs declared: learning is what the student does.

It is not surprising, therefore, that reflexion has not only retained its popularity but greatly increased its spread in contemporary theory and practice. In the influential suite of writings by the same John Biggs, reflexion sits alongside theorizing—and sometimes even above it—as the supreme stages of higher-order thinking; and for that reason reflexion is implicitly commended to teachers as the ultimate goal of learning.[3] Without a stage of reflexion, students are imagined to have achieved only shallow learning: the very nub of deep learning is the reflexion that the learners make upon the new material or the act of absorbing it. Reflexion is not only highly valorized in theory but for thirty years has been supplied with frameworks; practical methods for attaining or cultivating reflexion are variously put forward for students to reach the greatest phase of educational practice. Mostly, these frameworks, like that of Donald Schön, relate to the teacher's reflexion rather than the student's;[4] though it seems necessary to see the two in a relationship.

We now live in an epidemic of reflexion. In universities, reflexion is almost ubiquitously recommended as a stage for clinching the syllabus; indeed, reflexion has advanced to proportions that exceed our ability to imagine them, as can be quantified through a Google search. 'Reflective practice' scores about 4,750,000 results; even 'reflective practice definition' yields c.1,940,000 results. Then there are certain tools in common use, which again Google finds in staggering numbers: 'reflective essay' turns up about 1,950,000 results; and 'reflective journal' an astonishing 4,030,000 results. Each year, the pages proliferate; and the web engine only covers discrete pages, leaving aside the recommendations in learning management systems and intranets (an enormous local grey web) where lecturers exhort their students to reflect on the various moments of learning, presumably the better to learn or to

---

3   'To achieve most intended learning outcomes a range of verbs, from high to low
     cognitive level, needs to be activated. The highest would refer to such activities as
     reflecting and theorizing, the lowest to memorizing and recalling', John Biggs and
     Catherine Tang, *Teaching for quality learning at university: What the student does*, 4th
     edition (first edition 1999), Open University Press, McGraw-Hill, Maidenhead, 2011.

4   As in the four lenses of Stephen Brookfield, *Becoming a critically reflective teacher*, San
     Francisco, Jossey-Bass, 1995.

embed the learning and make it more sustainable or enduring. New pedagogy officially encourages reflexion.

At some point, usually after some task or attendance at a presentation has been completed, learners are encouraged to reflect. Sometimes, for efficiency's sake, reflexion is folded into assessment (despite the apparent incompatibility of a task that needs to be free of trepidation and another that is full of it) and hence the popularity of a so-called reflective essay. Sometimes, reflexion is suggested consistently throughout the semester and sometimes the moment proposed for reflexion lies beyond assessment, where it is therefore free of pressures, a safe hermitage of altruistic philosophical engagement on the other side of measurement and competition, a high-minded retreat, where the self-sufficiency of the learning experience extends its inspiration to a kind of selfless intellectual regrouping. Consciously or otherwise, reflexion as an educational strategy lays claim to a transcendental condition, a moment of reverie, where the learner—no longer facing an anxious challenge—can function in autonomous engagement with the material that has been learned.

Potentially, at least, there is great resonance between this practice and the subjective basis of creativity. Here, amid the noisy dynamics of active learning—fraught by a tense grid of learning outcomes and marking rubrics—is a beautiful window of private intellectual collectedness, where a meditative enjoyment of thought is encouraged. Reflexion, like a fragile vestige of educational liberality, reminds us that the project of socializing learning is incomplete. Learning ultimately requires a return to the self, a process where the ideas are bounced back or reflected in the mind of the unique individual. Of course it too has been gridded (in education, everything can be de-organicized), so that it is constrained to be about the learning that needs to be done; and that is the rub. Yes, we admit the primacy of a subjective self, a looking back on knowledge in relation to personal experience; but the framework is fixed rather than motile: it does not contemplate the movement of thinking beyond the stimulus, to put knowledge to another use, a moment of disruption, a scruple, a query, a reckoning with discomfort, perchance an eagerness to intervene, an impatience with everything so far encountered. If it did contemplate those wonders, it would be closer to the preconditions of creativity.

So what is reflexion? In fact there is little agreement on what reflexion is and what takes place during its inspired moments of musing, those precious minutes of independent intellectual flight that somehow clinch the learning. One wonders what confessional material is introduced into the framing of the syllabus, what unknown personal curiosity is entertained, what potential is spied for future engagement. Perhaps just because of a great fear of the unknown, the unmeasurable, the possibly specious, there have already been expressions of concern for the vulgarization of the practice, where learners are indiscriminately ordered to reflect; and these reservations have been published by scholars who were among the earlier systematic apologists for reflexion, like David Boud and David Walker,[5] who could legitimately worry about the vagueness and self-gratifying qualities of reflexion, especially when encouraged outside a framework of defined benefits: 'we believe that there are now many examples of poor educational practice being implemented under the guise and rhetoric of reflection.'[6] Some of the dangers arise from 'equating reflection with thinking, and yet others arise from teachers pursuing their own personal agendas at the expense of learners.' They worry that

> some practitioners … translate reflection and reflective practice into such simplified and technicist prescriptions that their provocative features—such as the importance of respecting doubt and uncertainty and distrust of easy solutions—become domesticated in ways which enable teachers to avoid focusing on their own practice and on the learning needs of students.

They identify 'recipe following' where students are taken through 'a sequence of steps of reflection and required to reflect on demand.' They are concerned about 'reflection without learning', with a mechanistic reflex of 'intellectualising reflection' where emotions are downplayed or the opposite, where students are unethically encouraged to reveal personal information. They warn about 'uncritical acceptance of experience' and exhort us instead to give 'consideration of the context in which reflective action is engaged', which 'is a seriously underdeveloped aspect of discussion of reflection. The context to which we are referring is the total cultural, social and political environment in which reflection takes place. This broader context is so all-pervasive that it is difficult to recognize its influence.' Their critique is powerful and has remained hard to answer. It implicitly recognizes an important element of the challenge, namely that reflexion is hard to direct: it cannot be another exercise or task to perform, else it loses its Platonic

---

5   David Boud and David Walker, 'Promoting reflection in professionals courses: the challenge of context', *Studies in Higher Education*, vol. 23(2), 1998, pp. 191–206.

6   *loc. cit.*

freedoms, where ideas and memories associate without pressure. Unlike 'self-evaluation', which in some regards it resembles, reflexion is not metrical, and it therefore frustrates some who would rather see a qualitative process of self-review with an evaluation rubric, possibly even yielding quantifiable standards.

For others, however, that is precisely the appeal of reflexion, a liberal and potentially idle moment that surmounts the strenuous surfeit of details in a stressful course of study and instead enables free thinking. To me the idea of reflexion has a marvellously romantic dimension, where my natural eagerness to meander and ruminate indulgently on subject matter of any kind is justified. At primary school, I would be accused of being a dreamer, of lacking concentration for the lessons that demanded exclusive attention. Now, however, I see that my foibles are valorized; my very waywardness is redefined as a necessary element in research method, a power that imaginative research cannot do without. For me, little could be more gratifying than this widespread approbation of the reflective impulse.

It would therefore be pleasurable to join in and celebrate our epidemic of reflexion, to enjoy the flattery which it bestows on the romantic learner and patch over the scruples of reflective sceptics like Boud and Walker. But even scrutinizing Boud and Walker's own texts, it appears that our ability to reflect on reflexion may be limited. In the masterful article cited, there are warnings about the mechanistic but there is no gesture to the contrary: there is no mention of 'imagination' nor talk of 'speculation', and concepts like 'the poetic' are not entertained. There is an acceptance of the emotional but there is no term like 'subjectivity' to make it meaningful. Alongside other stalwarts of learning taxonomies, like 'critical thinking', we find it difficult to act out the recommended virtue: we do not easily think critically about critical thinking and we do not reflect curiously upon reflexion. For something so widely accepted, it seems inordinately difficult to quiz ourselves about the substance and value of the construct. We readily accept a number of taxonomies, which (I would argue) artificially divide and invidiously rank thinking, about which we should be more suspicious. Thinking is mostly inscrutable and layered in such complicated patterns that we would not even succeed in comprehending a dog's analysis of a scent much less our excogitations over the mysteries of language. We blithely recommend both critical thinking and reflexion—assuming a relationship between them— without possessing a satisfactory definition that reassures a sceptic that our fondest beliefs are not based on waffle.

I would avoid the crisis of an absolute definition but instead historicize reflexion and from there attempt to fathom some of the phenomenological richness of the concept. I want to know when we first began talking about reflexion as a thinking process and what it meant in its several stages of development. There may be no absolute definition of reflexion. It may be inherently relative, given that even the concept of metacognition—a word synthetically hatched in 1979 by John Flavell—is less than absolute.[7] But the great advantage of reflexion is that it can indeed be historicized, yielding a perspective that allows us to be more reflective about it.

If we begin with a provisional general definition, reflexion means thinking about thinking or, more properly, the experience of thinking. It is close to metacognition, which is a more psychological way to describe awareness of thought process, also popularly described as thinking about thinking or learning about learning. It refers to an advanced kind of thinking ('high-order thinking'), uniquely ambitious and relaxed at the same time, conscious of the internal agency of ideas and their treatment by alternative impulses within the mind.

Reflexion is historically defined because there was a time when there was no word to describe the condition. In ancient Greek, for example, there is no good match for the concept. There are words to describe the physical condition of reflexion, to be sure; but they do not transfer to the intellectual by metaphor. Making use of prefixes like 'against' or 'back', Greek vocabulary described the reflexion of light with numerous conceptions[8] or representation as in a mirror (ἐνόπτρισις, εἰσοπτρισμός); there are verbal forms[9] but none of these terms suggested a meditative interval in cognition, where the mind wanders somewhat creatively.[10] On the contrary, if anything they suggest the sudden flash of the return of light, the glint or sparkle, which might be associated with polished weapons.

Meanwhile, there are plenty of words that describe thought itself, the condition of cogitation or mindedness (ἔννοια, verb ἐννοέω) or an idea that is turned out for communication (ἐπιλόγισμα) which, at a pinch, could be translated as a reflexion. There are powerful words to describe meditation

---

7   John Flavell, 'Metacognition and cognitive monitoring. A new area of cognitive-development inquiry', *American Psychologist*, vol. 34, no. 10, pp. 906–911 (doi:10.1037/0003-066X.34.10.906).

8   ἀντανάκλασις, ἀνταυγασία, ἀντίλαμψις, ἀντιφάνεια, ἀντιφωτισμός, κατάλαμψις, φραστύς.

9   ἀντιστίλβω, ἀνακυλίνδω, ἀντανακλάω, ἀνταυγέω, ἀντιφαίνω.

10   Greek words dated in Liddell, Scott, Jones (*LSJ*) *A Greek lexicon*, Oxford University Press, Oxford, 1968.

(σύννοια, συννοέω) which, like ἔννοια, draw from the root of thought or mind (νους);[11] one can meditate in the sense of weigh up or deliberate (μητιάω) and care for, be anxious about, think about, and hence meditate upon (μεριμνάω). Another strong root lies again with a synonym for thought (φροντίς, verb φρονέω) which also means care, attention bestowed upon a person or thing, but which can be used more abstractly to mean thought itself, arguably reflexion, meditation, for which lexicographers can adduce examples from the classical drama and histories.[12] The poet Pindar uses the word in an abstract sense,[13] which is hardly surprising, given that the whole aesthetic of lyric verse is so much constructed around speculative cues, a series of invitations, if you like, to reflexion.

As an example, Pindar's first *Olympian ode* begins with the memorable sentence 'Water is best'. It occurred to scholars of antiquity and more recently to ask the question 'best of what?'[14] Pindar does not say. He just says 'water is best'. True to the ethos of modern poetry, it is a phrase deliberately constructed to remain without closure, poetically incomplete, to be supplemented by speculation and hence encourage reflexion. In listening to poetry, we latch onto words, images and phrases that suspend the urgency of a narrative and hang around in the mind, as if awaiting more intimate connexions that we might bring to them.

It could therefore be argued that enough of the lexical preconditions of reflexion were met in ancient Greece and that the Greek mind was handsomely supplied with a vocabulary that allowed for ample reflexion. But still the process did not occur by an analogous word and it was impossible to ask a student in the lyceum to reflect upon his or her learning. Socrates could ask you in the *agora* to think about something, to think deeply, to think prudently and with penetration, even to meditate; but still the concept of reflexion is not quite there. As Bruno Snell argued in his beautiful book on the development of the mind in ancient Greece, the concept of thought or mind or spirit did not arise ready-made but had a long development from the Homeric period, where it was 'not yet' apparent (*noch nicht*).[15] It follows

---

11   Sophocles, *Antigone* 279, Plato, *Republic* 571d, *Laws* 790b, Aristotle, *Problems* 917ᵇ39.

12   Aeschylus, *Agamemnon* 912, *Persians* 142, Suppliants 407, Sophocles, *Oedipus the King* 67, *Oedipus at Colonna* 170, Xenophon, *Cyropaedia* 6.2.12, Herodotus 2.104, Euripides, *Fragments* 684.4, *Hippolytus* 436.

13   *Olympian odes* 1.19.

14   William H. Race, 'Pindar's "Best is water": Best of what?', *Greek, Roman, & Byzantine Studies*, vol. 22, 1981, pp. 119–124.

15   Bruno Snell, *Die Entdeckung des Geistes, Studien zur Entstehung des europäischen Denkens bei den Griechen*, Vandenhoeck & Ruprecht, 5ᵗʰ ed, 1980, p. 10. Snell is

that the same ideas continued their development from antiquity to the present time, which is the subject matter of the history of ideas. Reflexion in the current acceptation is a good example. It did not exist in antiquity and there is a question of when it arose closer to our times.

In tracing these histories, it is useful to observe the unique element of reflexion which appears in the tradition of our language. Our word is derived from Latin, with a preposition for 'back' or 'again' (re-) and the verb to bend (flectere). But the Romans had no substantive form and the verb means 'to turn around' or 'turn back', like the tusks of elephants or horns of other creatures.[16] Romans rarely used the verb metaphorically and, when they did, it seems safest to translate such instances as 'turn around in the mind'.[17] As in Greek, to describe what we mean by reflexion, they would say 'thinking' (cogitatio, with the famous verbal form cogito and even adverbial, cogitate, thoughtfully), meaning considering, deliberating, thought, reflection, meditation, imagination. Or they could invoke consideration (consideratio) which also had moral overtones, a 'sitting together' with an implicit sympathy for others. As for the physical dimension of reflexion, the Romans used different words, just like the Greeks.[18]

Our reflexion, even when abstracted from the physical image of the mirror, is rooted in a physical motif of bouncing back an image. The reflexion presupposes three elements: the object, the image of the object as returned by a mirror and the subject who sees. In the case of Narcissus and all self-admirers who follow, the object and the subject are collapsed as the one person, the unique individual whose image is bounced by the mirror and who simultaneously sees the image. In that instance the mirror turns the subject into an object (a specimen to be examined by someone) and vice versa: the object who is seen becomes animated as the person who sees.

---

circumspect: 'Wenn in Folgenden etwa behauptet wird, die homerischen Menschen hätten kein Geist, keine Seele und infolgedessen auch sehr viel anderes noch nicht gekannt, ist also nich gemeint, die homerischen Menschen hätten sich noch nicht freuen oder nicht an etwas denken können und so fort, was absurd wäre: nur wird dergleichen eben nicht als Aktion des Geistes oder der Seele interpretiert: in *dem* Sinn gab es noch keinen Geist un keine Seele'.

16   Instances given in Lewis & Short, *A Latin dictionary*, s.v.: '(elephantorum) dentes reflexi.' Pliny 11.37.62; 'cornu (with adunco aere)', Seneca Oedipus 731: 'cornicula (scarabaei)', Pliny 30.11.30; and, of the nape of the neck, Virgil, *Aeneid* 10.535.

17   I turned it around—or reflected—in my mind, 'animum reflexi.' Virgil, *Aeneid* 2.741.

18   Their idea of a reflexion was a bright flash, where things shine (*refulgeo*), are refulgent, to use our archaic word; they glitter, glisten (*renideo*) and are resplendent, with a certain *revibratio*.

Mirrors are spooky and loom large in the language-oriented psycho-analytical theory of Lacan, proposing the mirror phase as a kind of archetypical constant in human development. As applied to thinking in education, the mirror also seems uncannily more than a metaphor: it returns a useful image of thinking itself in that moment when it is reflexive. The quest for insight necessarily involves reflexion. In order to redeem 'thoughts of great value, worthy cogitations', Shakespeare's Cassius asks: 'Tell me, good Brutus, can you see your face?' To which Brutus says, 'No, Cassius, for the eye sees not itself / But by reflexion, by some other thing.'[19] This 'other thing' is the shiny mirror, the surface so perfect and hard that it has no comfort in it, no permeability, so that it immediately turns the rays back. The strategic Cassius offers to be that crystalline membrane himself: 'And since you know you cannot see yourself / So well as by reflexion, I, your glass, / Will modestly discover to yourself / That of yourself which you yet know not.' This glass or mirror for inner knowing is a precursor to reflexion in the contemporary sense.

At a similar time, the King James translators of the *Bible* rendered the lines of Paul with the same image: 'For now we see through a glass darkly'.[20] The rendering is colourful, because there was no 'darkly' in the Greek text, which reads: now we see through a mirror as by enigma (βλέπομεν γὰρ ἄρτι δι' ἐσόπτρου ἐν αἰνίγματι). But for the baroque interpreters, the mystery of the mirror is enigmatic because the image which is a mere semblance contains the truth: it is not the truth in a literal sense but an image of the truth, effectively a reflexion but which is still enigmatic because it is not itself the thing that it shows. So the King James translators installed darkness into the image of the glass, which in a shadowy way yields the sight that cannot be obtained from the mortal position that we occupy, so far beneath divinity. The enigma or symbol is like the reflexion in a mirror: it is 'there' but 'not there', showing something as more than a sign but still not actually being the thing that it shows.

The motif of reflexion as a mental process is riddled with enigma in the senses that we most want to identify. If Dewey and others position reflexion as the prime and indispensable circumstance of learning—and in turn we consider learning to be something like absorption, taking in material, embedding ideas and methods in our minds—the process of reflexion is an uncomfortable match. In learning, material is indeed absorbed, as if

---

19   *Julius Caesar* 1.2.
20   *1 Corinthians* 13.12.

entering a permeable membrane and thence obtaining intercourse with the substrates of memory and marrying the material already embedded within it by the urging of will and imagination. The mirror, on the other hand, has no quality of absorption. It entertains the rays only to deflect them immediately through the same glass. The light never sees the tain side of the glass: nothing is embedded. As the mirror remains impenetrably hard and unyielding, the moment of reflexion is of infinitesimally tiny duration, inscrutable, occurring in no space, a complete virtuality of impact and return that no one has ever witnessed. And yet the image is there, 'in the glass', as Lucretius says.[21] The paradox is the enigma already suggested: the reflexion—which in a sense is nothing, an immaterial event of imperceptible physics—is metaphorically the neuronal magic, potentially the moment of epiphany.

If the physical mirror bounces back rays in space, the optical phenomenon is called reflexion. If the reflexion is understood as a metaphor, the element through which events are bounced back is time. What is past has been; but when we reflect, it comes back—somewhat differently and regardless of how quickly—to memory, which is the salvageable record, so to speak, of events, sights, sounds or language. The reflexion is not simply an act of opening the door to the repository. It is a bend in time where the event or condition is apparently wilfully reconnected with your perception, so that you get to interpret it.

Reflexion as a physical phenomenon had been used in English since the renaissance and, if you examine the beautiful entry in the *Oxford English Dictionary* (*OED*), you could imagine that the motif proliferated in linear fashion from Gutenberg to Google. In fact, the uses of reflexion even as a physical phenomenon are relatively rare throughout early modern European literature. Reflect or reflexion does not appear in key writers like the fourteenth-century Petrarch, nor high-renaissance authors like Guiccardini or Castiglione, nor poets like Boiardo and Tasso. In the same sixteenth century, Ariosto uses the term once in describing extreme heat[22] but the instances even in baroque authors like Giambattista Marino are exiguous, given the enormous volume of their production and the temptations of visual seduction, where reflexion involves glowing light in a dynamic interchange between luminaries and surfaces. In his long poem, *L'Adone*, Marino mentions the harmonious reflexion of rays only once[23] which, however, is

---

21 'speculis apparent simulacra', Lucretius 4.98.

22 'del calor che si riflette a dietro', Ludovico Ariosto, *Orlando furioso* 8.20,1–4.

23 'meco amica e concorde i rai riflette', *Adone* 11.17.

not metaphorical. Reflexion tends only to arise when the visual spectacle of light bouncing around inspires the poet. It is not yet a figure of language, where one thing is compared to another as a reflexion, a critical moment of recall. As in Milton, the discourse is light itself.[24]

Following the physical side of reflexion, however, the seventeenth century distinguishes itself by attention to light in the art of painting. Of particular note is the development of still life, where the scene is contrived to relish reflexions in subject matter of little account by itself. The purpose of the painting is to devote attention to the form and surface of various objects in light, like the shine of grapes from one sphere to the next, a gourd, a silver charger or a glass or bottle. It also belonged to the genres of portraiture and figure-painting to register reflexions, as the proximity of the skin to a radiant textile would pick up heightened tone and colour. These subtleties were acknowledged in contemporaneous texts, such as in Francis Junius who goes so far as to propose that the very atmosphere becomes a vector of colour by reflexion: 'Goe to then, Painter, confound red roses with good store of lillies, and what reflexion the aire taketh of them, let that be the colour of her face.'[25]

In art, the seventeenth century loves spectacle and therefore relishes reflexions, almost like painting with paradoxes, because the reflexion is a part of a body which is not essential but contingent on a coincidental closeness to something else. Given the superb pictorial skill of modelling, *chiaroscuro* and reflexion, it is curious that there are so few baroque poetic rhapsodies on reflexions. In a beautiful amorous sonnet by Giuseppe Artale, a woman wearing glasses is described as heating up the ardours of the poet's love: 'if the sun nourishes heat with its reflexions, she—in order to make glances more fervid—wears two lenses so that lightning vibrates in place of wild flames'.[26] As a joke, a piece of wit or *argutezza*, the lines are perhaps reflective in another sense, because we are caused to ponder the curious attraction that the male poet finds in the sight-challenged lass, some layer of cuteness through her minor disability, a source of titillation not so much because of relish in a girl's disadvantage but the poet's command of hyperbole. This toying with attraction and witty gamesmanship is echoed in Shakespeare's

---

24   'that side which from the wall of Heav'n / Though distant far some small reflexion gains / Of glimmering air less vexed with tempest loud', *Paradise lost* 3.427–29.

25   Francis Junius, *Painting of ancients*, London, R. Hodgkinsonne, 1638, p. 285.

26   'Se co' riflessi il sol nutre il calore, / questa, per far più fervide le occhiate, / l'oppon due vetri, acciò che 'l suo folgore / vibri in vece di rai vampe adirate,' *La donna con gli occhiali* 5–8.

concern for a woman, that 'her beauty and her brain go not together. She's a good sign, but I have seen small reflexion of her wit';[27] to which a lord says as an aside to us, the audience: 'She shines not upon fools, lest the reflexion should hurt her', almost as if the utterance is an inverted reflexion of the insult, bouncing it back upon its rude originator.

In fact, the great metaphor of reflexion—where the beam is a bounce-back in the mind—predates Shakespeare and belongs to the sixteenth century. In a letter that prefaces one of his *novelle*, Bandello describes

> the appetite for revenge, which appears so sweet that little by little it draws a person beyond the limits of reason and somehow igniting anger, that with a blinded intellect, she or he cannot turn the mind to anything but thinking always how to offend the enemy; nor does she or he reflect upon the evaluation of so many and such diverse dangers that present all day long.[28]

It is a wonderful passage to introduce reflexion in the metaphorical sense, not merely a scintillation of light or heat that is bounced back, reflected or 'retorted', which Shakespeare once uses as a synonym, where man 'cannot make boast to have that which he hath, / Nor feels not what he owes, but by reflection; / As when his virtues shining upon others / Heat them, and they retort that heat again / To the first giver.'[29] Bandello's beautiful intuition that the physical word can be used to describe a psychological moment is also telling. He still needs the word 'evaluation' to fit alongside the term reflect (*né mai riflette la considerazione*): one never reflects, he says, the consideration of the many dangers. One is supposed to reflect not on the reality but on the thought of the reality, as if the act of reflexion is intrinsically deferred, as if tentative. And in any case, his usage is negative. It is a failure to reflect (a finite condition: reflexion did not occur) rather than a realization of the act (which is a potentially infinite realm of speculation). A similar example is cited in the *OED* from the end of the sixteenth century: 'To this all the company answered,

---

27   *Cymbeline* 1.2.
28   'E questo credo io che avvenga perciò che l'appetito de la vendetta che par cosí dolce, a poco a poco tira l'uomo fuor dei termini de la ragione e in modo l'ira accende che, accecato l'intelletto, ad altro non può rivolger l'animo che a pensar tuttavia come offender possa il suo nemico, né mai riflette la considerazione a tanti e sí diversi perigli che tutto 'l dí occorrer si vedeno.' (Il Bandello al molto illustre e valoroso signore il signor Cesare Fregoso) *Novelle* 2.13.
29   *Troilus and Cressida* 3.3.

that they had never much thought, nor made reflexion, upon any such circumstance.'[30]

In the tumultuous flow of history, the vigorous creative period from the renaissance to the end of the baroque was the wrong time to define reflexion as a thought process. The word existed and had occasionally been used metaphorically; but the times were showy, not reflective; they were energetic, glamorous and brilliant but not rich in absorption or intellectual intimacy. Voltaire summed up the spirit of the times in addressing his great satirical predecessor Boileau: 'I witnessed the tail-end of your brilliant century, a time of great talents rather than light'.[31] By Voltaire's estimation, then, the baroque had little light in the metaphoric sense of 'enlightenment' and less reflexion of it in the intellectual sphere. We could verify the suspicion philologically, because the eloquent masterpieces of Racine, for example, have no reflexion in them; and when the word is used in Racine's prose, the phrase could be translated equally by 'observation' or 'remark': 'here is the reflexion that Dio Cassius makes on the intentions of Mithridate'.[32] It is reflexion as a product rather than an activity; it is the result of thinking, the expression of a judgement rather that the thinking that might have led to it, and in fact might have led elsewhere pending a resolution.

It was left to the eighteenth century to discover reflexion. Known charmingly as 'the enlightenment', with light installed in the very epithet, the eighteenth century brought forth an enormous and adorable emphasis on reflexion. In the same way that the eighteenth century discovered the conversational and the intimate,[33] it clinched the metaphoric potential of reflexion to describe a process of mental review, a moment of contemplation or perhaps second thoughts, thinking back, and used the word prolifically. Most tellingly, reflexion appears on the comic stage which is dedicated to conversation, richly elaborating the spontaneous talk among individuals who are subject to somewhat chaotic impulses in the drama. Through amusing episodes, reversals of fortune and accidents, the act of reflexion presents a note of counterpoise, where the busy motives on stage are referred to second thoughts, thinking back, speculation, reservations, gentle relish or analysis.

---

30   *s.v.* cited as '1595 R. Parsons et al. *Conf. Next Succession* ii. 33'.

31   'De ton siècle brillant mes yeux virent la fin; / siècle de grands talents bien plus que de lumière,' Voltaire, *À Boileau, ou mon testament*, 6–7.

32   'Voici la réflexion que fait Dion Cassius sur ce dessein de Mithridate', Préface to *Mithridate*.

33   See my article 'The development of intimacy: history of an emotional state in art and literature', *Australian Journal of Art*, vol. 4, 1985, pp. 15–35.

In the plays of Marivaux, reflexion arises in all complexions. It is not necessarily confined to an encounter in the past but can be used of the future: hence the phrase, 'making reflexion on the pleasure that he is going to have'.[34] There is often a judgement involved in reflexion but sometimes not. Reflexions can be negative, not just in their subject matter but their value in occupying attention: there are 'sad reflexions for which there is no longer any time; when I am lost, wisdom lightens me up'.[35] Reflexions can be fallacious and unjust, as when the female sex is underrated.[36] Reflexion can argue a negative case or can be used to convey rejection: 'I've reflected that it's quite pointless for us to see one another'.[37] Consternation over a bad turn of events could lead to reflexions that might embarrass you.[38] A reflexion can put you in a bad mood;[39] reflexions might disturb you when someone talks in a maudlin or depressive manner.[40] A reflexion can be arresting because of wicked contradictions, as when 'it's cruel to be suspected of joy when one has nothing but trouble'.[41] Reflexion can be a way of being guarded and politely hedging your bets. Asked by the ambassador if he is rejecting a marriage proposal, Lélio says: 'I don't reject it at all; but it requires reflexion', meaning careful consideration.[42]

Though we identify reflexion with private mulling, it is expected that reflexions enter the social domain and are wilfully communicated as observations. No sooner is reflexion discovered than it is used for profit or broadcast. Once discovered, the private source of introspection is appropriated by the social, which is exactly what would happen in our own epoch in education, where the intimacy of the individual's private reflexions would be pressed into service through various exercises. But even so, reflexions are

---

34 'faisant réflexion au plaisir qu'il vient d'avoir', Marivaux, *Arlequin poli par l'amour*, single act, 11.

35 'Tristes réflexions, qu'il n'est plus temps de faire! / Quand je me suis perdu, la sagesse m'éclaire', *Annibal* 3.6.

36 'un récit que j'accompagne ordinairement de réflexions où votre sexe ne trouve pas son compte', *La surprise de l'amour* 1.7.

37 'Monsieur, depuis que nous nous sommes quittés, j'ai fait réflexion qu'il était assez inutile de nous voir. Oh! très inutile; je l'ai pensé de même. Je prévois que cela vous gênerait', *La surprise de l'amour* 2.2.

38 'tout cela amènerait des réflexions qui pourraient vous embarrasser,' *Le Prince travesti* 3.7.

39 'cette réflexion-là me met de mauvaise humeur', *La surprise de l'amour* 2.5.

40 'Ce butor-là m'inquiète avec ses réflexions,' *Le Prince travesti* 1.13.

41 'Cette réflexion m'arrête; mais il est cruel de se voir soupçonné de joie, quand on n'a que du trouble.' *Le Prince travesti* 1.8.

42 *Le Prince travesti* 2.8.

never public insofar as they are never owned by the social. If they are not yours, they are someone else's and you can be jealous of them, impatient, irked. They are obdurately removed from your control. You might find them importunate: I'm done with your reflexions;[43] and then, as Pasquin calls for, 'a little politeness in your reflexions!'[44] Constance advises Lisette to make her reflexions in private and not in communal conversation.[45] Against this, Arlequin can be seized by prudence and 'make a reflexion', that is, an observation with a considered dimension.[46] Lisette is not so sure, however, as to where this reflexion might lead.[47] Trivelin himself will cast some doubt on their merit by the degree of his enthusiasm for them: 'by deuce, your reflexions are rich stuff'.[48]

In the social realm, reflexions can be made, dispensed with, doubted. They are like a thing or act to which one reacts, evaluates, with which one possibly disagrees, like the Countess: 'as for me, I find the heart of woman is correct and does not deserve your satirical reflexion'.[49] Reflexion is an artefact produced for social consumption rather than an internal process; and for that reason it can be resented. Reflexion touches on the moral and is socialized conscience. Trivelin can abandon his non-materialistic principles; he will seize the opportunity to take property in spite of his reflexions,[50] literally 'despite the shame of my reflexions'. A man's heart, he adds, is a right rogue (*fripon*). The same crisis occurs with Marton in *Les fausses confidences*. Dorante suggests that she is tempted by 1,000 shillings in a failure to reflect (*faute de réflexion*) on the moral or sentimental consequences. But Marton replies 'On the contrary, it's thanks to reflexion that the shillings tempt her. The more I dream of them, the more I like them'.[51]

---

43 'Taisez-vous; je n'ai que faire de vos réflexions.' *Le Prince travesti* 2.11.

44 'un peu de politesse dans vos réflexions,' *La joie imprévue*, single act, 5.

45 'Faites vos réflexions à part, et point de conversation ensemble,' *La Joie imprévue*, single act, 14.

46 'Oui, mais la prudence m'a pris, et j'ai fait une reflexion'.

47 'à quoi vous a conduit cette réflexion-là?', *Le Prince travesti* 3.2; elsewhere, Trivelin's reflexions can be discounted in favour of the facts ('Tu m'obligerais de retrancher tes réflexions et de venir au fait,' *La fausse suivante* 2.3).

48 'Diantre ! tes réflexions sont de riche étoffe,' La fausse suivante ou le fourbe puni 2.5.

49 'ne mérite pas votre réflexion satirique', *L'heureux stratagème*, 2.10.

50 'j'en prendrais, à la honte de mes réflexions', *La fausse suivante ou le fourbe puni*, 1.1.

51 'Au contraire, c'est par réflexion qu'ils me tentent. Plus j'y rêve, et plus je les trouve bons.' *Les fausses confidences* 1.11. The same phrase arises when La Comptesse is threatened with innuendo of infidelity which looms large in the absence of reflexion (*faute de réflexion*). *L'heureux stratagème* 1.4.

Amid the mystifying charades and mascarades of the comic drama one can have a thought that all one's reflexions corroborate something,[52] as if reflexions are a suspicion. Reflexions find their place in a transactional economy of messages. Someone's reflexions can be to your advantage,[53] meaning your arguments or position or decision. Reflexion can be calculating, where wisdom is very much on the pragmatic side: 'a little reflexion … you're young, beautiful and a girl of means? Who can hold out against these three qualities?'[54]

Elsewhere, imperative verbs are used to command reflexion; because if individuals have proprietorship over their thoughts, you aim your effort to control them at the innermost squishiest core. This protected zone, the sanctum, the intimacy that is morally quarantined from social control, is precisely the target of anyone who wants to have power over you. With an air of urgency, the word 'reflect' means 'think about it' (*faites-y réflexion*). In bossy discourses, the word arises without much sense of the meditative: make your reflexions on that (*faites vos réflexions là-dessus*); or 'pay attention to the fact that I'm talking to you'.[55] Reflexion is also capable of being severe with remonstrations. Often, reflexion is a reckoning, stated in a slightly threatening way, to get a grip on yourself: 'make some serious reflexions of yourself; try to become aware of your foolishness'.[56]

However, the pragmatic and mediocre use of the concept in the social domain should not detract from the purer philosophical structure of reflexion, which remained in perfect credit at its core. A Marquis, pointing to his forehead, batches together 'judgement, reflexion, phlegmatism and wisdom'.[57] And later, completing the reflexive character of reflexion, the Chevalier says to the Marquis that one needs plenty of judgement to know that one has none; isn't that the reflexion that you want us to make?[58] Equally, reflexion can describe discretion, as when Parmenès says that 'we won't say what we

---

52   'Ce qu'il me dit là me fait naître une pensée que toutes mes réflexions fortifient', *La fausse suivante ou le fourbe puni* 3.1.

53   'vos réflexions sont à mon avantage', *La fausse suivante* 3.7.

54   'Madame, un peu de réflexion. Ne savez-vous pas que vous êtes jeune, belle, et fille de condition ? Citez-moi une tête de fille qui ait tenu contre ces trois qualités-là, citez-m'en une.' *L'Île de la raison ou les petits hommes* 2.6.

55   'faites donc réflexion que je vous parle', *La fausse suivante ou le fourbe puni* 3.6.

56   'faites de sérieuses réflexions sur vous ; tâchez de vous mettre au fait de toute votre sottise', *L'Île de la raison ou les petits hommes* 1.10.

57   'de jugement, de réflexion, de flegme, de sagesse, en un mot, de cela (montrant son front)', *L'Île de la raison ou les petits hommes* 1.1.

58   'il faut avoir bien du jugement pour sentir que nous n'en avons point. N'est-ce pas là la réflexion que tu veux qu'on fasse ?' *L'Île de la raison ou les petits hommes* 1.1.

think', to which the Countess replies: 'make reflexion, however'.[59] Reflexion can be a sweet and diplomatic way to point something out: 'I would be very upset to displease you; I would ask only to reflect on it'.[60] When reflexions are described as serious, it seems pompous, as when the Marquise asks what is in your book, to which Hortensius answers that it contains nothing but serious reflexions;[61] though this gravity would not compromise the serious-ness of a husband who abuses his wife.[62] In life, according to the drama, there are instants and reflexions that suddenly determine our actions.[63] You expect a reflexion to have something of the momentous. According to Silvia, her boyfriend thinks that he will shame his father in marrying her, betraying his fortune and birth: 'behold great subjects of reflexion'.[64]

Reflexion is the history of second thoughts. By the eighteenth century, the styles, manners, religiosities and patronage were ready for overhaul. From the painter Boucher to Greuze, the age would become more dialect-ical; its enchantment and loveliness would have a moral edge, where the care of the mind, relationships and personal property would be a topic of poetic scrutiny. It was an age of reflexion, where vanity would be subject to the judgement of satirical comedy. Following the baroque in the century of light, extravagance has its reckoning; and among all the jokes, the wit, the crazy plots and misunderstanding, the comic stage increasingly devotes itself to the stern redress of frivolity. Marivaux is far from an exception. If we go to Venice, whose baroque talents in architecture and painting rivalled those of Paris, the stage is also charged with reflexion, the need to countenance all stimuli—from good advice to errant behaviour—with some imaginative deliberation, an urge to ponder, to weigh up but also to rhapsodize, to extend, to muse upon. In that sense, we go beyond 'second

---

59 'nous ne disons point ce que nous pensons ... Faites pourtant réflexion que je suis étrangère ... ' *L'Île de la raison ou les petits hommes* 2.8; *cf.* 'faites-y vos réflexions', *Les Serments indiscrets* 4.4, and 'faites réflexion à ce que je vous dit', *Le Petit-Maître corrigé* 1.12.

60 'Madame, je serais bien fâché de vous déplaire; je vous demande seulement d'y faire réflexion.' *La seconde surprise de l'amour* 2.5.

61 'Ce ne sont que des réflexions très sérieuses,' *La seconde surprise de l'amour* 2.8.

62 'du malheur d'une femme maltraitée par son mari, je lui citais celle de Tersandre que je trouvai l'autre jour fort abattue, parce que son mari venait de la quereller, et je faisais là-dessus mes réflexions'.

63 'des instants et des réflexions qui nous déterminent tout d'un coup', *La seconde surprise de l'amour* 3.8.

64 'Ce qui lui en coûte à se déterminer, ne me le rend que plus estimable: il pense qu'il chagrinera son père en m'épousant, il croit trahir sa fortune et sa naissance, voilà de grands sujets de réflexion', *Le Jeu de l'amour et du hasard* 3.4.

thoughts', reflexion as the tempered moderation of impulse. Nor is reflexion merely a matter of testing assertions or subjecting them to proofs; it is an open-ended speculation that discovers how far the mind can enjoy the concept that is put before it, either the concept in its naivety or the critique that a contrary impulse prepares for it.

Among the authors in whom reflexion flourished is the Venetian playwright Carlo Goldoni. In Goldoni's drama, reflexion is demonstratively acted on stage, with stage-directions specifying reflexion for the actors, as with Geronte who, in a note within the text, 'reflects for a moment and then calls out (*riflette un momento, indi chiama*)'.[65] Reflexion is utterly part of the drama and is therefore not always a serene or rhapsodic affair. Facing the prospect of creditors repossessing his assets and establishing a dowry, Pancrazio says: 'I'm thinking, reflecting and don't know which side to grab onto'.[66] But like an actor who makes claims, reflexion is not to be believed without testing. Sometimes, the reflexion is part of the farce. And sometimes, it reveals an impatient character who is incapable of it. The audience often has to decide if the named reflexion is worthwhile or not. Reflexion is often dismissed as idleness: 'this is no time to lose heart nor to form reflexions on the events of the world'.[67] We have to remember that reflexions can be empty and in vain.[68] One can have second thoughts about reflexion itself.

There is therefore an issue in every case as to whether reflexion redeems stupidity or is the cause of it. There is no saying that reflexion will be automatically self-vindicating. As in the earlier Marivaux reflexion is sometimes conceived communicatively; it overlaps with advice and hence requires tact: I'm happy that that you're taking things so well; I praise and admire you. But allow me to make a reflexion.[69] And if there is no tact, there is sometimes rudeness. Reflexions in the transactional domain can be harsh. 'Daughter, if I show myself to be frank, it proceeds from the reflexions that your circumstances deserve'.[70] Because they closely reveal the integrity

---

65   *Il burbero benefico* 2.1.

66   'Penso, rifletto e non so a qual partito appigliarmi,' *I mercanti* 1.3.

67   'Signor padrone, ora non è tempo né di perdersi di animo, né di formare riflessi sulle vicende del mondo,' *I mercanti* 2.6.

68   'Vani riflessi e tardi: dovea pensarci in prima.' *Il Cavaliere di spirito ovvero La donna di testa debole* 2.4 or they can be downright useless in a despairing exlamation (*Inutili riflessi!*) *Il Moliere* 2.2.

69   'mi piace che voi prendiate la cosa in buona parte; vi lodo e v'ammiro. Ma permettetemi di far un riflesso. Chi si prenderà il pensiero de' preparativi necessari per una giovane che si fa sposa?', *Il burbero benefico* 2.5.

70   'Provien da quei riflessi che merta il caso vostro.' *Il padre per amore* 4.4.

of a person's deliberations, reflexions are handled anxiously in the social setting of the drama. There are legion exhortations to reflect before speaking or acting rashly.[71] 'Excuse me, for the love of heaven! These reflexions need to be done before giving the word'.[72] Timeliness in reflexion is everything: 'These wise reflexions would have been opportune before promising' what cannot be delivered.[73]

Goldoni, one of Italy's most entertaining moralists, is also conscious that literature itself is a source of reflexion, that one contemplates it in a discursive conversation with others, which must be very close to what we mean by reflexion as the higher faculty in education: 'we were accustomed to make reflexions on some fine book'.[74] The proper mood and occasion are important for reflexion, as important as the content. An event needs the right timing to achieve reflexion. When a letter arrives, Pantalone immediately wants to read it; but the Dottore says 'let's read it this evening with greater ease and with reflexion. For now, it's necessary to pay attention to looking after what is pressing.'[75] Often, however, the reflexion is the thing being reflected, reified as utterance, analogous to a poem which is beautifully written; hence Lelio's exclamation: 'what eloquence, what reflexions!'[76] For that reason, a cleverly stated observation can be called 'the best reflexion' (*Ottima riflessione!*).[77] Ottavio says: 'This business deserves some reflexion (or scrutiny)', to which Aure says: 'I have forestalled all your reflexions'.[78] The reflexion in that case is like a vote, a calling out, which can be prevented or annulled by someone else being ahead of the game.

Pictorially, Venice in the eighteenth century had a curious relationship with reflexions. In the paintings of masters like Canaletto and Guardi, the waterways cast gentle reflexions, weak traces of buildings on the

---

71   'Quando così si parla ci si riflette in prima.' *L'amante di sé medesimo* 3.7.

72   'Per amor del cielo, scusatemi. Queste riflessioni si dovevano fare prima di dargli parola.' *L'impostore* 3.10.

73   'Tutti questi saggi riflessi sarebbono stati opportuni prima di promettere.' *La donna di maneggio* 1.10.

74   'Avendo io avuto la fortuna di conoscere la signora Rosaura, quando era in casa della signora sua zia, ed essendo noi accostumati a far delle riflessioni su qualche buon libro, era venuto per non perder l'uso di un così bello esercizio.' *Il padre di famiglia* 1.18.

75   'Una lettera? Lassemela veder' ... 'La leggeremo poi questa sera con comodo, con riflesso. Per ora è meglio badare a sollecitar quel che preme.' *La bancarotta, o sia il mercante fallito* 1.13.

76   *La donna di garbo* 1.8.

77   *La donna di maneggio* 2.16.

78   'L'affare merita qualche riflesso' ... 'Tutti i vostri riflessi io li ho prevenuti', *La madre amorosa* 2.3.

canal—almost shadows rather than reflexions—as if the painter does not entirely trust them. They are far from the centre-stage that they would occupy during the nineteenth century with impressionism. Optical reflexions are of course not the issue, even if perhaps the concept played on a writer's mind by a tempting analogy. But if we can examine one contrast in the history of ideas, the evidence of painting might still be helpful as a touchstone. Reflexion, whether physical or metaphorical, is not solid, like the architecture. In the same way that a painter must use observation and conjecture rather than measurement in depicting reflexions, so we use our intuition and imagination in concert with memory to reflect on what we have learned. And in this somewhat tentative intellectual space, we depart from the rock of prudence, the knowledge and computational certainties that apply to objective fact and instead draw meaning from a comparison between realities and the subjectivity that interprets them.

In the eighteenth century, the place once held by prudence yields to reflexion. As witnessed in Titian's *Allegory of prudence* in the London National Gallery from c.1565, the concept of prudence is iconic, mystical, Serapic, with recondite associations in Hieroglyphic texts. In this haunting painting from renaissance Venice, the three-tiered composition portrays an old man's profile on the left, a mature man's frontal visage in the middle and a young man's profile looking to the right.[79] Below these archetypes of the three ages of man, there are respective depictions of a wolf, a lion and a dog; and above the human register, there is a Latin inscription which reads 'Out of the past the present acts prudently lest it spoil future action'. In many ways, this marvellous patriarchal statement of ancestral authority and wisdom represents the opposite mind-set to reflexion. We see prudence as priestly, a vision into the preordained which projects the future. The old man has prudently paved a path favorable for the mature man, who in turn reciprocates for the young man, making a kind of cycle of good fate for one another, a wilful destiny of powerful beasts and humans with links to the supernatural. These three figures are gifted with the quality of foresight (*prouidentia*) or prudence, a looking into the future with the oracular art of the soothsayer.

Reflexion is the opposite in that it casts a mirror back onto the recent past. It is a way of bringing the recent past into a vivid connexion with the present. We live in the present and make decisions that have an impact

---

[79] See the masterful study by Erwin Panovsky, 'Titian's *Allegory of prudence*: A postscript', in *Meaning in the visual arts*, University of Chicago Press, Chicago, 1982 ed. See also Simona Cohen, 'Titian's London Allegory and the three beasts of his selva oscura', *Renaissance Studies*, vol. 14, no 1, 2000, p. 46.

on the future; but while reflexion propitiates our next phase, it refers to the previous phase and enlivens it with relevance to further thought. It thus contributes to making the future, obliquely, as if through a glass darkly; and as Goldoni says of a decision based on reflexion: 'the choice will not be capricious nor ill-advised but the child of good reflexions, just and assiduous',[80] where of course any decision affects the future. Usually, reflexion contains prudence: he has the right point of view; one must reflect upon it.[81] In Goldoni, reflexion is often a stage of precaution, facing a deal or commitment. 'One shouldn't sign the papers so quickly', says one character. 'One has to reflect, to see if someone advises thus'.[82] One must not be precipitate: 'if I have said something without reflecting on what you said ... I have some good news for you'.[83] You expect a reflexion to be wise and memorable.[84] Reflexion is in essence identified with reason, especially whenever there is a contrast between reason and emotion, which is not to be trusted. 'Ah, reason and the heart speak to me in two different languages. This one prompts me to deceive myself and that one inspires me to the most justifiable and virtuous reflexions'.[85] Reflexions relate to balance, to a perception of things having a relationship when none is immediately apparent. In rhyming verse, Goldoni explains how the fortune of twin brothers is analogous, even though one serves at war and the other labours in court; the one task, if you reflect upon it, is equal to the other.[86] Reflexion means prudent council; the reasons deserve more time and more reflexion.[87] It is therefore identified with moral astuteness: whoever has a blotted conscience is always afraid of being discovered, whence I need to reflect and establish some resolution'.[88] But failing to reflect is not in itself a sign of bad character. 'He

---

80 'La scelta ch'io farò non sarà capricciosa, né sconsigliata, ma figlia di buoni riflessi, giusta e doverosa.' *La vedova scaltra* 3.25.

81 'Egli ha il punto di vista. Riflettere conviene', *Il Moliere* 3.3.

82 'Ah, non dovea sì presto scriver la carta ingrata' ... 'Riflettere conviene, se alcun l'ha consigliata.' *Il Cavaliere di spirito ovvero La donna di testa debole* 3.3.

83 'Ma se l'ho detto senza riflettere a quello che mi dicessi! Signora Beatrice, ho da darvi una buona nuova.' *Il contrattempo* 1.6.

84 'mi ricordo il vostro saggio riflesso', *Il ritorno dalla villeggiatura* 2.4.

85 'Ah! la ragione ed il cuore mi parlano con due diversi linguaggi. Questo mi stimola a lusingarmi, quella mi anima ai più giusti, ai più virtuosi riflessi.' *Il ritorno dalla villeggiatura* 2.11.

86 'L'una e l'altra incombenza, se si riflette, è uguale.' *Il padre per amore* 1.2.

87 'alcune ragioni dell'avversario, le quali meritano maggior tempo e maggior riflesso', *L'avvocato veneziano* 2.1.

88 'Chi ha la coscienza macchiata, ha sempre timore d'essere scoperto, onde mi conviene riflettere e stabilire una qualche risoluzione.' *L'impostore* 2.10.

always speaks without reflecting: it's his defect and I've corrected him many times. He doesn't seem to have a bad heart. He has protested a hundred times his gratitude and love'.[89] Sometimes reflexion is close to consideration or interest: 'What do you say, sir? Is my daughter worthy of your reflexions?' as if referring to interest in buying a property.[90]

We cannot trace every reflexion in every epoch. Into the romantic period, the word is more often physical than metaphorical, where, however, it takes on the uncanny glow of its luminary. A favourite is the reflexion of moonlight, as in a sublime passage in Goethe's *Werther*: 'when the moon appeared and rested over the black cloud, and the tide swelled and roared in fearful and awesome reflexion (*Widerschein*), then a shudder overcame me and a desire as well.'[91] The reflexion is physical, because made by the rays of the moon, but metaphysical because echoing in the psyche, as also in Goethe's *Letters from Switzerland*[92] or the spooky figure of a man who appears most pictorially in a mirror-like brook in Goethe's play *Torquato Tasso*.[93] Still on the precipice of mystical metaphor, in the second half of *Faust*, Goethe evokes the memory of blood spilled on the earth which the earth breathes back as a reflexion,[94] or similarly wasted human spirits.[95] It is also the way that Nietzsche uses reflexion, as an echo of something psychological or cultural, as in his invocation of dreams as more pressing than reality, which involves a description of the painter Raphael's *Transfiguration*, where the figures in the lower half are the reflexion (*Wiederspiegelung*) of eternal original grief,

---

89   'Egli è solito parlare senza riflettere. Questo è il suo difetto, e l'ho corretto più volte. Non mi pare poi ch'egli abbia un fondo cattivo. Mi ha protestata cento volte la sua gratitudine, l'amor suo.' *Il contrattempo* 2.2.

90   'Che dice, signore? Le pare che mia figliuola sia degna de' suoi riflessi?' *Il matrimonio per concorso* 2.19.

91   'Und wenn dann der Mond wieder hervortrat und über der schwarzen Wolke ruhte, und vor mir hinaus die Flut in fürchterlich herrlichem Widerschein rollte und klang: da überfiel mich ein Schauer, und wieder ein Sehnen!' Johann Wolfgang von Goethe, *Die Leiden des jungen Werther* 2, 12 December.

92   'Durch Fichtenwälder stiegen wir weiter den Jura hinan, und sahen den See in Duft und den Widerschein des Mondes darin.' Goethe, *Briefe aus der Schweiz* 2, 24 October.

93   'Und zeigt mir ungefähr ein klarer Brunnen / In seinem reinen Spiegel einen Mann, / Der wunderbar bekränzt im Widerschein / Des Himmels zwischen Bäumen, zwischen Felsen / Nachdenkend ruht,' *Torquato Tasso* 1.3.

94   'Der Boden haucht vergoßnen Blutes Widerschein', *2 Faust* 2, Klassische Walpurgisnacht. Pharsalische Felder.

95   'Verzeih, o Herr, das sind die Spuren / Verschollner geistiger Naturen, / Ein Widerschein der Dioskuren, / Bei denen alle Schiffer schwuren; / Sie sammeln hier die letzte Kraft.' *2 Faust* 4.

the only reason for the 'appearance' of things as the reflexion (*Widerschein*) of an eternal contradiction.[96] The poetic, throughout the nineteenth century, would seek some overlap between the physical and the psychological. For Baudelaire the word is preferred, for instance, when the wan complexion of his muse reflects cold and silent madness and horror,[97] or a mysterious eye reflects the indolence and pallor of the sky.[98]

Through this history of reflexion, several aspects of the concept are revealed which are congruent with creative processes and invite certain educational corollaries: first, the inscrutable relationship with physical reflexion where, like a mirror, the absolute impermeability of the surface furnishes an image that is paradoxically positioned for absorption. Second, reflexion emerges in dialectical circumstances, where things reflected could be good or bad and not necessarily helpful. Third, reflexion is stressful when socialized, where remarks proceeding from personal intuition are introduced into conversation under the name of reflexion, to be absorbed by others or debated and rejected. These observations all point to reflexion requiring imagination. To reflect means to energize intuitions across complicated matrices of information, opinion and experience, where one matches the several stimuli in lively connexions. It is not without reason that it has been highly esteemed in educational discourse as an advanced form of cognition. It is advanced because it is imaginative and yields consciousness as a creative act. It is similar, in that sense, to learning which I consider advanced at any dedicated level.

A cynic might argue that method is hereby advanced very little, because one vague term (reflexion) is triangulated with another vague term (imagination). That is why our task has not been to define reflexion but rather to analyse aspects of its phenomenology, especially as separated naturally through its historical development. In the process, however, the exigence of imagination emerges. Up to a point, the overlap of reflexion and

---

96 'die Wiederspiegelung des ewigen Urschmerzes, des einzigen Grundes der Welt der "Schein" ist hier Widerschein des ewigen Widerspruchs, des Vaters der Dinge.' Friedrich Nietzsche, *Die Geburt der Tragödie* 4.

97 'Ma pauvre muse, hélas! qu'as-tu donc ce matin? /Tes yeux creux sont peuplés de visions nocturnes, / Et je vois tour à tour réfléchis sur ton teint / La folie et l'horreur, froides et taciturnes.' *Les fleurs du mal* 7, *La muse malade* 1–4.

98 'On dirait ton regard d'une vapeur couvert; / Ton œil mystérieux (est-il bleu, gris ou vert?) / Alternativement tendre, rêveur, cruel, / Réfléchit l'indolence et la pâleur du ciel.' *Les fleurs du mal* 50, *Ciel brouillé*; cf. 'Nos deux cœurs seront deux vastes flambeaux, / Qui réfléchiront leurs doubles lumières / Dans nos deux esprits, ces miroirs jumeaux.' *Les fleurs du mal* 126, *La mort des amants* 6–8.

imagination is implied in the way that Boud and Walker (cited above) speak of the complexity and power of context in conditioning the way we reflect:

> Individualistic conceptions of reflection fail to take account of the subtle and powerful ways in which context legitimises and frames particular forms and approaches to reflection, and defines those outcomes from reflection which are accepted as valid. There are many circumstances in education and training in which it is inappropriate for teachers to be encouraging particular reflective activities ...
>
> Many discussions of reflection imply that it is a universal process which can be considered independently of context. However, if reflection is regarded as universal it more easily lends itself to abuse than if it is construed as a cultural practice located in a particular time and place.

The way that Boud and Walker address context is useful, describing the way all processes are framed and situated; but the discussion ends in a slightly mediocre way:

> Teachers need to consider themselves, the learners with whom they are working, the local context in which they operate, the processes they use, and the expected outcomes as defined by each party (including external ones, for example, the institution or accrediting body). They need to create a micro-context within which the kinds of reflection acceptable to learners and consistent with the values of learners and teachers can occur and which does not reproduce those aspects of the dominant context which impose barriers to learning.

The monitory outline is well and good; but the text already pulls away from the imagination and instead defaults to protocols. In recognizing the centrality of imagination to the reflective process, this chapter instead opens up the poetic side of reflexion in any discipline, which is also the primacy of imagination. European literature first discovered reflexion and then celebrated it in poetic forms which all, in one sense, are imaginatively dedicated to reflexion. All the plays, poems and paintings reflect upon the world in a way that encourages humorous and imaginative reflexion in us. If reflexion furthers thought, it does so by enjoining the imagination to extend an idea—possibly no further than into the stock of our own experience—and enlarging the contact with a new idea into the already received but freshly activated. Reflexion is a marriage of the new and the dormant, the stimulus and the sleeping, the fresh encounter and old potential. It is not imaginative to the extent of invention; but it is nevertheless a powerful motif in learning and research as well.

Reflexion occurs to a magical degree in a moment, say, when you put down a book and muse on the contents, perhaps repeating a refrain within it, and think: 'that's funny ... that's curious; there's something in this'. The thought is not immediately engaged in solving a problem or building a new construction but is the cue for a possibly inspired investigation. Reflexion is not as forceful as invention, which has an assertive dimension, envisioning something as yet unseen. It might be a precondition of invention; but that illustrious trajectory belongs to another investigation. Reflexion is more intimate and conversational within the person: it is a conversation that you have with yourself. And for that reason, it is hard to extricate from the self and take to the social. In reflexion, you recognize your thought, which enables you to become an interlocutor, to treat yourself as if you were another person; as Horace says, 'how often do you see someone else when you look at yourself in the mirror'.[99] This gentle dynamic which momentarily polarizes the psyche fulfils what Schiller hoped for in the genre of tragedy, where a person can deal with himself or herself as if a stranger.[100]

We have succeeded in making several reflexions on reflexion, none of which constitutes a comprehensive definition. But the element that emerges most vitally through the historical investigation is that reflexion is a poetic condition where an event in memory talks back to itself. It makes no sense to recommend that students perform some activity and then to reflect on it unless there is a cue to reflexion already installed in the material to be reflected upon. The material must, to some extent, be itself reflective—poetically so—else it will fail to induce reflexion in the metaphorical sense that we have identified as imaginatively productive. Boud and Walker are correct in their suspicion that reflexion cannot be handled mechanistically, as if syllabus is presented and students are subsequently told to reflect upon it. The command is hollow because no part of the initial circumstance is reflective. Reflexion presupposes two moments that look at one another, an encounter and an aftermath; but the subsequent period of pondering what might have occurred in the mind only takes shape by virtue of anticipation, an expectation that something is occurring that will require a fulfilment, something more inspiring than I can handle right now but which clearly

---

99   'quotiens te in speculo videris alterum', Horace, *Carmina* 4.10.6.

100   'uns dadurch in den Stand setzt, mit uns selbst wie mit Fremdlingen umzugehen', Friedrich Schiller, 'Über die tragische Kunst', *Sämtliche Werke*, Winkler Verlag, Munich n.d., vol. 5, p. 147.

has in it some beautiful potential, a great intellectual pregnancy that will warrant exploration, an activity in which I can enjoin my imagination. The corollary is that the teaching must itself have a reflective dimension for reflection to be induced naturally upon the student. It cannot be conceived as a completely distinct phase, to be activated by the command to reflect.

In today's climate of blended approaches to learning and teaching, the concern that Boud and Walker entertained—that reflexion had become an unthinking add-on without educational benefit—is heightened. As programs are increasingly structured around pre-class, on-campus and post-class elements, it is convenient to fill up the post-class activity with an invitation to reflect. But if nothing reflective has occurred from the overture to the denouement, the instruction to reflect is fake, artificial and vain. The reflective component has to be built in with every aria, so to speak, so that each element is suggestive, colourful, has a promise of intellectual growth and speculation. These suggestive moments of an inconclusive kind, where closure is deliberately resisted among cues to further questions, are difficult to express as learning outcomes. In a sense, they are not learning outcomes but learning itself as a continuum, as a lifelong source of wonder, the very openness and lack of finality that goad us into research. These structures of reflexion, wonder, research, creativity and imagination cannot be detonated by command and may be suspected of being antithetical to learning outcomes and the constructive alignment that serves them.

Reflexion means imaginatively matching ideas and experience, in no particular order but the one folded into the other in a fruitful rhapsody. In structure, reflexion depends on a special continuity of thought that has a fold in it, a point about which the ideas turn back on themselves. But just as in physics, where the angle of incidence equals the angle of reflexion, the reflective calibre of thoughts that come out is prefigured by the encounter that stimulates them. It is poetic because it involves a relaxation of semantic rules, where one thing equates with another through a jump, a fold, an uncertain parallel, which is symbolic: the return of a reality as an image, which creatively invites other realities and images in its train. It is always poetic, because the mind manages two conditions in one connexion, a memory and a desire to do something with it, to match it, to extend it, to marry it to a vision which includes emotional investments. In reflexion, one understands that all thoughts, no matter how much they reflect on the tangible, are themselves immaterial. This awareness is poetic and, at a certain point, transcends the most immediate purpose that we imagine we will put it to, and yields insight and pleasure that belong to a richer world.

Chapter 14

CONCLUSION

This book began with the claim that imagination is central to learning. We easily accept that imagination is necessary to an exceptional creative act, especially in art or music or a breakthrough in physics or economics. But I start with the contention that learning itself is a creative act—performed to some degree by anyone who learns—and that we build synapses in learning by the same processes in creating original works of art or science. Learning is creative because what we creatively build around the material yet to be learned is a projected picture of something marvellous and endearing, a part of us already, sometimes a fantasy, a hope, an entrancement. As you learn, your mind races in many directions and establishes links from flimsy and wayward cues that the unconscious throws up for reasons of identification and affection.

It might be objected that while some learning may occur in this fanciful way, surely not all learning does. For example, when we learn German grammar, we do not need fantasies and affection but a clear head for what is the correct conjugation or what kind of declension applies for a given noun … stuff, arguably, that is best learned by mental hammer, by rote or the mean old command of 'committing to memory'. Learning these technical features of the language is also necessary before we can progress to higher levels of German where the imagination may be rewarded with the poetic beauty of the language, as in the eloquence of Schiller or Musil. But there is no phase of learning German that is not magical, no matter how bogged down in mundane detail. A word and the way it changes shape according to the context are rich in imaginative potential. It is all rich and colourful. I can think about both in many ways that match the patterns in my native language and wherever I find a graft—either from English or my developing German itself—I exercise my imagination, even if it means pronouncing the words in an exaggeratedly comic way. If I cannot use my imagination, if I feel discouraged from making imaginative connexions and feel forced to learn just by concentrating harder, as if compelling myself, my learning is stressful, disagreeable and shallow. If I do not use my imagination, I try to constrain myself to learn; and little remains from my self-coercion that is endearing enough to retain.

Imagination is integral to the organic nature of learning because it draws the technical into the personal, the conceptual, the wilful, the joyful. Creativity is not unique to the great leap of a world-view or a major jump in paradigms. It belongs to the intimacy of learning anything, where facts and ideas are owned through an imaginative identification with a personal inclination and sympathy. Like reflexion, creativity is placed at the top of the educational hierarchy, because it is thought of as 'higher-order thinking', above and beyond the hard yards, the gruelling duty of learning that you undergo to gain aptitudes in grammar or calculus or scales in music. I do not share this view of creativity as something higher, as if it is only available at the top of a pyramid, presumably after one has gathered a great deal of knowledge and processing through lower-order thinking. I do not like the separation, because it ultimately denies the creativity of all learning, where the imagination is constantly jumping between the concrete and the abstract, the given and the provisional, the regular and the amazing. We learn best when we find something fascinating, that is where our mind actively toggles between the greater and the lesser; and this intellectually mobile process is not driven by a quality inherent in the subject matter but a personal appeal, a match with our personal view of ourselves, that we have created for ourselves.

If there is such a thing as higher-order thinking it enjoys constant and seamless interchange with lower-order thinking, memory, processing, hum-drum stuff that enjoys less glamour; and in a mind imaginatively engaged, they are as good as indivisible. My ownership of the facts is a function of my ability to identify with some aspect of them: it expands as I flicker between things that have a name and nameless ideas about myself that seduce me. Higher-order thinking and lower-order thinking are both necessary for every moment of intellectual ownership; and, as neither makes much sense without the other, we owe it in all cases to our imagination to create a lively infusion of the conceptual in the concrete and the concrete in the conceptual.

In reaching toward our creative potential, it is necessary to make room for several subjective preconditions of imaginative thinking. If learning is an imaginative act that links new material with a nascent view of ourselves, it relates to the affections, the elements of content that we can see ourselves identifying with. And because we must talk about appeal, the attraction that the imagination creates, we have to talk about the qualities in people and their interactions that favour the encouragement, the pedagogical themes that roll around our interests and growth like the intellectual satellites of love. This book has dwelt on a suite of themes that range from narrative enchantment to engagement, the simple motif of being nice, which is so necessary in a teacher, the ability to indulge in acts of telling, the intimate comfort with time that we might feel in waiting for ideas to arise without anxiety, the recognition of one's subjectivity in learning. Superintending these themes is the metaphor of colour, the imaginative inflexion that teachers install in their language and arguments that induce a parallel freedom of imagination in their students. Teachers themselves may be colourful, have dimensions of thought that race around by the motif of flux that we were describing as essential to the organic character of thought. These colourful themes that touch on imaginative growth might reasonably be available to everyone who ever learned. They are democratic and are not a mark of great distinction but a creative potential that we share. Alas, they are easily suppressed, tragically and structurally.

Nietzsche explained that the institution of genius was hatched out of vanity, to make us feel contented that creative activity is beyond us in the same way that the capacity inherent in Raphael's painting or Shakespeare's drama must be excessively marvellous (*das Vermögen dazu sei ganz übermässig wunderbar*), like a blessing from above. This positing of creative talent in exceptional genius absolves the individual from the challenge of creative engagement. The godly status of the genius is a signal to remain complacent yourself. To call a genius 'divine' means: 'we do not need to compete here'.[1] It is a condition of disengagement rather than modesty; we opt out of the creative on the pretext of not being a creative genius. The industrial period witnessed a grand promotion of the idea of genius, alas a disempowering trend of hero-worship, where native talents of unknown potential would abdicate in favour of the aggressive innovatory prowess of the genius. In previous times it was expected that any courtier, say, could turn out a polished sonnet; but from the industrial period, creative work would be alienated from the typical educated person—now greatly rising in number—and stressfully waged more and more by dedicated anxious pretenders to genius.

---

1   'Jemanden "göttlich" nennen heisst "hier brauchen wir nicht zu wetteifern".' Friedrich Nietzsche, *Menschliches, Allzumenschliches* 162 (Cultus des Genius' aus Eitelkeit).

No one ever meant to switch us off creatively but the discouraging tendency belongs to a frightened conservative streak in the industrial unconscious to suppress impulses and processes that are not standardized. In the period of industrialized education, we have witnessed a further wave of unconscious creative suppression, where study is co-opted by learning outcomes that press the learning experience into proximal relations with assessment. This book has argued that constructive alignment harms creativity and that both the constructivism behind it and the student-centredness that it supposedly serves do not make sense. The underlying reason for learning outcomes trumping creativity is an industrial discourse of certification and accreditation that dominates professional qualifications. Creativity is not just secondary in this discourse; it is obliterated. We do not do education to be creative. We are creative in spite of education.

Not to end on a negative note, this historicizing critique of constructivist pedagogy suggests pathways for a post-industrial view of education. Taking the long lens of history, it is easy to identify the features of education that have satisfied the creative mind for hundreds of years, conditions like the teacher being encouraging or 'nice' as we decided to call it; but above all, it is to connect with the subjectivity of the student in learning, to recognize the creative intimacy of learning, where the vital ingredient in learning is an imaginative rapport with the subject matter. If we could cultivate this more ontological view of education, whether in professional, research or creative programs, we would secure the post-constructivist future that our creative development deserves.

There remains a question of whether it is possible to graft a new ontological pedagogy onto the current constructivist dead-end of learning outcomes or whether we have to start again, perhaps reverting to teaching objectives or inventing something yet more open-ended which is based on the enthusiasm of the student. I am optimistic about the possibilities. There is still much that can be achieved within the current framework. At present, creative disciplines survive because they largely ignore the learning outcomes at every stage: the learning outcomes are platitudes that no one respects but everyone patronizes. Still, it is uncomfortable to recommend this subversive pragmatism to any discipline with less poetic licence.

One quick way to tackle the uncreative dimensions of coursework education is to change the assessment from a competitive structure to pass grade only. Nalini's problems will largely disappear, because she would not be discouraged through mediocre marks. Nalini could persist in her imaginative use of experience and interpret the critical feedback more positively, because it is not expressed as a justification for her mediocre mark. And because there would be less anxiety over the assessment, strategic Anastasia could also afford to relax and take an interest in Nalini's romanticism; she, too, could ease her way into creative approaches to learning.

The problem is not that we have assessment (because assessment can definitely accommodate creativity) but just that assessment according to constructive alignment is designed to conscript all academic attention in a strategic scoping exercise that annihilates the creative impulse. We do not have the same problem with research degrees in the ungraded tradition; and it is unclear why we deny ourselves the same latitude in coursework programs. One argument has been that students do not do their best if they are not graded; but the implicit reliance on competition to motivate students strikes me as uneducational, cynical, above all uncreative. It is a discourse of the ends justifying the means, stripping the educational process of good faith among students and teachers alike. Phillip Dawson and I examined the case that competition is energizing but came to the conclusion that it is more pernicious than helpful.[2] As a culture, we tend to accept the reality of competition because we expect that there will always be limited scholarships or higher degree places or some other mechanistic boon for a few at the end of a program; and it is therefore necessary to sort students to identify the elite candidates for receiving the privileges. These structures of limited opportunity—which are often *artificially* set up, as with scholarships—do not spell an eternal destiny for education, nor determine that all coursework has to be constructed invidiously as a competition. The tail is wagging the dog if education, which ought to be about learning, instead serves an entirely different bureaucratic purpose of sorting people into winners and losers.

Creativity and imagination are pivotal in this critique, because they can either be seen as exceptional gifts granted to an elite—thus supporting the competitive paradigm that we are saddled with—or, as this book has tried to demonstrate, creativity and imagination can be seen as integral with learning, to be developed in everyone who studies and who makes connexions between foreign academic material and a nascent view of themselves. At whichever level, if we engage our imagination, we identify the innocence of learning: it is the creative, the self-generating curiosity for something that augments the person studying or the inventive person at the

---

2   Robert Nelson & Phillip Dawson, 'Competition and education: connecting history with recent scholarship', *Assessment & Evaluation in Higher Education*, December 2015.

other extreme who develops new ideas. This pedagogical innocence, what I have described throughout as the intimacy of learning, is the ontological core of creative education. It is harmed by competition and it is harmed by the mechanistic grid of knowledge and skill acquisition described through learning outcomes.

To detach learning and teaching from their competitive structures is even less likely than the imminent abolition of learning outcomes; but if neither project is possible in the immediate future, we still have the assurance that creativity is larger than the structures that hem it. Once we understand how creativity permeates the very ontology of learning, we have a motive to push against the well-meaning shibboleths that restrict it; and when all is said and done, the motive—if it has been lacking but now stands up and looks at us—may be all that we need to restore creative colour to learning and teaching.

BIBLIOGRAPHY
OF RECENT SCHOLARLY LITERATURE

This list does not include classical and biblical texts. The numbering in the footnotes follows the standard reference system derived from the canonical editions used in lexicography. Different editions and translations have disparate pagination, whereas the canonical numbering is consistent. Similarly, the numbering used in renaissance and baroque texts follows the order of canto/stanza for epic poems, act/scene for plays or book/story for novelle or essays.

Abeysekera, L. & Dawson, P. 'Motivation and cognitive load in the flipped classroom: definition, rationale and a call for research', *Higher Education Research & Development*, vol. 34, 2015, Issue 1.

Abrahamson, C.E. 'Storytelling as a pedagogical tool in higher education', *Education*, vol. 118, no. 3, 1998, pp. 440–451.

Allam, C. 'Creative activity and its impact on student learning – issues of implementation'. *Innovations in Education and Teaching International*, vol. 45, no. 3, 2008, pp. 281–288.

Amabile, T. *The social psychology of creativity*, New York: Springer-Verlag, 1983.

Amabile, T. 'The three threats to creativity', *HBR Blog*, 2010, retrieved from http://blogs.hbr.org/2010/11/the-three-threats-to-creativit/

Anderson, K. 'The whole learner: The role of imagination in developing disciplinary understanding', *Arts and Humanities in Higher Education*, vol. 9, no. 2, 2010, pp. 205–221.

Anderson, R.C. 'Some reflections on the acquisition of knowledge', *Educational Researcher*, vol. 13(9), 1984, pp. 5–10.

Auerbach, E. *Mimesis: dargestellte Wirklichkeit in der abendländischen Literatur*, Bern: Francke, 1967.

Auslander, P. *Liveness: performance in a mediatized culture*, London and New York: Routledge, 1999.

Barr, J. & Steele, T. 'Revaluing the enlightenment: Reason and imagination', *Teaching in Higher Education*, 2003, vol. 8(4), pp. 505–515.

Beach, D. 'The paradoxes of student learning preferences', *Ethnography and Education*, vol. 3(2), 2008, pp. 145–159.

Beghetto, R. A. 'Nurturing creativity in the micro-moments of the classroom', in K. H. Kim, J. Kaufman, J. Baer & B. Sriraman (eds), *Creatively gifted students are not like other gifted students: Research, theory and practice*, Rotterdam: Sense Publishers, 2013.

Beghetto, R.A. & Kaufman, J.C. 'Intellectual estuaries: Connecting learning and creativity in programs of advanced academics', *Journal of Advanced Academics*, vol. 20(2), 2009, pp. 296–324.

Biggs, J. 'Enhancing teaching through constructive alignment', *Higher Education*, vol. 32, 1996, pp. 347–364.

Biggs, J. 'What the student does: teaching for enhanced learning', *Higher Education Research & Development*, vol. 18, no. 1, 1999.

Biggs, J. *Aligning Teaching and Assessment to Curriculum Objectives*, Imaginative Curriculum Project, LTSN Generic Centre, 2003.

Biggs, J. & Tang, C. *Teaching for Quality Learning at University* (1999), Maidenhead, Berkshire: Open University Press, McGraw-Hill, 4th edition, 2011.

Bleazby, J. 'Dewey's notion of imagination in philosophy for children', *Education and Culture*, vol. 28(2), 2012, pp. 95–111 (doi: 10.1353/eac.2012.0013).

Bloom, B.S., Engelhart, M.D., Furst, E.J., Hill, W.H. & Krathwohl, D.R. *Taxonomy of educational objectives: The classification of educational goals. Handbook I: Cognitive domain*, New York: David McKay Company, 1956.

Boud, D. & Walker, D. 'Promoting reflection in professionals courses: the challenge of context', *Studies in Higher Education*, vol. 23, no. 2, 1998, pp. 191–206.

Bourriaud, N. *Relational aesthetics*, translated by Simon Pleasance & Fronza Woods with the participation of Mathieu Copeland, original title: *Esthétique relationnelle*, Les presses du réel, 2003.

Brookfield, S. *Becoming a critically reflective teacher*, San-Francisco: Jossey-Bass, 1995.

Bruce, C. & Gerber, R. 'Towards university lecturers' conceptions of student learning', *Higher Education*, vol. 29, 1995, pp. 443–458.

Catmull, E. with Wallace, A. *Creativity Inc.: Overcoming the unseen forces that stand in the way of true inspiration*, London: Bantam Press, 2014.

Claxton, G., Edwards, L. & Scale-Constantinou, V. 'Cultivating creative mentalities: A framework for education', *Thinking Skills and Creativity*, 1, 2006, pp. 57–61.

Cole, D.G., Sugioka, H.L. & Yamagata-Lynch, L.C. 'Supportive classroom environments for creativity in higher education', *Journal of Creative Behaviour*, vol. 33(4), 1999, pp. 277–293.

Collins, M.A. & Amabile, T.A. 'Motivation and creativity' in R.J. Sternberg (ed.), *Handbook of creativity*, Cambridge: Cambridge University Press, 1999, pp. 297–312.

Cowdroy, R. & de Graaff, E. 'Assessing highly creative ability', *Assessment and Evaluation in Higher Education*, vol. 30 (5), 2005, pp. 507–518.

Craft, A. 'The limits to creativity in education: Dilemmas for the educator', *British Journal of Educational Studies*, vol. 51(2), 2003, pp. 113–127.

Craft, A., Jeffrey, B. & Leibling, M. *Creativity in education*, London: Continuum, 2001.

Creativity, Culture and Education (CCE). Change Schools CSDF Planning Form: Guidance, descriptors and form, UK, 2010.

Cropley, A.J. *More ways than one: Fostering creativity*, Norwood, New Jersey: Ablex, 1992.

Csikszentmihalyi, M. 'Where is creativity?' *Creativity: flow and the psychology of discovery and invention*, Harper Collins: 1996, pp. 23–50.

Csikszentmihalyi, M. *Beyond boredom and anxiety: Experiencing flow in work and play*, San Francisco: Jossey-Bass, 1975.

Csikszentmihalyi, M. 'Implications of a systems perspective for the study of creativity', in R. Sternberg (ed.), *Handbook of creativity*, Cambridge: Cambridge University Press, 1999, pp. 313–335.

Deleuze, G. & Guattari, F. *Mille plateaux*, Paris: Minuit, 1980.

Dennett, D.C. 'Memes and the exploitation of imagination', *The Journal of Aesthetics and Art Criticism*, vol. 48(2), 1990, pp. 127–135.

Derrida, J. *Donner le temps*, Paris: Galilée, 1991.

Dewar, J. M. 'An apology for the scholarship of teaching and learning', *InSight: A Journal of Scholarly Teaching*, vol 3, 2008, pp. 17–22.

Dewey, J. *How we think: A restatement of the relation of reflective thinking to the educative process* (1910), Mineola, NY: Dover Publications, 1997.

Doecke, B., Parr, G. & Sawyer, W. *Language and creativity in contemporary English classrooms*, Putney, NSW: Phoenix Education, 2014.

Donald, J. *Learning to think: Disciplinary perspectives*, San Francisco: Jossey Bass, 2002.

Duit, R. 'On the role of analogies and metaphors in learning science', *Science Education*, vol. 75(6), 1991, pp. 649–672 (doi: 10.1002/sce.3730750606)

Edwards, A. 'Let's get beyond community and practice: The many meanings of learning by participating', *Curriculum Journal*, vol. 16(1), 2005, pp. 49–65.

Egan, K. *An imaginative approach to teaching*, San Francisco: Jossey Bass, John Wiley & Sons, 2005.

Egan, K., Stout, Maureen, and Keiichi, Takaya (ed.), *Teaching and learning outside the box: Inspiring imagination across the curriculum*, New York: Teachers College Press, 2007.

Egan, K. & Judson, G. 'Values and imagination in teaching: With a special focus on social studies', *Educational Philosophy and Theory*, vol. 41(2), 2009, pp. 126–140 (doi: 10.1111/j.1469-5812.2008.00455.x).

Engeström, Y. 'Innovative learning in work teams: Analyzing cycles of knowledge creation in practice', in Y. Engeström, R. Miettinen & R. L. Punamäki (eds), *Perspectives on activity theory*, Cambridge: Cambridge University Press, 1999, pp. 377–404.

Engeström, Y. 'Expansive learning: Toward an activity-theoretical reconceptualization', in K. Illeris (ed.), *Contemporary theories of learning: Learning theorists … in their own words*. Abingdon, Oxon: Routledge, 2009, pp. 53–73.

Fiedler S. & Väljataga, T. 'Personal learning environments: concept or technology?'. *International Journal of Virtual and Personal Learning Environments*, vol. 2, issue 4, 2011, pp. 1–11.

Flavell, J. 'Metacognition and cognitive monitoring. A new area of cognitive-development inquiry', *American Psychologist*, vol. 34, no. 10, pp. 906–911 (doi:10.1037/0003-066X.34.10.906).

Frye, N. *The educated imagination*, Toronto, Ontario: Canadian Broadcasting Corporation, 1963.

Fryer, M. 'Facilitating creativity in higher education: A brief account of National Teaching Fellows' views', in N. Jackson, M. Oliver, M. Shaw & J. Wisdom (eds), *Developing creativity in higher education: An imaginative curriculum*, Abingdon: Routledge, 2006.

Fulcher, G. 'The unholy division between theory and practice: What does the recent discussion on language and text have to say about reflexivity and teaching?', *Teaching in Higher Education*, vol. 1(2), 1996, pp. 167–192.

Getzels, J.W. & Csikszentmihalyi, M. 'Creativity and problem finding in art', in F. G. Farley & R.W. Neperud (eds), *The foundations of aesthetics, art, and art education*, New York: Praeger, 1988, pp. 91–106.

Gibbs, R.W. & Matlock, T. 'Metaphor, imagination, and simulation: Psycholinguistic evidence'. In R. W. Gibbs (ed.), *The Cambridge handbook of metaphor and thought*, New York: Cambridge University Press, 2008.

Ginns, P. 'Learning by imagining', *Synergy*, vol. 19, May 2004.

Greene, M. *Releasing the imagination: Essays on education, the arts, and social change*, San Francisco: Josey-Bass Publishers, 1995.

Griffiths, T. 'History and the creative imagination', *History Australia*, vol. 6(3), 2009, pp. 71–74.

Hall, V. & Hart, A. 'The use of imagination in professional education to enable learning about disadvantaged clients', *Learning in Health and Social Care*, vol. 3(4), 2004, pp. 190–202 (doi: 10.1111/j.1473-6861.2004.00074.x).

Hansen, D.T. 'A poetics of teaching', *Educational Theory*, vol. 54(2), 2004, pp. 119–142 (doi: 10.1111/j.1741-5446.2004.00010.x).

Harris, A. *The creative turn: Toward a new aesthetic imaginary*, Rotterdam: Sense Publishers, 2014.

Harris, A. *Creativity and education*, Palgrave Macmillan, 2016.

Harris, A. & Ammermann, M. 'The changing face of creativity in Australian education', *Teaching Education*, vol. 27(1), 2015, pp. 103–113 (doi: 10.1080/10476210.2015.1077379).

Jackson, N. 'Creativity in higher education: Creating tipping points for cultural change', *SCEPTrE, Scholarly Paper* 3: March 2006, pp. 1–26.

Jackson, N. 'Nurturing creativity through an imaginative curriculum', *HERDSA News*, vol. 25 (no. 3), December, 2003, pp. 21–26.

Jackson, N. & Shaw, M. *Imaginative curriculum study: Subject perspectives on creativity: a preliminary synthesis*, The Higher Education Academy, 2006.

Jackson, N. J., Oliver, M., Shaw, M. & Wisdom, J. 'Developing subject perspectives on creativity in higher education', in N.J. Jackson & M. Shaw (eds), *Developing creativity in higher education: The imaginative curriculum*, London: Routledge, 2006, pp. 89–108.

Jackson, N., Martin, O. & Shaw, M. (eds), *Developing creativity in higher education: The imaginative curriculum*. London: Routledge, 2006.

Janesick, V.J. 'Intuition and creativity: A *pas de deux* for qualitative researchers', *Qualitative Inquiry*, vol. 7(5), 2001, pp. 531–540 (doi: 10.1177/107780040100700501).

Jeffrey, B. 'Creative teaching and learning: Towards a common discourse and practice', *Cambridge Journal of Education*, vol. 36(3), 2006, pp. 399–414.

Jeffrey, B. and Craft, A. 'Teaching creatively and teaching for creativity: Distinctions and relationships', *Educational Studies*, vol. 30(1), 2004, pp. 77–87.

Johnson, M. *Moral imagination: Implications of cognitive science for ethics*, Chicago: University of Chicago Press, 1993.

Kearney, R. *The wake of imagination*, London: Hutchinson Education, 1988.

Rasmussen, M. 'The narrative path', in Kemp, P. & Rasmussen, D. (eds), *The narrative path*, Cambridge, Massachusetts: The MIT Press, 1989.

Kiverstein, J. & Clark, A. 'Bootstrapping the mind', *Behavioral and Brain Sciences*, vol. 31(1), 2008, pp. 41–58.

Kleiman, P. 'Towards transformation: Conceptions of creativity in higher education', *Innovations in Education and Teaching International*, vol. 45(3), 2007, pp. 209–217.

Kloehn, L. 'Imagination and learning: Students living "real" lives during the Civil War', *English Journal*, vol. 99(2), 2009, pp. 37–41 (doi: 1899449791).

Koestler, A. *The act of creation*, New York: Macmillan, 1964.

Kohn, A. 'Four reasons to worry about "Personalized learning"', *Psychology today*, Feb 24, 2015.

Kuh, G.D. Kinzie, J., Schuh, J.H. & Whitt, E.J. *Student success in college: creating conditions that matter*, Washington: American Association for Higher Education, Jossey-Bass (Wiley), 2011.

Lachman, S.J. 'Learning is a process: Toward an improved definition of learning', *The Journal of Psychology*, vol. 131, issue 5, 1997, pp. 477–480.

Lakoff, G. & Johnson, M. *Metaphors we live by*, Chicago: University of Chicago Press, 1980.

Lave, J. 'The culture of acquisition and the practice of understanding', in Stigler, J. W., Shweder, R. A. & G. Herdt (eds), *Cultural psychology: essays on comparative human development*, Cambridge: Cambridge University Press, 1990, pp. 309–327.

Lee, K. W., Cho, N. S., Oh, E. S., Kwon, J. R., Kim, H. M., Chi, E. L. & Hong, W. P. *A study on the improvement of secondary school education to bring up students' creative talents*, Seoul: KICE Research report, Korea Institute for Curriculum and Evaluation, 2011.

Lehrer, J. *Imagine: The science of creativity*, Melbourne: Text, 2012.

Lucas, B. 'Creative teaching, teaching creativity and creative learning', in A. Craft, B. Jeffrey & M. Leibling (eds), *Creativity in education*, London: Continuum, 2001, pp. 35–44.

Lucas, U. 'Being "pulled up short": Creating moments of surprise and possibility in accounting education', *Critical Perspectives on Accounting*, vol. 19, 2008, pp. 383–403.

Madoc-Jones, G. 'Imagination and the teaching of literature: Interpretive and ethical implications', *Teaching and learning outside the box: Inspiring imagination across the curriculum*, Toronto: Canadian Broadcasting Corporation, 2007.

Marcus, G.E. *Ethnography through thick and thin*, Princeton, New Jersey: Princeton University Press, 1998.

Marginson, S. 'Freedom as control and the control of freedom: F. A. Hayek and the academic imagination', *International Perspectives on Higher Education Research*, vol. 4, 2007, p. 67.

Martindale, C. 'The biological basis of creativity', in R. Sternberg (ed.), *Handbook of creativity*, Cambridge: Cambridge University Press, 1999.

Marton, F. & Säljö, R. 'On qualitative differences in learning. 1—Outcome and process', *British Journal of Educational Psychology*, vol. 46, 1976, pp. 4–11.

Mazur, E. *Confessions of a converted lecturer*, video uploaded to YouTube on November 12, 2009 (www.youtube.com/watch?v=WwslBPj8GgI).

McWilliam, E. 'Is creativity teachable: Conceptualising the creativity/pedagogy relationship in higher education,' Paper presented at the 30th HERDSA Annual Conference: Enhancing Higher Education, Theory and Scholarship, Adelaide, 2007.

McWilliam, E. 'Teaching for creativity: From sage to guide to meddler', *Asia Pacific Journal of Education*, vol. 29(3), 2009, pp. 281–293 (doi: 10.1080/02188790903092787).

McWilliam, E. 'Creativity and innovation: An educational perspective', in L. Mann & J. Chan (eds), *ARC Learned academies project*, Melbourne: University of Melbourne, 2011.

McWilliam, E. & Dawson, S. 'Understanding Creativity: A survey of "creative" academic teachers: A report for the Carrick Institute for Learning and Teaching in Higher Education', 2007 (www.altcexchange.edu.au/system/files/handle/fellowships_associatefellow_report_ericamcwilliam_may07.pdf.)

McWilliam, E. & Dawson, S. 'Teaching for creativity: Towards sustainable and replicable pedagogical practice', *Higher Education*, vol. 56, 2008, pp. 633–643 (doi: 10.1007/s10734- 008-9115-7).

McWilliam, E. & Haukka, S. 'Educating the creative workforce: New directions for twenty-first century schooling', *British Educational Research Journal*, vol. 34(5), 2008, pp. 651–666.

McWilliam, E., Hearn, G. & Haseman, B. 'Transdisciplinarity for creative futures: What barriers and opportunities?', *Innovations in Education and Teaching International*, vol. 45(3), 2008, pp. 247–253.

McWilliam, E., Poronnik, P. & Taylor, P.G. 'Re-designing science pedagogy: Reversing the flight from science', *Journal of Science Education and Technology*, vol. 17(3), 2008, pp. 226–235 (doi: 10.1007/s10956-008-9092-8).

McWilliam, E.L., Dawson, S.P. & Tan, J. P. L. 'From vaporousness to visibility: What might evidence of creative capacity building actually look like?', UNESCO Observatory, Faculty of Architecture, Building and Planning, The University of Melbourne: *Multi-Disciplinary Research in the Arts*, vol. 1(3), 2008.

McWilliam, E. & Dawson, S. 'The creative application of knowledge in university education: A case study', Paper presented at the *Creative Industries and Innovation Conference*, 2007 (www.google.com.au/search?hl=en&source=hp&q=mcwilliam+the+creative+application+of+knowledge+in+university+education&btnG=Google+Search&meta=&aq=241f&aqi=&aql=&oq=).

Mezirow, J. 'An overview of transformative learning', in K. Illeris (ed.), *Contemporary theories of learning*. Abingdon: Routledge, 2009, pp. 90–105.

Moon, J.A. *A handbook of reflective and experiential learning: Theory and practice*, London: RoutledgeFarmer, 2004.

Moran, S. & John-Steiner, V. 'Creativity in the making: Vygotsky's contemporary contribution to the dialectic of creativity and development', in R. K. Sawyer, V. John- Steiner, S. Moran, R.J. Sternberg, D.H. Feldman, H. Gardner, J. Nakamura & M. Csikszentmihaly (eds), *Creativity and development*, New York: Oxford University Press, 2003, pp. 61–90.

Morley, D. *The Cambridge introduction to creative writing*, Cambridge: Cambridge University Press, 2007.

Morley, D. 'Creative recognitions: Science, writing and the creative academy', *LUMAS on-line journal*, 2007 (www.liv.ac.uk/poetryandscience/essays/creative- recognitions.htm).

Murphy, P., Peters, A.M. & Marginson, S. *Imagination: Three models of imagination in the age of the knowledge economy*, New York: Peter Lang, 2010.

Murray, E.L. *Imaginative thinking and human existence*, Pittsburgh, PA: Duquesne University Press, 1986.

Nelson, R. 'The courtyard inside and out: a brief history of an architectural ambiguity', *Enquiry, The ARCC Journal*, vol. 11, issue 1, 2014, pp. 8–17.

Nelson, R. 'Toward a history of rigour: an examination of the nasty side of scholarship', *Arts and Humanities in Higher Education*, vol. 10, no. 4, October 2011, pp. 374–387 (doi: 10.1177/1474022211408797).

Nelson, R. *The space wasters: the architecture of Australian misanthropy*, Carlton: Planning Institute of Australia, 2011.

Nelson, R. & Dawson, P. 'Competition and education: connecting history with recent scholarship', *Assessment & Evaluation in Higher Education*, December 2015.

Nickerson, R. 'Enhancing creativity', in R. J. Sternberg (ed.), *Handbook of creativity*, Cambridge: Cambridge University Press, 1999, pp. 392–430.

Nussbaum, M. *Upheavals of thought: The intelligence of emotions*, New York: Cambridge University Press, 2001.

Nussbaum, M. *Not for profit: why democracy needs the humanities*, Princeton University Press, 2010.

Oliver, B. *Assuring graduate outcomes*, Strawberry Hills, NSW: Australian Learning and Teaching Council, 2011 (www.olt.gov.au/resource-assuring-graduate-outcomes-curtin-2011).

Oliver, M. *Creativity and the curriculum design process: A case study*, York: Learning and Teaching Support Network, Generic Centre, 2002.

Onsman, A., & Paganin, D. 'Perturbative analogies: Fostering creativity in postgraduate research students', Paper presented at the *AARE International education research conference*, Adelaide. Conference of the Australian Association for Research in Education, 2006 (www.aare.edu.au/06pap/ons06061.pdf).

Onsman, A., & Paganin, D. 'Towards grasping the unknowable: Networked hierarchies of analogies', Paper presented at the *Australian Association for Research in Education*, Canberra, 2009.

Opdal, P.M. 'Curiosity, wonder and education seen as perspective development', *Studies in Philosophy and Education*, vol. 20 (4 July 2001), pp. 331–344.

Philip, R. 'Cultivating creative ecologies: Creative teaching and teaching for creativity', Paper presented at the *Research and Development in Higher Education: The place of learning and teaching*, AUT University, Auckland, New Zealand, 1–4 July 2013.

Phillips, A. & Taylor, B. *On kindness*, London: Hamish Hamilton, 2009.

Polanyi, M. *The tacit dimension*, Garden City, New York: Anchor Books, 1967.

Race, W.H. 'Pindar's "Best is water": Best of what?', *Greek, Roman, & Byzantine Studies*, vol. 22, 1981, pp. 119–124.

Reddy, M. 'The conduit metaphor', in A. Ortony (ed.), *Metaphor and thought*, Cambridge: Cambridge University Press, 1979, pp. 284–324.

Ricoeur, P. [1975]. *The rule of metaphor: The creation of meaning in language* (R. Czerny, K. McLaughlin & J. Costello, trans.), London: Routledge, 2003.

Ricoeur, P. 'The metaphorical process as cognition, imagination and feeling', in S. Sacks (ed.), *On metaphor*, Chicago: University of Chicago Press, 1979, pp. 141–153.Ricoeur, P. 'Narrative time', *Critical Inquiry*, vol. 7(1), 1980, pp. 169–190.

Ricoeur, P. 'The function of fiction in shaping reality: Reflection and imagination', in M. J. Valdes (ed.), *A Ricoeur reader*, Hertfordshire: Harvester Wheatsheaf, 1991, pp. 117–136.

Ricoeur, P. 'Imagination in discourse and in action' (K. Blamey & J. B. Thompson, Trans.), in J.M. Eadie (ed.), *From text to action: Essays in hermeneutics*, Evanston, Illinois: Northwestern University Press, 1991, vol. 2, pp. 168–187.

Rizvi, F. 'Imagination and the globalisation of educational policy research', *Globalisation, Societies and Education*, vol. 4(2), 2006, pp. 193–205.

Rizvi, F. 'Imagination and the globalisation of educational policy research', *Encountering education in the global: The selected works of Fazal Rizvi*, Routledge: London, 2014.

Robinson, K. *All our futures: Creativity, culture and education*, London: National Advisory Committee on Creative and Cultural Education (NACCCE), 1999.

Robinson, K. *Out of our minds: Learning to be creative*, Oxford: Capstone Publishing Limited, 2011.

Roth, W. M., Lee, Y. J., & Hsu, P. L. 'A tool for changing the world: Possibilities of cultural-historical activity theory to reinvigorate science education', *Studies in Science Education*, vol. 45(2), 2009, pp. 131–167.

Runco, M. 'Education based on a parsimonious theory of creativity', in R. Beghetto & J. Kaufman (eds.), *Nurturing creativity in the classroom*, New York: Cambridge University Press, 2010, pp. 235–251.

Schön, D. *Displacement of concepts*, London: Tavistock Publications, 1963.

Schön, D. 'Generative metaphor: A perspective on problem-setting in social policy', in A. Ortony (ed.), *Metaphor and thought*, Cambridge: Cambridge University Press, 1979.

Schön, D. *The reflective practitioner: How professionals think in action* (1983), New York: Basic Books, 1984.

Scott, G., Leritz, L., & Mumford, M. 'The effectiveness of creativity training: A quantitative review'. *Creativity Research Journal*, vol. 16(4), 2004, pp. 361–388.

Smolucha, F. 'The relevance of Vygotsky's theory of creative imagination for contemporary research on play', *Creativity Research Journal*, vol. 5(1), 1992, pp. 69–76.

Smolucha, L.W., & Smolucha, F.C. 'A fifth Piagetian stage: The collaboration between analogical and logical thinking in artistic creativity', *Visual Arts Research*, vol. 11(2), 1985, pp. 90–99.

Sneath, D., Holbraad, M. & Pedersen, M.A. 'Technologies of the imagination: An introduction', *Ethnos*, vol. 74(1), 2009, pp. 5–30 (doi: 10.1080/00141840902751147).

Snell, B. *Die Entdeckung des Geistes* (1975), Vandenhoeck & Ruprecht, Göttingen,

5ᵗʰ edn., 1980.

Solomon-Minarchi, A. *Authentic storytelling: The implications for students and teachers*, Masters Project in partial fulfilment of the requirements of Masters degree, The Evergreen State College, 2010 (http://archives.evergreen.edu/masterstheses/Accession89-10MIT/Solomon- Minarchi_AMIT2010.pdf).

Spencer, E., Lucas, B. & Claxton, G. 'Progression in creativity – developing new forms of assessment: A literature review', *Creativity, Culture and Education Series* (CCE), Newcastle upon Tyne, 2012.

Spoehr, J., Barnett, K., Molloy, S., Dev, S.V. & Hordacre, A. L. *Connecting ideas: Collaborative innovation for a complex world*, The Australian Institute for Social Research, University of Adelaide: Report prepared for Department of Further Education, Employment, Science and Technology, 2010 (www.adelaide.edu.au/wiser/pubs/pdfs/wiser201005_connecting_ideas.pdf).

Sternberg, R.J. & Lubart, T.I. 'The concept of creativity: Prospects and paradigms', *Handbook of creativity*, Cambridge: Cambridge University Press, 1999, pp. 3–15.

Stierer, B. & Antoniou, M. 'Are there distinctive methodologies for pedagogic research in higher education?', *Teaching in higher Education*, vol. 9(3), 2004, pp. 275–285 (doi: 10.1080/1356251042000216606).

Stout, M. & T. Keiichi (eds), *Teaching and learning outside the box: Inspiring imagination across the curriculum*, Toronto: Canadian Broadcasting Corporation, 2011.

Taber, K. S. 'The natures of scientific thinking: Creativity as the handmaiden to logic in the development of public and personal knowledge', in M. S. Khine (ed.), *Advances in nature of science research: Concepts and methodologies*, Dordrecht: Springer, 2012, pp. 51–74.

Tharp, T. *The creative habit: Learn it and use it for life*, New York: Simon & Schuster, 2008.

Tokumitsu, Miya. 'In defense of the lecture', *Jacobin*, 26 February 2017.

Trowler, P. 'Can approaches to research in Art and Design be beneficially adapted for research into higher education?' *Higher Education Research & Development*, vol. 32(1), 2013, pp. 56–69 (doi: 10.1080/07294360.2012.750276).

Vygotsky, L.S. 'Imagination and its development in childhood', *The development of higher mental functions*, Moscow: Izdatell'stvo Akademii Pedagogicheskikh Nauk RSFSR, 1960, pp. 327–362.

Vygotsky, L.S. *Thought and language* (E. Hanfmann & G. Vakar, Trans. E. Hanfmann & G. Vakar eds), Cambridge, Massachusetts: The MIT Press, 1962.

Vygotsky, L.S. 'Imagination and creativity in the adolescent', *The collected works of L.S. Vygotsky*, Moscow: Izdatelstvo Pedagogika, 1984, vol. 4, pp. 199–219.

Vygotsky, L.S. 'Imagination and creativity in childhood', *Journal of Russian and East European Psychology*, vol. 42(1), 2004, pp. 7–97.

Wagner-Lawlor, J. A. 'Kathleen Lennon, *Imagination and the imaginary*', *Notre Dame Philosophical Reviews*, 12 July 2015 (https://ndpr.nd.edu/news/59310-imagination-and-the-imaginary/).

Ward, T., Smith, S. & Vaid, J. (eds). *Creative thought: An investigation of conceptual structures and processes*, Washington, DC: American Psychological Association, 1997.

Weisberg, R. 'Modes of expertise in creative thinking: Evidence from case studies', *The Cambridge handbook of expertise and expert performance*, New York: Cambridge University Press, 2006.

Weisberg, R.W. 'Creativity and knowledge: A challenge to theories', in R. J. Sternberg (ed.), *Handbook of creativity*, Cambridge: Cambridge University Press, 1999, pp. 226–249.

Wenger, E. 'A social theory of learning', in K. Illeris (ed.), *Contemporary theories of learning: Learning theorists ... in their own words*, London: Routledge, 2009, pp. 53–73.

White, A. *The language of imagination*, Oxford: Basil Blackwell, 1990.

White, H. V. *Metahistory: The historical imagination in nineteenth-century Europe*, Baltimore: Johns Hopkins University Press, 1973.

White, J. 'Arias of learning: Creativity and performativity in Australian teacher education', *Cambridge Journal of Education*, vol. 36(3), 2006, pp. 435–453.

Whitton, J. 'Using Ricoeur to interpret acts of imagination in a university physics class', in M.A. Peters & T. Besley (eds), *Re-imagining the creative university for the 21st century*, Rotterdam: Sense Publishers. 2013, pp. 83–96.

Whitton, J. 'Looking through the lens of Ricoeur: Mastering the conditions for imaginative creation in history', *Departures in Critical Qualitative Research*, vol. 3(3), Fall, 2014, pp. 218–238.

Whitton, J. *Fostering imagination in higher education teaching and learning: Making connections*, PhD thesis, Monash University, 2016.

Young, L. 'Imagine creating rubrics that develop creativity', *English Journal*, vol. 99(2), 2009, pp. 74–79.

Zilsel, E. *Die Entstehung des Geniebegriffes. Ein Beitrag zur Ideengeschichte der Antike und des Frühkapitalismus*, Tübingen: Mohr, 1926.

INDEX